with **Lucy Holmes, Sarah Walker**
and **Rawdon Wyatt**

Series Adviser **Catherine Walter**

Photocopiable Materials Adviser **Jill Hadfield**

Navigate

Teacher's Guide
with Teacher's Support and Resource Disc
and Photocopiable Materials

B1 Pre-intermediate

OXFORD
UNIVERSITY PRESS

OXFORD
UNIVERSITY PRESS

Great Clarendon Street, Oxford, OX2 6DP, United Kingdom

Oxford University Press is a department of the University of Oxford.
It furthers the University's objective of excellence in research, scholarship,
and education by publishing worldwide. Oxford is a registered trade
mark of Oxford University Press in the UK and in certain other countries

© Oxford University Press 2015

The moral rights of the author have been asserted

First published in 2015

2019 2018 2017 2016 2015

10 9 8 7 6 5 4 3 2

All rights reserved. No part of this publication may be reproduced, stored
in a retrieval system, or transmitted, in any form or by any means, without
the prior permission in writing of Oxford University Press, or as expressly
permitted by law, by licence or under terms agreed with the appropriate
reprographics rights organization. Enquiries concerning reproduction outside
the scope of the above should be sent to the ELT Rights Department, Oxford
University Press, at the address above

You must not circulate this work in any other form and you must impose
this same condition on any acquirer

Links to third party websites are provided by Oxford in good faith and for
information only. Oxford disclaims any responsibility for the materials
contained in any third party website referenced in this work

Photocopying

The Publisher grants permission for the photocopying of those pages marked
'photocopiable' according to the following conditions. Individual purchasers
may make copies for their own use or for use by classes that they teach.
School purchasers may make copies for use by staff and students, but this
permission does not extend to additional schools or branches

Under no circumstances may any part of this book be photocopied for resale

ISBN: 978 0 19 456546 2

Printed in China

This book is printed on paper from certified and well-managed sources

ACKNOWLEDGEMENTS

Photos: iStockphoto p.17 (White digital tablet pc/hanibaram), Alamy Images
p.233 (futuristic robot/3C Stock); Corbis pp.231 (portrait serious girl/13/Regine
Mahaux/Ocean), 231 (portrait woman laughing/Hero Images), 231 (portrait
Chinese woman/Paul Burns/Blend Images); Getty Images pp.219 (designers
discussing ideas/Robin Skjoldborg), 226 (friends eating outside/Jake Curtis),
226 (friends walking at coast/Dougal Waters), 231 (portrait businesswoman/
Chris Ryan); Shutterstock pp.212 (paper money/2j architecture), 216 (bus
stop/Ints Vikmanis), 219 (students in lecture/wavebreakmedia), 230 (judge's
gavel/Peeradach Rattanakoses), 231 (portrait young man/lithian), 231 (portrait
man sitting outside/eurobanks), 231 (man with glasses/Ysbrand Cosijn),
231 (portrait angry man/Ollyy).

Illustrations: Paul Boston pp.210, 213, 247, 255; Dylan Gibson pp.214, 234;
Kerry Hyndman pp.245, 251, 253; Joanna Kerr pp.227, 235, 244, 246, 248.

Contents

Coursebook contents   4

Introduction to *Navigate*   8

***Navigate* overview**   10
Coursebook	10
Workbook	15
Teacher's guide; Teacher's Support and Resource Disc	16
e-Books	17
iTools	18
Online practice	19

The *Navigate* Approach   20
Reading	20
Listening	22
Grammar	24
Vocabulary	26
Photocopiables	28
The CEFR	30
Testing	32

Teaching notes   34
Unit 1	34
Unit 2	48
Unit 3	62
Unit 4	76
Unit 5	90
Unit 6	104
Unit 7	118
Unit 8	132
Unit 9	146
Unit 10	160
Unit 11	174
Unit 12	188

Photocopiable teacher's resource materials   202
Grammar	203
Vocabulary	220
Communication	238
Vox pops video worksheets	256

On the Teacher's Support and Resource Disc
Lesson overview videos with Catherine Walter
Photocopiable activities
Vox pops video worksheets
Tests
Wordlists
Audio and video scripts

Coursebook contents: Units 1–6

Contents

🗝 **Oxford 3000™** Navigate has been based on the Oxford 3000 to ensure that learners are only covering the most relevant vocabulary.

Unit	Learning objectives	Lesson	GRAMMAR
1 Time — page 6	■ Talk about your daily life ■ Ask questions ■ Talk about how often you do things ■ Talk about your free time ■ Predict before you read a text ■ Understand and use nouns and verbs with the same form ■ Talk about the weather ■ Talk about your likes and dislikes ■ Write a web post	1.1 Do you live in the past, present or future? p6 1.2 Free time p8 1.3 Vocabulary and skills development p10 1.4 Speaking and writing p12 1.5 ▶ Video *Adventure sports in Chile* p14 Review p15	Question forms p6 Present simple & adverbs of frequency p8
2 Inside outside — page 16	■ Talk about where you live ■ Talk about the present ■ Identifying things and people ■ Talk about things in your home ■ Use phrases with *on* ■ Understand sentences with missing words ■ Ask for and give directions ■ Write text messages	2.1 Street life p16 2.2 Home life p18 2.3 Vocabulary and skills development p20 2.4 Speaking and writing p22 2.5 ▶ Video *London's changing skyline* p24 Review p25	Present simple & present continuous p17 Identifying relative clauses p18
3 Going up, going down — page 26	■ Describe movement ■ Talk about the past (1) and (2) ■ Talk about feelings ■ Understand and use adverbs of manner ■ Understand *-t* and *-d* before a consonant ■ Tell and respond to a story ■ Write an informal email describing an event	3.1 The man who fell to Earth p26 3.2 Going up … One man's lift nightmare p28 3.3 Vocabulary and skills development p30 3.4 Speaking and writing p32 3.5 ▶ Video *The RRS Discovery* p34 Review p35	Past simple p27 Past simple and past continuous p2
4 Changes and challenges — page 36	■ Talk about life stages and events ■ Use verbs with *-ing* and *to* ■ Talk about using the internet ■ Talk about plans and arrangements ■ Understand connected speech (1) ■ Understand and use *get* ■ Invite and make arrangements ■ Write an email to make arrangements	4.1 Changing directions p36 4.2 Living without the Internet p38 4.3 Vocabulary and skills development p40 4.4 Speaking and writing p42 4.5 ▶ Video *Esplorio* p44 Review p45	Verbs with *-ing* and *to* p37 *going to* and present continuous for the future p38
5 Stuff and things — page 46	■ Describe objects ■ Use articles ■ Talk about money ■ Talk about quantity ■ Understand linkers for reason and result ■ Understand and use suffixes ■ Explain words you don't know ■ Write an email to return an online product	5.1 Your world in objects p46 5.2 It's all about the money p48 5.3 Vocabulary and skills development p50 5.4 Speaking and writing p52 5.5 ▶ Video *The Dubai Mall* p54 Review p55	Articles p47 Quantifiers p48
6 People — page 56	■ Describe character ■ Talk about similarities and differences ■ Talk about family ■ Talk about experience ■ Recognize linkers in fast speech ■ Understand and use adjectives prefixes ■ Use the present perfect simple with *just, already* and *yet* ■ Give and respond to news	6.1 The quiet revolution p56 6.2 A long way home p58 6.3 Vocabulary and skills development p60 6.4 Speaking and writing p62 6.5 ▶ Video *Nettlebed* p64 Review p65	Making comparisons p57 Present perfect simple and past simple p58 Present perfect simple with *just, already* and *yet* p62

VOCABULARY	PRONUNCIATION	LISTENING/READING	SPEAKING/WRITING
Daily life p6		▶ **Video** Vox pops 1 p7	
Free-time activities p9	Stress p9		
Nouns and verbs with the same form p11		**Reading** predicting before you read a text p10	
Talking about the weather p12			**Speaking** talking about likes and dislikes p12 **Writing** a web post about the best time to visit your country p13
Street Life p16	Compound nouns p26		
Household objects p19	*that* in relative clauses p19	▶ **Video** Vox pops 2 p19	
Phrases with *on* p20		**Reading** understanding sentences with missing words p20	
	Intonation in directions p23		**Speaking** asking for and giving directions p22 **Writing** text messages p23
Movement p26	Irregular past verbs p27		
Adjectives for describing feelings p28		▶ **Video** Vox pops 3 p29	
Adverbs of manner p30		**Listening** understanding *-t* and *-d* before a consonant p31	**Speaking** telling and responding to a story p32 **Writing** email (1): describing an event p33
Life stages and events p36			
Internet activities p38	*going to* p39		
Get p41		**Listening** understanding connected speech (1) p40	
			Speaking inviting and making arrangements p42 **Writing** email (2): making arrangements p43
Adjective for describing objects p46	Adjective word stress p46	▶ **Video** Vox pops 5 p47	
Money p48			
Suffixes p51		**Reading** understanding linkers for reason and result p50	
			Speaking explaining words you don't know p52 **Writing** email (3) returning an online product p53
Adjectives for describing character p56	*as* and *than* p57	▶ **Video** Vox pops 6 p57	
Family p58			
Adjectives prefixes p61		**Listening** recognize linkers in fast speech p60	
	Intonation in short expressions p63		**Writing** responding to news on social media p62 **Speaking** giving and responding to news p63

3

Coursebook contents: Units 7–12

			GRAMMAR
7 Travel page 66 ■ Talk about transport ■ Make predictions ■ Talk about holidays ■ Use *something, anyone, everybody, nowhere*, etc. ■ Recognize paraphrasing ■ Understand and use *-ed* and *-ing* adjectives ■ Check into a hotel ■ Write short notes and messages	7.1 On the move p66 7.2 Getting away p68 7.3 Vocabulary and skills development p70 7.4 Speaking and writing p72 7.5 ▶ Video *Beijing subway* p74 Review p75		Prediction (*will, might*) p66 *something, anyone, everybody, nowhere* etc. p68
8 Language and learning page 76 ■ Talk about ability ■ Talk about skills and abilities ■ Talk about obligation, necessity and permission ■ Talk about education ■ Understand connected speech (2) ■ Understand and use *make* and *do* ■ Ask for clarification ■ Complete a form	8.1 The amazing human brain p76 8.2 The secrets of a successful education p78 8.3 Vocabulary and skills development p80 8.4 Speaking and writing p82 8.5 ▶ Video *Career change* p84 Review p85		Ability (*can, be able to*) p76 Obligation, necessity and permission (*must, have to, can*) p78
9 Body and mind page 86 ■ Talk about greetings ■ Talk about possible situations and the results ■ Use present tenses in future time clauses ■ Talk about health and fitness ■ Use verbs and prepositions ■ Use sequencing words to understand ■ Ask for help and give advice ■ Write a formal covering letter	9.1 The rise and fall of the handshake p86 9.2 Going back to nature p88 9.3 Vocabulary and skills development p90 9.4 Speaking and writing p92 9.5 ▶ Video *Sports scholarship in the USA* p94 Review p95		*if* + present simple + *will/won't/might* p Present tenses in future time clauses p
10 Food page 96 ■ Describe food ■ Use the *-ing* form ■ Talk about food ■ Use the passive ■ Understand reference words in a text ■ Understand words with more than one meaning ■ Explain and deal with problems in a restaurant ■ Write a review of a restaurant	10.1 A question of taste p96 10.2 Canned dreams p98 10.3 Vocabulary and skills development p100 10.4 Speaking and writing p102 10.5 ▶ Video *Koreatown* p104 Review p105		Uses of the *-ing* form p97 The passive p98
11 World page 106 ■ Talk about unlikely situations in the future ■ Talk about global issues ■ Talk about past habits and situations ■ Talk about the news ■ Understand connected speech (3) ■ Express and respond to opinions ■ Give a presentation	11.1 Making the world a better place p106 11.2 Breaking news p108 11.3 Vocabulary and skills development p110 11.4 Speaking and writing p112 11.5 ▶ Video *The European Union* p114 Review p115		*if* + past tense + *would* p106 *used to* p108
12 Work page 116 ■ Talk about jobs and professions ■ Use the present perfect with *for* and *since* ■ Talk about what a job involves ■ Use the infinitive with *to* ■ Understand linkers for surprising information ■ Use phrases with *in* ■ Take part in a job interview ■ Write a CV	12.1 The working environment p116 12.2 The changing face of work p118 12.3 Vocabulary and skills development p120 12.4 Speaking and writing p122 12.5 ▶ Video *Personal assistant* p124 Review p125		Present perfect simple with *for* and *since* p116 Uses of the infinitive with *to* p118

Communication page 126   **Grammar Reference** page 134

4

VOCABULARY	PRONUNCIATION	LISTENING/READING	SPEAKING/WRITING
Transport p66			
Holidays p68	Word stress p68	▶ Video Vox pops 7 p69	
-ed and -ing adjectives p71		Reading recognizing paraphrasing p70	
			Speaking checking into a hotel p72 Writing short notes and messages p73
Skills and abilities p77	at p77	▶ Video Vox pops 8.1 p77	
Education p78		▶ Video Vox pops 8.2 p79	
make and do p81		Listening understanding connected speech (2) p80	
			Speaking asking for clarification p82 Writing completing a form p83
Body and actions p86		▶ Video Vox pops 9 p87	
Health and fitness p88	eat and bread p88		
Verbs and prepositions p91		Listening using sequencing words to understand p90	
			Speaking asking for help and giving advice p92 Writing a formal covering letter p93
Food p96	Words with shortened vowels p96	▶ Video Vox pops 10 p97	
Food containers p98			
Words with more than one meaning p101		Reading understanding reference words in a text p100	
			Speaking problems in a restaurant p102 Writing a restaurant review p103
Global issues p106			
The news p109		▶ Video Vox pops 11 p109	
Phrasal verbs p111		Listening understanding connected speech (3) p110	
	Expressing opinions politely p112		Speaking expressing and responding to opinions p112 Writing a presentation p113
Jobs, professions and workplaces p116	has and have p117	▶ Video Vox pops 12 p119	
Job responsibilities p118			
Phrases with in p121		Reading understanding linkers for surprising information p120	
			Writing a curriculum vitae p122 Speaking answering questions in a job interview p123

Audioscripts page 158   **Irregular verbs** page 166   **Phonemic symbols** page 167

5

Introduction to *Navigate*

Navigate is an English language course for adults that incorporates current knowledge about language learning with concern for teachers' views about what makes a good course.

Many English language courses today are based on market research, and that is appropriate. Teachers know what works in their classrooms, out of the many kinds of materials and activities they have available. However, relying only on market research discourages innovation: it ignores the wealth of knowledge about language learning and teaching that has been generated. *Navigate* has been developed in a cycle which begins by calling on both market research and the results of solid experimental evidence; and then by turning back to classrooms once more for piloting and evaluation of the resulting materials.

A course for adults

This is a course for adults, whether they want to use English for study, professional or social purposes. Information-rich texts and recordings cover a range of topics that are of interest and value for adults in today's world. Learners are encouraged to use their own knowledge and experience in communicative tasks. They are seen as motivated people who may have very busy lives and who want to use their time efficiently. Importantly, the activities in the course are based on how adults best learn foreign languages.

Grammar: accuracy and fluency

Adults learn grammar best when they combine a solid conscious understanding of rules with communicative practice using those rules (Norris & Ortega, 2000; Spada & Lightbown, 2008; Spada & Tomita, 2010). *Navigate* engages learners in thinking about grammar rules, and offers them a range of communicative activities. It does not skimp on information about grammar, or depend only on communicative practice for grammar learning. Texts and recordings are chosen to exemplify grammar features.

Learners are invited, when appropriate, to consider samples from a text or recording in order to complete grammar rules themselves. Alternatively, they are sometimes asked to find examples in a text that demonstrate a rule, or to classify sentences that fall into different rule categories. These kinds of activities mean that learners engage cognitively with the rules. This means that they will be more likely to notice instances of the rules when they encounter them (Klapper & Rees 2003), and to incorporate the rules into their own usage on a long-term basis (Spada & Tomita, 2010).

Navigate also offers learners opportunities to develop fluency in using the grammar features. Aspects of a grammar feature that may keep learners from using it easily are isolated and practised. Then tasks are provided that push learners to use the target grammar features in communicative situations where the focus is on meaning.

For more on *Navigate*'s approach to grammar, see pages 24–25 of this book.

Vocabulary: more than just knowing words

Why learn vocabulary? The intuitive answer is that it allows you to say (and write) what you want. However, the picture is more complex than this. Knowing the most important and useful vocabulary is also a key element in reading and listening; topic knowledge cannot compensate for vocabulary knowledge (Jensen & Hansen, 1995; Hu & Nation, 2000), and guessing from context usually results in guessing wrongly (Bensoussan & Laufer, 1984). Focusing on learning vocabulary generates a virtuous circle in terms of fluency: knowing the most important words and phrases means that reading and listening are more rewarding, and more reading and listening improves the ability to recall vocabulary quickly and easily.

Navigate's vocabulary syllabus is based on the *Oxford 3000*. This is a list of frequent and useful vocabulary items, compiled both on the basis of information in the British National Corpus and the Oxford Corpus Collection, and on consultation with a panel of over seventy language learning experts. That is to say, an initial selection based on corpus information about frequency has been refined using considerations of usefulness and coverage. To build *Navigate*'s vocabulary syllabus, the *Oxford 3000* has then been referenced to the Common European Framework of Reference for Languages (CEFR; Council of Europe, 2001), so that each level of the course focuses on level-appropriate vocabulary. For more information on the *Oxford 3000*, see pages 26–27 of this book.

Adult learners typically take responsibility for their learning, and vocabulary learning is an area where out-of-class work is important if learners want to make substantial progress. *Navigate* focuses on giving learners tools to maximize the efficiency of their personal work on vocabulary. One way it does this is to teach not only individual vocabulary items, but also a range of vocabulary systems, for example how common prefixes and suffixes are used. Another is to suggest strategies for vocabulary learning. In this way, learners are helped to grow their vocabulary and use it with greater ease.

Speaking: putting it all together

Based on a synthesis of research about how adults learn, Nation and Newton (2009) demonstrate that different kinds of activities are important in teaching speaking. *Language-focused learning* focuses explicitly and in detail on aspects of speaking such as comprehensible pronunciation, appropriately polite language for a given situation or tactics for holding the floor in a conversation. *Fluency development* gives learners focused practice in speaking more quickly and easily. *Meaning-focused output* provides opportunities to speak in order to communicate meaning, without explicitly focusing on using correct language.

Navigate covers all three kinds of activities. The course systematically teaches aspects of pronunciation and intonation that contribute to effective communication; appropriate expressions for a range of formal and informal situations; and ways of holding one's own in a conversation.

It offers activities to help learners speak more fluently. Very importantly, it offers a wealth of meaning-focused activities. Very often, these activities are tasks: they require learners to do something together to achieve something meaningful. These tasks meet Ur's (1981) criteria for a task that works: straightforward input, a requirement for interaction, an outcome that is challenging and achievable, and a design that makes it clear when learners have completed the task. Learners are not just asked to discuss a topic: they are asked to do something with some information that involves expressing thoughts or opinions and coming up with a recognizable outcome.

Reading: not just a guessing game

Typical English language courses tend to test rather than teach reading; and they often concentrate on meaning-focused strategies that assume learners should be helped to puzzle out the meaning in the text on the basis of prior knowledge. There is a large body of evidence that shows why this is inefficient, discussed in the essay on reading on pages 20–21 of this book. Activities such as thinking about the topic of the text in advance or trying to guess unknown words have limited benefit in helping learners to understand the text at hand. These activities have even less benefit in helping learners understand the next text they will read, and as Paul Nation (2009) notes, that is surely the goal of the classroom reading activity. *Navigate* focuses on explicit teaching of things like sound-spelling relations, vocabulary that appears often in certain kinds of texts, the ways that words like pronouns and discourse markers hold texts together, and techniques for simplifying difficult sentences. These will give learners ways of understanding the text they are reading, but more importantly the next text they will read.

Listening: a very different skill

Too many books treat listening as if it were just another kind of reading, using the same sorts of activities for both. *Navigate* takes into account that listening is linear – you can't look back at the text of something you're hearing – and that listening depends crucially on understanding the sounds of English and how they combine (Field, 2008). Practice on basic elements of listening will lead to faster progress, as learners acquire the tools to hear English better. People who read can stop, read again, and go back in the text; but listeners can't do this with the stream of speech. For listening, language-focused learning means starting with building blocks like discriminating the sounds of the language, recognizing the stress patterns of words, distinguishing word boundaries, identifying stressed and unstressed forms of common words, and holding chunks of language in mind for short periods. Concentrating on knowledge and skills like these will pay off more quickly than only focusing on meaning, and will make listening for meaning much more efficient. Fluency development in listening is important too: this means activities that teach learners to understand language spoken at natural speed, and give them progressive practice in getting better at it. *Navigate* includes activities that focus systematically on each of these areas separately, as well as giving opportunities to deploy this knowledge and these skills in more global listening. John Field's essay, on pages 22–23 of this book, gives more detail on this.

Writing for different purposes

Adults learning English for professional, academic or leisure activities will need to write different kinds of texts at different levels of formality. The *Navigate* writing syllabus is based on a so-called *genre* approach, which looks at the characteristics of the different kinds of texts students may be called upon to write. It implements this syllabus by way of activities that allow students to express their own meanings in drafting, discussing and redrafting texts. This has been shown to be an effective means of developing writing skills for adults (Hyland, 2011).

Navigate offers an innovative approach to developing reading and listening skills. This, combined with a solid speaking and writing syllabus, gives learners a sound foundation in the four skills. Grammar and vocabulary have equal importance throughout the course and learning is facilitated through the information-rich and engaging texts and recordings. It is the complete course for the 21st century adult learner.

Catherine Walter is the Series Adviser for the *Navigate* course. She is an award-winning teacher educator, materials developer and researcher. Catherine lectures in Applied Linguistics at the University of Oxford, where she convenes the distance MSc in Teaching English Language in University Settings, and she is a member of the Centre for Research and Development in English Medium Instruction.

References

Bensoussan, M. and Laufer, B. (1984). Lexical guessing in context in EFL reading comprehension. *Journal of Research in Reading*, 7(1), 15-32.

Field, J. (2008). *Listening in the Language Classroom*. Cambridge: Cambridge University Press.

Hyland, K. (2011). Learning to write. In Manchón, R. M. (Ed.), *Learning-to-Write and Writing-to-Learn in an Additional Language*, pp. 18-35. Amsterdam: John Benjamins.

Klapper, J. & J. Rees. 2003. 'Reviewing the case for explicit grammar instruction in the university foreign language learning context'. *Language Teaching Research* 7/3: 285-314.

Nation, I. S. P. (2009). *Teaching EFL/ESL Reading and Writing*. London: Routledge.

Nation, I. S. P. & Newton, J. (2009). *Teaching ESL/EFL Listening and Speaking*. London: Routledge.

Norris, J. M. and L. Ortega. 2000. Effectiveness of L2 instruction: a research synthesis and quantitative meta-analysis. *Language Learning* 50/3:417-528.

Schmitt, N. (2010). *Researching Vocabulary: A Vocabulary Research Manual*. Basingstoke: Palgrave Macmillan.

Spada, N. and Lightbown, P. M. 2008. Form-focused instruction: isolated or integrated? *TESOL Quarterly* 42/2, 181-207.

Spada, N. and Tomita, Y. 2010. Interactions between type of instruction and type of language feature: a meta-analysis. *Language Learning* 60/2:1-46.

Ur, P. (1981). *Discussions that Work: Task-centred Fluency Practice*. Cambridge: Cambridge University Press.

Navigate overview

Coursebook lesson 1

Unit topics
Navigate is created for adult students with content that appeals to learners at this level. The unit topics have been chosen with this in mind and vary from *Time* and *Work* to *Changes and Challenges*.

Goals
The goals show students what they will be working on and what they will have learnt by the end of the lesson.

Grammar focus box
At this level of *Navigate*, grammar is introduced inductively. Students are asked to complete the information in the Grammar focus box based on what has been introduced in previous exercises in the *Grammar & Speaking* or *Grammar & Reading* exercises. The Grammar focus box is followed by a number of spoken and written exercises in which the grammar is practised further.

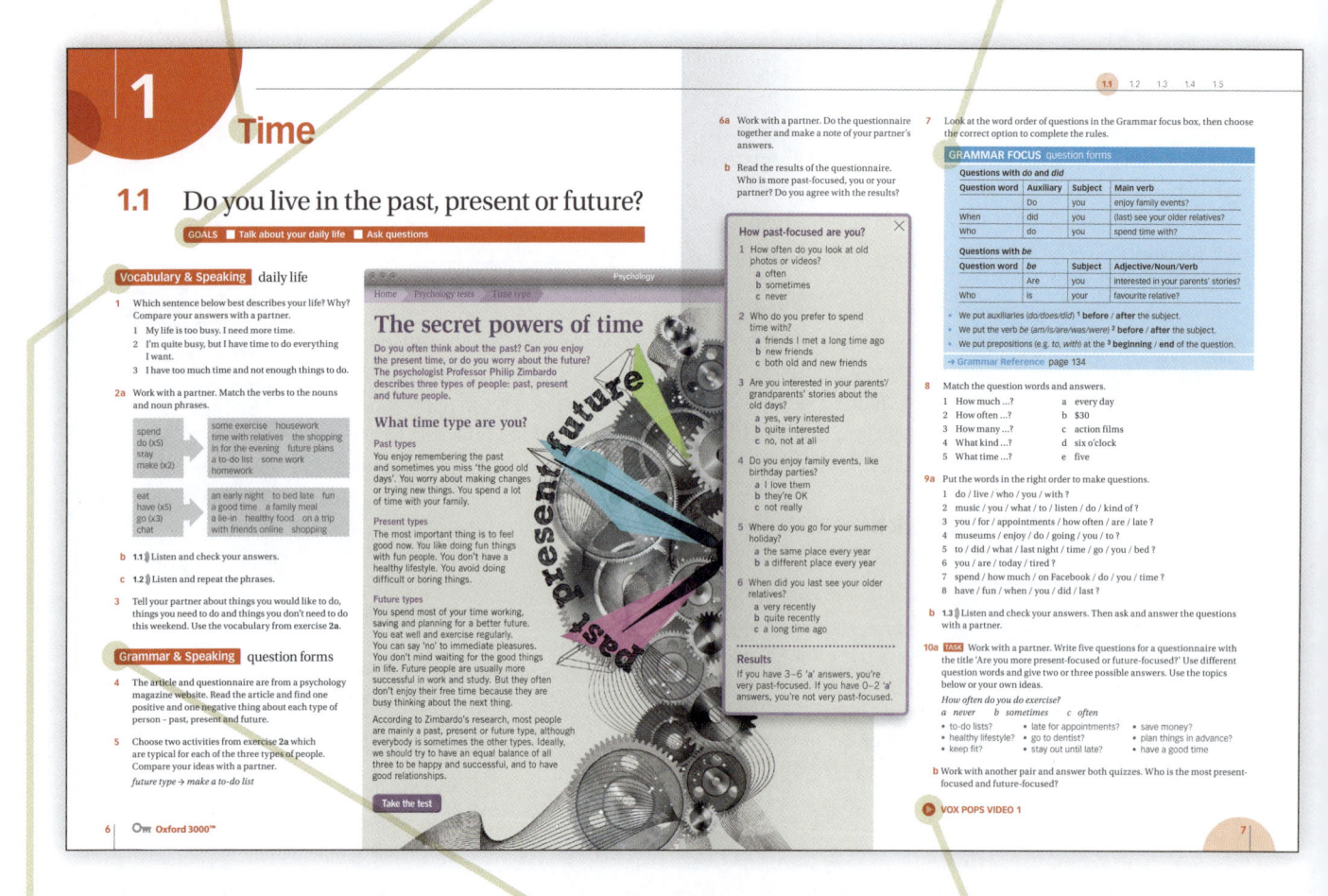

Vocabulary & Speaking
Navigate has a strong emphasis on active vocabulary learning. The first lesson in each unit starts with a *Vocabulary & Speaking*, a *Vocabulary & Listening* or a *Vocabulary & Reading* section in which essential vocabulary for the unit is introduced and practised. The vocabulary in lesson 1 and 2 is taught in topic sets, allowing students to build their vocabularly range in a logical and systematic way.

Grammar & Speaking
Grammar forms the 'backbone' of *Navigate*. Lesson 1 introduces the first grammar point of the unit. It is always combined with a skill, either reading or speaking. See page 24 of this book for more information.

Vox pops video
Most units contain a prompt to the Vox pops videos. The videos themselves can be found on the Coursebook DVD or Coursebook e-book, and the Worksheets that accompany them are on the Teacher's Support and Resource Disc. The videos themselves feature a series of authentic interviews with people answering questions on a topic that has been covered in the lesson. They offer an opportunity for students to hear real people discussing the topics in the Coursebook.

Coursebook lesson 2

Grammar & Speaking
Lesson 2 provides the second grammar point of the unit. It is always presented through a reading text or audio extract and is practised through controlled and freer exercises.

Grammar Reference
At the end of the Coursebook, the Grammar Reference section offers more detailed explanations of grammar and a series of practice exercises. This can be set as homework and then reviewed in class.

Vocabulary & Speaking
Navigate has a strong emphasis on everyday vocabulary that allows students to speak in some detail and in depth on general topics. Here students work on free-time activities. All target vocabulary in the unit can also be found in the wordlists on the Teacher's Support and Resource Disc, the e-book and the DVD packed with the Coursebook.

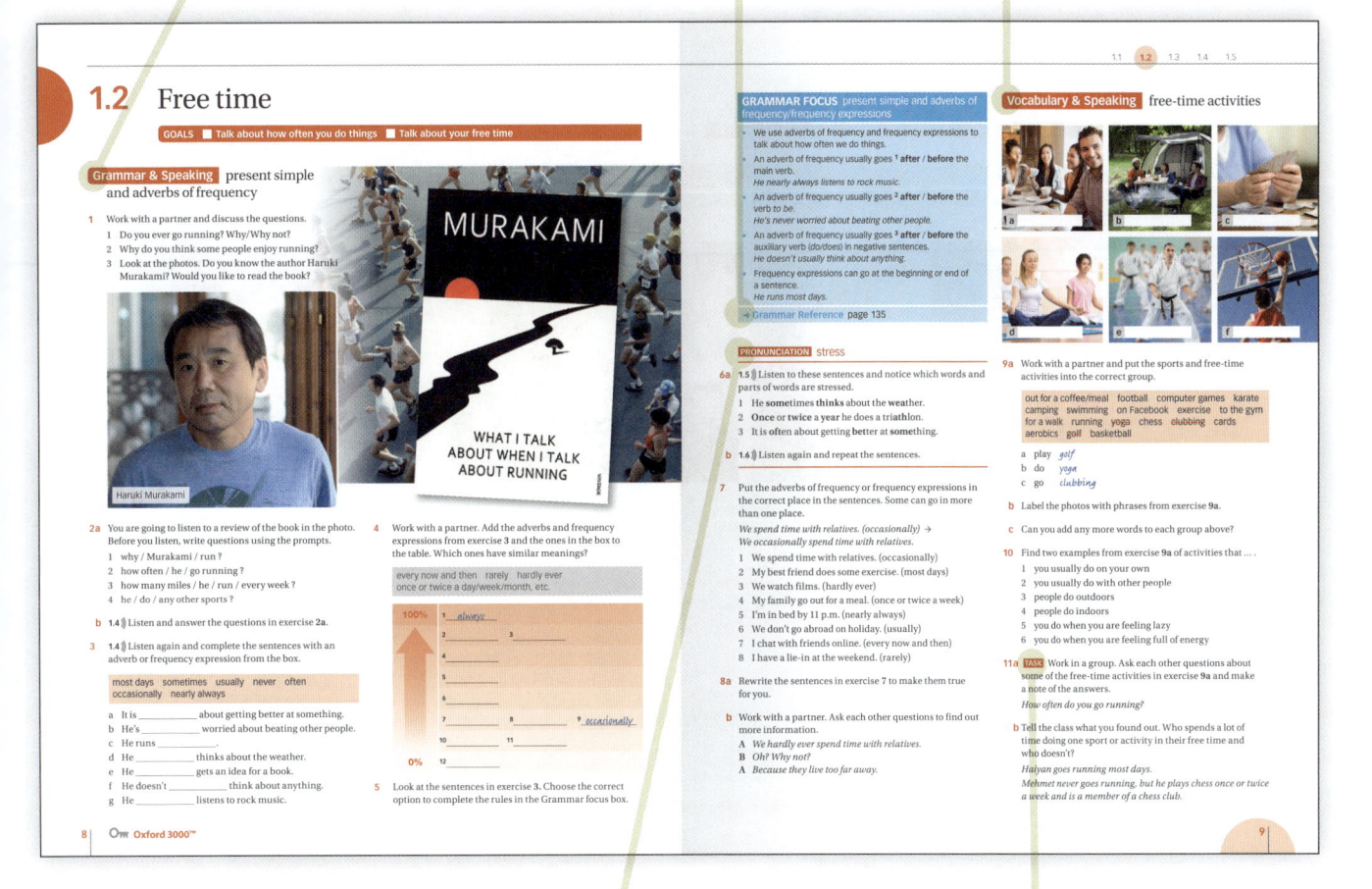

Pronunciation
Most units contain pronunciation work in either lesson 1 or lesson 2. Pronunciation in *Navigate* is always relevant to the grammar or vocabulary input of the lesson. The pronunciation exercises in the first two lessons focus mostly on speech production to improve intelligibility (for instance, minimal pairs and word stress). Pronunciation also appears in some Speaking and writing lessons and there it focuses mostly on teaching aspects of pronunciation that cause problems and confusion for listening comprehension (pronunciation for receptive purposes).

Task
Each lesson ends with a task which allows students to practise with others what they have learnt in the lesson. They often work in pairs or groups to complete the task.

11

Navigate overview

Coursebook lesson 3

Reading & Speaking
Navigate contains reading texts covering a wide variety of topics, text types and sources. As well as comprehension of interesting reading and listening texts, in this section students work on decoding skills to develop their reading or listening. These decoding skills, for example, predicting, connected speech, linking words, referencing words, etc., drill down to the micro level of reading and listening, and enable students to develop strategies to help them master these skills. See pages 20 and 21 of this book for more information.

Vocabulary and skills development
This lesson works on vocabulary and skills development. Students will, for instance, practise collocations, word building and word stress. The lesson also contains reading, writing, listening and/or speaking exercises.

Unlock the code
This section describes the decoding skill that is being taught in the reading or listening skills lesson. They are general tips which can be used as tactics for understanding when reading or listening to texts. This Unlock the code box is about predicting before reading.

Vocabulary focus
Vocabulary focus boxes appear in this lesson to draw attention to a particular vocabulary area, in this case nouns and verbs with the same form. The students go on to do some exercises where they use the information in this study tip. In other units, Vocabulary boxes deal with pre- and suffixes, adjectives, verbs and prepositions, etc.

Coursebook lesson 4

Speaking and writing
Navigate understands that classes can be made up of adults learning English for many different reasons. In lesson 4 of every unit, *Speaking and Writing*, *Navigate* provides appropriate communication practice for work, study or social life with an emphasis on language production. At the end of the speaking and writing sections, students complete a speaking or writing task. The lesson also contains two language focus boxes: *Language for speaking* and *Language for writing*.

Language for writing
The *Language for writing* box contains suggestions which students can use to complete their task in the writing section. There are various topics in this box throughout the Coursebook; here linking ideas with *and*, *but* and *so* are dealt with. In other units, the boxes focus on topics such as *Checking your writing*, *A formal letter* and *Opening and closing emails*.

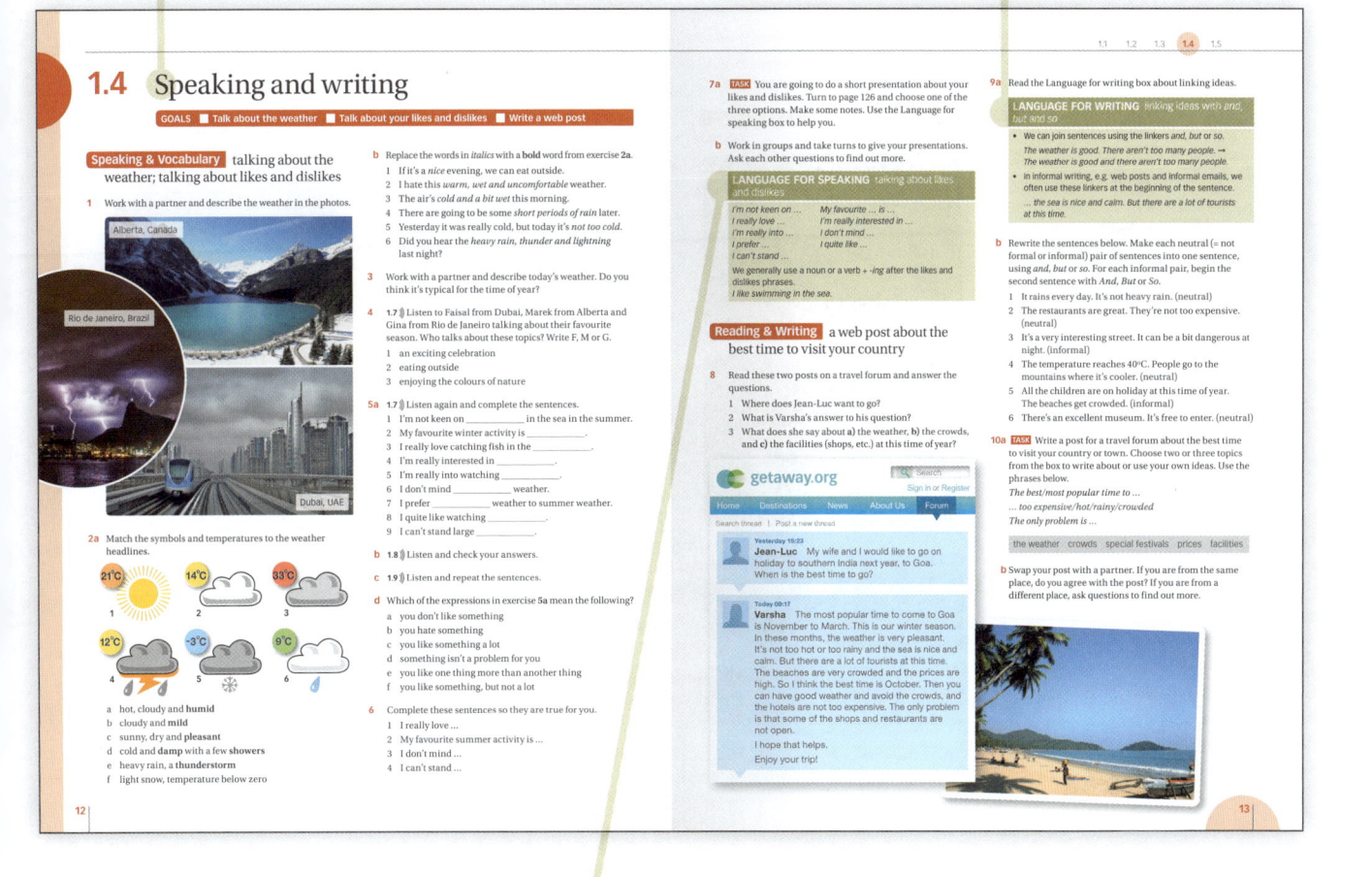

Language for speaking
The *Language for speaking* box contains phrases that students can use to complete a task about a particular topic. Here they have to talk about likes and dislikes in a presentation and they can use the phrases in the box. Other language for speaking boxes cover *Asking for help and giving advice*, *Explaining and dealing with problems* and *Asking for clarification*.

Navigate overview

Coursebook lesson 5

Video
The Video page contains activities that accompany the unit video. This video is a documentary video or authentic interview. The video page starts with one or two warmer activities which set the scene before the students watch the video, followed by two activities which check understanding of the video. The final activity is a task based on what the students have just watched.

In B1 the video topics are:
Unit 1: Adventure sports in Chile
Unit 2: London's changing skyline
Unit 3: The RRS *Discovery*
Unit 4: Esplorio
Unit 5: The Dubai Mall
Unit 6: Nettlebed
Unit 7: Beijing subway
Unit 8: Career change
Unit 9: Sports scholarship in the USA
Unit 10: Koreatown
Unit 11: The European Union
Unit 12: Personal assistant

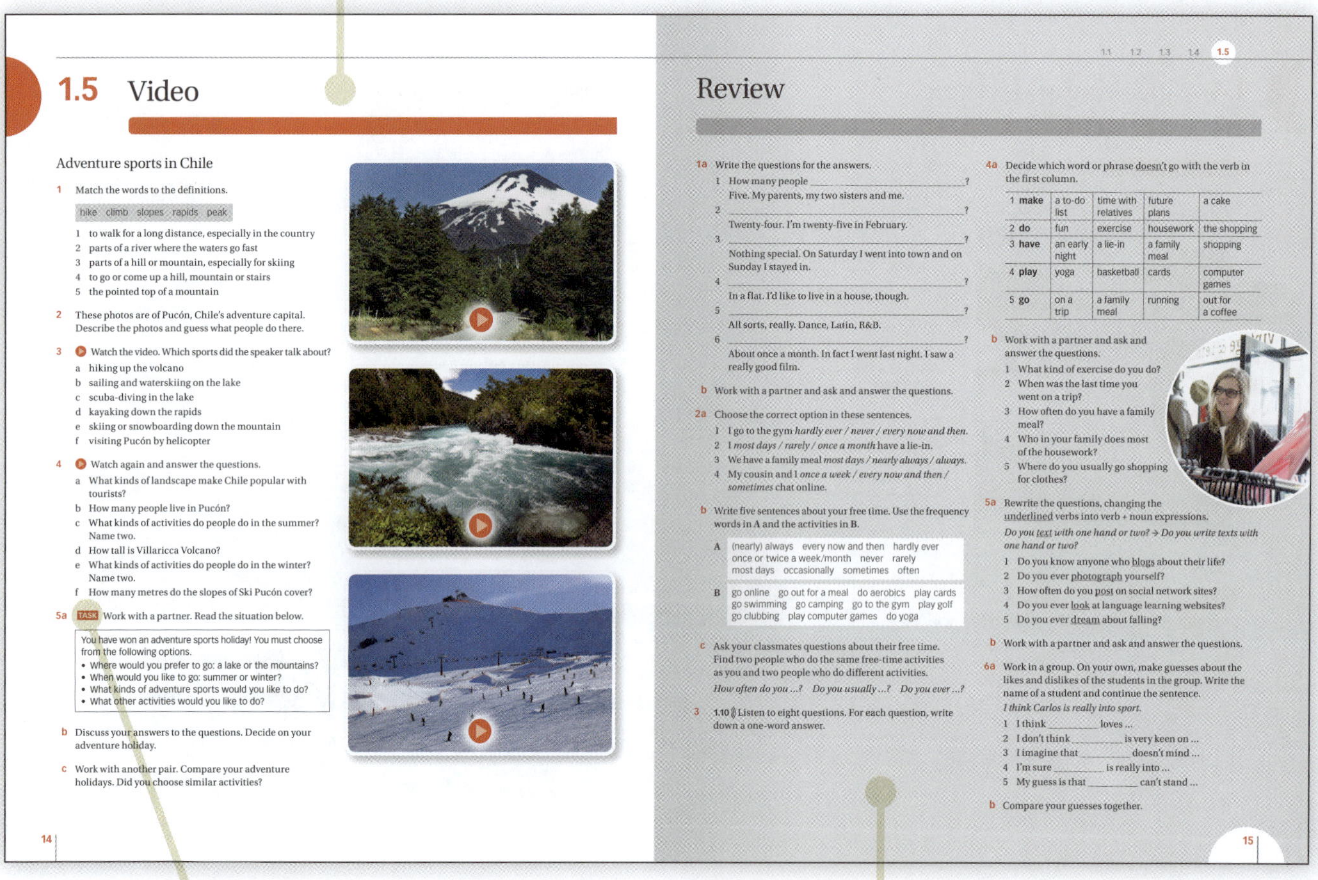

Task
The Task on the Video page is an outcome task which focuses on fluency. It can be a writing or speaking task. Here the students discuss their ideal adventure holiday in pairs and then compare their choice with another pair. Other tasks on Video pages are, for instance, making questionnaires, preparing a menu for a restaurant, creating a quiz and discussing ideas for an end-of-year event.

Review
The Review page contains revision of grammar, vocabulary and the skills practised in the unit. The Review activities can be set for homework, but are also specifically designed to be done in class incorporating pairwork and groupwork tasks to give learners additional opportunities to practise key language from the unit.

Workbook

Unit structure
The Workbook follows the Coursebook lessons. The first two spreads each have two pages of exercises which correspond with the Coursebook contents of the same lessons. Spreads 3 and 4 of the Workbook each have a page of extra practice which corresponds to the material in lessons 3 and 4 of the Coursebook. The Workbook also contains lessons for extensive reading and listening, review exercises, audioscripts of the listening material in the Workbook and answer keys (with key version only).

Grammar
In the Workbook, students find further practice of the grammar which they learnt in the corresponding lesson of the Coursebook. This page contains more exercises on making questions with *do/did* and *be* as introduced in the Coursebook.

I can …
At the end of each Workbook spread, the *I can* statements remind students which goals they should have reached. If they feel they need more practice, they can use the Online Practice materials (see page 19 of this book).

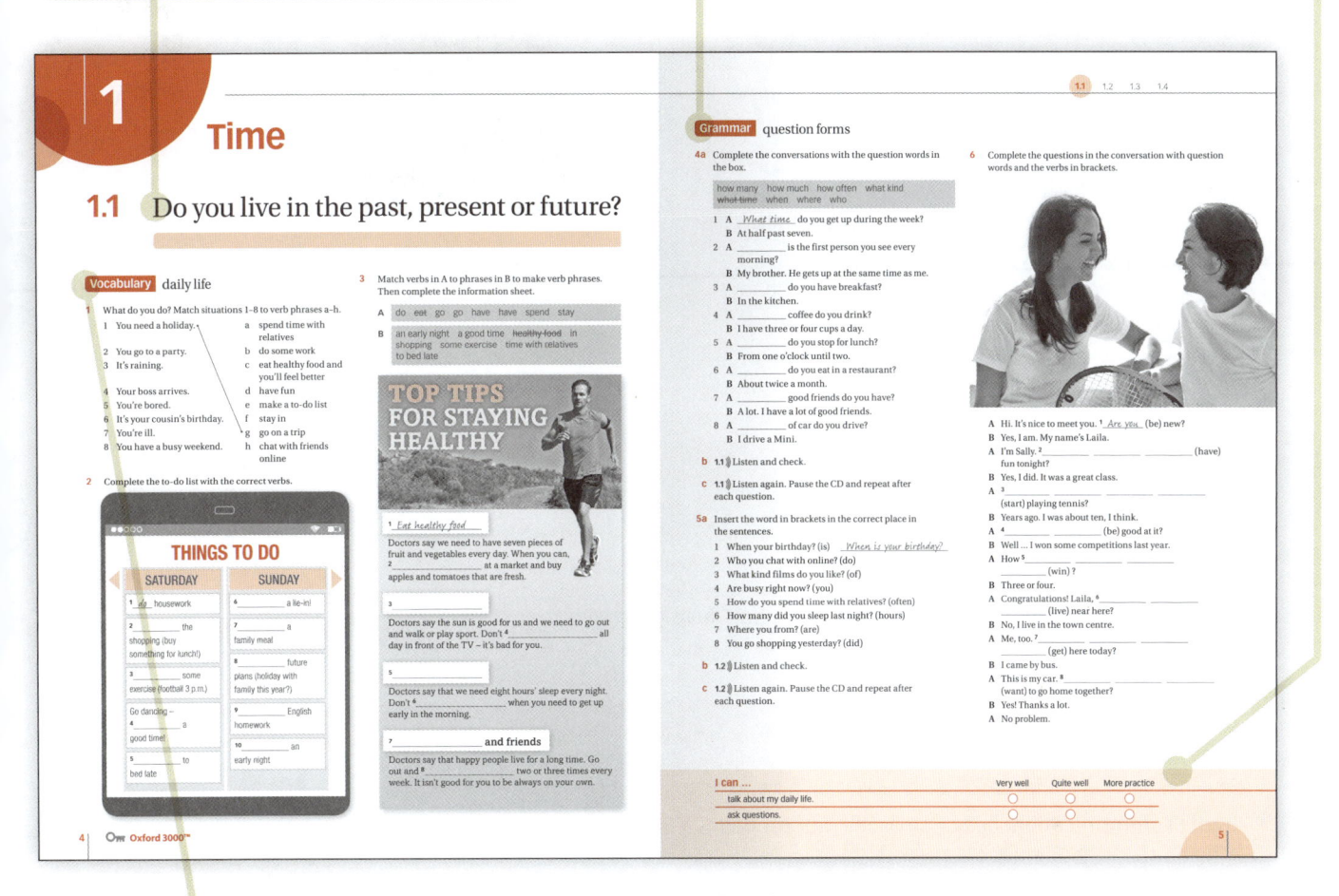

Vocabulary
In the Workbook, students find further practice of the vocabulary which they learnt in the corresponding lesson of the Coursebook. They can do this individually and at their own pace. On this page students practise the use of phrasal verbs with *spend, do, stay, make, eat, have, go* and *chat*.

Also in the Workbook

Reading for pleasure
The *Reading for pleasure* and *Listening for pleasure* pages appear once every two units in the Workbook. They offer students an opportunity for extensive reading or listening supported by a few exercises to ensure understanding. Here the students read an extract from a biography about Martin Luther King.

Review
As well as a Review page in every unit of the Coursebook, *Navigate* Workbook offers another chance for students to check what they have learnt with a Review page once every two units.

Navigate overview

Teacher's Guide and Teacher's Support and Resource Disc

The Teacher's Guide and Teacher's Support and Resource Disc Pack is a complete support package for teachers. It is designed for both experienced and new teachers and offers a wealth of resources to supplement lessons with Navigate.

What's in the Teacher's Guide?

The Teacher's Guide contains thorough teaching notes for teachers to follow as they go through the Coursebook in their lessons. Answer keys are provided to all activities where appropriate and the audioscripts are embedded within the teaching notes for ease of reference.

As well as this, though, the Teacher's Guide offers numerous ideas and extra support in the shape of the following features, to be found throughout the teaching notes:

- **Lead-in:** an extra activity at the start of every unit to encourage engagement with the topic of the unit.
- **Extra activity:** an activity that offers an alternative approach to the one in the Coursebook for variety or to tailor the material to a specific teaching situation.
- **Extension:** an idea on how to extend the activity in the Coursebook, useful especially if students have shown a strong interest in that topic.
- **Extra support/Extra challenge:** These are alternative ways of doing an activity where more staging may be required for learners who are struggling, or to keep stronger learners occupied in mixed ability classes.
- **Pronunciation:** tips and notes for teaching pronunciation.
- **Watch out!:** potentially problematic language points or language that learners might ask about.
- **Feedback focus:** guidelines on what to monitor in an activity and how to give feedback.
- **Dictionary skills:** moments when it may be useful to develop learners' dictionary skills and ideas on how to do it.
- **Smart communication:** tips on small talk, appropriacy, and communication strategies.
- **Critical thinking:** strategies to analyse and evaluate what learners read and hear, their work and that of their peers.
- **Study tips:** tips to help learners assimilate what they have learnt.

The Teacher's Guide also includes the following features:

- Essays by influential authors and experts in the fields of reading, listening, grammar, the CEFR, testing and photocopiable materials. These essays have been written by people who have contributed to the development of material used in Navigate.
- Photocopiable materials: Extra grammar, vocabulary and communication activities as photocopiable worksheets.
- Photocopiable worksheets to accompany the Vox pops videos found on the Coursebook DVD.

What's on the Teacher's Support and Resource Disc?

- **Lesson overview videos:** Catherine Walter, Navigate series adviser, offers one-minute overviews of each of the main lessons of the Coursebook, including the methodology behind it and the benefit to the learner.

- **Tests:** a full range of Unit, Progress and Exit tests to enable you and your students to monitor progress throughout their course. Available in PDF and Word format, and in A/B versions. See page 32 of this book for more details.
- MP3 audio for all of the tests.
- All of the photocopiable material that is found at the back of the Teacher's Guide as downloadable PDFs.
- Wordlists (A–Z and unit-by-unit)
- Audioscripts in Word of all Coursebook, Workbook and Test audio.
- Student study record: a self-assessment form to be filled in by the student after each unit is completed.

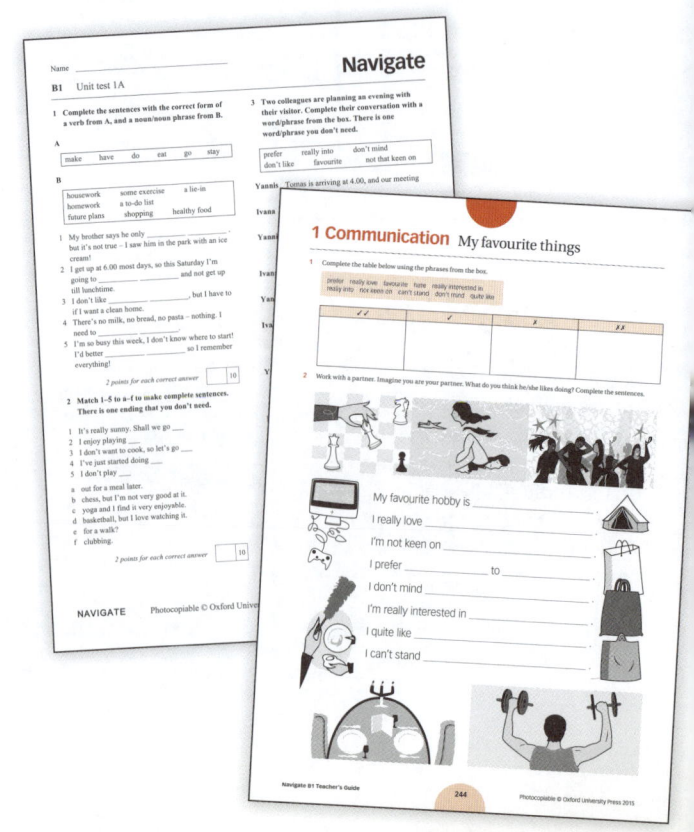

e-Books

The *Navigate* e-books are digital versions of the Coursebooks and Workbooks. Learners study online on a computer or on a tablet, and their work is safely saved in the Cloud. The *Navigate* e-book Teacher's edition is the Coursebook with integrated teacher's notes as well as selected pop-up images. You can use it as a classroom presentation tool.

To access an e-book:

1 Go to **www.oxfordlearnersbookshelf.com**.
2 To use your e-books on a tablet, download the app, and register or log in.
   To use your e-books on a computer, register or log in to the website.
3 **Note:** After you register, you can use your e-books on both a computer and a tablet.
4 Choose **Add a book**.
5 Enter your access code.

Watch this video for help on registering and using e-books: **www.brainshark.com/oup/OLBgetstarted**

In the *Navigate* e-Book Teacher's edition, the teacher's notes from the Teacher's Guide can be called up on the page where the information is needed.

Draw on the page or highlight text.

Find units quickly, jump to a page, or bookmark a page.

The listening materials that go with the course play straight from the page and are placed with the exercise where they are needed. The user can slow the material down to hear each word clearly and then speed up again. In addition, learners can improve pronunciation by listening to the audio, record their own and then compare to the original. The e-books also contain video material which can be played straight from the Video lesson page. The video material can be played full screen, or split screen to move around the pages and complete activities as you watch.

Automatic marking helps learners check progress and learn from their mistakes. They can also email a page to you to mark or to add to their learning portfolio.

The sticky note can be used to place comments with an exercise. These comments can either be written or recorded and can be placed anywhere on the page.

This tool allows the user to move back to the original page. For instance, if the user has moved from a lesson page to a grammar reference page, clicking on this arrow will move the reader automatically back to the page they came from.

Many images in the *Navigate* e-Book Teacher's edition can be enlarged by clicking on the image. This functionality can be used in class to discuss particular images in detail or to aid completion of exercises that go with the photos.

17

Navigate overview

iTools

Navigate iTools is a digital tool, specifically designed for use on whiteboards, that can also be used with data projectors, and PCs or laptop computers. Pages from the Coursebook and Workbook are seen on screen with various tools to help the teacher present the material in class.

This tool appears with each exercise and allows the teacher to discuss an exercise in class whilst calling up the answers. Clicking on the key will pop up a box containing the exercise rubric and spaces which can hold the answers when you click on the relevant buttons in the bottom of the box. There are three options: 'see next answer', 'see all answers', and 'hide all answers'.

The grammar reference page can be reached by clicking on the book icon placed near the Grammar focus box. The user jumps to the relevant grammar reference page and can return to the original page again by using the arrow button at the bottom of the page.

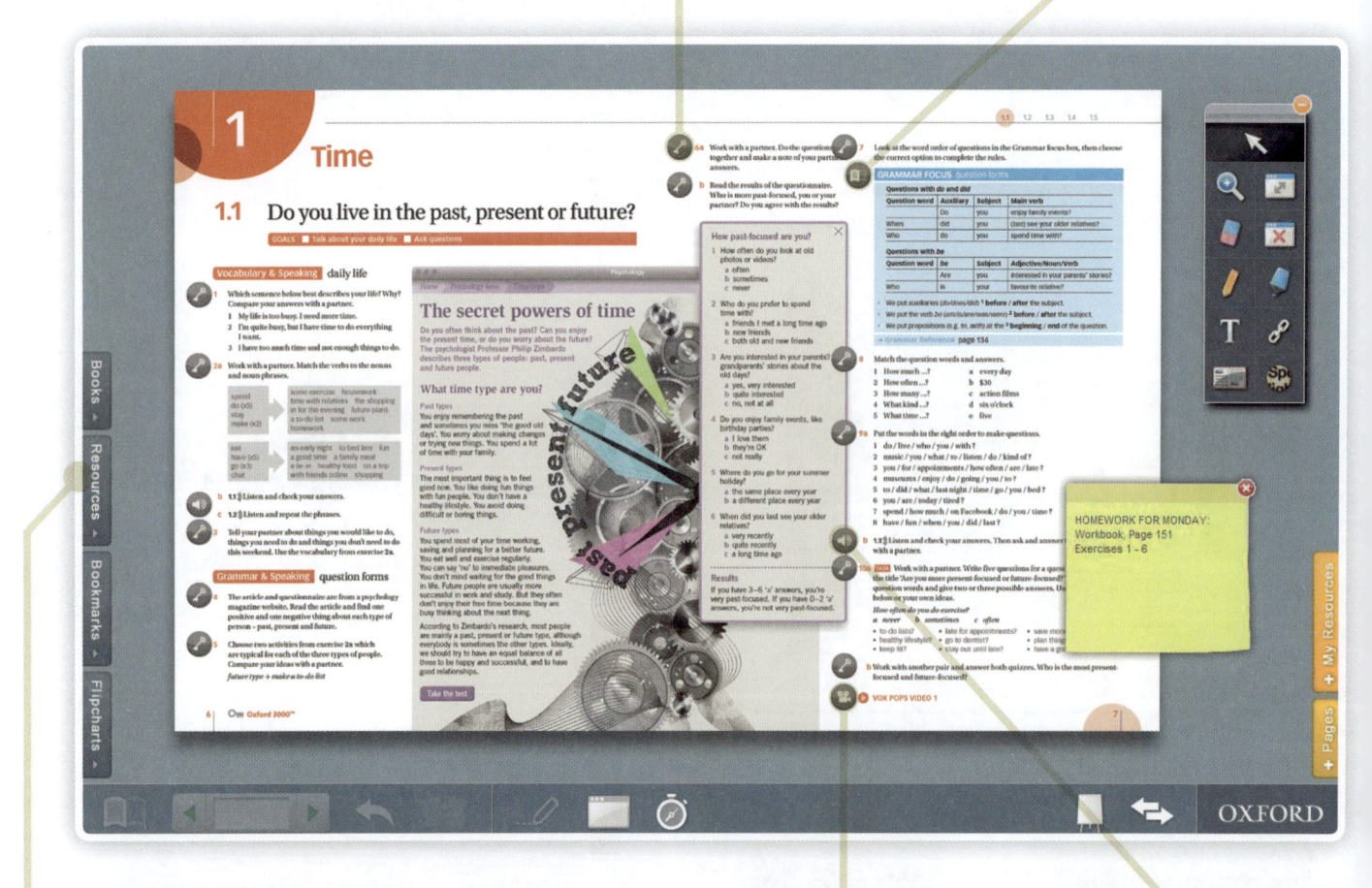

Resources

Navigate iTools includes a number of resources for use in the classroom:
- The Vox pops worksheets.
- Photocopiable materials from the Teacher's Guide are available to download here, as are wordlists.
- New Grammar Powerpoint presentations for display on your whiteboard help you teach the grammar from the Coursebook in a more interactive way.

Video can be played on your whiteboard by clicking the icon.

This tool allows the teacher to play the audio material that is relevant to the exercise. The teacher can also reveal the audio script so that students can read along whilst they listen.

Online practice

Our online practice courses give your learners targeted extra practice at the level that's right for them. Supported by the online Learning Management System, teachers and administrators can assign media-rich activities for the classroom or at home, and measure learners' progress.

Each learning module uses a step-by-step process, engaging learners' interest, then encouraging them to explore, practise and reflect on their learning.

Learners can study independently with a wide range of support materials: Cultural glossaries, Language models, Wordlists, Grammar and Vocabulary Reference, hints and tips, automatic marking and instant feedback.

You can monitor your learners' progress with a variety of management tools, including a Gradebook and User Progress statistics.

Create your own new content to meet the needs of your learners, including speaking and writing tasks, tests, discussions and live chat. You can also upload videos, audio and Powerpoint® presentations.

Oxford Online Skills
(General English, Bundle 2)
Helps learners focus on developing their Listening, Speaking, Reading and Writing skills, in the classroom or at home

- Engage learners with 30 hours of media-rich activities per level, including videos, interactive infographics and striking photography, on culturally diverse topics.
- Topics complement those found in *Navigate*. For example: My family, the past, giving opinions, writing emails or blog posts.
- Learners' access codes come on a special card included with their Coursebook.
- Variety of top-up materials if you'd like more skills practice for your learners. Choose more modules for general English with General English Bundle 1, or focus on Academic English, all four skills or paired skills (Reading & Writing, Listening & Speaking). The choice is yours. Find out more at **www.oup.com/elt**.

Oxford Online Language Practice
Puts the spotlight on building up learners' vocabulary and grammar

- With a topic-based approach, grammar and vocabulary is integrated in a meaningful and contextualized learning journey.
- Topic areas reflect those commonly found in Adult general English courses, and include Education, Personality, Work, Holidays, Storytelling, Crime and Entertainment.
- Comprehensive support for learners in every Module, with printable grammar and vocabulary references and wordlists, and notes on key differences in American and British English.
- Each CEFR level includes 12 Modules and 25 hours of learning and practice material.

Learners' access codes come on a special card included with *Navigate* Pack 3. If you do not have Pack 3, you can buy this course online from **www.oup.com/elt**.

Oxford English for Work
Telephoning, Socializing and Writing Skills

- Each level includes three skills: Telephoning, Socializing and Writing.
- Activities are highly practical and immediately transferable to the workplace.

Learners' access codes come on a special card included with *Navigate* Pack 3. If you do not have Pack 3, you can buy this course online from **www.oup.com/elt**.

The *Navigate* approach – Reading

Reading tomorrow's text better – Catherine Walter

Learning to play beautiful music does not start with playing beautiful music. No one would expect to start learning the cello by trying to play a concerto; rather, they would learn how to use the bow and to finger the notes, to transition quickly and accurately from one note to another, to relate the musical notation on the page with the physical movements needed to play, and to work on making all that happen smoothly.

In the same way, becoming skilled at reading comprehension in a second language is not best achieved solely by practising comprehension. Of course, the goal of reading activities in an English language course is to help learners achieve better comprehension of the English language texts that they read. However, this does not mean that all of the activities in the classroom should be comprehension activities.

To read well in a second language, readers need to decode written text accurately and fluently (Grabe, 2009). Accurate decoding means being able to make a connection between the words on the page, how they sound and what they mean. Making a connection between the written words and how they sound is important because readers of alphabetic languages immediately convert what they read to silent speech in their minds, using that silent speech to build a mental representation of the text (Gathercole & Baddeley, 1993).

- *Second language readers need practice in matching common spellings and the way they sound, and they need to recognize common words that are spelt irregularly.*

Just as fluent playing of a piece of music is not only achieved by playing it again and again, but by playing scales and doing other exercises, fluency in reading comprehension is not best achieved only by extensive reading – although this has a part to play. Fluency development activities can help (Nation, 2009).

- *Second language readers need to focus on reading fast and without hesitation.*

Knowing how the words sound is useless if the reader does not know what the words mean. Contrary to popular myth, skilled readers who are reading a text for information or pleasure do not spend a lot of time guessing unknown words, because they already know all the words. Skilled readers do not sample bits of the text and deduce what the rest of the text means; they process the entire text, rapidly and automatically (Grabe, 2009). Skilled readers do not use context to infer meaning as often as less-skilled readers do: they do not need to, because they know the words (Juel, 1999). Second language readers who guess unknown words usually guess them wrongly (Bensoussan & Laufer, 1984). To read a text comfortably without using a dictionary, second language readers need to know the meanings of 98% of the words in a text (Hu & Nation, 2000). Note that topic familiarity cannot compensate for second language proficiency (Jensen & Hansen, 1995).

- *Second language readers need to learn the most common and useful words at their level, and they need to be able to recognize them quickly and automatically.*
- *They need to be aware of vocabulary systems, such as how prefixes and suffixes work, so that they can recognize word families, and can learn more vocabulary independently.*
- *More time should be spent on learning vocabulary than on learning to guess unknown words; teaching about guessing unknown words should be strategic.*
- *Activating learners' prior knowledge about a text they are about to read has a very limited effect on how well they will understand it.*

To read well, second language readers need to be able, accurately and fluently, to break down the grammar of the sentences they are reading. They also need to know how these sentences are put together to make a text. Recognizing how sentences are assembled in a text means, for example, recognizing the uses of determiners like *this* and *that*, of words like *which* that link one part of a sentence to another, of expressions like *on the other hand* that say what the writer thinks about what follows.

- *Texts for language learners should contain high-frequency grammatical features in natural contexts.*
- *Second language readers should learn how ideas are linked within texts, e.g. with pronouns, lexical links and discourse markers.*

Paul Nation (2009) points out that what happens in many second language reading activities is that the learners are helped to understand the text in front of them. Nation says that the question for the teacher of reading should rather be:

How does today's teaching make tomorrow's text easier to read?

This is the aim of many of the teaching activities in *Navigate*. Some of the activities that contribute to better reading are not specifically labelled as reading activities. For example, there is work on matching spelling and sounds. There is a carefully staged vocabulary syllabus based on the Oxford 3000™ list of frequent and useful words (Oxford University Press, 2014). There is regular work on vocabulary systems.

In addition, each reading text

- has intrinsic interest, so that learners will want to read it
- contains high-frequency, useful vocabulary
- contains useful grammatical features in natural contexts
- exemplifies features of natural connected texts.

Generally, the reading texts in *Navigate* are the starting point for intensive language-focused learning of reading skills. That is to say, the activities surrounding them are part of a structured programme which aims to prepare learners to read the next text they will encounter more skilfully.

The activities do this by

- helping learners to read more accurately and/or more fluently
- focusing on aspects of the current text that commonly occur in other texts
- prompting learners to understand and reflect upon the ways in which important grammar and discourse features are exemplified in the text
- concentrating on working with features that occur more often in written than spoken language
- providing activities that help learners to understand the text as a whole
- providing teacher and learner with information about the learner's performance, as a basis for future work.

All these teaching activities contribute to a structured programme which will move learners more efficiently towards becoming better readers of English.

References

Bensoussan, M. and Laufer, B. (1984). Lexical guessing in context in EFL reading comprehension. *Journal of Research in Reading*, 7(1), 15-32.

Gathercole, S. E. & Baddeley, A. D. (1993). *Working Memory and Language*. Hove, England: Lawrence Erlbaum Associates Ltd.

Grabe, W. (2009). *Reading in a Second Language: Moving from Theory to Practice*. Cambridge: Cambridge University Press.

Hu, M. H. & Nation, P. (2000). Unknown vocabulary density and reading comprehension. *Reading in a Foreign Language* 13/1:403-430.

Jensen, C. & Hansen, C. (1995). The effect of prior knowledge on EAP listening-test performance. *Language Testing* 12:99-119.

Juel, C. (1999). The messenger may be wrong, but the message may be right. In J. Oakhill & S. Beard (Eds.), *Reading Development and the Teaching of Reading*, 201-12. Malden, MA: Blackwell.

Nation, I. S. P. (2009). *Teaching ESL/EFL Reading and Writing*. London: Routledge.

Reading in *Navigate*

Navigate includes micro-skills work on reading, helping learners to identify common aspects of reading texts, which in turn enables them to develop their reading skills in general. These *Unlock the code* boxes identify some specific areas of reading skills that are exploited in lesson 3 in six of the units.

> **UNLOCK THE CODE** linkers for reason and result
>
> - Words like *but*, *because* and *so* are 'linkers' or 'linking words'. It's important to understand them because they help you predict what kind of information comes next in a text.
> - *As*, *because* and *since* tell us the reason for something.
>   *He didn't buy the dishwasher, as his kitchen was too small.*
> - *So*, *therefore*, *as a result* and *for this reason* tell us the result of something.
>   *He had too many things. So his house was untidy.*

> **UNLOCK THE CODE** paraphrasing
>
> - To avoid repetition, writers use different words with a similar meaning.
>   *I love London, but I find the capital a difficult place to live in.*
> - To understand a text better, you need to recognize paraphrasing, otherwise you may think the writer is talking about two different things.

> **UNLOCK THE CODE** reference words in a text
>
> - We often use words like *this*, *that*, *these*, *those* to refer to a word or group of words earlier in a text.
>   Compare:
>   *One third of the world's food is wasted. This is a shocking figure.*
>   *One third of the world's food is wasted. This is shocking.*
> - Other words which refer back are *the one(s)* and *so*. *The one(s)* refers back to a noun(s). *So* refers back to a verb.
>   *The red apples look fresh. So do the green ones.*

5 Complete the text with *who*, *which* or *where*. Which ones could be replaced by *that*?

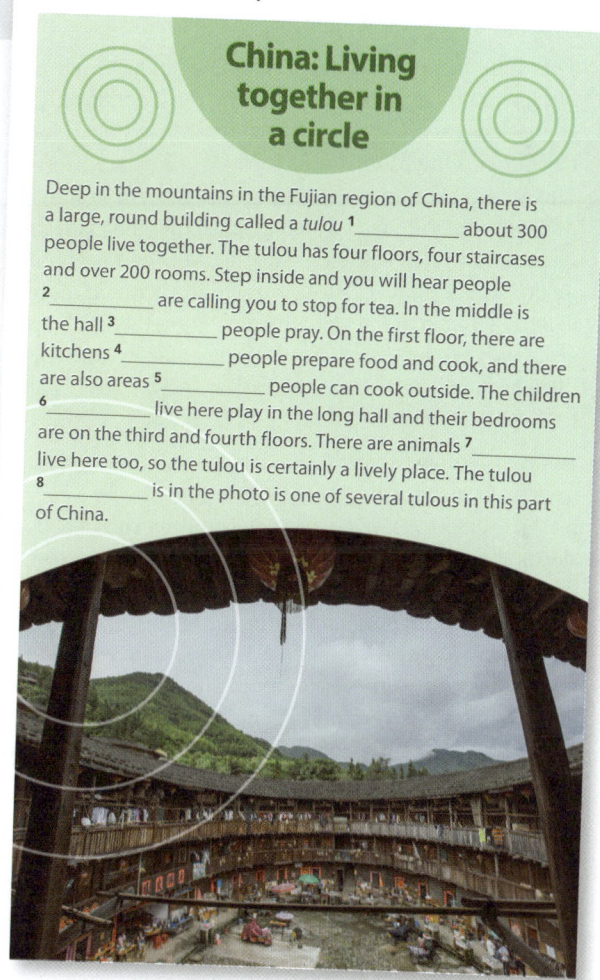

China: Living together in a circle

Deep in the mountains in the Fujian region of China, there is a large, round building called a *tulou* **1**_____ about 300 people live together. The tulou has four floors, four staircases and over 200 rooms. Step inside and you will hear people **2**_____ are calling you to stop for tea. In the middle is the hall **3**_____ people pray. On the first floor, there are kitchens **4**_____ people prepare food and cook, and there are also areas **5**_____ people can cook outside. The children **6**_____ live here play in the long hall and their bedrooms are on the third and fourth floors. There are animals **7**_____ live here too, so the tulou is certainly a lively place. The tulou **8**_____ is in the photo is one of several tulous in this part of China.

This approach is used in combination with a more top-down approach to reading where students read content-rich texts as vehicles for grammar or vocabulary learning, and to stimulate discussion on a topic of general interest to adults. All reading texts have been carefully graded. Vocabulary level in the texts is checked against CEFR levels to ensure that only a minimum number of words are above the level expected to be understood by learners at the level of the Coursebook.

The *Navigate* approach – Listening

Training better listeners – John Field

In the early days of ELT, listening was mainly employed as a means of presenting new language in a dialogue context. In time, teachers and teacher trainers came to recognize the importance of teaching the four skills for their own sake, but there remained the problem of precisely how to do it. For listening, they fell back on a method widely used in L1 and L2 reading, as well as in early listening tests – namely the comprehension question. More enlightened teachers played short sections of a recording and asked oral comprehension questions; but coursebook materials often relied on a conventional lesson format where the teacher sets comprehension questions in advance of listening, plays a three- or four-minute recording and then checks answers.

This approach became very entrenched in ELT methodology, but it was not without its critics. The most commonly expressed reservation was that it *tested* listening rather than *teaching* it. Other drawbacks were less often mentioned. The method is very teacher centred. The comprehension questions are often in written form so that the task taps into reading as well as listening. The focus on 'comprehension' diverts attention from the fact that there is much more to listening than just the end-product. Above all, if a learner gives the right answer to a question, it tells us nothing about the way in which they arrived at that answer, so we cannot help them to listen better.

Today, listening instruction has moved on. Current approaches treat listening as a form of expertise, like driving a car or learning chess. A novice trying to acquire expertise in any skill starts out by needing to focus a lot of attention on the basic processes that make up the skill (in the case of listening, an L2 learner might need to concentrate on just recognizing words). With time and practice, however, these basic processes become more and more automatic and demand less attention. This enables the novice to perform more efficiently – in the case of the L2 listener, to switch attention from word recognition to building up a wider picture of the speaker's purpose and the conversation as a whole.

This perspective suggests the need to practise the fundamentals of the listening skill as intensively as possible in the early stages of a teaching programme. It also suggests the wisdom of reserving some of the more complex processes associated with context, interpretation or line of argument for higher-level learners.

L2 listeners' needs can be tackled in three ways

Exposure to the input

Learners need to hear short clips which illustrate some of the phonetic features of English that prevent listeners from recognizing words. Words in connected speech do not have standard forms like they do in writing. Because speakers take short cuts in producing them, they are often subject to elision (*didn't* → *'dint'*), assimilation (*ten pounds* → *'tem pounds'*), liaison (*tie up* → *'tieyup,' go out* → *'gowout'*) or resyllabification (*find out* → *'fine doubt'*). Words that are of lesser importance in an utterance are often reduced. Function words in English have weak forms (*have, of, a* and *are* can all be represented by the single weak sound schwa /ə/), and words in commonly occurring chunks of language often get downgraded in prominence (*Do you know what I mean?* can be reduced to as little as '*Narp mean?*').

The best way of dealing with these perceptual problems is by using small-scale exercises that focus on examples of just one of the features mentioned. The teacher reads aloud these examples or plays a recording of them and learners transcribe them. But this is no conventional dictation exercise: it employs speech that is as natural as possible, not read-aloud; and learners are not penalized for spelling errors. For examples, see Field, 2008: Chap. 9.

Training in expertise

Psycholinguistic models of listening have demonstrated that the skill demands five distinct operations:

- Decoding: matching the signals that reach our ears to the sound system of the language
- Lexical search: matching groups of sounds to words in our oral vocabulary
- Parsing: combining groups of words into grammatical units to obtain a simple point of information
- Meaning construction: interpreting the information in terms of context and the goals of the speaker
- Discourse construction: adding the information to what has gone before.

All five can be practised by means of small-scale exercises. In terms of lexical search, a major challenge when listening to any language is that there are no consistent gaps between words in connected speech like those in writing. It is the listener who has to decide where one word ends and the next begins (Field, 2003). A useful exercise is therefore for the learner to listen to a short passage of natural speech and write down any words that he/she has recognized, then to replay the passage several times, each time adding more words. This kind of task is best done at the learner's own pace – for homework or in a listening centre. Parsing can be practised by playing half of a sentence and asking learners to use what they have heard so far to predict the rest. Discourse construction can be practised by asking learners to fill in a blank Table of Contents form. For multiple examples of these exercise types, see Field 2008: Chaps. 10–13.

Compensating for gaps

It has been suggested that lower-level L2 learners need a great deal of practice in cracking the code of speech before they can move on to building more complex meanings. This takes time, and learners feel frustrated when, despite their listening instruction, they find they understand little of what they hear on the internet or on TV, DVD and film. There is thus a further need to train learners (especially adults) in strategies which enable them to make the most of the little they are able to extract from a piece of real-world speech, at least until their listening improves. In one type of strategy practice, they listen to a short recording, try to work out the gist of what they have heard, share ideas in pairs, and then listen again (perhaps more than once) in order to check if they were right and to add new information. This type of task helps learners who dislike the uncertainty of not recognizing every single word, by encouraging them to make guesses. It also helps those who are more willing to take risks, by making them check their (sometimes rash) guesses against what comes next. The fact is that listening to speech (even in one's first language) is always a highly approximate process. Because words in speech vary so much, all listeners keep having to form hypotheses about what they have heard and revising those hypotheses as they hear more.

The tasks that have been suggested in this three-pronged approach focus on particular components of listening and are mainly small scale (some constituting just 5 minutes of intensive practice). So where does that leave the conventional comprehension task? Well, we do still need it. We need it in order to integrate many of the processes that have been mentioned. They do not operate in isolation and a listener has to learn to use them in conjunction with each other. The traditional comprehension recording also provides exposure to a wide range of voices, either in conversation or monologue. Adjusting to unfamiliar voices is a part of listening that we take for granted in our first language; but it can be demanding when the speaker is talking in a second language.

But we should perhaps rethink some aspects of the traditional comprehension task. Teachers and materials providers need to draw more heavily on authentic material – or at least use studio material that resembles natural speech in its pausing patterns, hesitations, overlaps, false starts, etc. Careful thought also needs to be given to the role of the comprehension question. It is quite possible to design questions that tap specifically into one of the five levels of processing identified above. This should be done in a way that reflects the capabilities of learners, with an emphasis at lower levels on questions that target word-level cues and factual information.

References

Field, J. 2003. Promoting perceptions: lexical segmentation in L2 listening. *ELT Journal* 57/4: 325–34

Field, J. 2008. *Listening in the Language Classroom*. Cambridge: Cambridge University Press

---

John Field is Senior Lecturer in the CRELLA research unit at the University of Bedfordshire, UK. He is especially known for his work on second language listening; and his *Listening in the Language Classroom* (CUP, 2008) has become a standard work in the field. His background in psycholinguistics (on which he has also written widely) informs much of his thinking. He is currently applying it to the notion of cognitive validity in L2 testing; and is developing new types of listening test which more accurately reflect the components of the skill. In another life, John was a materials writer and teacher trainer: writing coursebook series for Saudi Arabia and Hong Kong, radio programmes for the BBC World Service, and TV programmes for the Open University of China. He continues to advise publishers on materials design.

Listening in *Navigate*

The approach to listening in *Navigate* draws significantly on John Field's research, through a carefully graded listening skills syllabus focusing on features of the spoken language. These decoding skills for listening can be found in the skills development lessons and include the following areas:

UNLOCK THE CODE
connected speech

- When a word ends in a consonant and the next word starts with a vowel sound, speakers link the words together so they sound like one word. This can make it difficult to understand.

| went in | sounds like | wentin /wentɪn/ |
| the sound of it | sounds like | thesoundofit /ðəsaʊndʌvɪt/ |

- Sometimes words that end and start with consonants are also linked the same way.

| let's leave | sounds like | letsleave /letsliːv/ |

UNLOCK THE CODE
-t and -d before a consonant

- When a word ends in -t or -d and the next word begins with a consonant, we don't say the -t or -d.

Lift going up	sounds like	Lif going up
Second floor	sounds like	Secon floor
It isn't coming	sounds like	It isn coming

- Sometimes this happens with -t or -d inside a single word.

| politely | sounds like | poli-ly |
| friends | sounds like | friens |

UNLOCK THE CODE /w/ and /j/ sounds in connected speech

When a word ends with a vowel sound and the next word begins with a vowel sound, we sometimes add a /j/ sound or a /w/ sound to link the words.

/w/
I go out   do a challenge

/j/
the elevator   I agree

The *Navigate* approach – Grammar

Grammar: What is the best way to learn it? – Catherine Walter

Attitudes towards planned grammar teaching vary across the world. Some attitudes derive from theoretical stances that have not stood the test of time; yet they persist, here and there, in teacher education programmes, in national advice to teachers and in some language teaching materials.

One of the problems here may well be memories of classrooms where students learnt grammar rules, but didn't use them in communicative activities. It became clear that this was not a good way for learners to become good communicators in their second language. This led to proposals in which learning of grammar rules was seen as counterproductive.

One idea that emerged was that grammar should be taught only when the need for a particular grammar feature emerged spontaneously. The idea was that in the course of a communicative activity, the learner would want to say something, but lacked the necessary grammar. This was seen as the perfect time for the teacher to offer that grammar. However, there are three problems here. Firstly, in a classroom, different learners may be ready for a grammar point at different times. Secondly, it is not possible to construct a series of tasks from which every important grammar feature will emerge. Thirdly, classrooms are unpredictable. If the teacher is depending on what emerges in class for the whole grammar syllabus, they need to be able to give a clear, accurate, level-appropriate explanation of any feature that happens to emerge. This is not an easy task, and the chances of a teacher's improvising consistently good rules are small.

Some writers have proposed eliminating the teaching of grammar altogether. Krashen (1982) held that learners only need *comprehensible input*, a bit more advanced than the language they can already produce. He claimed that this would lead learners progressively towards proficiency. This approach has been clearly shown not to work, in careful studies by researchers such as Swain (1985) and Genesee (1987).

Another proposal is the Natural Order Hypothesis (Meisel, Clahsen & Pienemann, 1981): the idea that there is a natural developmental sequence for acquiring second language grammar features, no matter the order of teaching. This hypothesis has some evidence behind it, although only for a very few structures of the language. Even for those few structures, Goldschneider and DeKeyser (2005) demonstrated in a rigorous meta-analysis that the developmental order is strongly predicted by salience – how much the feature stands out in the language. Given this finding, it is clear that making a grammar feature more salient to the learner, for example by explicit teaching, should be a way of fostering learning.

It has also been claimed that peer-peer support, where students in a class help one another to learn, is an effective way of teaching grammar. This is based on a sound framework (Vygotsky, 1978), but the framework supposes an expert-novice pair, not two novices. Research has described some interesting interactions; but the peers almost always come up with a non-standard grammar form.

One respected framework for language acquisition that supports explicit grammar teaching is the input-interaction-output framework, in which the learner is gradually pushed to restructure their internal second language grammar so it approaches standard grammar more closely. Here, explicit grammar teaching is seen as valuable because it

- helps learners to notice grammar features in the input
- encourages learners to notice the differences between how they say something and how proficient speakers say it
- provides information about what *doesn't* happen in the language.

Another strong current approach, *task-supported instruction*, holds that it is important for learners to use their language in tasks, where the main focus is on meaning, but where the learners need to interact in their second language to reach an outcome. Early on, it was hoped that tasks would be enough to make grammar emerge. However, all serious scholars working in this paradigm (e.g. Skehan, 2003; Willis & Willis, 2007) now agree that pre-task and post-task explicit focus on grammar is necessary.

In a skills-based approach, where language learning is seen like learning to drive or to play a musical instrument, teaching grammar rules is highly valued. Learning the rules is seen as a precursor to being able to use those rules. As DeKeyser (1998) says, while you are learning to walk the walk, the rule is a crutch to lean on.

However, these are theories. What about the evidence? There have been rigorous meta-analyses finding that:

- explicit teaching of grammar rules yields better results than implicit teaching (Norris & Ortega, 2000)
- explicit teaching yields better results for both simple and complex forms (Spada and Tomita, 2010)
- explicit teaching of rules, combined with communicative practice, leads to unconscious knowledge of the grammar forms that lasts over time (Spada and Lightbown, 2008)
- there is no difference in results between integrating the teaching of rules with a communicative activity and teaching them separately (Spada and Tomita, 2010). In other words, presentation-practice-production works just as well as more integrated methods.

To summarise: there is theoretical support and hard evidence that teaching grammar rules, combined with communicative practice, is the best way for adults in classrooms to learn to use the grammar of their new language.

Navigate often teaches rules 'inductively': learners are given a bank of examples of the rule. Then they see part of the rule and are guided to think about how to complete it. There is evidence that for appropriate rules this works as well, and perhaps better, than giving the rule first (e.g. VanPatten & Oikkenon, 1996; Ming & Maarof, 2010).

Navigate also provides a wealth of communicative activities where the focus is on meaning, but which are structured so as to encourage the use of the rules that have been taught. This provides the second ingredient of the recipe that has been shown to be the best way for adults to learn to become more proficient users of second language grammar.

References

DeKeyser, R. 1998. 'Beyond focus on form: cognitive perspectives on learning and practicing second language grammar' in C. Doughty & J. Williams (eds.). *Focus on Form in Classroom Second Language Acquisition*. Cambridge: Cambridge University Press.

Genesee, F. 1987. *Learning through Two Languages*. New York: Newbury House.

Goldschneider, J. M. & DeKeyser, R. M. (2005). Explaining the "Natural Order of L2 Morpheme Acquisition" in English: A Meta-analysis of Multiple Determinants. *Language Learning* 55(S1):27-76

Krashen, S. 1982. *Principles and practice in second language acquisition*. Oxford: Pergamon Press.

Meisel, H., J. Clahsen & M. Pienemann. 1981. 'On determining developmental stages in natural second language acquisition'. *Studies in Second Language Acquisition* 3:109-135.

Norris, J. M. & L. Ortega. 2000. 'Effectiveness of L2 instruction: a research synthesis and quantitative meta-analysis'. *Language Learning* 50/3: 417-528.

Skehan, P. 2003. 'Task-based instruction'. *Language Teaching* 36/ 1:1-14.

Spada, N. & Lightbown, P. (1999). Instruction, first language influence, and developmental readiness in second language acquisition. *The Modern Language Journal* 83(i):1-22.

Spada, N. & P. M. Lightbown. 2008. 'Form-focused instruction: isolated or integrated?' *TESOL Quarterly* 42: 181-207.

Spada, N. & Y. Tomita. 2010. 'Interactions between type of instruction and type of language feature: a meta-analysis'. *Language Learning* 60/2: 1-46.

Swain, M. 1985. 'Communicative competence: some roles of comprehensible input and comprehensible output in its development', in S. Gass & C. Madden (eds.). *Input in Second Language Acquisition*. Rowley MA: Newbury House, 235-253.

Van Patten, B. & S. Oikkenon. 1996. 'Explanation versus structured input in processing instruction'. *Studies in Second Language Acquisition* 18/4: 495-510.

Vygotsky, L. S. 1978. *Mind in Society: the Development of Higher Psychological Processes*. Cambridge, MA: Harvard University Press.

Willis, D. & Willis, J. 2007. *Doing Task-Based Teaching*. Oxford: Oxford University Press.

Grammar teaching in *Navigate*

Grammar is taught in context through texts and audio recordings, and then followed up with Grammar focus boxes which offer the rules of the grammar point in a succinct and level-appropriate way.

Exercises to practise the grammar point offer controlled practice, and a speaking task gives learners the opportunity to reproduce the grammar point in a semi-controlled way.

The Grammar reference section at the back of the Coursebook offers more detailed grammar explanations and further controlled practice, to give learners as much opportunity as possible to assimilate the grammar point.

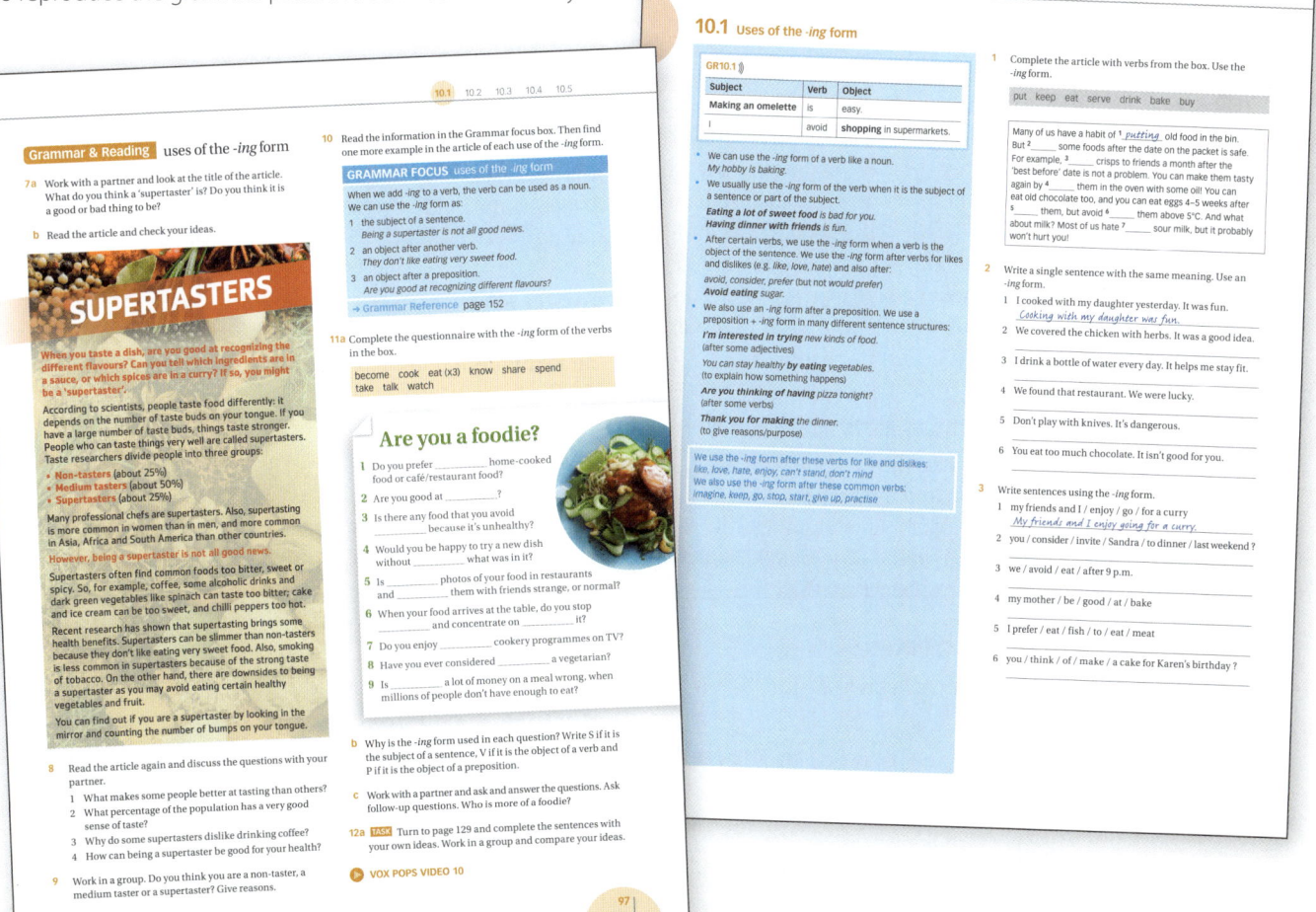

The *Navigate* approach – Vocabulary

Vocabulary and the Oxford 3000

Vocabulary is a crucial area of adult language learning and *Navigate* puts a strong emphasis on it. As well as useful and transferable vocabulary sets that allow students to speak in some detail and depth on general topics, there is a dedicated page in every unit on vocabulary development which covers areas like word families, prefixes or suffixes, collocations and fixed expressions.

In developing the vocabulary syllabus across the six levels of *Navigate*, special attention was paid to the Oxford 3000 – a tool to help teachers and learners focus on the key vocabulary needed to become proficient in English. The Oxford 3000 is integrated into the vocabulary syllabus and items from the coursebook that appear in the Oxford 3000 are indicated by a key symbol in the wordlists found on the Student's DVD, the Coursebook e-book, and on the Teacher's Support and Resource Disc. As you would expect, at the lower levels of *Navigate* a high proportion of words on these wordlists are in the Oxford 3000, and as students progress through the course to higher levels they will learn more vocabulary that sits outside this core 3000.

But what exactly is the Oxford 3000? Read on to find out.

The Oxford 3000 – The words students need to know to succeed in English

Which words should students learn to succeed in English?

The English language contains literally thousands of words and, as language teachers or language learners, it is often difficult to know which words are the most important to learn. To help with this, Oxford University Press's ELT dictionary team created the Oxford 3000 - a list of the 3000 words that students really need to know in English. It was drawn up in collaboration with teachers and language experts. The Oxford 3000 words are included in most OUP learner's dictionaries, including the Oxford Advanced Learner's Dictionary.

The Oxford 3000 words are marked with a key in OUP's learner's dictionaries, and are available on the www.oxfordlearnersdictionaries.com website. You can look up the entry for each word, and hear it pronounced in either British or American English. At elementary level OUP learner's dictionaries focus on the Oxford 2000, which includes 2000 of the words on the Oxford 3000 list.

How was the Oxford 3000 created?

There were three key requirements in creating the Oxford 3000:

1 sources – to provide evidence of how the English language is actually used

2 criteria – to use when analysing the sources

3 expertise – to provide insights into the vocabulary needs of learners of English.

1 Sources

The Oxford 3000 is a corpus-based list. A corpus is an electronic database of language from different subject areas and contexts which can be searched using special software. When lexicographers analyse a particular word in the corpus, the corpus shows all of the occurrences of that word, the contexts in which it is used, and the grammatical patterns of the surrounding words.

The Oxford 3000 is informed by the:

- British National Corpus (100 million words)
- Oxford Corpus Collection (developed by Oxford University Press and including different types of English – British English, American English, business English, etc.)

By using this combination of corpora, we can understand how English is currently used, and which words are used most frequently.

2 Criteria

When deciding which words should be in the Oxford 3000, corpus frequency alone was not used as a guide to inclusion. Three core criteria were identified:

- frequency – the words which appear most often in English
- range – the words which appear frequently AND across a broad range of different contexts
- familiarity – words that are not necessarily used the most frequently, but are important in general English.

The combination of frequency, range and familiarity means that the Oxford 3000 is more pedagogically informed than a list of words based on frequency alone. For example, when the corpus was analysed, it was found that we talk about 'Friday' and 'Saturday' more frequently than 'Tuesday' or 'Wednesday'. However, when learning the days of the week, it is useful to learn all of them at the same time – not just the most frequent ones. For this reason, all the days of the week appear in the Oxford 3000.

3 Expertise

A group of lexicographers and around 70 English language teachers from English language schools all over the world worked together on the Oxford 3000, bringing classroom experience and linguistic expertise together to create a list that truly supports the needs of language learners.

Why use the Oxford 3000?

When the research team looked at the corpora using the criteria mentioned above, they found that around 3000 words covered 80–85% of vocabulary in a general English text.

Here are the results of the research into frequency and coverage – that is, how much text is covered by the thousand most frequent words, the next thousand most frequent words, the third thousand most frequent words, and so on.

most frequent word families	coverage	total
1st 1000	74.1%	
2nd 1000	7.2%	2000 = 81.3% coverage (74.1% + 7.2%)
3rd 1000	3.9%	3000 = 85.2% coverage (81.3% + 3.9%)
4th 1000	2.4%	4000 = 87.6% coverage (85.2% + 2.4%)
5th 1000	1.8%	5000 = 89.4% coverage (87.6% + 1.8%)

12,500 word families cover 95% of text.

By learning the first 3000 words, students build a very strong vocabulary base which covers a significant majority of the words they will see in texts. The Oxford 3000 therefore provides a useful springboard for expanding vocabulary and is a valuable guide in vocabulary learning. If a learner comes across a new word and it is in the Oxford 3000, they can be sure that it is important to learn it.

Beyond the Oxford 3000
As students advance in their learning, the vocabulary they need will depend on the areas of English that they are interested in. The Oxford 3000 will give them a good base for expanding their lexical knowledge.

Dictionaries and the Oxford 3000

The Oxford 3000 app
Oxford 3000 is a list of the most important and useful words to know in English informed by corpus-based research. In a recent survey, over 60% of teachers told us they believe that learning the Oxford 3000 expands their students' vocabulary. The new Learn the Oxford 3000 app for iPad/iPhone™ helps students learn the Oxford 3000 with practice exercises and tests to check progress.

Oxford Wordpower Dictionary 4th edition
Updated with over 500 new words, phrases and meanings, *Oxford Wordpower Dictionary* is a corpus-based dictionary that provides the tools intermediate learners need to build vocabulary and prepare for exams. Oxford 3000 keyword entries show the most important words to know in English. This edition includes Topic Notes, Exam Tips and Writing Tips, and a 16-page Oxford Writing Tutor. Students can search the A-Z dictionary by word or topic on the CD-ROM, and use the exercises to practise for international exams.

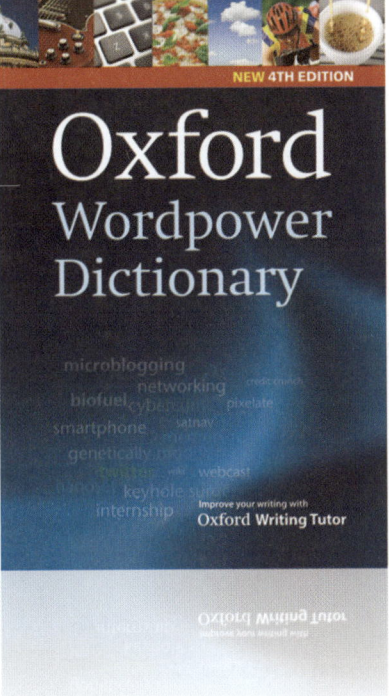

Oxford Advanced Learner's Dictionary 9
The *Oxford Advanced Learner's Dictionary* is the world's best-selling advanced learner's dictionary. The new ninth edition, featuring 185,000 words, phrases and meanings, develops the skills students need for passing exams and communicating in English. It is the ultimate speaking and writing tool, with brand new resources including the Oxford iSpeaker and Oxford Speaking Tutor.

The *Navigate* approach – Photocopiables

Photocopiable Teacher's Resource Materials – Jill Hadfield

What are photocopiable resource materials?

The resource materials in *Navigate* Teacher's Guide are one-page photocopiable activities that can be used to provide further practice of the target language in this book. There are 36 activities, divided into three sections: Grammar, Vocabulary and Communication, and they practise the target grammar, lexis and functions in the book.

What types of activity will I find?

There are two main types of activity in the photocopiable materials: linguistic activities and communicative activities.

Linguistic activities focus on accuracy and finding the right answer, inserting the correct word in a gap-fill, for example. These are familiar exercise types and require correct answers which are given in the Answer Key in the Teachers' Notes.

Communicative activities have non-linguistic goals: solving a puzzle or finding differences in two pictures, for example. The emphasis is more on fluency and on using the target language as a means to an end. The communicative activities in this book fall into two types: open-ended activities such as discussions or role plays with no fixed end-point or goal, and closed-task, game-like activities, such as board games or guessing games with a fixed goal.

Why use them?

The activities can be used to provide extra practice or revision in speaking, reading and writing the target language in each unit. The different types of activity provide different types of practice, which will appeal to different learner preferences. The linguistic activities provide practice in recalling the target language and using it accurately, and the communicative activities provide practice in recalling the target language and using it, integrated with other language, to complete a task. Some of these activities are designed with a game-like element: that is, they have a goal such as guessing or solving a problem, which students have to work together to achieve. This provides variety and a change of focus for the students and makes the practice fun and enjoyable. The element of play is also relaxing and lowers the affective filter (Krashen 1987) which makes learners less inhibited and more willing to use the language, and the fact that the activities have a goal is motivating for the learners and gives them a sense of satisfaction when they have achieved the goal. Other activities have a personalization element which is also motivating for the learners and leads to positive affect. Both personalized and playful activities involve the learners in investing more of themselves in the language, leading to deeper processing which helps retention of language items (Schmitt 2000).

When should I use them?

The activities can be used immediately at the end of each relevant section in the book for extra practice. Alternatively, they could be used later in the course for revision or review.

How should I use them?

The activities are for pair, group or whole class mingling work. This means you will have to think carefully about:

- how to arrange the groupings
- how to set up the activities and give instructions
- what your role will be during the activities
- what the different requirements of the 3 different activity types will be regarding monitoring, finishing off the activity and giving feedback.

Classroom layout

If you have desks arranged in groups of tables, you probably will have 4–6 students at each group of tables. This makes pairwork and groupwork easy. Mingling activities can be done in the spaces between the tables, or in a space at the front of the class if tables are pushed back a bit.

If you have desks in a U-shape, adjacent pairs can easily work together. Groups of three and four are best arranged by asking one or two students to move and sit opposite another pair of students. This makes it much easier for students to listen and talk to each other than if they are sitting in a line. Whole class mingling activities are easily arranged by asking students to move to the space in the centre of the U.

Even if you have fixed and immovable desks arranged in rows, you can adapt the arrangement to pair and group work by asking adjacent students to work with each other, or those in the row in front to turn around and work with the students behind them. Whole class mingling activities may cause more of a problem if space is limited, but you can adapt the activities so that only half the class is standing up and moving while the other half remain seated.

Setting up the activities

The activities often have several stages. This means you will have to be very clear in your own mind about how the stages follow each other. Here are some tips for giving instructions:

- Use simple language: simple vocabulary and simple sentence structure.
- One step, one sentence, then pause and make sure they have understood. Very often you may have to give an instruction, then wait for each group or pair to carry it out, before going on with the next, e.g. *Take a counter each … OK … have you all got a counter? … Place your counter on the START square …*
- Use checking questions, for example, *Are you working in pairs or on your own?*
- Use demonstration: show how to carry out an activity by doing it yourself for the class to watch, or by playing the first round of the game with one group while the class watches.

Teacher's role

Your role during the activity will vary. At the start you will be an Instruction Giver. During the activity you will have to be a Monitor, circulating and listening to the students in order to monitor progress, give help where needed, and note errors for feedback at the end of the activity. Depending on your class you may also have to be an Explainer if students have misunderstood what to do (if a number of them have misunderstood, you will need to stop the activity and give the instructions again), or a Controller, if students are off-task or not speaking English. Finally, you will need to stop the activity and give feedback. Your exact role during and at the end of the activities will vary according to the type of activity.

Linguistic activities

Some of these activities are to be done in pairs and some individually. If students are working individually (e.g. for a gap-fill), get them to check their answers in pairs before you give feedback. If they are working in pairs, get them to check with another pair. These activities are accuracy based and have one right answer. This means that you will need to go through the correct answers with the class at the end and explain any problems. It is a good idea to have visual support in the form of answers on the board or on a handout for students who may misunderstand the oral answers.

Communicative activities – open-ended

These activities do not have an outcome or come to a pre-arranged end. You will therefore have to keep a close eye on students to see when they are running out of ideas. If they come to a stop early while you feel the activity has more mileage, you may have to encourage them, or suggest new ideas. You will have to decide when to stop the activity – make sure students have come up with enough ideas, but don't let it go on so long that they get bored. There are no 'right answers' to these activities, so feedback is a matter of 'rounding off' the activity by asking students to share ideas.

Communicative activities – closed task

These game-like activities will come to an end automatically when the goal has been achieved. Some groups may achieve their goal earlier than others. You can keep them occupied by putting groups together and asking them to compare solutions. These activities often have an answer or 'solution,' so feedback will involve going through solutions and checking answers in much the same way as for the linguistic activities.

References

Hadfield, J *Elementary Communication Games* Pearson 1987.

Krashen, S. *Principles and Practice in Second Language Acquisition* Prentice-Hall International, 1987.

Schmitt, N. *Vocabulary in Language Teaching* Cambridge: Cambridge University Press, 2000

Jill Hadfield has worked as a teacher trainer in Britain, France and New Zealand and worked on development projects with Ministries of Education and aid agencies in China, Tibet and Madagascar. She has also conducted short courses, seminars and workshops for teachers in many other countries. She is currently Associate Professor on the Language Teacher Education team in the Department of Language Studies at Unitec, New Zealand and has been appointed International Ambassador for IATEFL. She has written over thirty books, including the *Communication Games* series (Pearson), *Excellent!*, a 3 level primary course (Pearson), the *Oxford Basics* series, *Classroom Dynamics* and *An Introduction to Teaching English* (OUP). Her latest book, *Motivating Learning*, co-authored with Zoltan Dornyei, was published in 2013 by Routledge in the *Research and Resources in Language Teaching* series, of which she is also series editor.

Photocopiable Teacher's Resource Materials in *Navigate*

The photocopiable Teacher's Resource Materials for *Navigate* can be found at the back of this Teacher's Guide, as well as on the *Teacher's Support and Resource Disc*, packaged with the *Teacher's Guide*, as downloadable PDFs. They are also available to download from the *Navigate iTools* classroom presentation software product.

The *Navigate* approach – The CEFR

The CEFR – Anthony Green

The *Common European Framework of Reference for Languages* (or CEFR), published by the Council of Europe in 2001, is intended to help teachers and others to develop and connect language syllabuses, curriculum guidelines, examinations and textbooks. It takes what it describes as an 'action-oriented approach' to language education: the purpose of learning a language is to enable the learner to communicate increasingly effectively in a growing range of social situations that are relevant to his or her individual needs.

For many educational systems, the CEFR's concern with effective communication represents a shift in emphasis. Instead of focusing on what learners know about a language – how many words they know or how accurately they can apply grammar rules – the key question for the CEFR is what learners might actually want to do with the language or languages they are learning – the activities they might need to carry out and the ideas they might want to express. Achievement in language learning is measured by the learner's degree of success in using languages to negotiate their way through the world around them.

Although practical communication is seen to be a fundamental goal, the CEFR does not try to suggest how this goal should be reached. It is not a recipe book that tells course designers what to include or that tells teachers how to teach. Instead, it offers a common set of terms that can apply to learners of different languages in different countries within a variety of educational systems. These common terms make it easier to draw comparisons and connect what happens in language education in one setting to what happens elsewhere.

It is part of the Council of Europe's educational philosophy of lifelong learning that learners should be able to move easily between informal learning, schools, universities and workplace training courses in different places to pick up and keep track of the practical skills that they need. This is much easier if everyone shares the same basic terms for talking about teaching and learning. If a 'Beginner' level class in one school is like an 'Elementary' level class in another school, or a 'Preliminary' class in a third and the 'Getting Started' book in textbook series X is like the 'Grade 2' book in series Y, life in the English classroom can soon get very confusing.

Having a shared descriptive language is very useful for course designers because it helps us to see how a particular course can fit into a learner's individual language learning career. In the CEFR, levels of language ability are set out – running from *Basic* (A1 and A2), through *Independent* (B1 and B2) up to *Proficient* (C1 and C2). These levels are based on teachers' judgements of the relative difficulty of 'Can Do' statements describing how learners are able to use language. For example, at the A1 level a learner, 'can use simple phrases and sentences to describe where he/she lives and people he/she knows', but at B2 'can present clear, detailed descriptions on a wide range of subjects related to his/her field of interest'. The system helps learners to monitor their progress, find suitable learning materials and identify which qualifications might be within their reach.

Of course, not every learner will need or want to 'present clear, detailed descriptions on a wide range of subjects'. The framework is not a specification of what learners ought to know, it simply provides examples of what is typically taught and learned at each level. Users are free (in fact they are encouraged) to add to the comprehensive, but far from exhaustive range of Can Do activities presented. People do not all choose to learn languages for the same reasons: they prioritise different skills and aspire to reach different objectives. Nor does everyone progress in their language learning in quite the same way. Someone who has learned a language informally while living in a country where that language is spoken may chat confidently with friends and colleagues, but find it more difficult to read a novel. On the other hand, someone who has learnt from books may read and translate with assurance, but struggle to keep up with the dialogue in films.

The framework captures such differences by providing a terminology for the range of social situations where learners may need to use languages and the kinds of knowledge, skills and abilities – competences – they might bring into play to achieve effective communication. Developing language abilities can involve 'horizontal' growth – coping with new contexts for language use – as well as 'vertical' progression through the CEFR levels. Horizontal progress could include shifts in the focus for learning between the written and spoken language, between more receptive language use (reading and listening) to more interactive (exchanging text messages and emails or participating in conversation) as well as shifts between different social domains (such as shifting from more academic to more occupational, workplace related language use).

Increasingly, English language textbooks include Can Do objectives derived from the CEFR in each unit. However, unlike *Navigate*, most have only incorporated the CEFR retrospectively, often after publication. This can certainly help to situate them in relation to other courses and systems of qualifications, but using the framework in the development process can bring much greater benefits. This is because in addition to providing a shared terminology, the framework poses challenging questions that help designers and other users to think about, describe and explain why they choose to learn, teach or assess language abilities in the way that they do. These questions keep the language learner at the heart of every decision. Examples of the wide range of issues that developers are invited to consider include, 'the communicative tasks in the personal, public, occupational and/or educational domains that the learner will need to tackle', 'how communicative and learning activities relate to the learner's drives, motivations and interests' and the 'provision … made for learners to become increasingly independent in their learning and use of language'.

Although the CEFR can provide us with shared terms, it is clear that people working in different places may sometimes understand the framework in quite different ways. The Can Do statements are inevitably open to a range of interpretations. For example, phrases and sentences that are considered 'simple' by one teacher may seem rather 'complex' to another. There have been complaints that the A2 level represented in one text book is as difficult as the B1 level in another. This has serious implications: if there is not at least a similar understanding of the levels among users of the framework, many of the potential benefits of the CEFR will be lost.

Recognizing the need to build shared interpretations and to provide more concrete guidance, the Council of Europe has called for the production of 'Reference Level Descriptions' which can show in much greater detail how the CEFR applies to specific languages. For English, a good deal of work has already been done. *Threshold* (first published in 1975, but updated in 1990) is effectively a specification of B1 level objectives. Other books cover CEFR A1 (*Breakthrough*), A2 (*Waystage*) and B2 and above (*Vantage*). All of these are available in print or as free e-books via the English Profile website at **www.englishprofile.org**. At the same site, you can find information about the ongoing work of English Profile which aims to further build our shared understanding of the CEFR as it applies to English.

To make the most of the CEFR and its place in the *Navigate* series, I would encourage teachers to learn more about the framework and the ways in which it can help to guide the teaching and learning process (as well as some of the many criticisms that have been made of its use). It is worth taking the time to find out about the overall descriptive scheme as well as the more familiar levels. The best place to start is the Council of Europe Language Policy Division website (**www.coe.int/t/dg4/linguistic**) where the rather more reader-friendly *Guide for Users*, the CEFR itself and many related resources can be downloaded free of charge.

Anthony Green is Professor of Language Assessment at the University of Bedfordshire, UK. He has published widely on language assessment issues and his recent book *Language Functions Revisited* (2012) sets out to fill the gap between the broad descriptions of levels provided in the CEFR and the level of detail required for applications such as syllabus or test design. His main research interests concern the design and use of language assessments and relationships between assessment, teaching and learning.

Reference to the CEFR in *Navigate*

The contents pages of *Navigate* Coursebook show not only what language points are taught in each unit, but also what the communicative goals are. Teachers and learners can relate their learning to real world situations and see at a glance what Can-do activities they will become competent in.

Each lesson shows clear communicative goals.

The *Navigate* Workbook allows students to self-assess on Can-do statements at the end of every section, giving them the opportunity to check their progress and manage their learning.

Teachers can also download a CEFR mapping document from the *Navigate* Teacher's website (**www.oup.com/teacher/navigate**) to see full details of how the competencies from the CEFR are covered in each level of *Navigate*.

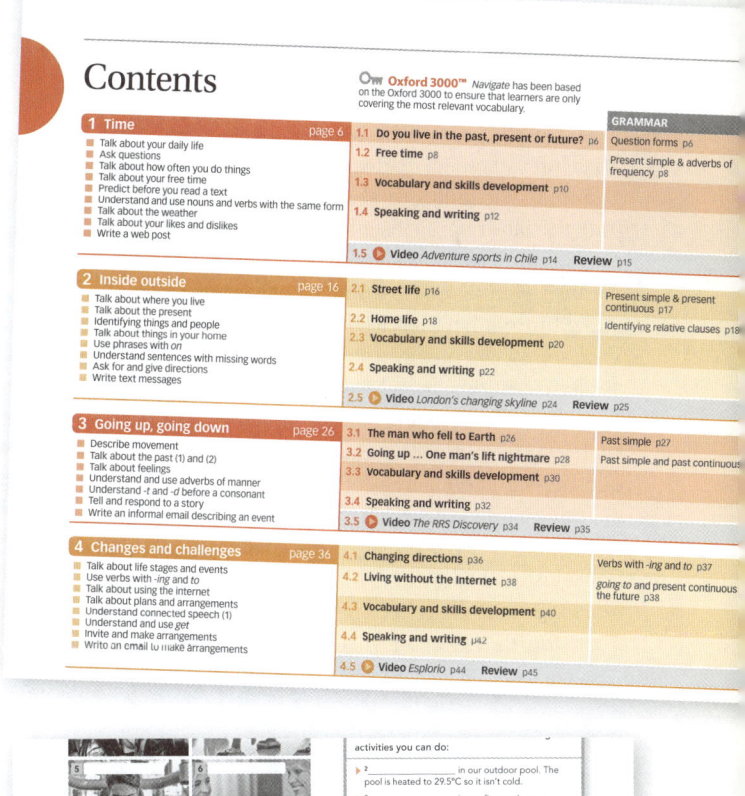

The *Navigate* approach – Testing

The *Navigate* Testing Package – Imelda Maguire-Karayel

As all teachers know, assessment is central to effective syllabus design and is an essential part of effective teaching and learning. It not only allows learners to recognize their achievements and make progress, but it enables instructors to shape and adapt their teaching to specific needs. This is especially true in the case of busy adult learners who often have limited time for attending language courses. Two of the main constructs in modern language testing are validity and practicality. Validity is key, a test has to measure what it claims to, and practicality is essential as tests should be easy both for teachers to administer and learners to take.

The *Navigate* course comes complete with its own testing package. This is included in the Teacher's Guide and is published in both Word and PDF formats. At each of the six levels, the teacher is provided with a complete set of tests designed to test learners' understanding and proficiency: twelve Unit tests, four Progress tests and one End-of-course test. Reflecting the course ideology, the tasks in the tests present learners with content that is both information rich, and international in flavour, while allowing them to practise newly acquired language in a range of contexts.

Unit tests

The Unit tests measure learners' understanding of the key grammar, vocabulary and decoding skills presented in the unit, the latter being tested in a similar context to the one in the unit. Unit tests are intended to last up to sixty minutes and comprise ten tasks. Greater weight is given to vocabulary and grammar which is tested across five different task types. Vocabulary is typically tested through tasks such as multiple-choice questions, matching sentence endings, gap fill, word formation or first letter tasks. Grammar is tested through tasks such as multiple-choice cloze, open cloze, or right/wrong questions, sentence transformation. The reading and listening decoding skills covered in the third lesson of each unit are tested across two tasks so that teachers and learners can see how effectively they have attained a command of potential blockages to comprehension. The functional language taught in the fourth lesson is also tested in an authentic context.

Each Unit test also includes two exam-style tasks, modelled on those in Cambridge Main Suite exams or IELTS. Tasks include those found in Cambridge English: Key, Preliminary and First, and have been especially written to reflect the theme of the unit. As they give exposure to task format and simulate exam conditions to some extent, the inclusion of the exam-style tasks is likely to be very beneficial for learners who go on to take certificated exams. The exam-type tasks learners will do in the Unit tests include multiple matching, matching headings, note-taking, true/false/not given, sentence transformation, multiple-choice reading comprehension, gapped text, short answer questions and open cloze. The accompanying Answer Key to each test allows busy teachers to mark unit tests quickly and accurately, thereby reducing demands on teachers' time.

Learners take Unit tests once they have completed the corresponding unit, and teachers and learners alike can evaluate if the learning objectives for that particular unit have been achieved. Teachers can then, if necessary, spend more time covering language points which need more attention. If they think it is more appropriate for their learners, teachers may also administer certain sections of the test only to match the sections of the unit that have been covered in class. Times can be adjusted accordingly.

Progress tests

There are four Progress tests in the *Navigate* testing package, each one intended to last approximately 60 minutes and to be administered after every three units. Progress tests are designed to test learners' proficiency. The content of each Progress test relates to the material covered in the units, but the Progress tests differ from the Unit tests in that they more closely resemble established international English Language exams. The vocabulary and grammar of the three units is tested by task types such as open or multiple-choice cloze. All four language skills are tested in the Progress tests. The Listening tasks comprise two question types, such as true/false, gap fill and multiple choice questions, and it can also cover some of the functional language from the three units. The Reading tasks also comprise two different task types, such as multiple matching, true/false/not given or multiple choice. Writing is tested through two tasks; the first is a short task testing discrete language items and the second is a longer task which requires the learner to produce a piece of extended written discourse. Writing tasks are authentic in that they reflect the real-world communication likely to be undertaken by learners. Genres include emails, text messages, form completion and social media posts. The Speaking task also assess learners' grasp of the units' functional language by asking them to carry out a transactional role-play based on a set of prompts. It appears at the end of the Progress test on a separate page and can be done at a later time than the rest of the test, either in pairs or with the teacher acting as one of the speakers in the task.

General mark schemes are provided to assist teachers in marking both the Speaking and Writing tasks. Care has been taken to ensure that the topic in each of the tested skills relates to as many units, thereby keeping the face validity of the Progress test high. For example, the content of the Listening section will usually relate to a different unit to the content of the Reading task. The same usually applies in the case of the Speaking and Writing skills.

End-of-course test

The End-of-course test also focuses on the four skills and tests target language from the entire course. As vocabulary and grammar are at the heart of the *Navigate* syllabus, these language systems are rigorously tested in the End-of-course test through task types such as gap-fill, open cloze and multiple-choice questions, with the course's functional language incorporated across tasks. The main part of the test covers tasks on Vocabulary, Grammar, Reading and Listening. There are 100 points available for the main test. Teachers are also provided with optional Speaking and Writing tests worth 20 points each, so if students take all parts of the test, they can achieve a maximum score of 140. The Writing task can easily be set along with the main test, but this will increase the time needed to complete the test, so teachers may prefer to set that part on a separate occasion. The Speaking tasks can be done at a time that is convenient for the teacher and students. This could be during normal class hours, by giving the class an extended task to do, and then taking pairs of students to a quiet space to do the Speaking test. Or the teacher may wish to set aside a different time for the Speaking test. It is advisable to do the Speaking test as soon as possible after the main test. As in the Progress tests, all tasks are exam-like in nature and general mark schemes are provided.

The *Navigate* tests are written by experts in the field of language assessment, many of whom also have years of EFL-teaching experience. As the test writers have extensive experience of writing for leading exam boards or assessment bodies, they bring knowledge of good practice in language assessment. The use of assessment experts also means that a consistent approach has been applied throughout the production of the tests. The test writers also contribute a deep understanding of aligning language to the CEFR. The result is a reliable, robust end-to-end testing package, which we are confident teachers and students using *Navigate* will find useful and rewarding as they work their way through the various levels of the course.

Imelda Maguire-Karayel has over twenty years' experience in ELT. She is an EFL/EAP teacher and teacher-trainer, a materials writer, and an educational consultant for adapting a BBC language education series for television.

She has taught in private language schools, ECIS-accredited schools and universities in Hong Kong, Greece, Turkey and the UK.

She has worked for Cambridge English and now works as an English language assessment consultant in the production of exam materials, exam practice materials, course-based assessment materials, and course books.

She has written course-based assessment and exam practice materials for *New Headway* (OUP), *English File* (OUP), *Touchstone* (CUP), and *Foundation IELTS Masterclass* (OUP)

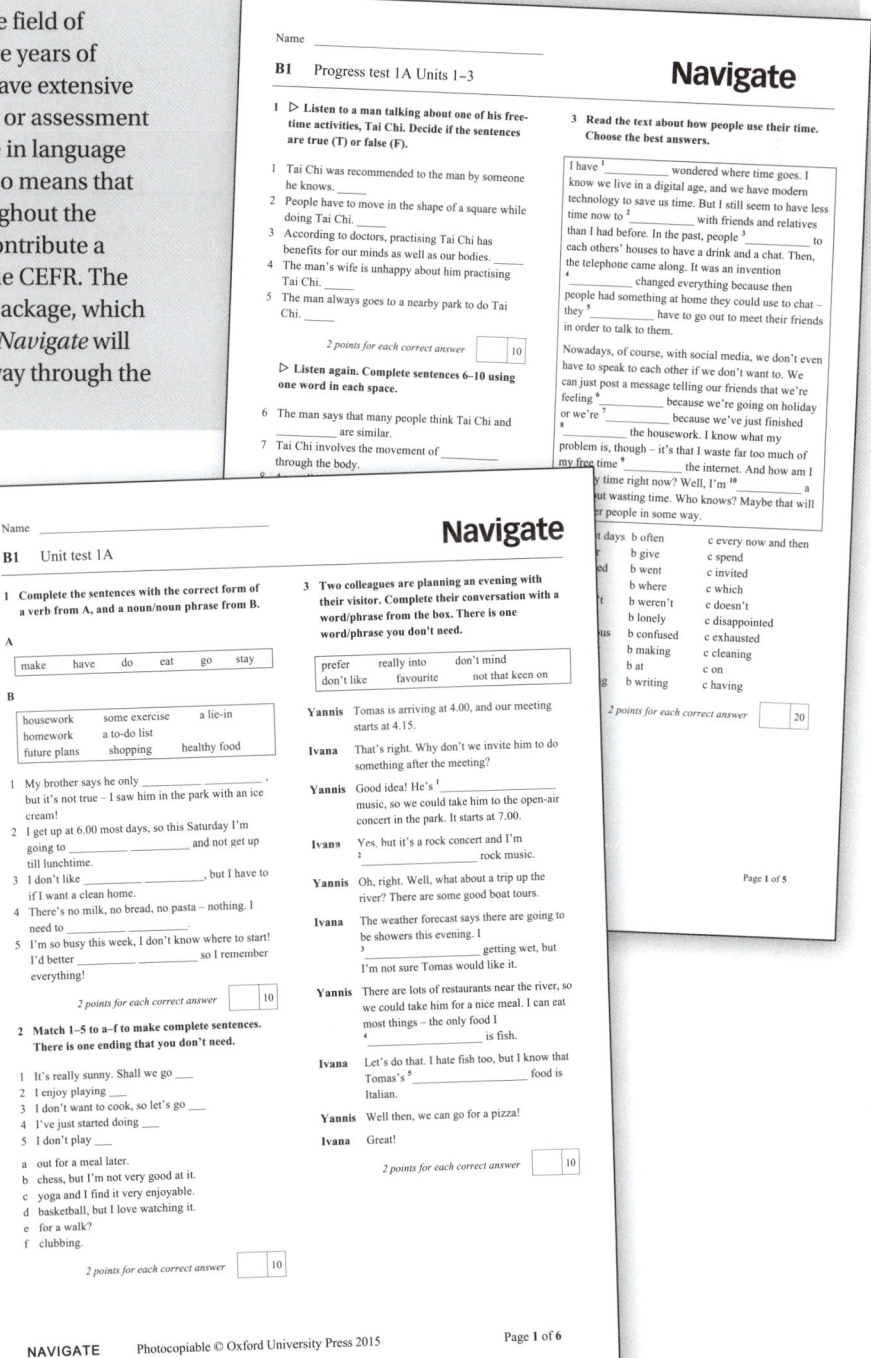

The *Navigate* tests

All the tests for *Navigate* can be found on the Teacher's Support and Resource Disc that is packaged with the Teacher's Guide.

Tests are supplied as PDFs and as Word documents for those occasions where teachers may wish to edit some sections of the tests. There are A and B versions of each test – the B version containing the same content as the A version but in a different order, to mitigate potential cheating if learners are sitting close to each other whilst doing the test.

Audio MP3 files for the tests are also available on the Teacher's Support and Resource Disc. All tests that contain a listening task begin with this task so that there are no timing issues with the listening during a test.

1 Time

Unit overview

Language input

Question forms (CB p6)	• Are you interested in your parents' stories? • Do you enjoy family events? • Who is your favourite relative? • How often do you exercise?
Present simple and adverbs of frequency (CB p8)	• He nearly always listens to rock music. • Mehmet never goes running.
Grammar reference (CB pp134–5)	

Vocabulary development

Daily life (CB p6)	• Spend time with relatives • Go shopping
Free-time activities (CB p9)	• Play golf • Do yoga • Go clubbing
Nouns and verbs with the same form (CB p11)	• Dream about flying / have a dream about flying
Talking about the weather (CB p12)	• hot, cloudy, mild, pleasant … • heavy rain, light snow …

Skills development

Reading: Predicting before you read a text (CB p10)

Speaking: Talking about likes and dislikes (CB p12)

Writing: A web post about the best time to visit your country (CB p13)

Video

Documentary: Adventure sports in Chile (Coursebook DVD & CB p14)

Vox pops (Coursebook DVD & TG p259)

More materials

Workbook	• Language practice for vocabulary, grammar, speaking and writing
Photocopiable activities	• Grammar: Three questions, three answers (TG p208 & TSRD) • Vocabulary: Something in common (TG p226 & TSRD) • Communication: My favourite things (TG p244 & TSRD)
Tests	• Unit 1 test (TSRD)
Unit 1 wordlist (TSRD)	

1.1 Do you live in the past, present or future?

Goals
- Talk about your daily life
- Ask questions

Lead-in
- Write *daily life* in the centre of the board and help the class to create a mind map of common activities that they do every day, e.g. *work, shopping, sleeping, housework, eating, studying*, etc.
- Alternatively, students could brainstorm and make mind maps in small groups, then compare with another group.
- Point out that one of the goals for this lesson is to talk about your daily life.

Vocabulary & Speaking   daily life

Exercise 1
- Write the word *busy* on the board. Elicit the meaning.
  WATCH OUT! Point out that in this word the letter 'u' is pronounced like the 'i' in 'sit'. Drill the pronunciation /bɪzi/.
- Students work alone and read sentences 1–3.
- Give them a moment to decide which sentence reflects their life and the reasons why they have chosen that sentence.
- Put students into pairs and allow time for them to compare their answers and discuss them.
- Conduct a class discussion. Encourage some students to tell the class which sentence they chose and why.

ANSWERS
Students' own answers
EXTRA CHALLENGE You could ask students to report on what their partner said. This ensures that they practise the 3rd person singular, including remembering to use the 's' ending for verbs in the present simple, e.g. *Anna need**s** more time because she ha**s** two children and she also work**s**.*

Exercise 2a
- Ask students to look at the nouns and noun phrases in the boxes to find out if any of the activities are the same as the mind map(s) from the lead-in.
  STUDY TIP Point out to students that this kind of brainstorming is very beneficial as it allows them to think about what they already know before extending their knowledge through further study. This is a good habit and something they should practise as often as possible. For example, before completing English homework tasks or before writing a business email on a particular topic in English.
- If necessary, do an example together as a class. Point out that some verbs must be used more than once.
- Students work in pairs.
  EXTRA CHALLENGE Ask students who finish early, to think of other nouns or noun phrases which collocate with *do* and others which collocate with *make*. Don't forget to check that these extra ideas are correct or encourage them to check this for themselves using a good monolingual dictionary. If you think they are useful collocations, you could teach them to the class and elicit or give them an example sentence.

Exercise 2b   1.1
- Tell students to listen carefully to the track and check their answers.
- Play track 1.1.
- Before moving on to the next exercise, check that the students heard all the answers. Explain any they didn't hear or understand.

AUDIOSCRIPT 1.1
spend time with relatives
do some exercise, do housework, do the shopping, do some work, do homework
stay in for the evening
make future plans, make a to-do list
eat healthy food
have an early night, have fun, have a good time, have a family meal, have a lie-in
go to bed late, go on a trip, go shopping
chat with friends online

Exercise 2c   1.2
- This time, the focus is on pronunciation so tell the students you are going to play the same track so they can repeat each phrase aloud.
- Play track 1.2, pausing and replaying when necessary so that students can repeat.
- Encourage students to mark the stress on the phrases so that they see how, in many cases, there is a common pattern with stress on the verb and on the final word in each phrase, e.g. **go** to bed **late**, **have** an early **night**, **have** a good **time**.
  EXTENSION Ask students to find more phrases which follow this pattern: **do** some **exercise**, **do** the **shopping**, **do** some **work**, **have** a family **meal**, **have** a **lie-in**, **go** to bed **late**, **go** on a **trip**. Check together and practise the pattern as a class.

AUDIOSCRIPT 1.2
spend time with relatives
do some exercise, do housework, do the shopping, do some work, do homework
stay in for the evening
make future plans, make a to-do list
eat healthy food
have an early night, have fun, have a good time, have a family meal, have a lie-in
go to bed late, go on a trip, go shopping
chat with friends online

Exercise 3
- Students work in pairs to think about the weekend ahead.
- Check which three things they should talk about and, if necessary, explain they need to talk about what they would like to do, need to do and don't need to do.
- Remind them that they should try and use the vocabulary from exercise 2a.
  EXTRA SUPPORT You could give students sentences about your weekend as a model for students who need extra support. Also, if necessary, give the students thinking time;

Unit 1   35

You have two minutes to think about this weekend and make notes. Don't write full sentences.
- Set a time limit for the task and monitor the pairs carefully.
- **FEEDBACK FOCUS** Focus on how much of the vocabulary they are using from exercise 2a. Remind students to use the phrases.
- Make a note of good sentences and which students said them.
- Conduct class feedback. Ask students to share one or two things about their weekend and encourage other members of the class to ask questions or make comments to extend the discussion.
- Point out the good sentences and praise those students.

ANSWERS
Students' own answers

Grammar & Speaking question forms

Exercise 4

> **Text summary:** An article from a psychology magazine website about different types of people: past, present and future types. The article explains what each type is like, and leads into a questionnaire for the students to do.

EXTRA ACTIVITY This activity will work best with a group of strong students. Write headings *past*, *present* and *future* on the board. Tell students that these labels are for three different kinds of people. Put students into pairs or small groups to think about what kinds of things are important to each type of person.
- Tell students they are going to read an online magazine article and they can find out if their ideas from the extra activity are the same as in the article.
- Elicit or teach the meaning of *psychology*, /saɪˈkɒlədʒi/, and drill the pronunciation. Point out that the 'p' at the beginning of this word is silent and 'ch' is pronounced /k/.
- Ask them to read the text, finding one positive and one negative thing for each type of person.
- Go through the answers together.

ANSWERS
Possible answers:
Past: Positive – enjoy remembering the past, spend time with family; negative – worry about making changes and trying new things
Present: Positive – do fun things; negative – don't have a healthy lifestyle
Future: Positive – eat well, exercise regularly, don't mind waiting for the good things in life, successful in work and study; negative – don't enjoy free time

Exercise 5
- Tell students to look back at the vocabulary in exercise 2a. Allow time for them to make their choices.
- Put students into pairs to share and discuss their ideas.
- Then conduct a class discussion.

ANSWERS
Possible answers:
Past: spend time with relatives, have a family meal
Present: go to bed late, have fun, have a good time, have a lie-in, go shopping, chat with friends online

Future: have an early night, stay in for the evening, do some exercise, eat healthy food, make future plans, make a to-do list

Exercise 6a
- Tell students that they are going to do a questionnaire to find out how 'past-focused' they are (= how much of a past type of person they are).
- Focus their attention on the questionnaire and ask them to read the questions. Go through any unknown vocabulary.
- Tell students to ask their partner the questions and record the answers.

Exercise 6b
- Ask students to look at the results at the bottom of the questionnaire and apply them to their partner's answers.
- Tell them to share the results with their partner and decide which of them is more past-focused.
- Conduct a class discussion, including asking students whether they agree with the results.

ANSWERS
Students' own answers

CRITICAL THINKING Encourage discussion about questionnaires so students can reflect on their opinions. Ask *Do you think questionnaires like this are ever scientific? Do you enjoy answering questionnaires? Why/Why not? Would you try to change anything about yourself according to the results of a questionnaire? Why/Why not?*

Exercise 7
- Focus students' attention on the Grammar focus box on question forms. Tell them to look carefully at the examples of questions with *do* and *did* and questions with *be*. Then ask them to delete the wrong word in each rule.
- Go through the answers together.

ANSWERS
1 before
2 before
3 end
- Refer students to *Grammar reference* on p134. There are three more exercises here which students can do for homework. See answers on p37.

Exercise 8
- Students do the task alone. When they have finished, encourage them to check their answers in pairs.
- Go through the answers together.

ANSWERS
1 b
2 a
3 e
4 c
5 d

EXTENSION You could write *How long… ?* on the board and elicit possible answers for this question (time or distance answers would be acceptable: 10 minutes, 6 months or 10 centimetres, 5 km).

Exercise 9a
- Explain that students must make questions from the jumbled words. Do number 1 together as a demonstration if necessary. Ask *Which is the first word?*
- Encourage students to refer to the rules in the Grammar focus box to be sure that they are putting the words in the right order, e.g. *In number 1, 'with' is a preposition so we know it goes at the end of the question.*
- Students complete the task then check their answers in pairs.

STUDY TIP Students often choose to do this kind of task by just writing numbers next to the words to indicate the order they go in. Encourage them to write the questions out in full as it is believed that this helps your brain to process the information better and it is more helpful for visual learners.

Exercise 9b 1.3
- Ask students to listen carefully and check their answers to exercise 9a.
- Play track 1.3.
- Play the track again for any students who are struggling.
- When you have checked the answers, tell students to ask and answer the questions with a partner and make a note of any interesting answers.

EXTRA ACTIVITY You could teach the expression *to have a lot in common* (= to have the same interests, ideas, etc. as another person) and also *to have nothing in common* (= to have none of the same interests, ideas). Example sentences: *I have a lot in common with my brother. We have a lot in common. They have nothing in common. Ibrahim has nothing in common with Carlos.*

- Now tell students that as they ask and answer the questions, they will discover things they have in common and they should try to remember them.
- Conduct class feedback and find out which pairs had the most/least in common with their partner.

ANSWERS/AUDIOSCRIPT 1.3
1 Who do you live with?
2 What kind of music do you listen to?
3 How often are you late for appointments?
4 Do you enjoy going to museums?
5 What time did you go to bed last night?
6 Are you tired today?
7 How much time do you spend on Facebook?
8 When did you last have fun?

Exercise 10a
- Explain to students that they are going to write their own questionnaires in pairs.
- Point out that the aim of the questionnaire is to find out whether the person answering the questions is present-focused or future-focused. You should also highlight that the questions need to give two or three answers to choose from as in exercise 6. Make sure they look at the example. (You could elicit or teach them that these kinds of questions are called *multiple-choice* – particularly if any of your students are going to take exams in English.)
- Monitor pairs carefully and help students to self-correct any mistakes in the formation or word order of the questions. Note points for correction with the class.

- When a few pairs have nearly finished, set a time limit to the end of the activity.

ANSWERS
Students' own answers

EXTRA CHALLENGE Encourage students who finish early to check their grammar and tell them to write two extra questions using their own ideas. Check these carefully.

Exercise 10b
- Put two pairs together in a group of four. Then students in each pair take turns to ask the other pair their questions.
- Tell them to make a record of the answers as they did in exercise 6.
- When they have all finished asking all the questions, tell them to analyse the results and discuss them in their group.
- In their group they should decide which member is the most present-focused and which the most future-focused.
- Conduct whole class feedback and discussion.

EXTENSION Ask students to ask you (the teacher) their questions to find out whether you are present- or future-focused. After five or six questions, ask them to tell you the overall result. You could ask *Is it better for a teacher to be present-focused or future-focused? Why?*

GRAMMAR REFERENCE ANSWERS
Exercise 1
1 f 2 e 3 g 4 d 5 c 6 a 7 b
Exercise 2
1 When does Laura get up?
2 How much (money) did you save?
3 Do you both enjoy painting?
4 Why are we worried about Jon?
5 How well do the children speak French?
6 Was Helen busy last weekend?
7 What do you remember from school?
8 Who does Mum play in the garden with?
Exercise 3
1 What did Hofstede write?
2 Who did he give the survey to?
3 Where were the students from?
4 What do East Asians work hard for?
5 What do Americans care about?

Unit 1 37

1.2 Free time

Goals
- Talk about how often you do things
- Talk about your free time

Lead-in
- Ask students to think of three things they enjoy doing in their free time and write them down.
- Monitor and help any students to find words they need for their free-time activities.
- Tell them that later in the lesson they will be able to talk about their free-time activities.

Grammar & Speaking present simple and adverbs of frequency

Exercise 1
- Tell students to look at the photos.
- Ask them to read questions 1–3 and discuss their answers in pairs.
- Conduct a class discussion, giving any background information about the author that you think your students will find interesting. They may not have heard of an ultramarathon before – this is any race longer than a marathon and some last more than 24 hours, covering up to 1000 miles.

> **Background note:** Haruki Murakami was born on 12th January 1949 in Kyoto, Japan. He is a novelist who has won many prizes for his writing. He has also translated English books into Japanese. *What I talk about when I talk about running* is a non-fiction book about his love of running. He started running when he was 33 and has run marathons, triathlons and an ultramarathon of 100 kilometres

Exercise 2a

> **Audio summary:** In this book review programme, two speakers discuss Haruki Murakami's non-fiction book on running. The recording focuses on the content of the book – when he started running, why and how often he does it.

- Check that all students understand what a book review is. You could ask *Where could I read a book review?* (online, in a newspaper/magazine) *Why do people read book reviews?* (to help them decide whether to buy/read a book or not) *Do book reviews give factual information about books?* (Yes) *Do book reviews give the reviewers opinion?* (Usually yes) *Do you read book reviews to help you choose books to read? Why/Why not?*
- Tell them that they are going to listen to part of a review of Murakami's book about running and answer questions.
- Point out that they need to make the questions before they can answer them. They do this task alone or work in pairs.
- Go through the questions with the class, checking that the grammar is correct.

ANSWERS
1 Why does Murakami run?
2 How often does he go running?
3 How many miles does he run every week?
4 Does he do any other sports?

Exercise 2b 1.4
- Ask students to listen and answer the questions.
- Play track 1.4.
- Allow them time to discuss their answers in pairs and then go through them together as a class.

ANSWERS
1 He runs to keep fit. It is also about getting better at something. He doesn't really enjoy team sports or beating other people. He prefers to go for a run and achieve his own goals.
2 He runs most days. He usually has one day off a week.
3 36 miles every week
4 swimming, cycling and running.

AUDIOSCRIPT 1.4
P Hello and welcome to Great Books of Our Time. Today, we're talking about the book, What I talk about when I talk about running by Japanese novelist, Haruki Murakami. Here to tell us about it is this week's reviewer, Maria Corbett. Maria, thanks for joining us today.
MC My pleasure.
P So Maria, what's this book about?
MC Well, it's about running but it's also about Murakami's life. He talks about why running and writing are important to him.
P And why is running important to him? Why does he run?
MC Well, it's certainly about keeping fit, but, um, it's more than just that. For Murakami, and I suppose for many runners, it's often about getting better at something. He says he doesn't really enjoy team sports, you know, playing soccer or baseball, because he's never worried about beating other people. He prefers to go for a run and achieve his own goals.
P How did he start running?
MC Well, he had a jazz bar in Tokyo but he sold it in 1982 and became a writer. At the same time, he started running and a year later, he completed a race from Athens to Marathon in Greece.
P And how often does he go running?
MC In the book, he says he runs most days. He usually has one day off a week, but he does 36 miles every week.
P Phew, that's amazing! And does he do any other sports?
MC Well, he does triathlons – that's swimming, cycling, and running, but he likes running best. He does at least one marathon every year.
P Ah, so he spends quite a lot of time on his own when he's running. Does he get lots of ideas for his books? Does he think about work?
MC Well, no, not really. He says he sometimes thinks about the weather and he occasionally gets an idea for a book. Actually. he says he usually doesn't think about anything – he just runs. Oh, and he nearly always listens to rock music!

Exercise 3 1.4

- Ask students to read the sentences a–g.
- **EXTRA CHALLENGE** With a strong class, ask them to try to remember the order the sentences came in the recording before they listen again. They could talk about this in pairs.
- Play track 1.4 again.
- Ask students to complete the sentences with an adverb or frequency expression from the box.

ANSWERS

a often   b never   c most days   d sometimes
e occasionally   f usually   g nearly always

Exercise 4

- Write on the board *adverbs of frequency* and *frequency expression*. Elicit or teach the meaning of these grammar terms.
- Point out or elicit what the arrow from 0% to 100% illustrates (= how often something happens.)
- Check that students know the meaning of the words and expressions in the box and also drill pronunciation (especially *rarely* /ˈreəli/ and *occasionally* /əˈkeɪʒnəli/ which can be difficult to pronounce well).
- You could demonstrate the task using one of the numbers – number 10 (*never*) is the easiest one to use for this.
- Students do the task in pairs.
- Go through the answers together.

ANSWERS

1 always	7 once or twice a year
2 nearly always	8 every now and then
3 most days	9 occasionally
4 usually	10 hardly ever
5 often	11 rarely
6 sometimes	12 never

Exercise 5

- Focus students' attention on exercise 3 again. Tell them to use these sentences as examples to help them work out the grammar rules for adverbs of frequency and frequency expressions.
- Tell them to read the information in the Grammar focus box and delete the incorrect word in the grammar rules.
- Allow them time to think carefully about the rules and analyse the sentences.
- Go through the rules together.

ANSWERS

1 before   2 after   3 after

- Refer students to *Grammar reference* on p135. There are three more exercises here students can do for homework. See answers on p40.

Pronunciation stress

Exercise 6a 1.5

- Highlight that this exercise focuses on word and sentence stress.
- Tell students to read the sentences 1–3 and notice which parts of the sentence are in bold.
- Now ask them to listen and notice how these parts of the sentence sound.
- Play track 1.5.

PRONUNCIATION Dynamic physical movement can help some students focus better on word and sentence stress. Try demonstrating stress punching to your students; hold your hand ready in a fist and bend your arm up at the elbow. Now say sentence 1 or play the track and punch your hand up into the air each time a syllable is stressed, bringing it down again for unstressed syllables. Encourage the students to do the same as you play the track.

AUDIOSCRIPT 1.5

1 He sometimes thinks about the weather.
2 Once or twice a year he does a triathlon.
3 It is often about getting better at something.

Exercise 6b 1.6

- Play track 1.6, pausing where necessary.
- Ask students to repeat each sentence.
- Correct any mistakes and play the track again if necessary.

AUDIOSCRIPT 1.6

See track 1.5.

Exercise 7

- Tell students to read the instruction and the example.
- Remind students to refer to the Grammar focus box if they cannot decide where the words/phrases go in each sentence. You could also elicit which ones can go in more than one place (= frequency expressions – at the start or at the end).
- Students work alone to do the task.
- Go through the answers together as a class. Elicit two possible sentences for numbers 4 and 7.

ANSWERS

1 We occasionally spend time with relatives.
2 Most days my best friend does exercise OR My best friend does exercise most days.
3 We hardly ever watch films.
4 My family go out for a meal once or twice a week. OR Once or twice a week my family go out for a meal.
5 I'm nearly always in bed by 11 p.m.
6 We don't usually go abroad on holiday.
7 I chat with friends online every now and then. OR Every now and then I chat with friends online.
8 I rarely have a lie-in at the weekend.

Exercise 8a

- Tell students that now they need to make the sentences in exercise 7 real. They should change any untrue sentences so that they are true about them.
- **WATCH OUT!** Some students find the adverb *hardly ever* confusing and try to use it with negatives, e.g. *We ~~don't~~ hardly ever see them. I am ~~not~~ hardly ever free in the evenings.* Explain that *hardly ever* = almost never. We never use a negative with *never* e.g. *I ~~don't~~ never play tennis.*
- **EXTRA CHALLENGE** Point out that they can change the frequency expressions in order to be more specific: e.g. *once or twice a month/once or twice a year/most days/some days/every day.*
- Monitor and check that the changed sentences are grammatically correct.

ANSWERS

Students' own answers

Unit 1   39

Exercise 8b

- Put students into pairs. Choose one pair to read out the example dialogue to demonstrate the activity.
- Tell them to take turns reading their sentences to each other.
- The student who is listening should ask questions to get more information.
- **FEEDBACK FOCUS** Monitor carefully and check that the questions are correct. Note any mistakes in word order.
- When they have finished, elicit interesting information some of them found out about their partner.
- Remind them that they studied questions in 1.1. Write any question form errors on the board and elicit corrections.

Vocabulary & Speaking free-time activities

Exercise 9a

- Remind students that at the start of the lesson they wrote down their favourite free-time activities. Ask them to look in the box and see if any of their activities are mentioned. If not, explain that they will get a chance to talk about them later.
- Tell them to work in pairs and categorize the vocabulary in the box with the correct verbs.
- Allow them plenty of time to discuss the groups of words.
- Go through the answers together.

ANSWERS
a play: football, computer games, chess, cards, basketball
b do: karate, exercise, aerobics
c go: out for a coffee/meal, camping, swimming, on Facebook, to the gym, for a walk, running

Exercise 9b

- Tell students to look at the six photos a–f.
- Ask them to label each photo with an expression from exercise 9a. Remind them to include the correct verb.
- Go through the answers together.

ANSWERS
a go out for a coffee/meal
b go camping
c play cards
d do yoga
e do karate
f play basketball

Exercise 9c

- Ask students to work in pairs or small groups to think of other sports or free-time activities for each verb group.
- Conduct a class discussion to share their ideas.

ANSWERS
Students' own answers
EXTENSION Students could look to see if there are patterns in the types of activities which collocate with each verb. Generally sports involving a ball or a team need the verb *play*. Activities which we call a game usually need the verb *play*. Activities where the noun is a gerund (*-ing* form) need the verb *go*. These are not rules, as there are exceptions.

Exercise 10

- In their pairs or groups, ask them to find two activities from exercise 9a which fit each category 1–6.
- Point out that there are some activities which can fit in more than one category, e.g. *You can play computer games on your own but also with other people.*
- Conduct a class discussion about their ideas.

POSSIBLE ANSWERS
1 on your own: play computer games, go on Facebook, go to the gym, go for a walk, go out for a coffee, go running
2 with other people: go out for a coffee/meal, play computer games, play golf, play cards, play chess, go camping, go clubbing, go for a walk, go running, play football, play basketball
3 outdoors: go out for a coffee/meal, play golf, go swimming, go for a walk, go running, go camping, play football, play basketball
4 indoors: go out for a coffee/meal, go swimming, play computer games, go on Facebook, go to the gym, play cards/chess, do yoga, do aerobics, play football, play basketball
5 lazy: play computer games, go on Facebook, play cards, play chess
6 full of energy: go running, go to the gym, go clubbing, do aerobics, play football, play basketball

Exercise 11a

- Put students into small groups and tell them to ask questions to find out how often the members of their group do the different free-time activities in exercise 9a. Remind them to write down the answers.
- Set a time limit. Tell them when there is only a short time left to the end of the task so they finish together.

Exercise 11b

- Conduct class feedback on their group discussions.
- Focus their attention on the question: *Who spends a lot of time doing one sport or activity? Who does not?*

EXTENSION Ask students whose real free-time activities are different from those in exercise 9c, to tell the class about them. The class should ask how often they do the activities.

STUDY TIP In pairs, students recall what they know about Haruki Murakami and his free time activity (running). After a few moments, ask them to summarize what they know orally or in writing. Summarizing in English is an essential skill and students could keep pages in their notebooks for summarizing each recording or text in the course.

GRAMMAR REFERENCE ANSWERS
Exercise 1
1 always
2 sometimes
3 hardly ever
4 nearly always
5 occasionally
6 sometimes
7 every now and then

Exercise 2
1 Is James nearly always at the gym?
2 My parents don't often go on Facebook.
3 I never do karate.
4 Does his brother occasionally play cards in the evening?

5 Katy isn't usually keen on watching basketball.
6 Sandra and I sometimes don't cook on week days.
7 Ben is always happy when he wins his chess matches.
8 Do you both swim every now and then?

Exercise 3
1 Marathon runners nearly always train four to six times a week
2 They are usually not satisfied with their performance …
3 they nearly always eat healthy food
4 and have rest days once or twice a week
5 Sometimes they need a lot of support
6 their families often find it difficult

1.3 Vocabulary and skills development

Goals
- Predict before you read a text
- Understand nouns and verbs with the same form

Reading & Speaking predicting before you read a text

Lead-in
- Tell students that they are going to read a blog. Elicit or teach the meaning of this word. (= a website where a person writes regularly about recent events or topics that interest them, usually with photos and links to other websites that they find interesting. The word blog is a shortened version of weblog, i.e. a diary or record (log) on the web.)
- Find out about the students' experience of blogs to start them thinking about this particular genre of writing. Ask them: *Have any of you written a blog? Would you like to? Why/Why not? Do you ever read blogs? If so, what kind of blogs do you read and why?*

Exercise 1
- Focus students' attention on the photographs.
- Put the students into pairs to discuss questions 1–3.
- Monitor their discussions and then conduct discussion together.
- Encourage students to say what they think and give reasons if they can.

EXTENSION You could teach some adjectives to describe this kind of situation/behaviour: *annoying, unnecessary, stupid, strange, silly, rude*.

Exercise 2a

Text summary: This is a blog post where the writer is complaining about people taking photos and video of art exhibitions and live music. The writer thinks this behaviour is foolish as they should be interested in seeing the real thing (and it also blocks other people's view)..

- Unless you are sure that your students know these terms, elicit from them *What is the title?* and *What is the sub-heading?*
- Ask them to look at the photos, title, sub-heading and first line and discuss in their pairs whether the blog is positive or negative about taking photos.

- Elicit their answers but do not accept or reject them yet. You could say something like *OK, we will see if you're right when we read the whole article.*

ANSWERS
Students own answers

Exercise 2b
- Individually, students make a list of five key words or phrases they think will be used in the text.
- Then ask them to compare their lists with their partner.
- Conduct feedback as a class. Write some of the students' key words and phrases on the board. It is fine if they have many of the same key words – this is quite likely and shows good predicting skills.

EXTRA CHALLENGE Encourage students to say why they picked these key words if possible, e.g. *We think 'exhibition' will be in the blog because the first line is about going to an art gallery., We think 'mobile phone' will be in the blog because we can see them in the photograph.*

- Explain that in exercises 2a and 2b they have been practising a skill we use to decode text even before we read it. They are predicting (and it's quite likely they do this in their own language if they are good readers).

Exercise 2c
- Ask students to read the Unlock the code box about the skill of predicting.
- You could ask them whether they automatically predict content, type of text and vocabulary in their own language.

STUDY TIP Explain that sometimes skills like this are transferred without thinking from your first language to your second, but not always. Often you need to concentrate on using them more in a new language. Predicting key vocabulary is particularly useful for understanding text in another language, so they need to practise it in English.

Exercise 3
- Allow students plenty of time to read the blog.
- Conduct a class discussion about how successfully they predicted. For the key words/phrases, you could base a discussion on the vocabulary list you made on the board in exercise 2b.

Exercise 4
- Put students into pairs.
- Tell them to read the questions and answer them together. They don't need to write the answers, just discuss.
- Go through the answers together.

CRITICAL THINKING Often we need to explain how we know something, i.e. point clearly to the evidence. It is especially important in another language in order to make your argument strong. Encourage the students to refer to the blog in their answers. *How do you know that? What exactly does the writer say? Which paragraph is that?*

ANSWERS
1 going to the Louvre Museum in Paris to see the *Mona Lisa* painting; going to a rock concert in London
2 tourists are filming and taking photos of the *Mona Lisa*; people are filming the concert

Unit 1   41

Exercise 5
- Ask students to read the question.
- Allow them time to think about how to answer.
- Students could discuss their answers in pairs or small groups. Otherwise, elicit some answers from the class all together and encourage other class members to agree or disagree, giving their reasons.

ANSWERS
Students own answers

EXTENSION With a strong group, you could extend the discussion to talk about what photography and filming is allowed and not allowed at concerts and in galleries. At most concerts there will be an announcement to say that recording is not allowed. This may be because a performer only wants high quality film to be seen or they want to make money from selling official films of their performance. It may be illegal to sell home-made videos of a concert. Nowadays many people have mobile phones which take films so it is not possible to enforce a no-filming rule. In galleries and museums, taking films and photographs is often permitted but not flash photography because it could damage the exhibits.

Vocabulary & Speaking nouns and verbs with the same form

Exercise 6a
- Point out that the focus of this page is on vocabulary.
- Students read the blog and focus on the highlighted words. Do one as an example together if necessary.
- When they have finished the task, go through the answers together.
- Drill pronunciation of the longer words *photograph* /ˈfəʊtəgrɑːf/ and *experience* /ɪkˈspɪəriəns/ to ensure accurate word stress.

ANSWERS
Nouns: blog, photograph, film, look, experience
Verbs: record, post

Exercise 6b
- It is important that the students understand that all the words in the box can be used as nouns or verbs.
- Ask them to read the Vocabulary focus box.

EXTRA SUPPORT Answer any questions the students have about this aspect of vocabulary. Give examples to illustrate the words in noun and verb form and underline or highlight them in different colours, e.g. *We experience many challenges in our lives. Winning the game was a great experience. It is good to have new experiences.*

Exercise 6c
- Students read the instruction.
- Tell them to transfer the verb + noun example from the Vocabulary focus box (*have a look*) into the table. Do another example together if necessary.
- Students work individually on the task.

EXTRA CHALLENGE Remind early finishers that some nouns may go in more than one column and ask them to check this.
- Go through the answers together.

WATCH OUT! There is a difference in pronunciation between *record* (noun) /ˈrekɔːd/ and *record* (verb) /rɪˈkɔːd/. The main difference is where we put the stress on these words but this also has an effect on how we pronounce the 'e'. The exercises which follow use the noun so you could focus on the pronunciation of that form but just point out that the pronunciation of the verb is different.

ANSWERS

make	have	take	write
a film	a look	a look	a blog
a record	an experience	a photograph	a post

Exercise 6d
- Tell students that the box contains four more words which can be nouns or verbs.
- Students add the four words from the box to the table.
- Go through the answers together.

ANSWERS

make	have	take	write
a promise	a dream		a text
a plan	a plan		

Exercise 7a
- Highlight that each gap is a combination of verb + noun from the table.
- Students work on this task individually.
- Put them into pairs to discuss and check their answers.
- Go through the answers together.

ANSWERS
1 have dreams
2 have a look
3 have/make a plan
4 takes a photograph
5 make a promise
6 write a blog
7 write a text
8 make a film

Exercise 7b
- Put students into pairs.
- Tell them that they should ask the questions in exercise 7a and also ask follow-up questions. Point out that they are not restricted to using the words as nouns but can use them as verbs too.
- Monitor their discussions.

FEEDBACK FOCUS Make a note of any mistakes they make in using the words as a noun or as a verb.
- Conduct class error correction if there are many mistakes or a lot of students are making the same mistake with a particular word or words.

Exercise 7c
- Conduct class feedback on the discussions, eliciting two interesting facts from each student about their partner.
- Encourage the rest of the class to make a comment if their experience is the same or to ask a further question if the fact is particularly interesting.

42

EXTRA ACTIVITY The following words related to technology can be nouns or verbs: *blog, post, email, text, download, copy, search, click, video*. For homework, the students could collect sentences in written or spoken English which contain any of these words. Then they could analyse whether the word is used as a noun or verb (and, if used as a noun, also may find verb + noun combinations). You could make a chart of the words and example sentences on the wall and continue to add to it during the course.

1.4 Speaking and writing

Goals
- Talk about the weather
- Talk about your likes and dislikes
- Write a web post

Lead-in
- Write *Canada*, *Brazil* and *United Arab Emirates* (*UAE*) on the board.
- Put students in pairs and ask them to find out anything that their partner knows about each of these countries.
- After one or two minutes focus their attention on the *climate* /ˈklaɪmət/ of the three countries. Teach this word if necessary (= the regular pattern of weather conditions of a particular place).
- Elicit some answers from the class. Add information from the background note below if you wish.

Speaking & Vocabulary talking about the weather; talking about likes and dislikes

Exercise 1

Background note:

Canada – The second largest country in the world, covering six different time zones. It is very cold in the north but most Canadian cities are within 300 km of the border with the USA.

Brazil is the largest country in South America. Summer time is hot. The north east of Brazil is the driest region and temperatures can reach 38 degrees Celsius.

United Arab Emirates (UAE) is in the south-east of the Arabian Peninsula, bordering Saudi Arabia and Oman. Temperatures in summer can reach 45 degrees Celsius. The lowest temperature in winter is 10–14 degrees Celsius.

- Focus students' attention on the photos.
- Put students into pairs to describe the weather in each photo. They could also say which season they think it is.
- Conduct a class discussion. Write any useful weather words from the discussion on the board.

Exercise 2a
- Ask students to look at the symbols 1–6 and match them with the weather headlines a–f.

- Tell them not to worry if there are words in a-f that they don't understand. They will learn them in exercise 2b. Encourage them NOT to look them up in a dictionary yet.
- Go through the answers with the class.

ANSWERS
1 c   2 b   3 a   4 e   5 f   6 d

Exercise 2b
- Ask students to read the sentences 1–6 and focus their attention on the words in italics.
- Tell them to find a word in bold in exercise 2a which means the same as one of the phrases in italics.
- Allow them time to check their answers in pairs and then go through them together as a class.

ANSWERS
1 pleasant
2 humid
3 damp
4 showers
5 mild
6 thunderstorm

Exercise 3
- Put students into pairs.
- Elicit or teach the adjective *typical*.
- Monitor the descriptions and discussions. Make a note of good use of the weather vocabulary they have studied.

EXTENSION With a multilingual class, encourage them to describe the weather in their own countries today and answer the question about it. If the class is monolingual, you could ask about the weather in other places they've been to on holiday or business, or places where their friends, family or colleagues live.

EXTRA ACTIVITY If you have access to computers, you could give each pair a different destination to research, such as *What's the weather like today in Moscow?* and/or *Find out about the climate in Moscow*. Alternatively, this could be given as a homework task to be discussed in class the following day.

SMART COMMUNICATION The weather is one of the most important topics for small talk. It is easy to discuss, needs no particular level of formality or informality and it is unlikely to cause offence. In Britain, it is very common to talk about the weather and people expect you to do it.

Exercise 4   1.7

Audio summary: Monologues by three different speakers; one from UAE, the second from Canada and the third from Brazil. All three speakers talk about their favourite season and the climate of the place they live.

- Tell students that they are going to listen to three people from the places in the photos talking about their favourite season.
- Check that students understand what they have to do.
- Play track 1.7.
- Go through the answers together.

ANSWERS
1 G   2 F   3 M

Unit 1 43

AUDIOSCRIPT 1.7

1 **Faisal from Dubai:** Winter's my favourite season. In summer it's too hot to enjoy outdoor activities. But in winter the temperature is really mild and pleasant – perfect for walks and picnics in the desert, or in the city's beautiful parks. Also, the sea's wonderful in the winter. I'm not keen on swimming in the sea in the summer. The water's too warm and there are sea snakes and other nasty animals. In winter it's safer and fresher. My favourite winter activity is fishing. I really love catching fish in the sea and then cooking them on a barbecue on the beach.

2 **Marek from Alberta:** I love autumn, when the days are sunny but cool. I'm really interested in photography and autumn's a great time for that as the leaves are a beautiful golden colour. In late autumn we get our first snowfalls and the snow looks amazing against the bright blue skies. Also, I'm really into watching ice hockey and autumn is when the new ice hockey season starts. The only problem with autumn is that it comes before winter and our winters are so long and cold. I don't mind cold weather but when the temperature goes down to 35 below zero, well, that's another story!!

3 **Gina from Rio de Janeiro:** My favourite season here in Rio is summer. I'm an English teacher, so I have long summer holidays, when I can relax and spend time with my children. To be honest, I prefer spring weather to summer weather. Summers here are extremely hot and humid. We get a lot of thunderstorms then too, but actually I quite like watching storms. Another thing I love is New Year's Eve, which of course is in the middle of summer here. There's an amazing firework display on the beach. I don't go down there because I can't stand large crowds, but we have a great view from our apartment.

Exercise 5a   1.7

- Allow plenty of time for students to read sentences 1–9.
- Tell them to listen again and complete the sentences.
- Play track 1.7 again.
- Encourage students to check their answers with a partner, but don't give them the correct answers yet.

ANSWERS
1 swimming   2 fishing   3 sea   4 photography
5 ice hockey   6 cold   7 spring   8 thunderstorms
9 crowds

Exercise 5b   1.8

- Tell them to listen and check their answers to exercise 5a.
- Play track 1.8.
- If you think the students may have any difficulty with spelling, write the answers on the board for them to check.

AUDIOSCRIPT 1.8 & 1.9

1 I'm not keen on swimming in the sea in the summer.
2 My favourite winter activity is fishing.
3 I really love catching fish in the sea.
4 I'm really interested in photography.
5 I'm really into watching ice hockey.
6 I don't mind cold weather.
7 I prefer spring weather to summer weather.
8 I quite like watching thunderstorms.
9 I can't stand large crowds.

Pronunciation stress

Exercise 5c   1.9

- Tell them that this time the focus is on pronunciation.
- Ask them to listen and repeat the sentences.
- Tell them to mark the stressed syllables on the sentences.
- Play track 1.9, pausing where necessary.
- Listen carefully and drill any problem sentences a few times.

AUDIOSCRIPT 1.9

See track 1.8.

PRONUNCIATION You could use back-chaining to help them pronounce the stress and intonation well. Start with the last word or phrase in the sentence, then add the previous word or phrase and so on until they are repeating the whole sentence. Example: *In the summer* (students repeat), *in the sea in the summer* (students repeat), *swimming in the sea in the summer* (students repeat), *keen on swimming in the sea in the summer* (students repeat), *I'm not keen on swimming in the sea in the summer.*

Exercise 5d

- Ask the students to read the meanings a–f and match them with phrases from exercise 5a. Point out that they will need to use some of the meanings more than once.
- When they finish, ask them to check their answers in pairs.
- Go through the answers together.

ANSWERS
a not keen on   b can't stand   c really love, really interested in, really into   d don't mind   e prefer
f quite like

Exercise 6

- Students read the instructions. If necessary, complete one sentence yourself to demonstrate the task.
- Give a suitable time limit for thinking about and completing the sentences.
- When they all have complete sentences, ask them to compare what they have written with a partner. Tell them to ask and answer questions to get more information.
- Conduct class feedback.

ANSWERS
Students' own answers

Exercise 7a

- Tell students they are going to give a short presentation. Ask them to turn to page 126 and choose one of the options 1–3.
- They should write notes about their likes and dislikes in relation to their chosen topic using the ideas to help them.
- This is individual work, but you should monitor and check that they are focused on likes and dislikes.

EXTRA CHALLENGE For fast finishers, ask them to think what kinds of questions their audience may ask them and how they will answer them.

Exercise 7b

- Focus students' attention on the Language for speaking box. Point out that these are phrases from exercise 5a.
- **WATCH OUT!** Make sure they notice the grammatical point at the bottom of the box about using the *-ing* form.
- Students should plan how they can use these phrases in their presentations. Allow plenty of time for them to think about this.
- Put the students in small groups to give their presentations.
- Highlight that students who are listening should make notes of any questions they want to ask.
- At the end of each presentation, the presenter should say *Any questions?* and the listeners should ask questions to get further information.
- When monitoring the presentations, focus on how well they are expressing their likes and dislikes, using the language for speaking. Make a note of any serious errors.
- In feedback, you could ask some students what was most interesting/surprising about the presentations they heard.
- Do error correction if necessary.

EXTRA ACTIVITY Put students in new pairs, working with someone who hasn't heard their presentation. They tell their new partner about their likes and dislikes, but this time it is not a presentation but a more informal chat. Encourage the listener to be involved in the discussion by using common phrases such as *Me too* if they share an opinion or *Really?* to get more information about an opinion.

Reading & Writing   a web post about the best time to visit your country

Exercise 8

- Write on the board *forum* and *web post*. Elicit that they are connected with writing and reading on the internet and go through the meanings if necessary.

EXTENSION You could also elicit the verb *to post* and some common words we use with it, e.g. *a message, a comment, a link, a picture, a photo, results, a video*.

- Students read questions 1–3. Then read the posts on the travel forum to find the answers.
- Go through the answers together.

ANSWERS

1 Goa
2 The best time to go is October.
3 a The weather is still good.
   b It's not too crowded.
   c Some of the shops and restaurants are not open.

Exercise 9a

- Tell students that one way to improve their written English is to link their ideas clearly.
- Focus their attention on the Language for writing box and ask them to read it.
- Ask questions to check their understanding: *Which linker can we use to … ?*

Exercise 9b

- Write the first example sentence on the board: *The weather is good and there aren't too many people.* Using a different colour pen, add a full stop after *good* and change *and* to *And*. Ask the students *Is this sentence more formal now?* They should answer *No, it's informal*.
- Explain that they need to use linkers to join sentences 1–6. Point out that each has a label *neutral* or *informal* Tell them that for informal sentences, they should use the linker as shown on the board, with a capital letter.
- Allow time for them to add the linkers and change punctuation where necessary.
- Go through the answers together carefully.

ANSWERS

1 It rains every day but it's not heavy rain.
2 The restaurants are great and they're not too expensive.
3 It's a very interesting street. But it can be a bit dangerous at night.
4 The temperature reaches 40°C so people go to the mountains where it's cooler.
5 All the children are on holiday at this time of year. So the beaches get crowded.
6 There's an excellent museum and it's free to enter.

Exercise 10a

- Ask the students to look at the topics in the box. Go through any unknown words.
- Tell them that they are going to write a post similar to Varsha's in exercise 8 about the best time to visit their country or town.
- Focus their attention on the useful phrases.
- Ask them to choose two or three topics from the box (or their own ideas). For students who need more challenge, tell them to choose four topics.
- Remind students to use linkers to write longer sentences.
- Set a time limit for the writing task. Tell them to write clearly because another student is going to read their post.
- Monitor, assist and correct as they write.

ANSWERS

Students' own answers

Exercise 10b

- In pairs, students give their post to their partner to read.
- Choose the focus for their reading to fit your students, according to whether they are a multilingual or monolingual group.
- Conduct class feedback.

EXTENSION 1 If you think it is appropriate, you could ask them to give each other feedback on their writing. They should focus only on the linkers in their partner's writing. They can circle every linker which is used well and can underline any linker which has been used incorrectly. In an adult class, this kind of analysis of another student's work can be very useful. But some students may be sensitive to criticism and only wish the teacher to do this, so it is not suitable for all classes.

EXTENSION 2 You could also make a gallery of all the posts on a classroom wall/notice board or if your college has a real website, students could post their writing on the internet or intranet. Students from your class and even other classes could read and add comments or questions.

Unit 1   45

1.5 Video

Adventure sports in Chile

VIDEOSCRIPT

Chile is a long, narrow country between the Andes Mountains and the Pacific Ocean.
It has deserts, lakes, mountains and volcanoes.
This incredible landscape makes Chile very popular with tourists.
But what do they do? Some tourists visit cities like Santiago, the capital of Chile.
Others travel north to see the Atacama Desert, the driest desert in the world.
But many tourists travel south, to a small town called Pucón, Chile's adventure sports capital.
Pucón is a fantastic destination for anybody interested in adventure sports.
This small city has a population of around 20,000 people.
It's between a volcano and a lake so there are lots of different sports and activities here.
What kinds of activities? It depends on the season.
In summer, many tourists climb to the top of Villarrica Volcano. The volcano is almost 3,000 metres high, so these hikes aren't easy.
At the bottom of the volcano is Lake Villarrica, a popular location for water sports including sailing, rafting and waterskiing. Every year, around 70,000 tourists visit the lake.
They often come here to Playa Blanca, a peaceful location with warm clear waters and a beautiful forest.
Some visitors go up to Trancura River, where they can kayak down some of the best rapids in Chile!
But at the moment the volcano, the lake and the river are quiet. This is because it's winter and most people here are skiing!
This is Ski Pucón, a small resort on the slopes of Villarrica Volcano. There are 20 different runs here for all kinds of skiiers and snowboarders.
These slopes cover a drop of 900 metres, and there are nine ski lifts to take visitors to the top.
From here, the peak of the volcano towers over the whole resort. And, as you travel towards it, you can sometimes see steam rising from the crater!
From the top, there are amazing views of the lake and the surrounding mountains. It's an incredible landscape to ski in.
Visitors to Pucón enjoy lots of different adventure sports.
In the summer, they hike up the volcano or spend time on the lake.
In the winter, they race down the volcano's slopes – either on skis or snowboards.
And, whatever the season, they can always enjoy the beautiful scenery.

VIDEO ANSWERS

1 1 hike   2 rapids   3 slopes   4 climb   5 peak
3 a, b, d, e are mentioned in the video
4 a mountains, lakes, deserts and volcanoes
   b around 20,000
   c climbing to the top of the volcano, sailing, kayaking, rafting, water-skiing
   d almost 3000 metres
   e skiing, snowboarding
   f 900 metres

Review
ANSWERS

Exercise 1a
1 How many people are there in your family?
2 How old are you?
3 What did you do at the weekend?
4 Do you live in a house or a flat?
5 What kind of music do you like?
6 How often do you go to the cinema?

Exercise 2a
1 every now and then
2 rarely
3 most days
4 sometimes

Exercise 2b
Students' own answers

Exercise 3   1.10
1 housework
2 family
3 late
4 internet
5 good
6 future
7 night
8 football

AUDIOSCRIPT 1.10
1 When you clean the floor, is this homework or housework?
2 Are your relatives your friends, or your family?
3 If you have a lie in, do you get up early or late?
4 If you are online, are you on the internet or the telephone?
5 Is healthy food good or bad for you?
6 When you write a to-do list, is it for the future or the past?
7 Do people go clubbing in the day or at night?
8 Do you need more energy for football or chess?

Exercise 4a
1 time with relatives
2 fun
3 shopping
4 yoga
5 a family meal

Exercise 5a
1 writes a blog
2 take photographs of
3 write posts
4 have a look
5 have dreams

Unit 1

2 Inside outside

Unit overview

Language input

Present simple and present continuous (CB p17)	• *The art happens outside.* • *Every now and then, my boss checks my work.* • *My luck is changing now.* • *What hours are you working today?*
Identifying relative clauses (CB p18)	• *Quinjun is a photographer who travels around China.* • *The photos show the huge changes which are taking place in China.*
Grammar reference (CB pp136–7)	

Vocabulary development

Street life (CB p16)	• *souvenir seller, street performer, stall …* • *dull nightlife, crowded pavement …*
Household objects (CB p19)	• *towel, candle, dustpan and brush …*
Phrases with *on* (CB p20)	• *on business* • *on the left*

Skills development

Reading: Understanding sentences with missing words (CB p20)	
Speaking: Asking for and giving directions (CB p22)	
Writing: Text messages (CB p23)	

Video

Documentary: London's changing skyline (Coursebook DVD & CB p24)	
Vox pops (Coursebook DVD & TG p259)	

More materials

Workbook	• Language practice for vocabulary, pronunciation, grammar, speaking and writing • Reading for pleasure • Review: Units 1 & 2
Photocopiable activities	• Grammar: Relative clauses game (TG p209 & TSRD) • Vocabulary: Household objects (TG p227 & TSRD) • Communication: Giving directions (TG p245 & TSRD)
Tests	• Unit 2 test (TSRD)
Unit 2 wordlist (TSRD)	

2.1 Street life

Goals
- Talk about where you live
- Talk about the present

Lead-in
- Write *village*, *town* and *city* on the board and elicit the difference between them (i.e. that *village* is the smallest and *city* is the largest). Drill the pronunciation of these words, /ˈvɪlɪdʒ/, /taʊn/, /ˈsɪti/.
- Put students in pairs or small groups. Ask them to talk about the place where they live: *Is it a village, town or city? What is it called? What is one good thing about living there? What is one bad thing about living there?* If all the students come from the same town/city, they could just discuss the last two questions.
- Conduct a brief class discussion and point out that one of the goals for this lesson is to talk about where you live.

Vocabulary & Speaking street life

Exercise 1
- Focus students' attention on the photo.
- Ask them to read questions 1–4 and discuss their answers in pairs.
- Conduct a class discussion.

EXTENSION Ask students to give their reactions to the street art in the photo and to pavement art in general. You could ask: *Do you think a pavement artist is really an artist? What is good or bad about pavement art? Should people give pavement artists money?* Students could also discuss other forms of street art: singing, playing music, circus skills, magic tricks, etc. Encourage them to share different experiences from places they may have travelled.

> **Background note:** Edgar Mueller. Mueller, born in Germany in 1968, is famous for his 3D pavement paintings and has won a number of awards. His art is large-scale, usually taking more than one day to create. If you stand at a particular point, his paintings give the impression of different dimensions. Like most street art, his creations wash away when it rains.

Exercise 2a
- Tell students to look at the mind map and the words in the box below.
- Students work in pairs to decide where to add the words in the box to the mind map and to help each other understand any unknown words.

DICTIONARY SKILLS Students should be encouraged to use monolingual or bilingual dictionaries if they are available.
- Go through the answers together.

ANSWERS
1 souvenir seller, pavement artist, street cleaner, street performer
2 safe, crowded, dirty, huge, lively, dull
3 stall, statue, market place, pedestrian area, rubbish, parking space

Exercise 2b
- Write *pedestrian area* on the board. Explain that these two nouns form a compound noun with a specific meaning.
- Tell students to work alone making compound nouns using one word from list 1–5 and another from a–e.
- Tell them to check their answers in pairs and then check answers together.

ANSWERS
1 c   2 a,e   3 b   4 a,e   5 d

Pronunciation compound nouns

Exercise 3a 2.1
- The focus is on word stress in compound nouns.
- Explain that they have to underline the stressed word.
- Play track 2.1.
- Students underline the stressed words. Go through the answers – the students should soon notice that the stress falls on the first word of a compound noun.

ANSWERS/AUDIOSCRIPT 2.1
<u>market</u> place
<u>souvenir</u> seller
<u>pavement</u> artist
<u>parking</u> space
<u>street</u> cleaner
<u>pedestrian</u> area
<u>street</u> performer

Exercise 3b 2.2
- Tell students to repeat the words after the recording.
- Play track 2.2 and ask students to repeat each compound noun.
- Repeat any which the students find difficult. Encourage them to count syllables. Count them yourself holding up your fingers as a visual reference and highlight the stressed syllable by clearly indicating the appropriate finger.

Exercise 4a
- Students read the example. Tell them that if a sentence is true, they don't need to change it. But they must add another sentence to give more information.
- Students work alone on this task.
- Monitor carefully to ensure they are adding information

ANSWERS
Students' own answers

EXTRA CHALLENGE Ask fast finishers to write more sentences about their town/city using words from exercise 2a or compound nouns from exercise 2b.

Exercise 4b
- Put students into pairs to compare their answers.
- If students are from the same town or city, they can focus on whether they have written the same things. They could discuss any differences of opinion.
- If students come from different towns or cities, they can ask further questions about their partner's sentences.
- Monitor their discussions and note any good sentences, particularly ones which use the vocabulary from 2a or 2b.

Unit 2   49

EXTENSION Ask students to look at their true sentences again and discuss with their partner which is the best and worst thing about their town.

Exercise 5

- Put students in small groups. Try to group students from the same country together.
- This is primarily a speaking exercise, but one member of the group can write notes so they remember what they have said.
- If students come from the same place, they should use the prompts to describe the place where they live. Students from different places can choose a town they all know.
- Allow enough time for the groups to work together on the task. Set a time limit if necessary.
- Ask each group to present their description to the class. They can choose one student to speak for them or take turns to speak using the prompts.

FEEDBACK FOCUS Monitor closely, noting good and bad examples of word stress on the compound nouns.

EXTENSION Encourage other groups to ask questions if you wish to extend the speaking task.

Grammar & Speaking present simple and present continuous

Exercise 6   2.3

Audio summary: Three different interviews with people who work in the street, talking about their work. The people are a pavement artist, a tea-seller and a street cleaner.

- Tell students they are going to listen to three people who work in the street speaking about their work. Elicit words for different people who work in the street (from exercise 2). Elicit spellings and pronunciation where necessary.
- Ask them to read the notes 1–6. If necessary, go through any unknown vocabulary.
- Play track 2.3.
- Students listen and match the notes to the people.
- Go through the answers together.

ANSWERS
1 L   2 H   3 E   4 H   5 E   6 L

AUDIOSCRIPT 2.3

Interview 1: Edgar Mueller
I Good morning and welcome to the show. Today, we're talking to three very different people about their work outside in the street: Edgar Mueller, an amazing 3D pavement artist, Laxman Rao, a tea-seller and Harry Bakewell, a street cleaner. So, first of all, Edgar, why do you think 3D pavement art is so popular nowadays?
EM The art happens outside, so people can enjoy the art on their way to work – they don't have to go to art galleries or museums to see it. They love getting close to the art and exploring it.
I Your painting, *Ice Age*, was 330 square metres and broke a world record. Why do you do such huge paintings?
E Well, er, I want to change how the street looks …
I Hmm … but why's that important?
E Because I'm interested in the way people see the world: people watch and ask questions when I'm working. Also, I want them to walk on the paintings, become part of the art.

Interview 2: Laxman Rao
I Laxman Rao is a tea-seller and a writer in New Delhi, India. So Laxman, please tell me about your work.
LR Well, every day I serve tea at a stall in central Delhi – it's crowded and noisy, but my job for the last twenty years! I also write novels and plays in Hindi, India's national language.
I Uh-huh, but why does a writer have to sell tea?
LR Well, actually, I'm the writer, publisher and the salesman! Before, I never made enough money from my books, but I think my luck is changing now … .
I Oh really? Why's that?
LR Well, more and more people are reading books and newspapers in Hindi these days. Did you know it's the third most spoken language in the world? And one of my novels is selling well, so …

Interview 3: Harry Bakewell
I Finally, Harry Bakewell is a street cleaner from London in England. Good morning, Harry, could you tell us a little bit about your job now. Do you work alone?
HB Yeah, I do, but I work in a very lively neighbourhood and I know everyone, so it's fine. There's plenty to do and all kinds of people to chat to, so it's never dull! I have to be careful though because every now and then, my boss checks my work and I get in trouble if I'm chatting or drinking tea when he arrives!
I And what hours are you working today?
HB Well, er, today I'm working from 7 a.m. to 3 p.m.
I And how do you find this work?
HB Well, er, I work in a pedestrian area near the city centre. We do have a huge problem with rubbish so it's hard work, but I prefer working outdoors and I'm not embarrassed about my job. The people who drop their rubbish on the pavement instead of putting it in the bin should be embarrassed, not me!

Exercise 7   2.3

- Ask students *How many words are missing from each sentence?* to check they understand that there may be more than one.
- Play track 2.3 again, or more than once if necessary.
- Go through the answers together.

ANSWERS
1 happens
2 love
3 are reading
4 is changing
5 checks
6 are (you) working
7 'm working

Exercise 8

- Focus students' attention on the Grammar focus box. Make sure they, know what they have to do – write PS or PC next to sentences 1–4 and complete sentences 5–6.

EXTRA SUPPORT Students can do this in two stages; tell them just to read sentences 1–4 and decide which tense they are. Check those answers. Then ask them to complete the rules.

- Go through the answers together.

ANSWERS
1 PS
2 PC
3 PC
4 PS
5 simple
6 continuous

WATCH OUT! Take this opportunity to point out the 3rd person 's' in the present simple sentences 1 and 4. Most students are aware of this change in the verb form in theory but it is often missed out in practice.

- Refer students to *Grammar reference* on p136. There are three more exercises here students can do for homework. See answers in next column.

Exercise 9

Background note: Dustbot is a real technology project, partly funded by the European Commission and involving Italy, UK, Sweden, Switzerland and Spain. It started in 2006. Another part of the project is Dustclean which is a robotic street cleaner which sucks up rubbish like a vacuum cleaner.

EXTRA ACTIVITY Ask students to look at the photo of Dustbot and ask *What is it? What does it do? Where is it from?* Tell them to quickly read the text to check their answers.

- Ask them to read the text again and underline the correct form of the verb 1–8.
- Go through the answers with the class. Encourage strong students to explain their choice of verb form, using the rules from the Grammar focus box if possible.

ANSWERS
1 are developing   5 want
2 call   6 don't find
3 comes   7 are trying
4 takes   8 are recycling

Exercise 10

- Explain to students that each of the time expressions in the box is usually used with one of the two tenses.
- Do an example together. *Is 'always' used with present simple or present continuous?* (present simple) *How do we know?* (it's not only about now).
- Students work alone to categorize the time expressions.
- Go through the answers, eliciting 'why' if possible.

ANSWERS
present simple – always, usually, occasionally, every Sunday, never
present continuous – at the moment, right now

Exercise 11a

- Write the first question together as a demonstration.
- Students work alone to make the questions.
- When they finish, ask them to check their answers in pairs.
- Go through the answers together as a class.

ANSWERS
1 What do you do every Sunday?
2 How often do you go into the city centre?
3 What do tourists usually visit in your town?
4 How is your life changing at the moment?
5 What do you like about your home town?
6 What is happening outside right now?

Exercise 11b

- Put students into pairs to ask and answer the questions.
- Monitor carefully, paying attention to the tenses they use in their answers. Make a note of good uses as well as errors.

FEEDBACK FOCUS Read out or write on the board any good responses. Highlight that answers generally use the same tense as in the question.

Exercise 12a

- Ask students to read questions 1–3.
- Put them into small discussion groups.
- If students aren't discussing the same town, city or country, they could try to find similarities between the different places they're discussing.

CRITICAL THINKING In these kinds of discussions, students should try to give reasons for their opinions, with examples if possible. This makes their arguments clearer and will also help when they need to decide which are the strongest arguments (see exercise 12b below).

Exercise 12b

- In their groups, students choose the three most positive and the three most negative changes.
- Set a time limit so they all finish their discussions at the same time.
- Conduct class feedback. Encourage groups to present their ideas to the class and respond to what their classmates say.

GRAMMAR REFERENCE ANSWERS
Exercise 1
1 are living   2 exists   3 are sleeping   4 have   5 isn't going   6 cost   7 work   8 are organizing
Exercise 2
1 always visit   2 are sitting   3 are returning   4 Do you usually meet   5 don't usually visit   6 aren't performing   7 go   8 Are you and Sarah doing
Exercise 3
1 not possible
2 I am enjoying living here.
3 not possible
4 I am working in a factory.
5 not possible
6 not possible
7 People are driving quickly down our street.
8 I am watching football on my laptop.

2.2 Home life

Goals
- Identifying things and people
- Talk about things in your home

Lead-in
- Write three things on the board (e.g. *sofa, TV, bed*) and say that these are three items in your home. Tell students that

Unit 2   51

you love two of the items, but you don't like the other one.
- Students need to ask you questions to identify the one you don't like. E.g. *Do you like your TV? What's wrong with your bed?* Answer their questions and give information about the items so students can find out which you don't like.
- Ask students to think of two things in their home that they love and one thing that they don't really like and write these three items down in any order.
- In pairs, students ask questions about their partner's three items.
- Conduct a class discussion if you have time.

Grammar & Reading identifying relative clauses

Exercise 1
- Put students into pairs.
- Ask them to study the photo and read questions 1 and 2.
- Students discuss their answers with their partner.
- Conduct a class discussion. (They will find the real answers in the next exercise.)

POSSIBLE ANSWERS
1 It shows people standing outside their home with their possessions.
2 The photographer took it to show the huge changes that are taking place in China right now.

Exercise 2

Text summary: An article about Huang Quingjun, a photographer working in China, who takes photos of people outside their homes with all of their possessions outside too.

- Ask students to read the topics a–d.
- Tell them that they are going to read an article and should match each paragraph of the article to one of the topics.
- Allow plenty of time for them to read and do the task.
- Go through the answers together.

ANSWERS
a 2   b 4   c 1   d 3

Exercise 3a
- Check students understand that they need to choose how they think/feel from the two options and make **true** sentences, giving their reasons.
- They work alone to complete the sentences.
- Monitor and help them finish the sentences if necessary.

ANSWERS
Students' own answers

Exercise 3b
- Put students into small groups.
- Tell them to compare their answers and find out whether they have the same opinions.

EXTRA CHALLENGE Strong students can try to discuss any different opinions in greater detail. They should ask questions to get more information about the opinions expressed.

- Conduct a class discussion and encourage students to share their different opinions.

Exercise 4a
- The grammar focus is about identifying relative clauses. You could elicit or explain that a clause is one part of a sentence. You could also write *who, which, where* on the board and explain that these are called 'relative pronouns'.

EXTRA SUPPORT It may be simpler for some students if you ask them questions about relative pronouns, e.g. *Do we use 'who' to talk about people or places?* This helps to give them extra confidence before doing the task.

- Focus the students' attention on the Grammar focus box. You could read the first paragraph aloud to them.
- Tell students to complete the rules. Highlight that there are five gaps but only four relative pronouns so one must be used more than once.
- Students work alone on the task.
- Go through the answers together as a class. Point out that *that* is very commonly used in spoken English because it is flexible and can be used for things or people.

WATCH OUT! It is a common mistake for students to want to use *what* as a relative pronoun. E.g. *This is the new phone what I told you about* instead of ... *that (or which) I told you about*. Make sure you correct this error if it happens or try to avoid this problem by explaining that we use *who, which*, or *that* but not *what* in identifying relative clauses.

ANSWERS
1 who   4 that
2 that   5 where
3 which

Exercise 4b
- Students find the first identifying clause together.
- Encourage students to check that they have found all the examples with a partner.
- Go through the answers together.

ANSWERS
Huang Qingjun is a photographer <u>who</u> travels around China and takes photos of people <u>that</u> are standing outside their homes.
The photos show the huge changes <u>which</u> are taking place in China.
The photo of elderly farmers <u>who</u> are standing outside their house ...
Some people feel it is strange to take all the things <u>which</u> are in their house outside.
It is easier to take the photos in places <u>where</u> people don't have many possessions.
He visited one location <u>where</u> a couple had to move.
You can see the Chinese word <u>which</u> means 'destroy'.

EXTRA ACTIVITY Ask students to look at the photo in detail. Ask *Which of these things do you have in your home?* and tell them to answer the question with their partner. As a class, ask them *Do you have more possessions in your home than this? Are all your possessions necessary? Do you have a lot of space in your home to put your possessions?*

- Refer students to *Grammar reference* on p137. There are three more exercises here students can do for homework. See answers on p54.

Exercise 5

> **Background note:** Around 46 of these Fujian tulous have been added to the UNESCO list of World Heritage Sites in recognition of how unique they are and because some date back to the 12th century.

- Make sure students know they should complete the text using *who*, *which* or *where*.
- Students work alone to read and complete the text.
- When they finish, ask them to read the text again and find the relative pronouns they could replace using *that*.
- Go through the answers together.

ANSWERS

1	where	5	where
2	who	6	who
3	where	7	which
4	where	8	which

2, 6, 7 and 8 could be replaced by *that*

CRITICAL THINKING Encourage personal reactions to the text. You could ask: *Why do you think 300 people live together in the same building like this? How is it similar to and different from living in an apartment block? Would you feel happy living in this building? Why/why not? Would you like to visit this building? Why/why not?*

Pronunciation *that* in relative clauses

Exercise 6a 2.4

- Tell students that they are going to listen to sentences 1–3. The stressed words are in bold. They should focus on how the speakers say *that* in the sentences.
- Play track 2.4.
- Ask students to tell you what they noticed about *that*. The key thing for students to notice is that *that* is not stressed. We say /ðæt/ when we say the word on its own but in a sentence like this we pronounce *that* as //ðət//. It is a weak form which means the vowel sound is reduced, in this case to /ə/.

PRONUNCIATION It's important that students understand the concept of weak forms. Not all words are pronounced fully because English is a stress timed language. We tend to stress the content words and other grammar words such as auxiliary verbs, prepositions and articles become weaker. This helps the speaker to talk more quickly and easily.

AUDIOSCRIPT 2.4 & 2.5
1 It's something that you see in the street.
2 It's something that doesn't move.
3 It's something that birds sit on.

Exercise 6b 2.5

- Play track 2.5 so students can repeat each sentence.
- If you ask them to over-exaggerate the stressed words, this will give them less time to say the other words in the sentence and may help to make *that* quicker and weaker.
- Play track 2.5 again if necessary.
- Elicit what the students think the three sentences describe.

ANSWER
It's a statue.

Exercise 7a

- Check students understand what to do.
- Remind them NOT to say or write the name of the two things.

EXTRA SUPPORT To simplify the task, tell them the two things must be normal things you find in a house. You could specify that the first sentence must give the location of the thing, e.g. *It's something that you find in the bathroom.*

- Students work in pairs and write down their three sentences about each thing. Both students need to write down the sentences (as they will be separated in exercise 7b).
- Monitor carefully and check that their sentences make sense and use *that* correctly.

Exercise 7b

- Regroup the pairs so that each student works with somebody different.
- Tell them to take turns reading their three sentences to their new partner who has to guess what the things are.
- Remind them before they start to pronounce the sentences as naturally as possible, including the weak form for 'that'.

FEEDBACK FOCUS As you monitor, note examples of natural pronunciation, including who said it – it is motivating for individuals to get targeted positive feedback.

- After the activity, elicit sentences about things which were difficult to guess. Praise good examples of natural pronunciation (see Feedback focus above).

Vocabulary & Listening household objects

Exercise 8 2.6

> **Audio summary:** Three different monologues where the speakers talk about living away from home. They talk about different household objects and mention positive and negative things about living in a different house.

EXTRA ACTIVITY As a lead-in, ask what situations take them away from home for a while? (a holiday, visiting relatives, living abroad, a business trip, going to university, etc.)

- Tell them they are going to listen to three speakers talking about living away from home. Ask them to look at situations a–c.
- Teach the meaning of *doing a house swap* (= you live in another person's house and they live in yours) and *house-sitting* (= you live in another person's house while they are away). Students may know a similar word: *to babysit*.
- Play track 2.6.
- They match each speaker to a situation a–c.
- Go through the answers together.

ANSWERS
1 b   2 c   3 a

AUDIOSCRIPT 2.6
Speaker 1
The house where we're staying is huge. I suppose they always say things are much bigger in the States, don't they? They have some beautiful things. I love all the candles in the bathroom and the soft, white towels, oh and the Egyptian cotton sheets on the bed are wonderful! It's a really lovely place, but I'm still missing certain things from

Unit 2   53

home, such as my own bed and even my duvet! Also, one thing which I don't like – they don't have a proper cooker, just a microwave oven. Hard to believe in such a big place, and a bit disappointing for me, as I love cooking. Another thing which surprises me is that they don't have any mirrors – very strange!

Speaker 2
I'm staying at my friend's flat for a couple of months – looking after it while he's away. It's really modern and I absolutely love the bathroom! The wash basin looks like a sheet of paper, and at first, I couldn't even work the taps! There are no carpets, just white rugs everywhere. I don't really like them because I'm so worried about spilling something – especially as I can't find his cleaning stuff, not even a cloth or a dustpan and brush! It's my first experience of house-sitting and I'm finding it quite hard to relax. My friend doesn't have much stuff at all, but I'm the opposite: I have loads of stuff and I miss all my things. Also, there's nowhere to put my clothes – no wardrobe or chest of drawers in the bedroom. I'm quite surprised about that.

Speaker 3
I'm enjoying living with friends, and the room here is OK. I mean it has all the basics, you know, a bed, a desk, bookshelves and a wash basin. But I honestly can't believe how much I'm missing home! I really hate not having my own washing machine, dishwasher and fridge! I also miss our big, comfortable sofa and satellite TV with all the channels. It's surprising because I never usually think about these things, but now I can't wait to go home for Christmas!

Exercise 9   2.6

- Ask students to read the questions a–f.
- Tell them to listen to the track again and match speakers 1–3 to each question.
- Play track 2.6.
- Go through the answers together.

ANSWERS
a 1
b 2
c 1
d 3
e 2
f 3

Exercise 10a

- Check that students know what to do.

DICTIONARY SKILLS Encourage students to explain the meaning of words to each other, but say it is also useful to practise using dictionaries. If they use dictionaries or translators on their mobile phones or tablets, remind them that they can search images for this kind of vocabulary. A picture can explain concrete vocabulary instantly.

- Allow plenty of time so that students can use dictionaries.
- Remind all the students that they need to explain why the underlined item is different. Give them a little extra time to think about this if necessary.

EXTRA CHALLENGE For fast finishers, ask them to think of an extra word to add to each group. Remember to check these after checking the answers or check them as you monitor.

- Go through the answers together. Drill any words with unusual or difficult pronunciation, e.g. duvet /ˈduːveɪ/, oven /ˈʌvn/, drawers /drɔːz/.

ANSWERS
1 towel
2 mirror
3 candle
4 dishwasher
5 satellite TV
6 pan

Exercise 10b

- Tell students to read the groups numbered 1–7. Tell them to find a suitable group for each of the words in exercise 10a.
- Categorize the first word together as a demonstration: towel = group 3.
- Students work on this task alone. Then check their ideas in pairs.
- Go through the answers together.

EXTENSION Put students into small groups and give each group one category 1–7 from this exercise. Tell them to think of more words for their category. Set a time limit. Elicit new words. Encourage students to explain/teach unknown words.

ANSWERS
1 duvet, sheet
2 candle
3 towel, mirror, tap, (candle), wash basin
4 mirror, carpet, rug, satellite TV, candle
5 cooker, microwave oven, pan
6 chest of drawers, wardrobe
7 cloth, dustpan and brush, dishwasher

Exercise 11

- Ask students to read the questions and discuss in small groups.
- Conduct class feedback. Ask them to tell the class any surprising or interesting things about the people in their group. If short of time, you could ask whether they had similar or very different answers.

Exercise 12a

- Students work alone on this task. They turn to page 126 and choose five examples from the table.
- Tell them to write only the names down and no other information. Demonstrate the activity yourself if necessary.

Exercise 12b

- Put students into pairs to ask and answer questions about the people, places and things they have written down.
- Ask them to read the example conversation.
- Monitor the conversations for correct and incorrect use of *who, which, where* and *that*.
- Conduct class feedback. Do error correction if necessary.

GRAMMAR REFERENCE ANSWERS

Exercise 1
1 which   2 where   3 which   4 which   5 who
6 which   7 which   8 who   9 which   10 where

Exercise 2
1 Can you light the candle ʌ that we bought and put it over there?

2 In the old museum there are some rooms ∧ that you mustn't enter.
3 The man and woman ∧ who bought our house are lovely people.
4 This is the gallery with the famous painting ∧ which cost 7 million dollars.
5 The park ∧ where people go jogging is on the other side of the town.
6 Stephen is the man in the office ∧ that I play tennis with.

Exercise 3
1 This is the new rug which/that we bought last week.
2 Mr Reynolds is the architect who designed our home.
3 In the bedroom there is a chest of drawers where you can put your things.
4 This is the room where we study.
5 I wouldn't like to stay in a house which/that doesn't have bathroom.
6 Who is the boy who/that lives opposite us?
7 There are two towns near here that/which have railway stations.

2.3 Vocabulary and skills development

Goals
- Use phrases with *on*
- Understand sentences with missing words

Vocabulary & Listening phrases with *on*

Lead-in
- Write on the board: *Which city in the world do you know best? Do you have positive or negative feelings about it? Why?*
- Give your own answers to the questions as an example.
- Put students into groups to ask and answer the questions.
- Conduct brief class feedback.

Exercise 1a
- Put students into pairs to talk about the advantages and disadvantages of living in a city.
- Ask them to make a note of their ideas.
- Monitor their discussions and then conduct feedback.
- Write the advantages and disadvantages on the board.

EXTRA CHALLENGE Some aspects of living in a city could be an advantage or a disadvantage, depending on your point of view. For example, *Cities have a lot of people in them: disadvantage: they are over-crowded, and advantage: it is interesting to live with different kinds of people.* Ask stronger students to explain why something is an advantage or disadvantage and give their reasons.

Exercise 1b 2.7

Audio summary: An informal conversation between two speakers (one male and one female) about living in the city.

- Tell students that they are going to listen to a discussion between two speakers, Mike and Emma, on the topic of living in a city.

- Ask them to listen to find out how each speaker feels about living in a city.
- Play track 2.7.
- Go through the answers. Ask which words helped them to decide.

ANSWERS
Students' own answers
Mike isn't enjoying it.
Emma loves the city.

AUDIOSCRIPT 2.7
E How do you find city life then, Mike?
M Oh well, I've only been here for a few weeks. But to be honest, I'm not enjoying it at all.
E How come?
M I think it's because I'm from a small town in the country but I just can't get used to it. Everybody's so rude!
E How do you mean?
M Well, for example, nobody's ever on time for anything. I was at a business meeting last week and three of the six people were late!
E That's because public transport here is so rubbish. I was on the way to the city centre yesterday and the tram just stopped for half an hour. That's life.
M But it's crazy. There are so many people who come here on business, but if you can't get to your appointments on time, you'll go somewhere else to do business. And another thing, I always get lost, this city's like a maze.
E But you've got a smartphone. If you get lost, you just look it up on the internet. Come on, Mike, maybe you come from the country, but you know how to use a smartphone!
M And the tourists! You can't move. I was in Bath Street the other day, trying to get to a business appointment. All the tourists and shoppers – I was blocked. I really don't understand why they come here on holiday.
E Probably because of all the great museums, art galleries and shops! I love all the people here, all the different nationalities, all the buzz … .
M The buzz?
E Yes, I feel excited all the time. I love it!

Exercise 1c 2.7
- Ask students to read sentences 1–5.
- Tell them that you're going to play the track again and they need to listen for these sentences and write down who says each one. They should write M for Mike and E for Emma.

EXTRA CHALLENGE Encourage strong students to try to remember or guess which person said each sentence. Then they listen in order to confirm or correct their ideas.

- Play track 2.7 again.
- Go through the answers together.

ANSWERS
1 M 2 E 3 M 4 E 5 M

Exercise 2a
- Focus students' attention on the Vocabulary focus box.
- Tell them to read the information and point out that there are example phrases with *on* in the sentences in 1c.

Unit 2 55

- Go through the information from the Study tip if necessary.

STUDY TIP You could tell them that there has been research which shows that learning 'chunks' of language can make language learning more efficient. There are certainly a large number of common prepositional phrases such as these (with *on* and many other prepositions). It is sensible for students to record these chunks in their notebooks. They can organize them under the same preposition and add phrases as they learn them.

WATCH OUT! Draw students' attention to *Learn these as complete phrases* in the Vocabulary focus box. These kinds of chunks are best learned as phrases together rather than learning the individual words.

Exercise 2b
- Tell students to use the phrases in the box to complete questions 1–8.
- They work alone on the task.
- Encourage them to check their answers with a partner.
- Go through the answers together.

ANSWERS
1 on holiday
2 on the left
3 on public transport
4 on the internet
5 on the way
6 on TV
7 on time
8 on business

Exercise 3
- Put students in pairs.
- Tell them to ask each other the questions in exercise 2b.
- To keep this discussion interesting, you could tell them to ask each other the questions in random order or start by asking the questions they find most interesting first.
- Set a time limit for the task if necessary.

EXTRA CHALLENGE Fast finishers could make their own questions using some of the phrases with *on*. Check carefully. They could ask each other these new questions straight away or you could include them during feedback.

- Conduct class feedback about anything interesting they found out about their partner.
- You could also ask: *Which of these phrases with 'on' did you already know before this lesson?*

EXTRA ACTIVITY Ask students to remember their partner's answers to the questions and write them down using full sentences containing the phrases with *on*. It doesn't matter if they cannot remember all the answers, but they should write down what they think. They are not allowed to ask their partner again. Then when they have eight written answers, they can pass them to their partner to check. Students can make changes to the sentences if they are factually wrong or, if all students feel comfortable with peer-correction, you can ask them to correct any grammatical mistakes they find.

Reading & Speaking understanding sentences with missing words

Exercise 4a
- Ask students to read the sentence and decide which word is missing.
- Check the answer together.

ANSWER
she

Exercise 4b
- Ask them to read sentences 1–4 and, again, find which word is missing. Sometimes it is more than one word.
- Encourage them to check their answers in pairs.
- Go through the answers together.

ANSWERS
1 We were in a traffic jam in Oxford Street and **we** didn't move for an hour.
2 A What's the capital of Canada?
 B **I** don't know.
3 They're walking along the street and **they're** looking at the shop windows.
4 They're going to write a blog and **they're going to** post it on their website.

Exercise 5
- Focus students' attention on the Unlock the code box and give them time to read it.
- You could use the sentences in exercise 4b to highlight the kinds of words which are generally missed out.

Exercise 6a

> **Text summary:** An article about *pavement rage* which is when people get angry with slow pedestrians blocking their way. It is the pavement equivalent of *road rage* – where drivers become angry with each other.

- Students read the questions and discuss their ideas in pairs.

EXTRA SUPPORT If you think your students do not know the word *rage* you could teach it (= a feeling of very strong anger that is difficult to control).

- Elicit ideas from the class but do not confirm whether they are right – they will read the article to find the answer.

Exercise 6b
- Point out that students should read only the first paragraph of the article to check whether their ideas about 'pavement rage' were right.

EXTRA SUPPORT To further check their general understanding, you could ask *So the writer says that some pedestrians are very slow. What reasons does he give for this?* (They are texting, window shopping or talking on their mobile phones.)

- Don't encourage discussion of the article at this stage. It is important that the focus is on understanding sentences with missing words. They will have a chance to give their views in exercise 7b.

Exercise 7a
- Focus students' attention on sentences a–e and point out that there is a symbol to show where a word is missing.

- Students work alone on the task.
- Encourage them to check their answers with a partner.
- Go through the answers together.
- The most natural answer for sentence b is *they're* because we are thinking about the tourists (but *they are* is grammatically possible).

ANSWERS
a I'm
b they're
c they
d I
e Have you

STUDY TIP As well as understanding where words are missing when you read in English, missing out unnecessary words is a useful skill to transfer to your own writing. Encourage students to review each piece of writing they do and check whether there are any unnecessary words which they could take out in order to avoid repetition. You could also use a specific symbol when marking so that they can see where they could have left out a word.

Exercise 7b
- Put students into pairs or small groups and ask them to think of any times when they have experienced pavement rage, or perhaps they have caused it. Encourage them to talk about when, where and why it happened.
- After a few minutes, interrupt their discussions to ask the second question *Can you think of a good solution?*
- Allow enough time for them to discuss possible ideas in their pairs or groups.
- Conduct a class discussion together and elicit solutions to the problem.

Exercise 8
- Tell students to read the rest of the article and answer questions 1–4.
- They work on this task individually.
- Put them into pairs to discuss and check their answers.
- Go through the answers together.

EXTENSION Focus the students' attention on the first line of the last paragraph. Ask them to find a place in this sentence where a word has been missed out. *What is the word?* (they) (*The city council have seen the plans for the fast lane and like the idea …*)

ANSWERS
1 tourists and slow pedestrians
2 people in the fast lane
3 people not following the rules
4 the city council

Exercise 9
- Put students into pairs.
- Ask them to discuss the idea of having pedestrian fast lanes in cities. Highlight that they need to think of two good points and two bad points.
- When they have thought of good and bad points in general, ask them to discuss in their pairs whether they would like a pedestrian fast lane in their own town or city. Encourage them to give reasons for their opinions.
- Elicit good and bad points from some students and conduct a class discussion on the topic.

2.4 Speaking and writing

Goals
- Ask for and give directions
- Write text messages

Lead-in
- Write on the board *Have you ever been lost?*
- Put students into pairs or small groups to talk about their experiences. Tell them to describe where, when, who they were with, what happened.
- Monitor their discussions and if any experiences are particularly interesting or well-described, invite students to tell the whole class.
- You could also elicit feelings for this situation – worried, stressed, scared, frightened.
- Elicit what you can do to help yourself when you get lost (look at a map, ask for directions, check on your smartphone maps app).

Listening & Speaking asking for and giving directions

Exercise 1

Background note: Bangkok is the capital of Thailand. Over 8 million people live in Bangkok and 14 million in the surrounding metropolitan area. It is a modern, commercial city but there are many ancient sites, popular with tourists. In Thai, the traditional name for Bangkok is listed as the longest place name in the Guinness Book of Records.

- Put students into pairs to discuss what they know about Bangkok. They can also look at the photograph of Bangkok and say what they can see.
- Conduct a class discussion. Ask if anyone has visited Bangkok. Find out who would like to go to Bangkok and why. Also elicit reasons for any strong 'no' answers.

Exercise 2 2.8

Audio summary: A conversation in Bangkok, Thailand, between a visitor who is asking directions and a local who is giving directions.

- Focus students' attention on the map of Bangkok.
- Check that they know they have to draw the route and identify which building is the Jim Thompson House. Check the meaning of the word *route* /ruːt/ if necessary and drill pronunciation.
- Play track 2.8.
- Go through the answers with the class. If possible, display the map on an interactive whiteboard and draw the route.
- You could give background information about the Jim Thompson House at this point if you wish.

ANSWER
The Jim Thompson House is building B.

Unit 2   57

AUDIOSCRIPT 2.8

T Excuse me, do you speak English?
L Er, yes.
T Sorry, please could you tell me how to get to the Jim Thompson House?
L Yeah, sure. Er … Let me see. You go straight along this road, you'll see the MBK shopping centre on the left. Go past that and keep going until you reach a crossroads. At the crossroads, turn left down Rama 1 Road, then, er, take the second right. Just go down that street and it's the building with flags outside on the left. There's a sign outside anyway.
T OK, so it's left at the crossroads? Is that right?
L Yes, that's right, then the second right.
T And it's the building on the left?
L Yeah.
T And, er, is it far?
L No, er, it takes about ten minutes, I should think.
T OK, thanks very much.

> **Background note:** The Jim Thompson house is a museum. It is named after an American architect who moved to Bangkok after the Second World War. He is famous for rebuilding the Thai silk industry. In 1967, Jim Thompson went on holiday to Malaysia with friends, went for a walk in the jungle and never returned.

Exercise 3a

- Ask students to read sentences 1–8 and complete them with one of the words or phrases from the box.
- Do the first sentence together as a demonstration if necessary.
- Students work on this task alone.
- Encourage them to check their answers with a partner.

Exercise 3b 2.8

- Ask students to listen to the track again to check their answers.
- Play track 2.8 again.
- Confirm any answers they may have missed.

WATCH OUT! The word *right* is used in the dialogue with two different meanings – the noun *right* is the direction, opposite of *left* and the adjective *right* is correct, opposite of *wrong*. This may sound strange to the students. The word is also used in exercise 4 – and at that point you could elicit which meaning it is: *Is this the right way to the library?* And *Yes, that's right*. (Both examples are adjectives, meaning correct.)

ANSWERS
1 how to get to
2 straight along
3 on the left
4 keep going until
5 turn left
6 second right
7 that right
8 takes

Exercise 4a

EXTRA ACTIVITY Ask *What is the difference between the two illustrations?* One is a map/street map and the other is a map of the inside of a building – a floor guide or floor plan. Students may not know the phrase *floor guide*, /flɔː(r) gaɪd/. Ensure they understand the meaning and drill the pronunciation.

- Check that students know what to do. Point out that the first line is given to them.

EXTRA SUPPORT To make sure weaker students understand the context, before they do the task, you could ask questions: *Where is the tourist now? Who is she talking to?*

- Students write numbers 1–5 next to a–e in the correct order. They can check their order with a partner before they listen.

ANSWERS
1 c 2 a 3 e 4 d 5 b

Exercise 4b 2.9

> **Audio summary:** A guide inside the Jim Thompson House museum gives directions to a female visitor.

- Tell students that you will play the track and they should listen and check their dialogue order is correct. Also ask them to decide which room on the floor plan is the library.
- Play track 2.9.
- Play it again if necessary.
- You could ask whether the students think the guide's directions were clear. Also *Why did the tourist repeat the instructions?* See information in Smart Communication box.

ANSWERS
The library is letter E.

AUDIOSCRIPT 2.9

T Excuse me, is this the right way to the library?
G Yes, well, you're on the terrace now, so you need to go through the drawing room and cross the garden. It's in the corner on the left by reception, you know, where you come in.
T So I need to go through the drawing room, cross the garden and it's next to reception?
G Yes, that's right. You can't miss it.
T Thank you.

SMART COMMUNICATION When someone is giving you directions, it is a good idea to repeat the main instructions back to the speaker for them to confirm. We often begin this checking phase with *so, … .*
When giving directions, it is useful to clearly indicate landmarks, i.e. places which everybody knows, are big and easy to see or are special for some reason (e.g. *the MBK shopping centre* in the first conversation). This is easier than only talking about the directions to move in.
Sometimes when you have asked for directions, you will be answered with another question *Do you know the MBK shopping centre?* – this is to check whether a particular landmark is a good reference point for you.

Pronunciation intonation in directions

Exercise 5a 2.10
- Tell students that the focus of this task is pronunciation. They especially need to listen for intonation, i.e. how the speaker's voice goes up and down.
- Ask them to read the instruction. Point out the arrows. You could also use hand gestures to indicate the intonation. This can really help visual and physical learners.
- Play track 2.10 several times so that the students can copy the intonation.
- You could ask students if their own language has varied intonation like this.

AUDIOSCRIPT 2.10
1 Excuse me, is this the right way to the library?
2 Keep going until you reach the crossroads.

Exercise 5b 2.11
- Tell students to read sentences 1–4 and try to imagine where the voice goes up and down.
- They should compare what they think by saying the sentences to each other.
- Tell them to listen to track 2.11 and repeat the sentences.
- It is a good idea if they can mark the intonation patterns with arrows as in exercise 5a.
- Play track 2.11 as many times as necessary for them to have good, natural intonation.

ANSWERS

AUDIOSCRIPT 2.11
1 Please could you tell me how to get to the Jim Thompson House?
2 You'll see the shopping centre on the left.
3 You can't miss it!
4 So it's left at the crossroads? Is that right?

Exercise 6
- Tell students to imagine that they are in the Jim Thompson House. They should look at the floor plan in exercise 4b.
- Put students into pairs, one Student A and one Student B.
- Tell Student As to turn to page 126 and Student Bs to look at page 130. Make sure they look at exercise 6.
- They read and follow the instructions, writing the names on their maps. Remind them NOT to let their partner see their map.
- Students practise asking for and giving directions.
- Tell them to start at reception each time and to take turns being the tourist and the guide.

FEEDBACK FOCUS Monitor their directions and focus on whether the guide gives clear directions and whether the tourist checks the directions well.
- Conduct a class discussion on how easy or difficult it was to ask and give directions.
- Give feedback on good use of the directions phrases and correct any mistakes.

EXTENSION If this task was not very successful, you could pair the students again so that they have different partners and give them a different starting point in the Jim Thompson House. Ask them to do the task again.

Exercise 7a
- Focus students' attention on the Language for speaking box. Ask them to try to use the phrases in their practice.
- Tell them to work in their pairs. Student As are to turn to page 126 and Student Bs are to look at page 130. Make sure they look at exercise 7a.
- Ask them to read the different options 1–3 and choose one.
- Student A tells Student B which option he has chosen. Together they practise asking for/giving directions.
- Then it is Student Bs' turn.
- Allow plenty of time for their speaking practice.
- Monitor and make a note of any particularly natural dialogues or good use of the phrases.
- Give a time limit to the end of the activity if necessary, to help all the students finish at the same time.
- Give feedback to those students who performed very well. If there is time, invite some pairs to act out their dialogues to the class.

Exercise 7b
- Ask them to choose a different option from 1–3 and change roles.
- Students practise again asking for and giving directions.

EXTRA CHALLENGE Tell students who think they remember the phrases to now focus on using natural intonation as they practised in exercise 5.
- Monitor the speaking practice and note any errors in pronunciation or grammatical accuracy.

EXTRA CHALLENGE Fast finishers could use the remaining option for further practice.
- Conduct class feedback and error correction.

EXTRA ACTIVITY For extra practice, you could tell them to ask for and give directions around their school or college, e.g. *from the classroom to the toilets, from the car park to the classroom* or *from the classroom to the coffee machine,* etc. Obviously this will be specific to your learning environment and depends on the students' knowledge of the building.

Writing text messages

Exercise 8
- Tell students that they are going to practise writing text messages or SMS (short message service) in English. Tell them that they are going to learn about *text speak* and elicit or teach the meaning of this phrase (= special, short forms of words used in text messages).
- Put students into small groups.
- Ask them to read questions 1–3 and ask and answer them together to find out about each other's texting habits.
- Conduct a class discussion.

Exercise 9
- Tell students that they are going to read some examples of texts in English.
- Ask them to read the three text messages and identify the sender for each one.
- Students work alone on this task.

Unit 2   59

- Go through the answers together.
- You could ask them if there is anything surprising or interesting about these text messages.

ANSWERS
1 a   2 c   3 b

Exercise 10
- Focus students' attention on the highlighted words and elicit that these are *abbreviations* (= short forms of words).
- Tell them to discuss with a partner what they think these abbreviations mean.
- They should cover the Language for writing box while they are guessing, so they can't see it.
- When they have discussed and guessed as much as they can, they may look at the Language for writing box and check their answers.
- Conduct a class discussion of these examples of text speak. Point out that often these abbreviations are based upon sound, e.g. *GR8 is useful because eight sounds like the end part of great*. Ask which other ones are based upon sound. (CU, U, RU)
- Other text speak abbreviations are just shortened words (pls, asap, sry). The text speak for *thanks* (thnx) is a combination of shortening and sound because 'x' sounds like 'ks'.
  WATCH OUT! We also use 'x' to represent a kiss on informal, friendly letters, greetings cards and emails to friends and family.

Exercise 11
- Tell students to work with their partner.
- Explain that they are going to have a written conversation now, as if they were sending texts to each other.
- Ask them to read the situation and decide which person is going to be A and which B.
- Remind them to work on one piece of paper, write clearly and quickly, then pass their 'text' to their partner who will reply.
- Set a time limit if necessary. Monitor and encourage them to use the abbreviations.
  EXTRA CHALLENGE For fast finishers, encourage them to continue the text conversation – say one of them has a problem and they have to change the arrangement.
- Conduct class feedback. Elicit some of the text exchanges.
  EXTENSION If you think it is appropriate, encourage students to exchange mobile phone numbers with one or two classmates and send at least one text in English to the other person/people before the next lesson. Make it clear that this is optional homework.

2.5 Video

London's changing skyline

VIDEOSCRIPT
Hi, I'm Toby. Today I'm visiting King's Cross, a new development in the centre of London. There are building sites like this all over the city.
Traditionally, most of London's buildings weren't very tall. For over 300 years, St Paul's Cathedral was the city's tallest building. In the sixties and seventies, some property developers built towers, but for most of the twentieth century, London's buildings weren't as tall as other major cities.
Over the last fifteen years this has changed. London is now one of the world's most important financial centres and its population is growing.
The city is expanding all the time. Its new businesses need new offices and its new residents need new houses. Suddenly there are skyscrapers everywhere!
When The Shard opened in the summer of 2012, it was the tallest building in Europe with 87 floors. It is over 300 metres high, has 306 flights of stairs and on the outside there are 11,000 glass panels!
Like many of London's skyscrapers, The Shard is a multi-purpose building. It is a home, a workspace and a tourist attraction. It has offices, apartments, several restaurants, a 5-star hotel, and at the top there's a 360 degree viewing platform.
This is another iconic London tower. Its official name is 30 St Mary Axe, but everybody calls it The Gherkin because of its unusual structure. It isn't the tallest building in the city, but it's an important part of London's architecture.
It has 41 floors and you can find some of London's biggest businesses here. It has become a symbol of the city.
Buildings like The Shard and The Gherkin have completely changed London's skyline. This famously low-rise city now has some of the most famous skyscrapers in the world. And building isn't stopping. Property developers are planning to build over 200 towers around the city.
But many Londoners disagree with these plans. They say the city can meet the demands of a growing population without towering skyscrapers.
This new development at King's Cross is a great example of this. The developers here are building 2,000 homes, 20 streets, ten public squares and 50 workspaces. Around 35,000 people will work here. But they aren't building any towers.
A major part of the development is Google's new headquarters. It will be larger than The Shard, but it will only have eleven floors. Instead, it will be 330 metres long and will sit on a two and a half acre site.
People are still arguing over London's development. The towering Shard and the lower but longer Google HQ show each side of this argument.
People will probably never completely agree on this, but it will be interesting to see how London's skyline changes in the future.

VIDEO ANSWERS
1 skyscraper, high-rise, low-rise, building site, financial centre, skyline, tourist attraction
3 a hasn't   b new   c more   d bigger   e disagree
4 a K   b G   c S   d K   e G   f S

Review
ANSWERS

Exercise 1a
1 have
2 'm sitting
3 'm reading
4 come
5 is wearing
6 have

Exercise 2a
1 who
2 which
3 where
4 who
5 that
6 where

Exercise 2b
1 souvenir seller
2 dull
3 flower stall
4 street cleaner
5 safe
6 rubbish bin

Exercise 3a
1 c 2 e 3 a 4 b 5 f 6 d

Exercise 3b
1 bedroom
2 kitchen
3 kitchen
4 sitting room
5 bathroom
6 kitchen/bathroom

Exercise 4a 2.12
1 He's going away because of his work.
2 I normally travel by metro or bus.
3 Please can you arrive punctually.
4 I'm coming right now.
5 They're having a vacation this week.
6 I bought it online, using my computer.

AUDIOSCRIPT 2.12
1 He's going away because of his work.
2 I normally travel by metro or bus.
3 Please can you arrive punctually.
4 I'm coming right now.
5 They're having a vacation this week.
6 I bought it online, using my computer.

Exercise 4b
1 He's going away on business.
2 I normally travel on public transport.
3 Please can you arrive on time.
4 I'm on the way.
5 They're on holiday this week.
6 I bought it on the internet.

Exercise 5a
1 me
2 turn
3 until
4 take
5 see
6 miss

Exercise 5c 2.13
ANSWERS/AUDIOSCRIPT 2.13
(Answers in square brackets)
A Excuse me, could you tell me how to get to the railway station?
B Sure. Go out of the coach station and turn right [left]. Keep going along Kingland Road until you reach the George Roundabout. You'll see the shopping centre [hospital] on the left, then turn left into Towngate Street.
A OK, so left at the George Roundabout.
B Yeah. Then take the first [second] right into Serpentine Road and right again into Station Road. You'll see the station straight ahead. You can't miss it.
A Great, thanks very much.

3 Going up, going down

Unit overview

Language input

Past simple (CB p27)
- *His journey started at 3.16 p.m.*
- *Did he have any problems during the jump?*

Past simple and past continuous (CB p28)
- *It was 11 p.m. and nobody was working.*
- *He began to get anxious.*
- *I was walking through a forest.*

Grammar reference (CB pp138–9)

Vocabulary development

Movement (CB p26)
- *towards, along, through …*
- *climb out of, jump backwards, fall over …*

Adjectives for describing feelings (CB p28)
- *guilty, embarrassed, anxious …*

Adverbs of manner (CB p30)
- *I smile politely.*
- *In my job I need to dress smartly.*

Skills development

Listening: Understanding -*t* and -*d* before a consonant (CB p31)

Speaking: Telling and responding to a story (CB p32)

Writing: Email (1): describing an event (CB p33)

Video

Documentary: The RRS *Discovery* (Coursebook DVD & CB p34)

Vox pops (Coursebook DVD & TG p260)

More materials

Workbook
- Language practice for vocabulary, grammar, pronunciation, speaking and writing

Photocopiable activities
- Grammar: A new hobby (TG p210 & TSRD)
- Vocabulary: Don't hide your feelings (TG p228 & TSRD)
- Communication: What a story! (TG p246 & TSRD)

Tests
- Unit 3 test (TSRD)
- Progress test: Units 1–3

Unit 3 wordlist (TSRD)

3.1 The man who fell to Earth

Goals
- Describe movement
- Talk about the past (1)

Lead-in
- With books closed, write the title of the lesson on the board *The man who fell to Earth* and ask the students to predict what they think the lesson is going to be about.
- Conduct a class discussion, eliciting ideas.

Vocabulary & Listening   movement

Exercise 1a

> **Background note:** Felix Baumgartner, born Salzburg, Austria in 1969. He started skydiving when he was 16 and was part of the Austrian military display team. As well as skydiving he is a BASE jumper and drives for Audi motorsport.

- Focus the students' attention on the photograph.
- Put students into pairs.
- Ask them to read the questions and discuss possible answers together.
- Conduct a class discussion. Some students may remember or know quite a lot of information about this event and the man involved.

Exercise 1b   3.1

> **Audio summary:** A radio programme about Felix Baumgartner's record-breaking jump from a balloon in space.

- Tell students they can check their answers to the questions in 1a by listening to a radio programme.
- Play track 3.1.
- You could elicit which questions in 1a they had answered correctly. Go through the answers together.

ANSWERS
1. In space.
2. Jumping out of a balloon 38 km above the Earth.
3. He was thinking: 'I want to get home alive.'
4. 14 October 2012
5. In the desert in New Mexico.

AUDIOSCRIPT 3.1
Hello and welcome to *Making History*, the programme where we look back at human achievements that have changed history. And it was on October the 14th 2012, that Felix Baumgartner, a pilot from Austria, made history when he became the first person to go faster than the speed of sound. Eight million people watched live on YouTube as Baumgartner made the amazing jump out of a balloon from a height of 38 kilometres above the Earth. Baumgartner's journey started at 3.16 p.m. when the large balloon slowly lifted him up into space. As he went up he tweeted from his phone. 'Live from space! World, you are beautiful!'

At 5.37 p.m. it was time to jump. He slowly moved his seat forward out of the capsule. He sat still and looked down for a few seconds. He didn't think about the beautiful view or breaking the speed record. He had only one thought: 'I want to get home alive.' Then he jumped. But immediately something went wrong. He fell too fast and he suddenly started to turn round and round. The rest of his skydiving team saw this on their computer screens and were worried he was in terrible danger. Luckily, he got into the correct diving position quickly, with head down and arms out behind him … like Superman.
When Baumgartner's parachute finally opened and he floated down towards the desert in New Mexico, everybody shouted and jumped up and down. They were so pleased he was safe. His mother cried with happiness. Baumgartner landed on his feet. He was so happy to be safe that he fell down on his knees.
A few days later, he told a TV reporter his next goal was 'to go faster than the speed of light'. It was a joke, of course.

Exercise 2   3.1
- Tell the students to read the sentences a–h.
- Put them into pairs to discuss/remember the order of the events and write 1–8 next to them.
- **EXTRA SUPPORT** You could find the first sentence together as a class to start them off.
- Ask students to listen again to check their order.
- Play track 3.1 again.
- It's a good idea to write the order on the board for clarity and to help visual learners.

ANSWERS
1 c   2 b   3 e   4 f   5 h   6 a   7 g   8 d

Exercise 3
- Students read the questions.
- Put them into small groups to discuss them or conduct a whole class discussion.
- **EXTENSION** You could ask them to brainstorm other extreme sports; diving, snowboarding, rock climbing, skateboarding, surfing, wind-surfing, etc. and discuss the questions with those in mind to maximize their speaking practice. If they have experience of extreme sports, they should be encouraged to talk about it.

Exercise 4
- Students read the instruction and work alone on the task.
- **DICTIONARY SKILLS** With a list of words like this (not presented in the context of a sentence), using a dictionary is a good idea. Encourage them to do this if they need to.
- Allow them to check their answers in pairs.
- Go through the answers as a class.
- Check that all the students are pronouncing *climb* /klaɪm/ accurately. Drill if necessary.

ANSWERS
Up: lift, rise, climb, take off, jump
Down: drop, land, dive, fall

Unit 3   63

Exercise 5

- Focus students' attention on the movement words 1–9 above the pictures.
- Tell them to find a picture which illustrates each word.
- Students work alone or in pairs on the task.
- Go through the answers together.
- Drill pronunciation of all the words, particularly 'through' /θruː/.

WATCH OUT! Although similar in spelling, make sure the students notice the difference in pronunciation and word stress between these words: *towards* /təˈwɔːdz/ and *backwards* /ˈbækwədz/ *forwards* /ˈfɔːwədz/.

ANSWERS
1 c 2 d 3 h 4 f 5 g 6 a 7 b 8 i 9 e

Exercise 6

- Ask the students to read the instruction carefully.
- Point out that they need to use vocabulary from both exercises 4 and 5 and that they may need to change the form of verbs they use.
- Students work alone to complete the sentences.
- Go through the answers together.

ANSWERS
1 drop, into
2 climb through
3 jump backwards
4 falling, towards
5 lift, out of

Grammar & Speaking past simple

Exercise 7

- Focus students' attention on the Grammar focus box.
- Ask them to read the rules carefully.
- Tell them to refer back to exercise 2 and find all the past simple forms.
- They should then add them to the table in the Grammar focus box.
- Allow enough time for students to work on this alone.
- Go through their answers together.
- Elicit the infinitive/base form of each of the verbs as you go through them.

ANSWERS
Regular: shouted, jumped, landed, parachuted
Irregular: took, came, got, made, fell, began

EXTRA CHALLENGE You could conduct brief discussion on the topic of irregular verbs. Possible questions: *Do you have irregular verbs in your language? How do you know if a verb in English is regular or irregular?* (Check on a list and learn them.)

- Refer students to *Grammar reference* on p138. There are three more exercises here students can do for homework.

Pronunciation regular past verbs

Exercise 8a 3.2

- Explain that the focus now is on how we pronounce past simple forms.
- Ask them to read the instruction. Then play track 3.2.
- Elicit the pronunciation of *lifted* /lɪftɪd/ and *landed* /lændɪd/ and check that they have understood that this extra syllable is because there's /t/ or /d/ before the *-ed* ending. Drill pronunciation.
- Drill pronunciation of the other past simple forms which don't have the extra syllable.

AUDIOSCRIPT 3.2
1 watch – watched
2 look – looked
3 lift – lifted
4 land – landed
5 dive – dived

Exercise 8b 3.3

- Put students into pairs so that they can say the words together and decide which ones have an extra syllable.
- Play track 3.3 so that they can check their answers.

ANSWERS
Extra syllable: started, decided, needed

AUDIOSCRIPT 3.3 & 3.4
1 start – started
2 work – worked
3 decide – decided
4 move – moved
5 need – needed

Exercise 8c 3.4

- Tell them to repeat the words on the track.
- Play track 3.4 as many times as necessary to ensure good pronunciation.

Exercise 9

- Ask the students to read the Fact file about Felix Baumgartner and use the verbs in the box to complete it.
- Remind them to change the verbs to the past simple form.
- Students work alone on the task.
- Go through the answers together.

ANSWERS
1 was   6 took
2 grew   7 didn't like, needed
3 began   8 didn't sleep
4 set   9 married
5 flew, wore

Exercise 10

- The focus in this exercise is on time expressions.
- Tell students to look at the time expressions in the *Saying when something happened* box.
- Point out the key words in bold in the box, so that they understand that each phrase on each line of the box includes that word, i.e. they need to add a word to the

first set which goes with *in*. You could do this one as an example together.
- Students work alone on this task.
- Encourage them to check their answers with a partner when they have finished.

EXTRA CHALLENGE Fast finishers could try to think of one more time expression to add to each set in the box. (Check these after you go through the answers.)

- Go through the answers together. Ensure the students understand all the time expressions. They may not know that *the other day* refers to a non-specific day in the recent past. You could also elicit that *the year before last* has the same meaning as *two years ago* and that *the day before yesterday* is *two days ago*.
- Elicit the pattern of how we use the prepositions *in* (with months, seasons, years) and *on* (with days, dates). Don't forget to check any extra time expressions that fast finishers have thought of.

WATCH OUT! Point out to students that *last night* is correct, but *last* + any other part of day (e.g. *last evening*) is incorrect. Elicit that for other parts of the day they need *yesterday*, e.g. *yesterday evening/morning/afternoon*.

ANSWERS
1 2014
2 New Year's Day
3 year before last
4 three months
5 week
6 she was 13

STUDY TIP Encourage students to record vocabulary in a systematic and easy to access way. One suggestion is to start different pages for commonly used expressions or patterns which they see in the language. In Lesson 2.3, prepositional phrases with *on*, they could start a page of Time expressions and include a table with *on*, *at* and *in*. Then during their studies they can add to these pages and build up their own reference tool. Other useful pages could be prepositional phrases with other prepositions or collocations with common verbs such as *get*, *make* and *do*.

Exercise 11

- This exercise is primarily speaking. Students work with a partner.
- Monitor their conversations carefully.

FEEDBACK FOCUS Focus on their use of the past simple forms and the time expressions. Note both good and incorrect sentences.

- When the first students finish, get all the students' attention and elicit interesting facts they have found out about each other.
- Do error correction and praise good use of the past simple and time expressions.

EXTENSION Ask the students to think of two other things similar to the ones in this exercise that they would like to ask their partner about, using a *When did you last … ?* question. Allow time for them to ask and answer the questions in pairs.

EXTRA ACTIVITY Each student writes the numbers 1–5 and chooses five of the time expressions from exercise 10 to write down. He/She passes the paper to his/her partner. His/Her partner then finishes the sentences so they are true for

him/her using the past simple form (e.g. *In March I went to a concert.*). The students then take turns to ask each other at least two questions about each sentence to find out more details.

Exercise 12

- Divide the class into two halves.
- One half of the class is 'A' and they should turn to page 127. The other 'B' half should turn to page 131.
- They each read their fact file.
- Student B asks Student A questions based on the prompts to find out about James Cameron.
- Then it is Student A's turn to ask Student B questions about Bertrand Piccard, using the prompts.
- Monitor all questions, making sure they are using the past simple of the auxiliary verb *do* (did).

EXTENSION You could put all Student As together and all Student Bs together to share the information they got or you could ask students individually to write full sentences answering the six questions they asked.

- Go through answers together if necessary.

ANSWERS
Student A
1 What did he do in 1999?
2 When did his trip begin?
3 Who did he go with?
4 Where did the balloon start from?
5 How long did the trip take?
6 Did anybody attempt this trip before him?

Student B
1 What is/was his job?
2 Where did he go?
3 Who did he go with?
4 How did he get to the bottom?
5 How long did it take?
6 Why did he do it?

GRAMMAR REFERENCE ANSWERS
Exercise 1
1 grew
2 copied
3 moved
4 cut
5 watched
6 wore
7 took
8 needed
9 wrote
10 played
11 did
12 chatted

Exercise 2
1 joined
2 applied
3 began
4 wanted
5 selected
6 was
7 learned
8 travelled
9 married
10 had

Unit 3   65

Exercise 3
1 Did Armstrong land on the moon in 1967?
2 Did she dive into the freezing pool?
3 The passengers weren't all from Russia.
4 We didn't get tired after running 5 km.
5 Did our children play in the tree house all afternoon?
6 I didn't have a bad experience on the journey.
7 Did Paula eat a delicious meal in the restaurant?
8 They didn't spend the afternoon watching tennis.

> **Background note:** There is a 1976 film with the title *The Man Who Fell to Earth*, directed by Nicolas Roeg and starring David Bowie. This film is about an alien who crash lands on Earth. Note: This is not the topic of the lesson but may come up in discussion.

3.2 Going up … One man's lift nightmare

Goals
- Talk about feelings
- Talk about the past (2)

Lead-in
- Ask students *What is the difference between 'an elevator' and 'a lift'?* The first is American English and the second is British English.
- Put students into pairs. Ask them to find out whether their partner prefers to use the stairs, a lift or an escalator to go up and down in a building and find out why. (Perhaps it depends what kind of building they are in or whether they are carrying anything.)
- Conduct a class discussion.

Vocabulary & Speaking adjectives for describing things

Exercise 1a
- Ask students to read the title of the lesson. Elicit whether they think it's going to be a positive or negative story. (*Nightmare* strongly suggests negative.)
- Ask them to focus on the photos and discuss with a partner which words from the box describe how the person is feeling in each photo.
  EXTRA CHALLENGE For stronger students, ask them to cover the vocabulary box and try to think of words to describe the feelings. Then they can check whether any of their words are in the box.
  EXTRA SUPPORT Encourage students to peer-teach the meanings of any unknown words in the box. Provide good dictionaries if possible. If you believe a lot of these words will be new to the students, you could go through them together before starting the task.
- Monitor their discussions. Encourage them to move on if they get stuck and go back to any difficult photos at the end.
  EXTRA CHALLENGE Ask fast finishers to think of possible reasons for the person's feelings in each photo.
- Conduct a class discussion and go through the answers.

POSSIBLE ANSWERS
1 anxious, lonely, disappointed, stressed
2 confused, nervous
3 anxious, nervous, stressed, scared, embarrassed
4 stressed, angry
5 embarrassed, guilty
6 in a good mood, pleased

Exercise 1b 3.5
- Draw two columns on the board, labelled *positive* and *negative*.
- Ask students to copy the columns into their books and then categorize the words in the box into positive feelings and negative feelings.
- Students work alone on this task. Encourage them to use dictionaries if they have them.
- Tell them to listen to track 3.5 to check their answers.

ANSWERS
a positive: in a good mood, pleased, calm, excited
b negative: guilty, scared, nervous, exhausted, embarrassed, disappointed, confused, lonely, angry, anxious, stressed

AUDIOSCRIPT 3.5 **&** 3.6
positive: in a good mood
pleased
calm
excited
negative: guilty
scared
nervous
exhausted
embarrassed
disappointed
confused
lonely
angry
anxious
stressed

Exercise 1c 3.6
- Ask students to listen and repeat the words for pronunciation practice.
- Play track 3.6. Pause where necessary. Play the track again if you need to.
- Drill any problem words more times to ensure good pronunciation. Highlight which parts they are getting wrong and model the correct version. It might help them to mark the word stress on words of two syllables or more.
  PRONUNCIATION It's important for students to say a word several times when trying to improve their pronunciation. To avoid this becoming boring, try to vary how you drill the students. You can split the class into two halves and drill one half, then the other. You can ask them to say the word in different ways; whisper, shout, slowly, quickly. You can allow them to take charge – you say a student's name and he/she says the word, then he/she says another student's name and that person says it and so on.

66

Exercise 2 3.7

> **Audio summary:** There are short extracts from eight different individual speakers in different situations. Each person displays a certain feeling.

- Tell students that they are going to hear short extracts of different people speaking. They should decide how each person is feeling and why they think this.
- Put students into pairs.
- Play track 3.7. Pause after each speaker so that the students can discuss in their pairs. Move on when they are ready.
- When they have listened to and discussed all eight speakers, play the recording again and elicit the answers from the class. Encourage them to give reasons for their suggestions. They should say where they think the speaker is and what's happening.

ANSWERS
1 anxious, stressed
2 scared
3 disappointed
4 lonely
5 embarrassed
6 in a good mood, pleased, excited
7 guilty
8 nervous

AUDIOSCRIPT 3.7
1 Come ON … Traffic lights … TURN GREEN … Come ON … I'm going to be so late for my meeting!!
2 David! Look! Those cows … They're … They're coming … They're coming towards us! Run!!
3 Oh no! I don't believe it! The restaurant's closed. Now where are we going to go?
4 Well, here I am … on my own in a foreign country. I miss my friends and family so much. I know I can skype them but it's not the same …
5 Good evening ladies and gentlemen and welcome to … oops … that's my phone … er, I'm so sorry …
6 Yes!! I'm on holiday. No more work for two whole weeks!!
7 Oh dear. It was Jake's birthday yesterday and I completely forgot! I didn't ring him or anything … Now I feel really bad!
8 I'm really sorry, but I can't speak now. I've a job interview in five minutes. Argh! Wish me good luck. I really need it!

Exercise 3
- Students read the instruction and work with a partner.
- Monitor their discussions and encourage students to ask for more information.
- Conduct class feedback. Ask some students to report on what their partners told them.

Grammar & Reading past simple and past continuous

Exercise 4

> **Text summary:** This is an online article about Nicholas White who was stuck in a lift for 41 hours. It describes what happened and his feelings. It is based on a true story which took place in New York in 2008.

- Ask students to cover the main part of the text and focus only on the introduction and photo(s).
- Tell them to read the introduction and then discuss questions 1 and 2 with a partner.
- When they have had time to do the task, elicit answers from one pair and encourage others to comment on the choice and order so that the class discusses this together.

ANSWERS
calm, anxious, lonely, scared, stressed, angry, exhausted

Exercise 5
- Tell them to read the whole article and check their answers to exercise 4.
- Allow plenty of time for the students to read and think about the feelings Nicholas White had.
- Discuss the feelings as a class.

Exercise 6
- Put students into pairs to discuss the questions.
- Monitor their discussions and give a time limit to the end of the activity when some are close to finishing.
- Conduct a class discussion.

EXTENSION You could ask extra questions: *Do you think it would be worse to be stuck in a lift alone or with other people? Why? Do you think Nicholas White takes lifts now?* (Apparently, he does. He told reporters: 'Living in Manhattan, I'd be seriously limiting my life if I didn't take elevators.')

Exercise 7
- Focus students' attention on the Grammar focus box.
- Tell them to refer to the text and look at the highlighted sentences.
- They should match each sentence to the uses 1–4.
- Students work alone on this task.
- Refer students to *Grammar reference* on p139. There are three more exercises here students can do for homework.

ANSWERS
1 It was 11 p.m. and nobody was working.
2 He calmly pushed the alarm button and waited for an answer.
3 He was working late at the office when he decided to go outside for a quick cigarette.
4 He rang it a few more times.

Exercise 8
- Point out that this is what happened next in the story of the man in the lift.
- Students work alone to complete the story with the correct form of the verb in brackets.
- Ask them to check with a partner when they have finished.
- Go through the answers together. You could ask them if they are surprised by anything in this final part of the story.

EXTRA ACTIVITY You could ask the students to write an email from Nicholas' female colleague to another worker at the company explaining what she did that evening and how she felt when she heard what had happened to Nicholas. This is an alternative way to get the students to summarize what they have read.

Unit 3 67

ANSWERS
1 was lying
2 wasn't wearing
3 jumped
4 asked
5 opened
6 did (he) do
7 was waiting
8 did (you) go
9 felt

Exercise 9a 3.8
- This is a dictation exercise.
- Tell students to write the questions they hear.
- Play track 3.8.
- Students write down the questions. Allow them to check what they have written with their partner.
- Play the track more than once if necessary, pausing between the sentences.
- If possible, display the answers on the board for the class to check.
- You could ask the students why the past continuous tense is used in each of the questions, referring back to the Grammar focus box if appropriate.

ANSWERS/AUDIOSCRIPT 3.8
1 Was it raining when you went out this morning?
2 What were the other students doing when you came to class today?
3 What was happening when you got home yesterday?
4 What were you doing this time last week?
5 Where were you working or studying five years ago?

Exercise 9b
- Put students into pairs so that they can ask and answer the questions.
- **FEEDBACK FOCUS** Monitor their discussions, paying particular attention to their use of tenses – in this exercise they should mainly be using the past continuous.
- Conduct class feedback. You could highlight good use of the past continuous by writing some of their sentences on the board.

Exercise 10a
- Check that students understand what to do. Elicit the meaning of *invented* (= not real) and *persuade* (= make somebody agree with or believe something).
- **EXTRA SUPPORT** This task is not difficult when students understand what they need to do. For students who need extra support, the clearest way to demonstrate what to do is to do it yourself. Write three sentences on the board, only two of which are true (you could use the suggested ideas). Ask the students to ask you questions so that they can work out or guess which is the invented idea.
- Ask students to read the suggested ideas and the example sentences.
- Allow them enough time to write their three sentences and monitor to check that they are correct.

ANSWERS
Students' own answers

Exercise 10b
- Tell students that now they are going to try to discover which of the three sentences is invented.
- Put the students into pairs and name them Student A and Student B.
- Elicit or explain that *convince* is similar in meaning to *persuade*.
- Tell them to read the example dialogue. You could choose a strong pair to demonstrate the activity at this point.
- Before all the Student As begin, highlight that they should use the past simple and past continuous forms.
- Monitor to ensure that they are successfully following the instructions.
- Note any problems with using the past forms.
- Give a time limit to the end of the first student's turn.

Exercise 10c
- Get students' attention and instruct them to change roles so now student Bs read out their three sentences and respond to their partner's questions.
- When some students have almost finished, give a time limit to the end.
- Get all the students' attention and conduct class feedback.
- Give feedback on the use of the past tenses. Do any necessary error correction.

GRAMMAR REFERENCE ANSWERS
Exercise 1
1 noticed
2 was
3 was helping
4 told
5 ran
6 lived
7 were standing
8 was
9 was getting
10 got
11 was holding
12 went
13 broke
14 helped
15 did
16 said

Exercise 2
1 were sending
2 was crying
3 were putting
4 was taking
5 were planning
6 was lying
7 were feeling

Exercise 3
1 We were driving when the sun rose.
2 Was the balloon landing when the accident happened?
3 I didn't put my hand up while the teacher was talking.
4 Was Dad walking down the stairs when he fell?
5 While you were climbing the Eiffel Tower, did you feel ill?
6 Paul dropped his ticket as he got off the train.
7 We weren't wearing jackets when the rain started.

3.3 Vocabulary and skills development

Goals
- Understand and use adverbs of manner
- Understand –t and –d before a consonant

Vocabulary & Speaking adverbs of manner

Lead-in
- Write the words *stranger* and *foreigner* on the board.
- Elicit the meanings and the difference between these commonly confused words (= stranger: a person that you do not know; foreigner: a person who comes from a different country).
- Students will need to know *stranger* for the first exercise.

Exercise 1a
- Tell students to read the instruction and the sentences below before they start.
- Check they all understand the meaning of *it doesn't bother me* (= it isn't a problem for me/it doesn't annoy or upset me).
- Students work on this task alone.

Exercise 1b
- Ask students to compare their answers and discuss their reasons.
- Put them into pairs.
- **EXTRA CHALLENGE** Fast finishers can also try to explain why they DON'T do the other things.
- Monitor and make a note of any adverbs of manner they use in their discussions.
- When they have finished talking, conduct a class discussion on the topic. You could find out whether everyone behaves in a similar way and the reasons for their behaviour.
- **CRITICAL THINKING** If you want students to reflect further on the discussion, you could ask them to apply their own experience to the topic: *From your experience, do you think people behave the same on public transport in different countries?* You could elicit which countries the different class members come from or have visited. Encourage them to think of concrete reasons to support their answers to the first question: *Do you have any examples of behaviour from your own experience which surprised you?* Make a note of any adverbs the students use.

Exercise 2
- Explain they are going to learn about adverbs in this part of the lesson. Point out the adverbs in bold in exercise 1a and give examples of any adverbs they used in exercise 1b.
- Tell them to read the Vocabulary focus box about adverbs.
- Ask checking questions if necessary: *Do adverbs describe nouns or verbs?* (verbs) *To make an adverb do we add -ly to a noun or an adjective?* (adjective) *When we make an adverb from an adjective ending in –y, what happens to the spelling?* (–y changes to –i, so it's –ily at the end) *Do all adverbs end in –ly?* (no, there are irregulars).

Exercise 3a
- Check students understand that there are two steps in the exercise (make the adverb, put it into the sentence).
- If necessary, do the first one together to demonstrate.
- Students work on this task alone. Encourage them to check with a partner when they have finished.
- Go through the answers together. Refer students back to the Vocabulary focus box when necessary.
- **WATCH OUT!** Highlight answers 1 and 5 where a common mistake is to separate the verb from its object, i.e. make quickly decisions or speak fluently two languages. Make sure they are aware of this and that they need to be careful not to just automatically put the adverb after the main verb.

ANSWERS
1 quickly: I can make decisions **quickly.**
2 easily: I can start a conversation with a stranger **easily**.
3 smartly: In my job I need to dress **smartly**.
4 fast: I get nervous when people drive **fast.**
5 fluently: I would like to speak two languages **fluently**.
6 loudly: I hate it when people speak **loudly** on their mobile phones.

Exercise 3b
- Tell students to think about the sentences for a moment and decide whether any of them are true for them.
- Put them into pairs to discuss.
- **EXTRA CHALLENGE** Fast finishers can go back to the sentences that are not true for them and explain why or try to change them to make them true.
- **EXTENSION** You could get all the students' attention and ask questions to the class: *Do you do the things in sentences 5 and 6? Do you know anybody who does? How about number 4? Do you drive fast? Do you know anybody who does?* This will give students another opportunity to use the adverbs.

Exercise 4a
- This is further practice but in question form.
- Tell students to read the instruction and look at the example.
- If necessary, check everyone knows the word *typist* in the box. (You could elicit the verb *to type*)
- Students work on this task alone.
- Go through the answers together.

ANSWERS
Are you a good cook? Do you cook well?
Are you a careful driver? Do you drive carefully?
Are you a quick typist? Do you type quickly?
Are you a slow eater/walker? Do you eat/walk slowly?
Are you a regular traveller? Do you travel regularly?
Are you a fast runner? Do you run fast?

Exercise 4b
- Ask students to ask and answer the questions. You could ask two students to read the example dialogue aloud.
- Put students into pairs.
- Monitor their discussions and note any adverbs they use which have not come up so far in the lesson. Also note any errors in word order when using adverbs.
- Conduct class feedback and do any necessary error correction.

Unit 3 69

EXTRA ACTIVITY With a strong group, you could ask them to think of more verbs for common everyday actions and write them in a list. They then swap lists with a partner and think of more questions using verbs from the list with adverbs of manner. Examples: *Do you sleep well? Do you wait patiently for buses or trains? Do you do your homework quickly?*

Listening and Speaking understanding *-t* and *-d* before a consonant

Exercise 5
- Tell students to read the list of places.
- Elicit ideas from the class or put the students into small groups to discuss.
- Ask them to explain why/why not for each different place. You could also ask what kind of greeting they use and why (e.g. *smile, nod, say something*).

Exercise 6a 3.9
- Tell them that the focus now is on listening and understanding natural pronunciation.
- Ask them to read the Unlock the code box.
- When they have read it, tell them that you're going to play the track so they can hear what happens.
- Play track 3.9.
- You could ask students if they had noticed this before.

AUDIOSCRIPT 3.9
When a word ends in *-t* or *-d* and the next word begins with a consonant, we don't say the *-t* or *-d*.

lift going up	sounds like	lif going up
second floor	sounds like	secon floor
it isn't coming	sounds like	it isn coming

Sometimes this happens with *-t* or *-d* inside a single word.

politely	sounds like	poli-ly
friends	sounds like	friens

Exercise 6b 3.10
- Point out that they should write the missing word with its complete spelling (including *t* or *d* at the end).
- Go through the answers together, writing them on the board.

ANSWERS/AUDIOSCRIPT 3.10
1 <u>behind</u> me
2 <u>first</u> floor
3 <u>next</u> stop
4 <u>don't</u> look
5 <u>fastest</u> lift
6 <u>old</u> people
7 <u>second</u> time
8 <u>stand</u> back
9 <u>cold</u> morning
10 <u>World</u> Cup
11 I <u>found</u> this
12 <u>lift</u> going up

Exercise 6c 3.11
- Tell students that they are going to listen and write like they did in exercise 6b but this time they may need to write down more than one word.
- Play track 3.11. You may need to play it more than once so that they can hear all the words and phrases. Pause where necessary.
- Go through the answers together, again writing them on the board.

ANSWERS/AUDIOSCRIPT 3.11
1 opposite corner
2 act normally
3 third person
4 next time
5 look at the floor
6 immediately
7 quietly
8 make contact with

Exercise 7 3.12

> **Audio summary:** A radio programme where a psychologist talks about how people behave in lifts; specifically where they stand. (A presenter introduces the topic and speaker.)

- Tell students that they are going to listen to the first part of a radio programme about *lift etiquette*. Elicit that this means how people behave in lifts.
- Give them time to read the instruction and look at the diagrams.
- You could physically show them what to do on the board, e.g. *So if you hear that a person stands in the corner, you put an 'x' here.*
- Play track 3.12.
- Go through the answers together.

ANSWERS

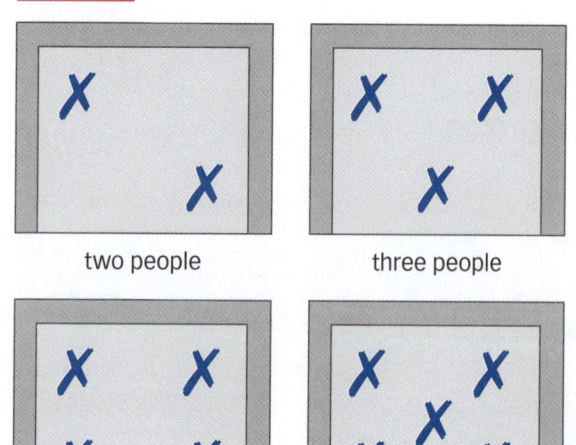

two people

three people

four people

five people

AUDIOSCRIPT 3.12
P Many of us use lifts several times a day without really thinking about it. But if you watch what people do in lifts, you'll see some very interesting behaviour. Here to tell us more is psychologist, Dr Len Mills.
LM Yes that's right. Lifts are very interesting social spaces. When we're alone in a lift. we act normally. But when another person comes in, suddenly we behave strangely. Next time you're in a lift, watch where people stand. If there are two people, you stand in opposite corners. If a third person enters, you change position quickly and make a triangle. Four people and you make a square, with one person in each corner. A fifth person will probably stand in the middle.

Exercise 8   3.13

> **Audio summary:** This is the continuation of the radio programme about how people behave in lifts. This part is about where people look and what they do.

- Tell students you are going to play the next part of the radio programme. Explain that they have to write down three things people do in lifts.
- Explain that more than three things are mentioned, but they only need to write down three of them.
- Play track 3.13.
- Students write down three (or more) things.
- Encourage them to check their answers with a partner.
- Play the track again so that they can listen for any things their partner heard or just try to hear some more.
- Go through the answers together. You could ask volunteers to act out the behaviour to demonstrate that they understand.

ANSWERS
Any three of the following:
Say hello politely or smile.
Turn around as soon as they enter the lift.
Look at the door, the floor or at the lift buttons.
Look at the floor, their phones, their hands or their ring.
Stop their conversation or start speaking quietly.

AUDIOSCRIPT 3.13
LM Now watch what people do. Some people say hello politely or smile. Others don't. But everybody turns around as soon as they enter the lift. Some people look at the door, the floor or at the lift buttons. Others look at their phones, their hands or their ring. But they never make eye contact with the other people. When two people come in at the same time, they stop their conversation or start speaking quietly.
The reason why we do this is that when we are in small spaces, we feel anxious and we act in a way that stops other people feeling nervous. That's why we don't stand near people, look at or speak to each other.

Exercise 9   3.13

- Tell students to read the instruction.
- Play track 3.13 again. You may need to do this more than once.
- Go through the answers together.

ANSWERS
1 turns around
2 lift, look, hands
3 speaking quietly
4 stand

Exercise 10

- Conduct a class discussion of these questions. Alternatively, the students could discuss in small groups.

Exercise 11a

- Check they all know the meaning and pronunciation of *queue* /kjuː/.
- Remind them to use adverbs of manner if possible as this is the focus of the lesson.
- Put them into pairs to think what the rules of behaviour are for the different places.
- Monitor to check whether they are using adverbs of manner and that their word order is good.
- Give a time limit to the end of the discussions to ensure they all finish at the same time.

Exercise 11b

- Put two pairs together to compare their rules. They should find which ones are similar and which are different.
- Encourage them to discuss the reasons for their rules, particularly if they are different.
- Monitor these discussions, again with a focus on adverbs of manner and word order.
- Conduct a class discussion and any necessary error correction from exercises 11a and 11b.

3.4 Speaking and writing

Goals
- Tell and respond to a story
- Write an informal email describing an event

Lead-in
- Write the word *story* on the board. Ask students whether they think this means something true or invented. If necessary, explain that it can be either – novels and fairytales are invented stories but news stories or stories about things that happened in our lives are based on fact.
- You could ask *Why do people tell stories?* (to entertain, to share information, to give examples or advice, as a way of explaining something, e.g. *…so that's why I never go by train*, etc.).
- Students sometimes confuse *story* and *history*. If necessary, elicit the difference in meaning (= history is always supposed to be factual and it is about the past events concerned with the development of a particular place, subject, etc., e.g. *The history of the European Union*).

Listening & Speaking telling and responding to a story

Exercise 1a

> **Audio summary:** Two speakers Ryu (from Korea) and Marta (from Mexico) tell stories of recent events. Ryu tells an embarrassing story about when he accidentally squirted blackcurrant juice on a fellow passenger on a train. Marta tells a story about when the plane she was on failed to land at the first attempt and she was scared.

- Focus students' attention on the two photos.
- Put students into pairs to predict what they think each story will be about. Tell them to help each other understand any new words in the boxes.
- Elicit some ideas from the class but don't confirm any of them yet.

Exercise 1b   3.14

- Tell students that they're going to listen to the stories so they can check whether their predictions were correct.

Unit 3 71

- Play track 3.14.
- Ask students how close their predictions were. You could put them back into their pairs to discuss what was the same and different from their discussions.

AUDIOSCRIPT 3.14
Story 1
A funny thing happened this morning. I was on the train on my way to work and there was this young woman sitting on the seat opposite me. She was dressed quite smartly, she was obviously travelling to work too. It was quite a hot day so she wasn't wearing a jacket – she was just wearing a white blouse and a skirt. So, anyway, I was feeling a bit thirsty so I got some juice out of my bag. It was one of those little cartons of juice that comes with a little straw. I was drinking it – and it was a blackcurrant fruit juice, a kind of dark purple colour. Anyway, I don't know how this happened, but suddenly the straw just jumped out of my mouth and a little stream of purple juice flew up in the air and landed on the woman's white shirt!! [Oh no!] I said, 'Oh I'm so sorry!' She didn't say anything, she just looked at me angrily. [Really!] Everybody was looking at us. I was so embarrassed!!

Story 2
I had a bad experience last year when I was flying back home to Mexico City from Hong Kong. We were just going to land. We were flying over the city. It was a beautiful clear morning. The sun was shining and I was looking out my window and enjoying the view. So, anyway, we were just beginning to land – the wheels were just touching the ground, when suddenly the plane took off again over the sea. [You're joking!] Yes. I was really scared, to be honest. [So then what happened?] Well, it flew over the sea for a minute or two. We didn't know what was happening and then the pilot made an announcement. A plane was stuck in the middle of the runway and he needed to avoid it. [Oh, right.] So, it was all OK in the end.

Exercise 2 3.14
- Ask students to read the questions about the two stories before you play the track again.
- Play track 3.14.
- Students write the answers.
- Allow them time to check their answers in pairs and then go through them together.

ANSWERS
1 A white blouse and a skirt.
2 The straw jumped out of his mouth and a stream of purple juice landed on the woman's blouse.
3 She didn't say anything.
4 It was clear and sunny.
5 It took off again.
6 Another plane was stuck in the middle of the runway.

Exercise 3a 3.15
- Focus students' attention on the words in the box. Go through any unknown vocabulary.
- Students work alone to complete the sentences.
- When they have finished, play track 3.15.
- Make sure they have completed the sentences correctly.
- It would be good to check the meaning and function of some of these phrases: Possible questions to ask: *What does 'funny' mean in sentence 1?* (could mean *amusing* but may also mean *strange*) *Why does the speaker use 'anyway?'* (to return to the main story) *Which words are used to emphasize feelings?* (so and really) *When you say 'Oh no!' what feeling are you expressing?* (surprise, shock, that you can understand how they're feeling) *When you say 'You're joking!' what feeling are you expressing?* (surprise, that you can't believe what they're saying).

WATCH OUT! Point out that we often use the phrase *in the end* to talk about the outcome of a series of events in a story (often a series of negative events). It would be incorrect to use *at the end* here.

- Point out that these phrases are highlighted in the Language for speaking box below.

ANSWERS
1 happened
2 anyway
3 no
4 embarrassed
5 experience
6 joking
7 really
8 what
9 in the end

AUDIOSCRIPT 3.15 & 3.16
1 A funny thing happened this morning.
2 So, anyway, I was feeling a bit thirsty …
3 Oh no!
4 I was so embarrassed!
5 I had a bad experience last year, when I was …
6 You're joking!
7 I was really scared!
8 So then what happened?
9 So it was all OK in the end.

SMART COMMUNICATION Being able to respond in the right way and with the right level of feeling is important when someone is telling you about something that happened to them. This is natural in your first language but students need to learn appropriate phrases in English which they can recall quickly when they need them. Practising the kind of phrases in this lesson will help. You could also encourage them to think about phrases they commonly use in their own language and how these might be translated into English.

Exercise 3b 3.16
- Ask students to repeat the sentences after the recording so that they pronounce them naturally.
- Play track 3.16, pausing wherever necessary. You may need to play it more than once.

PRONUNCIATION If the intonation seems flat in sentences such as *Oh no!*, *I was so scared* and *You're joking!*, encourage the students to 1) exaggerate the feeling expressed and 2) slow them down. It's really important in these phrases to sound as if you mean it, which we tend to convey by changing our tone of voice and lengthening the keywords. If the intonation is flat, a phrase like this can sometimes be taken as sarcasm.

Exercise 4a
- This is primarily a speaking task, though students have planning time.

- Ask students to read the instruction carefully. Point out the bullet-pointed questions which are there to help them plan their story.
- Students work alone writing notes and planning.
- Monitor this stage and help any students who seem to be struggling.

EXTRA SUPPORT For less confident students, one thing they could do is practise saying their story to themselves, just mouthing the words or whispering. If you think they would feel embarrassed, ensure all students turn their chairs to face the classroom walls so that they don't focus on each other while they do it.

Exercise 4b

- Tell students that they are going to tell their stories now.
- Focus their attention on the Language for speaking box and tell them to try to use some of the phrases in their stories and also, importantly, to respond to their classmates' stories.
- Put them in groups to tell their stories.
- Monitor and note examples of where students use the phrases correctly and effectively plus any errors in use or pronunciation. Try to notice students who use them with good natural intonation, which conveys feeling well.
- Keep an eye on the time and give a time limit to the end of the activity if necessary.
- Praise students who were responsive to their partner's story.

EXTRA CHALLENGE Fast finishers should ask each other more questions about the stories to check they have fully understood, get further information and find out about how the speaker was feeling at particular moments in the story.

Exercise 4c

- Tell students that they need to choose the most interesting story from their group to be told to the rest of the class.
- As a whole class, elicit the best stories from each group. Encourage the class to respond to the stories as they hear them.

EXTRA CHALLENGE Instead of a whole class story-telling session, you could remix the groups and tell them that they should tell their new group the story they chose as the most interesting one – as if it were their own story.

- Give feedback to the class together and conduct any error correction you feel necessary.

EXTRA ACTIVITY If students are able to take video clips on their smart phones, check whether they are happy to film and be filmed. If so, you could ask them to record the members of their group telling their stories. Then they can play the clips back and analyse how well the listeners responded to the stories, e.g. *Did they use suitable phrases? Did their pronunciation show an appropriate level of feeling?*

Reading & Writing   email (1): describing an event

Exercise 5

> **Text summary:** An informal email between friends describing a snowboarding accident.

- Tell students to read the email from Juliana to her friend Petra. They should find the answers to the two questions.
- Remind them that they are reading for specific information and may not need to read it all or in detail. You could make this a race or set a time limit.
- Elicit the answer. Find out how much of the email they had to read to get the information (only the first paragraph). You could point out that we often do this – give the basic information first, followed by more detail or order of events.
- Encourage them to read the email again more slowly to find out more information about the accident.
- Ask more questions to check their understanding if you wish: *How did the accident happen?* (She crashed into a tree when she was avoiding a little boy.) *What was the problem with phoning for help?* (The signal was really bad.) *How did Juliana get help?* (She snowboarded down to a café.) *Did Juliana take Martina to hospital?* (No, a rescue team did.) *Is Martina back at college now?* (No, she has to take a month off.)

ANSWERS
She went on holiday to go snowboarding.
Her friend had an accident and broke her leg.

Exercise 6

- Focus students' attention on the Language for writing box about time sequencers and ask them to read it.
- Tell them to find which sequencers are in the email. You could go through these with them, eliciting the function of each sequencer by referring to the box.

ANSWERS
suddenly, when, then, at first … but after, after a few minutes, in the end, a short time later

Exercise 7

- Students work alone to choose the correct sequencer.
- Go through the answers together.

ANSWERS
1 when
2 Then
3 in the end
4 later
5 At first, after

Exercise 8

- Tell students that they need to write an email about a recent event that went wrong. Explain that the story does not have to be true.
- Ask them to choose one of the situations.
- Highlight the tenses and vocabulary that they need to remember to use.
- Set a time limit if necessary or just monitor and give a time limit to the end of the activity when you see most have nearly finished.

Ideas for feedback on the emails:

- You could ask students to swap emails. They should read their partner's email and then act out making a telephone call to that person to react to what they have written.
- Students could swap their email with a partner and concentrate on the four writing criteria; past simple, past

Unit 3 73

continuous, linkers and adverbs of manner. They should underline all examples of these things and check that they are correctly used.
- The teacher may need to collect these emails in order to mark them and give feedback.

ANSWERS
Students' own answers

EXTENSION You could ask students to leave the emails they have written on their desks and walk around the classroom reading all the emails by other students. Tell them to write a response or question for at least five of the emails they read, adding their name to each response/question they write. When they return to their seats they should read what others have written, get up and find those people and answer any questions orally.

3.5 Video

The RRS *Discovery*

VIDEOSCRIPT

Hello and welcome to Dundee. It's a small city on the east coast of Scotland, where the River Tay meets the North Sea.

The city has a long history of building boats, and the city's most famous ship is the RRS *Discovery*.

In 1900, the British government wanted a boat that could explore the undiscovered continent of Antarctica.

They built a boat with sails and steam engines that was so strong it could sail through large blocks of ice.

On the 6th August 1901, *Discovery* left the UK.

After a five month journey via Cape Town and Lyttelton Harbour in New Zealand, the ship arrived on the coast of Antarctica on the 8th January 1902.

Some of Britain's most adventurous explorers, Captain Robert Falcon Scott and the Third Officer Ernest Shackleton, were on board.

There were scientists too, who wanted to learn more about the area's plants and animals.

When they arrived, this group of scientists, sailors and explorers made a camp.

They built a large hut, where they lived and worked.

It was all going well, but while they were working the Antarctic ice froze around *Discovery*.

The ship didn't break, but the crew couldn't leave. They needed to wait for the ice to melt. While they were waiting, Scott and Shackleton left camp and tried to walk to the South Pole.

They walked through storms and blizzards, but unfortunately they didn't reach the Pole.

But they survived and when they returned to camp, two ships –*Morning* and *Terra Nova* – were there to help them.

After two years in freezing conditions, the *Discovery* crew sailed home.

On the 10th September 1904, the ship arrived back in London.

The crew quietly returned home. But soon, the story of the expedition became famous and Captain Scott became a national hero.

Both Scott and Shackleton later returned to Antarctica.

On one of Shackleton's expeditions his ship – *Endurance* – sank.

He and a small group spent five days in a lifeboat. Finally, they reached South Georgia, where they contacted the navy to send help.

And one of the boats that came to the rescue? The RRS *Discovery*.

Discovery became a symbol of British heroism. For years it was a popular tourist attraction in London. But in 1986, *Discovery* returned home to Dundee where it is part of the city's history and culture.

VIDEO ANSWERS

Exercise 1
1 *Titanic* 2 *Santa Maria* 3 *Black Pearl* 4 *Yamato*
5 *Vostok 1*

Exercise 3
1 Antarctica
2 August 1901
3 they made a camp
4 they could not leave
5 2 years
6 continued to sail

Exercise 4a
Students' own answers

Review
ANSWERS

Exercise 1b
1 were working
2 fell
3 were losing
4 received
5 had
6 dropped
7 lifted
8 didn't move
9 arrived
10 were waiting
11 made

Exercise 2a
1 jump; dive
2 climb
3 lifted
4 rise

Exercise 3a
Possible answers:
1 nervous, anxious, stressed
2 angry
3 exhausted
4 embarrassed
5 pleased, in a good mood, excited

Exercise 4 3.17
1 They are shouting angrily.
2 The person is playing the piano badly.
3 The door is opening slowly.
4 The person is eating noisily.
5 The person is laughing loudly.
6 The car stopped suddenly.

Exercise 5a 3.18
1 experience 2 when 3 carefully 4 anyway 5 later
6 joking 7 so 8 then 9 no

AUDIOSCRIPT 3.18
A I had a bad experience the other day. I was having lunch with a friend in a café when a man came over and asked for directions to the station. He put a map down on the table and my friend showed him where to go. I noticed that the man wasn't listening carefully to my friend. He was looking nervously at the table.
B Really? That's strange!
A So, anyway, a few minutes later, I wanted to make a phone call, but I couldn't find my phone.
B You're joking! Don't tell me … the phone was on the table and the man lifted it up with the map?
A Exactly! I was so angry!
B So then what happened?
A I called the police. But it was too late.
B Oh no! That's terrible!

Unit 3 75

4 Changes and challenges

Unit overview

Language input

Verbs with -ing and to (CB p37)	• *He likes playing the piano.* • *She hopes to be a politician.*
Going to and present continuous for the future (CB p38)	• *I'm meeting a friend for lunch at one o'clock.* • *I'm going to change a few things.*
Grammar reference (CB pp140–1)	

Vocabulary development

Life stages and events (CB p36)	• *teenager, in your twenties, middle-aged, …* • *Pass your exams* • *Leave home*
Internet activities (CB p38)	• *blog and tweet, download films, chat online …*
Get (CB p41)	• *When did you get your first job?* • *The days are getting warmer.*

Skills development

Listening: Understanding connected speech (1) (CB p40)	
Speaking: Inviting and making arrangements (CB p42)	
Writing: Email (2): making arrangements (CB p43)	

Video

Documentary: Esplorio (Coursebook DVD & CB p44)	
Vox pops (Coursebook DVD & TG p260)	

More materials

Workbook	• Language practice for vocabulary, grammar, pronunciation, speaking and writing • Listening for pleasure • Review: Units 3 & 4
Photocopiable activities	• Grammar: Let's get together (TG p211 & TSRD) • Vocabulary: A full life (TG p229 & TSRD) • Communication: Where, when, what? (TG p247 & TSRD)
Tests	• Unit 4 test (TSRD)
Unit 4 wordlist (TSRD)	

4.1 Changing directions

Goals
- Talk about life stages and events
- Use verbs with *-ing* or *to*

Lead-in
- Put students into pairs or small groups.
- Write *important life events* on the board.
- Elicit the meaning of *important* and give an example of a life event, e.g. *getting married*.
- Ask students to brainstorm other life events like this in pairs. Put their ideas on the board. You could make a list or mind-map.
- Point out that one of the lesson's goals is to talk about life stages and events so the list may be useful later on.

Vocabulary & Reading life stages & events

Exercise 1a
- Ask students to read the words in the box and put them in order of age. They should start with the youngest.
- Students work alone on this task.
- When they are ready, tell them to check their answers in pairs.
- Go through the correct order together.
- You can elicit age ranges to check they understand the different phrases including *twenties* (early = 21–23, mid = 24–26, late = 27–29). Also check that they understand another way to say *about thirty-five* is *in your mid-thirties*.

ANSWERS
child /tʃaɪld/
teenager /ˈtiːneɪdʒə/
in your early twenties /ɪn jər ˈɜːli twentiːz/
in your mid-twenties /ɪn jə ˈmɪd twentiːz/
in your late twenties /ɪn jə ˈleɪt twentiːz/
about thirty-five /əˈbaʊt θɜːti ˈfaɪv/
middle-aged /mɪdl ˈeɪdʒd/
in your sixties /ɪn jə ˈsɪkstiːz/
elderly /ˈeldəli/

PRONUNCIATION Ask students to mark the stressed syllable on the words and phrases and then check together. Point out that most of the stress in the phrases with *twenties* falls on the word *twenties* /jə ˈtwentiːz/. Similarly, the main stress in *middle-aged* /mɪdl ˈeɪdʒd/ falls on the second part of the word.

EXTRA CHALLENGE Ask *What is the difference between 'elderly' and 'old'?* Explain the word *elderly* is more polite than *old*, e.g. *My aunt is an elderly woman.* is more polite than *My aunt is an old woman.*

Exercise 1b
- Tell students that they are going to describe people in their family using the words in exercise 1a.
- Put them into pairs to talk about as many people in their family as possible.

EXTRA SUPPORT For less confident students, ask them to think of five people in their family who they can describe

with one of these words or phrases. Give them two minutes thinking time.
- Monitor the discussions.

WATCH OUT! Make sure students remember to change the pronoun *your* to *his* or *her* for each person they describe.

EXTRA CHALLENGE Ask fast finishers to continue the task but think of friends and colleagues they can describe.

- Conduct a class discussion. You could ask questions, e.g. *Do you know a lot of people in their sixties? Did you describe any children? At what age do you stop being a child? What age do you think is 'elderly'?*

Exercise 2a
- Tell students to look at the list of life events.
- Go through any unknown vocabulary. You could ask *What is the difference between 'job' and 'career'?* (career = when somebody has a series of jobs in a particular area of work which they do for a period of years)
- Ask them to tick which life events they have experienced.

Exercise 2b
- Students read the instruction and the example.
- Highlight the need to say what you did, when and why. You could elicit these three points from the example: *What did she do? When did she do it? Why did she do it?*

FEEDBACK FOCUS Monitor what the students say, paying particular attention to their use of the past tenses, which they studied in Unit 3. Note any problems with past tense irregular verbs and any errors in choosing between past simple and past continuous.

- Ask a few students to report anything particularly interesting about their partner.
- Conduct error correction of past tense mistakes. Write problem sentences on the board and encourage all the students to find mistakes and correct them together.

Exercise 3
- Demonstrate the activity to the class by asking *Which is the best age to get married?* and managing the discussion of this question. Encourage students to try to explain why they have chosen a particular age.
- Ask them *Is it ever too late to get married?* and elicit some answers and reasons.
- Students read the instruction. Then put them into small groups for a discussion. Set a time limit.
- Monitor the discussions and encourage students to give reasons and examples where possible.
- Conduct a class discussion. Ask them which things they believe you can be too old to do and why.

EXTENSION You could ask students to think of one thing from the list that they think they did particularly early or late in life. Alternatively they could think of a person they know who experienced one of the life events earlier or later than usual. Ask them to take turns to tell each other in their pairs.

Exercise 4

Text summary This is a biographical text of João Carlos Martins, a famous Brazilian conductor. It gives details of the many different events and experiences of his life.

Unit 4   77

- Ask students to look at the photo and guess the age of the man. Elicit ideas from the class. Tell students they are going to read about a famous conductor from Brazil who has experienced many different changes in his life and had a number of different careers. (Elicit the meaning of the word *conductor* /kənˈdʌktə/ if necessary.)
- Ask them to read the article quickly and find out how many different careers he has had and to confirm whether they were right about his age.
- Check the answer together.

ANSWER
Four careers – classical pianist (three times), conductor, manager of a boxer, politician

Exercise 5
- Ask students to read the article again in more detail, and complete the table with information about the career changes and reasons why he changed career.
- Students work alone. Allow plenty of time for this task.
- Go through the answers together.

EXTENSION Put students in pairs and ask them to ask and answer questions about João Carlos Martins. Examples: *What do you think of the choices Martins has made during his life? Do you think he is lucky or unlucky? What is your opinion of this man?*

ANSWERS
2 Boxing manager
3 He had RSI – extreme pain in his hands
4 Politician
5 He hated it.
6 Two men attacked him and he suffered a brain injury and lost all movement in his right hand. Later he lost movement in his left hand.
7 Conductor

Exercise 6
- Students read the questions. Explain that it doesn't matter if they or their family haven't experienced any big changes, but encourage them to invent some if necessary. The point of the exercise is to encourage students to talk about changes in the past. Put students into small groups and ask them to discuss the questions.
- Note that some students may talk about rather personal events such as divorce, health problems or the death of a loved one. It is important to be sensitive and encourage students to be sensitive to each other.

EXTRA SUPPORT Allow students who need it some thinking time before they start their discussion.

- Monitor their discussions.
- Invite a few students to report what their partner said.

Grammar & Speaking verbs with *-ing* and *to*

Exercise 7
- Focus students' attention on the Grammar focus box and ask them to read points 1 and 2 in the box.
- Tell them to find highlighted words in the text and focus on what kind of verb form follows each word in order to add them to the Grammar focus box. Do an example together if necessary, e.g. *learned to play*. Explain that 'learned playing' would be incorrect. Add *learn* to point 2 in the Grammar focus box.
- Students work alone to complete this task. Then go through the answers together.

ANSWERS
1 stop, can't stand, keep
2 learn, decide, want

- Refer students to *Grammar reference* on p140. There are three more exercises here students can do for homework. See answers on p79.

Exercise 8
- Ask students to look at the verbs in the box.
- Tell them to decide which group (1 or 2) in the Grammar focus box each verb belongs to.
- They can discuss this task in pairs if you wish.

EXTRA SUPPORT/EXTRA CHALLENGE The students have no context for these verbs, i.e. they aren't from the reading text. Encourage them to think of example sentences for each verb in order to try out both verb forms if they are unsure which is correct. This is one of the best ways to analyse verb patterns. You can ask stronger students to think of a negative example for each. (NB We often use *can't imagine* as the negative of *imagine*.)

- Go through the answers together.

ANSWERS
1 enjoy, imagine, hate
2 need, would like, plan

EXTRA ACTIVITY Give students a few minutes to study/memorize the list of verbs with *-ing* and verbs with *to*. Put them into pairs and give each a role; Student A or Student B. Ask Student A in each pair to choose three of the verbs from exercises 7 and 8 to test their partner (who must not look at the book). Student A says the verb and asks *-ing* or *to*? Then Student B in each pair has a turn to test his/her partner. (There are enough verbs for them to test each other twice if you have time.)

STUDY TIP There are no specific rules about these verb patterns. They have to be memorized. Students need to find their own most effective ways to record vocabulary patterns like these which they need to learn. Encourage them to make 'a verb with *-ing* and *to*' page in their notebooks which they can add to when they read or hear another verb used with one of these patterns.

Exercise 9a
- Students read the instruction, then work alone on the task to complete the questions with the *-ing* form or infinitive with *to*.

EXTRA CHALLENGE Tell students to cover the Grammar focus box before doing this exercise.

- When they have finished, encourage them to check their answers with a partner and refer to the Grammar focus box if necessary.
- Go through the answers together.

ANSWERS
1 to live
2 to have
3 to move

4 to take up
5 moving
6 changing
7 trying
8 to change
9 reading

Exercise 9b
- Put students into new pairs and tell them to take turns asking and answering the questions in exercise 9a.
- Point out that the instruction says *ask for more information*.
- Monitor their discussions and give a time limit to the end of the activity so the class finishes at the same time.
- Encourage them to think for a moment about the answers that their partner gave and what this means. Ask *Does your partner have a positive or negative attitude to change? Explain why.*
- Tell them to share their conclusions with their partner and find out what their partner believes about their own attitude.
- Conduct a class discussion if appropriate. You could share your own attitude to change with the students.

EXTENSION You could ask students to write down their opinions about their partner's attitude or their own attitude to change. They should give examples of a few things from their conversations to support their opinions.
For example: *I don't think I like change because I said I hope to have the same career forever and I don't plan to move home. Some small changes are good. For example, I enjoy trying new food and I don't like reading the same blogs because that's boring.*
Go round and check that they are using verb with *-ing* and verb with *to* correctly (or collect their writing and mark it).

GRAMMAR REFERENCE ANSWERS

Exercise 1
infinitive with *to*:
agree
need
'd like
hope
plan
want

-ing form:
hate
can't stand
like
keep
imagine

Exercise 2
1 to live
2 to get
3 getting
4 to share
5 having
6 to buy
7 to be

Exercise 3
1 to swim
2 moving
3 to have
4 to retire

5 to leave
6 changing
7 living
8 to take
9 to get
10 being

4.2 Living without the internet

Goals
- Talk about using the internet
- Talk about plans and arrangements

Lead-in
- Put students in pairs. Tell them to ask their partner two questions, 1) what kind of mobile phone they have and 2) what kind of electronic equipment they regularly use. Ask them to note down their partner's answers.
- Conduct class feedback, eliciting different kinds of devices.

Vocabulary & Speaking internet activities

Exercise 1
- Put students into pairs to brainstorm ideas.
- Conduct a class discussion.

EXTENSION Ask students how much they use the computer or smartphone for work and how much for leisure.

Exercise 2a
- Ask students to read the different activities and check which ones they had already thought of in exercise 1.
- Go through any unknown vocabulary. If Facebook, Instagram and Twitter are not used by the students, elicit the names of social networking sites they use instead.
- Ask students to work in their pairs to discuss how often they do the activities. You could remind them that they studied adverbs of frequency in Unit 1.

Exercise 2b
- Students work alone to think about and choose two activities.

EXTRA SUPPORT If necessary, tell students to write brief notes about their reasons to help organize their thoughts. You can also give them sentence starters to help them, e.g. *The most important activity for me is … /One of the most important activities for me is … /Another important activity is … /The second activity I have chosen is …*

- Put students into pairs to discuss which activities are most important for them. Tell them they should explain why.
- Conduct a class discussion and highlight any patterns that appear, i.e. which activities seem the most or least important to many class members.

CRITICAL THINKING Being able to put things in order of priority or importance is a useful skill to practise. By putting things in order, students can make choices more easily. In a second language it is a good idea to learn useful phrases for outlining and explaining rankings and choices (see sentence starters in exercise above).

Unit 4 79

Exercise 3a
- Ask students to look at the photo and read the two questions. Check their understanding by asking, *What is Sylvie's job?* (Check they know what a fashion blogger does.) *What is she doing for one day? Why do you think she's doing it?*
- Tell them to look back at the list of activities in exercise 2a and decide which things she normally uses in her job and which she will miss most in her job.
- Students make notes alone and then discuss in pairs.
- Elicit some ideas from the class.

Exercise 3b 4.1

> **Audio summary:** A podcast by a fashion blogger who is trying life without the internet for the day. She explains what effects this has on her.

- Tell them that you are going to play the podcast to check whether their ideas were correct.
- Play track 4.1.
- Elicit the answers as a class. Ask if they are surprised by what she missed most.

ANSWERS
1 She normally checks and uses social media, goes online, checks her emails, reads the news, shares/posts photos.
2 She misses social media most.

AUDIOSCRIPT 4.1
Today, I'm going to spend 24 hours without the internet. Usually, before I go to bed, I check Instagram, Twitter, Facebook, my email and the weather and my calendar for the next day! I never completely switch off and stop thinking about work. When I get up, I always look at my phone and then go online and read the news. Most of my social life is online too, so I think I'm going to find it really hard.
Social media is very important for my job. Usually, I take photos of what I'm wearing, post them online, count the 'likes' and read people's comments. I can't do that today. So this morning I'm visiting a fashion show with colleagues, then I'm meeting a friend for lunch at one o'clock. I'm going to look through some magazines this afternoon, and hopefully get ideas for a new post. Then I plan to finish work early today. I'm going to see my sister later on, and perhaps have an early night.
So, now it's ten o'clock in the evening. Well, I can't lie, I'm *really* looking forward to being back online tomorrow. I missed social media so much at work, but I do feel differently about it now. I felt so much more relaxed today and really liked spending more time with family and friends, having interesting conversations with colleagues, and a bit more time for myself. So, in future, I'm going to change a few things and think more carefully about my internet use. I'm not going to deal with work emails outside work, I'm not going to waste as much time online and I'm not going to check my phone all the time.

Grammar & Listening *going to* and present continuous for the future

Exercise 4 4.1
- Tell students that you will play track 4.1 again so that they can complete the script. Explain that some gaps may need more than one word to complete them.
- Point out that this script is just 'extracts', not the whole podcast.
- Allow students time to read the script before listening.
- Play the track. You may need to do this twice as the gaps are close together and students need to accurately complete the gaps with the correct form of the verbs.
- Go through the answers together.

ANSWERS
1 visiting 2 meeting 3 going to look 4 going to see
5 going to change 6 going to waste 7 going to check

Exercise 5
- Put students into pairs to ask each other the questions and give and explain their answers.
- Conduct a class discussion. Ask students to respond to each others' answers and ask further questions.

EXTRA ACTIVITY In the same pairs, ask students to discuss how their life outside work would be affected if they could not use the internet. Ask them to discuss what the advantages and disadvantages would be.

Exercise 6a
- Focus students' attention on the Grammar focus box.
- Tell them to choose the correct options, then go through the answers together.
- Refer students to *Grammar reference* on p141. There are three more exercises here students can do for homework. See answers on p82.

ANSWERS
1 present continuous
2 *going to*

Exercise 6b
- Ask students to look back at the extract in exercise 4.
- Tell them to find and underline examples of the two different future forms – *going to* and present continuous.
- Ask them to check with a partner that they have found all the examples then go through the answers together.

ANSWERS
1 I'm visiting
2 I'm meeting
3 I'm going to look
4 I'm going to see
5 I'm going to change
6 I'm not going to deal
7 I'm not going to waste
6 I'm not going to check

Exercise 7a 4.2

> **Audio summary:** Lucas calls Sophie to tell her about/invite her to the school reunion he is organizing.

- Elicit which person makes the phone call (Lucas).

80

- Play track 4.2 and tell students to listen for the answers to the two questions.
- Go through the answers together.
- Write *school reunion* /ˈskuːl ˌriːˈjuːniən/ on the board, drill the pronunciation and check all students know the meaning. You could ask whether any students have been to a school reunion and/or what they think of the idea.

WATCH OUT! A word similar to *reunion* exists in a number of other languages but with a different meaning so make sure students understand the meaning here.

ANSWERS
Lucas calls Sophie to invite her to the school reunion next year. He also invites her to meet some old friends from school next Saturday.
He is planning to organize a school reunion on 14 July. He is visiting three hotels next week and is going to take photos and post them on the reunion website. He's going to book a live band for the evening. He's meeting old school friends next Saturday.

AUDIOSCRIPT 4.2
S Hello.
L Hi Sophie, it's Lucas.
S Lucas, I haven't spoken to you for ages! How are you?
L Very well, thanks. And you?
S Yeah, fine too, thanks. What a lovely surprise!
L Well, I'm calling because I'm organizing a school reunion on the 14th of July next year. Are you interested?
S Yeah, it'd be great to see everyone again! Where are you having the party?
L Well, I'm not sure yet. I've made a few appointments and I'm visiting three hotels next week. I'm going to take some photos and post them on the reunion website, so everyone can vote which they like best.
S Oh, that's a good idea. And have you got any other plans?
L Yeah, I'm going to book a live band for the evening, but I haven't done that yet.
S Uh-huh, sounds great! And how did you find everyone?
L Well it's much easier these days with the internet. I found a lot of people through Facebook. In fact, a few of us are meeting next Saturday at 7.30 if you're free?

Exercise 7b
- Tell students to look back at the Grammar focus box and remind them that both forms are often possible.
- Students work alone to choose the more likely option.

Exercise 7c 4.2
- Tell them that you're going to play the track again so they can check their answers.
- Play track 4.2 and go through the answers together.

ANSWERS
1 organizing 2 having 3 visiting 4 going to take
5 going to book 6 meeting

Pronunciation *going to*

Exercise 8a 4.3
- Explain that the focus of this part of the lesson is on pronunciation – specifically the pronunciation of *going to*.
- Play track 4.3.
- Explain we don't tend to stress *going to* and so at normal speed in connected speech it sounds more like /ˈgənə/.

AUDIOSCRIPT 4.3 & 4.4
1 I'm going to take some photos.
2 I'm going to book a live band.

Exercise 8b 4.4
- Play track 4.4 and ask students to repeat the sentences.
- You may need to play the track several times to ensure they produce /ˈgənə/ naturally.

WATCH OUT! We say /ˈgənə/ when *going to* is followed by a verb. If followed by a noun, we generally pronounce it a little more fully /ˈgəʊɪŋ tə/. Example: *She's going to hospital.*

STUDY TIP Encourage students to learn phonemic symbols as this will help them to a) record the pronunciation of new words and b) understand how to pronounce a word if they only have a dictionary. Good monolingual dictionaries have a list of the phonemic script with example words for each sound.

Exercise 8c
- Put students into pairs. Remind them that their conversations need to include *going to* as often as possible.

EXTRA SUPPORT Help students to create new conversations by putting a picture prompt of a party (food, DJ, balloons, etc.) on the board. One student should start with *I'm gonna have a party*.

- Monitor the conversations carefully and ensure they are pronouncing *going to* as /ˈgənə/ where appropriate.

Exercise 9a
- This 'find someone who …' task can be done as a whole class activity or in small groups of 3–4.
- Ask students to read sentences 1–8 and check that they understand all the vocabulary.
- Check they know how to make the questions and point out that /ˈgənə/ is used in questions too.
- Set a time limit to ask as many questions as they can to different people in the class/group. Tell them to make notes of any 'yes' answers with the student's name.

Exercise 9b
- Stop the activity but don't ask the students to sit down if they are mingling. Read out the next instruction.
- Ask them to take turns to ask and answer questions. They should make notes of any interesting plans they discover.
- Start the activity again, but set a time limit.

FEEDBACK FOCUS The focus of your monitoring should be the two future forms. Generally, in this exercise they should be using more present continuous as they are talking in more detail about plans and giving specific information such as dates, times and places.

Exercise 9c
- Encourage whole class feedback from exercises 9a and 9b. Ask them to report on interesting plans they discovered.
- Conduct error correction of any mistakes with the future forms which you noticed when monitoring exercises 9a and 9b.

Unit 4

Exercise 10a
- Check the meaning of *venue* and *entertainment* if necessary. Then put students into small groups.
- Tell them before they begin that they should ensure everyone has a chance to speak in their group.
- Allow plenty of time for students to discuss and make decisions.
- Monitor the discussions and make sure everyone has a chance to speak and give their opinion. After a set time, pause the activity and explain exercise 10b.

Exercise 10b
- Tell them that now they have the date, time, place, food and entertainment they must make practical arrangements.
- Tell them to discuss all aspects of the planning together and make notes of who will organize each part and what they will do.

  EXTRA SUPPORT Make it clear that they are going to present their ideas and plans to the class. Give less confident students time to choose a speaker (or speakers) and to practise presenting in a group first.

Exercise 10c
- Ask students to present their plans to the class.
- If there is limited time, divide the time so each group has the same amount of time and tell them this time limit in advance.

  EXTRA ACTIVITY For students who may need to practise note-taking for university or meetings, encourage them to write notes in English about the presentations. This can also help weaker students with the next exercise when they have to vote for which group's plan is the best.

Exercise 10d
- Ask students to judge which group has the best plan overall for the class reunion. (Not their own group.)
- Remind them that they should be ready to give reasons for their choice if asked.

  CRITICAL THINKING You could set this task up in a different way to practise critical thinking skills. Conduct several different votes based on different criteria which you give to them in groups to discuss, e.g. most detailed plan, most organized group, most original ideas, most practical/realistic plan, use of English language.
- Conduct a class vote. Then give your own feedback, which could be based on some of the criteria above.

GRAMMAR REFERENCE ANSWERS

Exercise 1
1 are going to stay
2 are not going to spend
3 am going to do
4 are going to make
5 is my son going to do
6 is going to watch
7 are we going to eat
8 am not going to cook
9 are going to order

Exercise 2
1 is going jogging
2 are arriving
3 is meeting
4 aren't playing
5 am chatting
6 Is Mike doing, isn't

Exercise 3
1 I'm going to update my Facebook page later.
2 We are having a chat online at 9.30 p.m.
3 Are you going to share that photo of us?
4 Akemil isn't going on holiday this year.
5 Ella and I aren't getting married on the 5th July, but on the 6th!
6 Are you and Roberta going to call when you arrive?
7 My brother is going into hospital this evening.
8 What time is the taxi coming tomorrow?

4.3 Vocabulary and skills development

Goals
- Understand connected speech (1)
- Understand and use *get*

Listening understanding connected speech (1)

Lead-in
- Ask students to look at the photos. Tell them to find one lifestyle change in the list in 1a which matches the photos.

Exercise 1a
- Focus students' attention on the list and tell them that these are changes some people make to their lifestyle.
- If necessary, check they know all the vocabulary. You could point out useful collocations for this lesson, e.g. *make changes to …* and *do things/something*.
- Allow them plenty of time to do the task alone.

  EXTRA CHALLENGE Ask fast finishers to think about their reasons why they would like to make these changes.

Exercise 1b
- Put students into pairs to discuss their choices.

  EXTRA SUPPORT This can be a two-stage process for students who need extra support. 1) Tell them to explain why they ticked and crossed the different things. You could give them some sentence starters, e.g. *I've always wanted to …/I think …ing is a good idea/I'm not interested in …ing/I don't feel I need to …*. 2) Tell them to focus on the ticks and try to explain what is stopping them from doing those things.
- When they have had enough time to discuss, conduct class feedback. Elicit sentences about why they haven't done the things they ticked. If appropriate, you could share information about your own life, changes you'd like to make and reasons why you haven't made the changes yet.

Exercise 2

> **Text summary** An article about a man who decided to do a 30-day challenge, trying something new and doing it every day for 30 days.

- Students read questions 1–3. They read the article to find the answers.

EXTRA SUPPORT Pre-teach the meaning of *challenge* and *habit* as these are key words for understanding the text.

- Go through the answers together.

ANSWERS
1 He thought his life wasn't moving forward.
2 cycle more, watch less television, eat less sugar, write a novel, climb a famous mountain
3 He learned that if you do something for 30 days, it becomes a habit; and if you stop doing something for 30 days, you can break the habit. He learned that if he really, really wanted to do something, he could.

EXTENSION Conduct a class discussion – elicit the students' opinions of the 30-day challenge. Possible questions: *Do you think 30 days is enough to break a habit or create a new one? Are there any things you think take longer than 30 days to change? Do you believe if you really, really want to do something, you can? Why/why not?*

Exercise 3a 4.5

- Explain that the next part of the lesson focuses on pronunciation and listening.
- Tell them to read the Unlock the code box.
- Explain that you're going to play a track so that they can hear the sentences which contain the linking sounds.
- Play track 4.5.
- This may be new for the students so play the track again if necessary. Point out that we include these extra sounds because they make linking vowel sounds easier.

AUDIOSCRIPT 4.5
When a word ends with a vowel sound and the next word begins with a vowel sound, we sometimes add a /j/ sound or a /w/ sound to link the words.
I go /w/ out
do /w/ a challenge
the /j/ elevator
I /j/ agree

Exercise 3b 4.6

- Ask students to read the phrases with the extra /w/ sound.
- Put students in pairs and tell them to practise saying the phrases aloud, including the linking /w/ sounds.
- Play track 4.6. Students check to see if they were pronouncing the phrases naturally.
- Then play the track again and ask students to repeat the phrases.

AUDIOSCRIPT 4.6
quarter to /w/ eight   we're going to /w/ eat soon
so /w/ am I   who /w/ are you   go /w/ inside
do /w/ it now

Exercise 3c 4.7

- Tell students that this exercise is the same as exercise 3b but the phrases have an extra /j/ sound.
- Follow the same instructions as exercise 3b.

AUDIOSCRIPT 4.7
me /j/ and you   she /j/ eats a lot   the /j/ easy way
three /j/ o'clock   we /j/ aren't ready   be /j/ a

Exercise 3d 4.8

- Tell students that they need to write two words in each space.
- Play track 4.8.
- Students listen and complete the sentences. Then they mark the linking sounds.
- Ask them to check their answers with a partner, saying them aloud. Then go through the answers together.
- Play the track again for students to repeat the phrases.

ANSWERS
1 you /w/ in
2 the /j/ other
3 go /w/ on
4 do /w/ I
5 she /j/ isn't
6 three /j/ apples

AUDIOSCRIPT 4.8
1 see you /w/ in two minutes
2 the /j/ other side
3 go /w/ on holiday
4 so do /w/ I
5 she /j/ isn't ready
6 three /j/ apples, please

Exercise 4 4.9

> **Audio summary** An informal discussion between Mia (female) and Dino (male) about the 30-day challenge and which challenges they will face.

- Tell students that they will now hear a conversation about the 30-day challenge between two people, Mia and Dino.
- Explain they need to write down any five sentences they hear. It might be easier for students to just make notes first and then turn the notes into sentences.
- Students compare their sentences with one another.

ANSWERS/AUDIOSCRIPT 4.9
1 How are you going to do it?
2 Was it a free app?
3 It's not going to be easy.
4 We aren't going to eat meat for 30 days.
5 To be honest, it's not good to eat too much meat.

Exercise 5 4.10

- Ask students to read the table and explain they will need to complete it as they listen to the whole conversation.
- Play track 4.10.
- Students check in pairs, then go through the answers together.
- You could ask students to discuss whether they think Mia and Dino will be successful. Why/Why not?

Unit 4   83

ANSWERS

	Mia	Dino
What challenge?	Walk 10,000 steps a day	Give up eating meat for 30 days
Alone? With people?	Alone	With his partner
What to get or buy?	Nothing	A vegetarian cookbook

AUDIOSCRIPT 4.10

Mia I think this 30-day challenge idea is great. I'm definitely going to try it.
Dino Me too. So, what are you going to do first?
Mia I'm going to walk 10,000 steps a day.
Dino Good idea. So, how are you going to do it?
Mia Well, when I go out to the shops, I'm going to walk, not drive. I'm going to take the stairs instead of the elevator and twice a week I'm going to walk to work, not get the bus.
Dino Are you going to get one of those little things which count your steps … um … ?
Mia A pedometer? Well, actually, I've got an app on my phone that does that.
Dino Was it a free app?
Mia Yeah. You just put it in your pocket and it counts your steps.
Dino Excellent. Well, good luck.
Mia Thanks. So what about you? What's your first challenge?
Dino Well, me and my partner are going to do a challenge together.
Mia What's that then?
Dino We aren't going to eat meat for 30 days.
Mia Really?! But you love eating meat!
Dino I know, but, to be honest, it's not good to eat too much meat.
Mia True, I agree with that.
Dino It's not going to be easy, but we're going to get a vegetarian cookbook to help us. My parents are coming for lunch on Sunday. My dad's a big meat-eater so I need to cook something very tasty!
Mia Well, best of luck!

Exercise 6

- Refer the students back to the list in exercise 1a.
- In pairs, students tell each other their plans for a 30-day challenge. They should ask each other questions to get more information.

EXTRA CHALLENGE For strong students, tell them to choose three different challenges and decide what order they are going to do them in. They should be able to explain what they are going to do, give extra information about each challenge and give reasons for the order of the three challenges.

FEEDBACK FOCUS When monitoring, focus on the pronunciation of *going to* and check the use of linking /w/ or /j/ sounds. Note down good examples or examples of phrases where linking sounds were missing.

- Conduct a class discussion and error correction of the pronunciation if necessary.

Vocabulary & Speaking *get*

Exercise 7

- Ask students to read the instruction and sentences 1 and 2.
- Students work alone to think about the meaning of *get*. Then discuss their ideas with their partner.
- Go through the answers together.

ANSWERS
1 catch
2 buy

Exercise 8

- Ask students to read the Vocabulary focus box about *get*.
- Ask students if they had already noticed that this very common verb has a number of meanings.

Exercise 9a

- Tell students to match the six sentences with the correct meanings. If necessary refer them to the Vocabulary focus box.
- Go through the answers together.

ANSWERS
1 c 2 e 3 f 4 a 5 b 6 d

Exercise 9b

- Put students into pairs.
- Tell them to take turns to ask and answer the questions in exercise 9a.

EXTRA CHALLENGE Fast finishers can return to the most interesting question and ask further questions to get more information.

- You could point out that in all these questions *get* is far more natural than using the equivalent verb (a–f). Help them to realize that it's neutral rather than informal. We use *get* with these meanings in normal everyday English, but it's also common in business.

Exercise 9c

- Ask students to look at the phrases with *get* in the box.
- Ask them to refer to the Vocabulary focus box and identify which meaning *get* has in each of the phrases.
- Students work alone, but can check their ideas in pairs.
- Go through the answers together. (NB We say *catch a bus* but not *catch a taxi*.)

ANSWERS
get with adjectives:
become: get engaged, get angry, get cold
get with nouns:
arrive: get home late
receive: get a present, get a text
obtain: get enough sleep
buy: get some bread
catch: get the bus, get a taxi

Exercise 10

- Ask students to use the phrases in the box to complete the sentences.
- Students work alone on the task. Then go through the answers together.

84

EXTENSION Ask students to talk in pairs and identify the correct meaning of *get* for each of the phrases in exercise 10.

ANSWERS
1 gets her some (buys)
2 get a new pair (buy)
3 getting (becoming)
4 get the bus (catch)
5 gets there (arrives)
6 get some (buy)
7 get, get (become, buy/obtain)
8 got one (obtain)

Exercise 11
- Ask students to read the actions in the list.
- Highlight the second question *How are you going to achieve them?*
- Put students into pairs. Ask one pair to act out the example dialogue.

EXTRA SUPPORT For students who need extra support, give them 2–3 minutes thinking time before they talk. They can make brief notes to help them speak more confidently during the task.

- Monitor the students' conversations. Remind them to pronounce *going to* the way they have studied in connected speech /ˈgənə/.
- Give a time limit to the end of the activity so that all students finish at the same time.
- Conduct class feedback. Ask some students to repeat one of their conversations in front of the class.
- Students could also ask you which you would like to do and how you are going to achieve it/them.

EXTRA ACTIVITY Tell students to look through the exercises in the Vocabulary & Speaking section and select five phrases with *get*. They should write a question for each of the phrases to ask another student in the class. These questions do not have to use *going to*. Examples: *When did you get married? How long does it take you to get to school?*

- Monitor the question-writing stage carefully to ensure accuracy. Then put students into small groups so that they can ask their questions. They can report back on any interesting facts they found out about the members of their group.

STUDY TIP Encourage students to collect examples of *get* in sentences from TV, radio, internet and printed sources. They need to be careful to write down the whole sentence and information about the context, e.g. a formal newspaper article or an informal conversation. They can then use a good dictionary to check the meaning of *get* in their examples.

4.4 Speaking and writing

Goals
- Invite and make arrangements
- Write an email to make arrangements

Lead-in
- Write the word *invite* on the board. Ask *Is this a noun or a verb?* (It is a verb. However, it is increasingly used informally as a noun, e.g. *Thanks for the invite.*)

- Elicit or teach the noun *invitation*. Drill pronunciation of both *invite* (verb) /ɪnˈvaɪt/ and *invitation* /ɪnvɪˈteɪʃn/.
- Put students into small groups to brainstorm different things they might receive invitations to (party, wedding, conference, informal invitations to the cinema, etc.).
- You could elicit ideas and build a mind map on the board.

Listening & Speaking inviting and making arrangements

Exercise 1
- Put students into pairs. Ask them to talk about recent invitations they have made. If they haven't made any, they could also talk about invitations they have received recently.
- Conduct a class discussion. Find out about a few students' invitations. You could also ask whether the person they asked accepted or refused the invitation. The verbs *accept* and *refuse* are key vocabulary for this lesson.

Exercise 2 4.11

Audio summary Two voicemail messages left by Max Weber – one is an invitation Max makes to a work colleague, the other is an informal refusal of a friend's invitation.

- Write *diary* /ˈdaɪəri/ on the board and drill pronunciation. You could elicit other things which the students use for planning their time (calendar, personal organizer, smartphone, etc.)

WATCH OUT! *Agenda* is not used in the same way as *diary* in English – an agenda is a list of things which will be talked about at a meeting.

- Tell students that they are going to hear two separate voicemail messages and they need to choose the correct answer in each sentence.
- Play track 4.11 then go through the answers together.

ANSWERS
1 makes
2 refuses
3 colleague
4 informal

AUDIOSCRIPT 4.11
Voicemail 1 (to his colleague Seyit Samyeli)
Hello Seyit, this is Max Weber from Weber Design Solutions. I'm just ringing to let you know that I'm visiting Izmir the week of the 27th March, and, I was wondering, would you like to meet for lunch?
Please call me back on 00 49 64 19 81 64 02. OK, thank you, bye.
Voicemail 2 (to his friend Agneta)
Hi Agneta, it's me. Sorry, I can't make it on Thursday – did you get my Facebook message? Anyway, do you fancy doing something at the weekend instead? OK, er, hope you have a great time with Jens. Speak soon.

Unit 4

Exercise 3a 4.12

> **Audio summary** Two different telephone conversations in response to the voicemail messages. Max makes plans with his colleague Seyit and his friend Agneta.

- Ask students to read the instruction. Elicit that they are going to listen to Max's colleague and Max's friend responding to the voicemail messages they just heard.
- Tell them to make a note of the arrangements Max makes with each person.
- Play track 4.12.
- Go through the answers together.

ANSWERS

Max arranges to have lunch with Seyit on 29th March during his trip to Izmir.
Max arranges to go to a Chinese restaurant for dinner with Agneta on Sunday at 8 p.m.

AUDIOSCRIPT 4.12

Phonecall 1 – Max & Seyit
M Hello, Weber Design Solutions.
S Oh hello, Max, this is Seyit Samyeli. I'm sorry I missed your call, but I …
M Ah, Seyit, good to hear from you. Thanks for returning my call.
S Yes, I'm pleased to hear you're coming over soon.
M Thank you, I'm looking forward to it. Er, are you free that week at all?
S Yes, it's fine for me.
M Great, so would you like to meet for lunch?
S Yes, I'd like to very much, thanks.
M OK, so how about the 28th? Is that OK for you?
S Oh, sorry, I'm afraid I can't make the 28th because … er … I have another meeting that day. How about the 29th instead?
M No problem, that's fine for me too.
S OK, shall I find a nice restaurant and book a table for us?
M That sounds perfect.
S I'll email you with the details nearer the time.
M Great, so, see you soon. Thanks for ringing, bye.
S Thank you, bye.

Phonecall 2 – Max & Agneta
M Hello.
A Hi it's me! Thanks for your messages. Are you OK? How was your week?
M Yeah, it was good thanks, a bit tiring with work. But how about you? Are you OK?
A Yeah, yeah, I'm fine thanks, busy week too. Eh, so, I was wondering, do you still fancy doing something this weekend or are you …?
M Yeah, yeah, that'd be lovely. How about you? Are you doing anything tomorrow?
A I'm really sorry but I can't make it tomorrow – I'm working. Is Sunday any good for you? Could we meet then instead?
M Yeah, yeah, that'd be fine. We could try that new Chinese restaurant? What do you think?
A Yeah, sounds great! I've heard the food's really good there. Shall we meet outside the restaurant at eight, then?
M Yes, good idea. See you on Sunday. I'll ring and book a table now while I remember.
A OK, thanks. So see you soon, bye!
M Bye!

Exercise 3b 4.12

- Students read questions 1–3.

EXTRA CHALLENGE Stronger students can try to remember the reasons and then listen to check their ideas.

- Play track 4.12 again.
- Students listen and write/check their answers.
- Discuss the answer to question 3. You could ask whether this is the same in the students' culture/language too (see Smart Communication box).

ANSWERS
1 Because he has another meeting.
2 Because she is working.
3 Because it's polite to give a reason when you refuse an invitation.

SMART COMMUNICATION When refusing an invitation in English, it is possible to use the phrase *I'm busy* but we make it softer by adding *I'm afraid* or *Sorry, but …* in front of this phrase. It is generally considered normal and more polite to give a more detailed reason why you cannot accept.

Exercise 4a

- Tell students that they need to match the two halves of the sentences. Do the first sentence together as an example.
- Students work alone on this task. Monitor and ensure all students have finished matching before you move on.

ANSWERS
1 b 2 e 3 i 4 f 5 g 6 h 7 d 8 a 9 c

Exercise 4b 4.13

- Tell them that you will play the track again and they should listen and check their answers. (Tell them that you're not playing the full conversation this time, but only the sentences 1–9.)
- Play track 4.13.
- You could point out that in the UK when we make arrangements and talk about time, we don't say 'a.m.' or 'p.m.' but only the number, e.g. *outside the restaurant at 8*. You could also say *8 o'clock*. In the rare case that it is not clear whether the time is 8 a.m. or 8 p.m., we tend to say *8 in the morning* or *8 in the evening*.

ANSWERS
1 Are you free that week at all?
2 Would you like to meet for lunch?
3 I'm afraid I can't make the twenty-eighth.
4 How about the twenty-ninth instead?
5 Do you fancy doing something this weekend?
6 That'd be lovely.
7 Is Sunday any good for you?
8 Sounds great!
9 Shall we meet outside the restaurant at eight?

AUDIOSCRIPT 4.13 & 4.14
1 Are you free that week at all?
2 Would you like to meet for lunch?
3 I'm afraid I can't make the twenty-eighth.
4 How about the twenty-ninth instead?
5 Do you fancy doing something this weekend?

6 That'd be lovely.
7 Is Sunday any good for you?
8 Sounds great!
9 Shall we meet outside the restaurant at eight?

Exercise 4c 4.14
- Tell them that you are going to play the track again for them to practise their pronunciation.
- Play track 4.14. Students repeat the sentences.
- **PRONUNCIATION** Encourage students to think about how their voice goes up and down (intonation). This helps to show interest in what the speaker is saying.

Exercise 4d
- Tell students to look back at exercise 4a and find the answers.
- Go through the answers together, then elicit why we do this. Ask if this is usual in the students' own language too. These questions are important because if the answer is no, then there is no point in trying to continue to make an arrangement. Asking this kind of question first saves time.

ANSWERS
Are you free that week at all?
Do you fancy doing something this weekend?

Exercise 5
- Focus students' attention on the Language for speaking box.
- Mention that two of these phrases are more suitable for informal discussions rather than business situations. Elicit or teach them that *Are you doing anything … ?* and *Do you fancy … ?* are quite informal.
- Put students into pairs. Encourage them to use the phrases for inviting and making arrangements.
- Monitor their conversations carefully. If you notice that they are always accepting or always refusing, encourage them to practise the other response too.
- Set a time limit to the end of the activity. It doesn't matter if they have not all completed conversations for all the situations but it is useful to end at the same time.
- Invite one or two of the most accurate pairs to act out a conversation in front of the class.

EXTRA CHALLENGE Ask students to note how many phrases from the box their partner uses.

EXTENSION Ask students to write one or two more situations similar to 1–6 when you might need to make an invitation. They could do this alone or in pairs. Use these new situations for further practice in their pairs.

Reading & Writing email (2): making arrangements

Exercise 6
- Tell students they are going to read emails to Max from Seyit and Agneta.
- Ask them to read both emails and answer questions 1–3.
- Go through the answers together.

ANSWERS
1 They need to change the arrangements they made.
2 Seyit has an important meeting with his boss. Agneta forgot that she is going to her grandmother's eightieth birthday party.
3 Seyit suggests meeting on 28th instead. Agneta suggests meeting next weekend instead.

Exercise 7a
- Focus students' attention on the Language for writing box.
- Point out that there are phrases for four different functions.
- Tell them to find and underline similar phrases in the two emails.
- Students work alone, then check their answers with a partner.
- Go through the answers together.

ANSWERS
1 Hi Max, Dear Max,
2 How's it going? I hope you're keeping well.
3 Speak soon. I hope to hear from you soon.
4 Love, All the best,

Exercise 7b
- Explain that there are differences in formality between the two emails and these are shown in the phrases that Seyit and Agneta choose to use.
- In pairs, ask them to discuss which expressions are particularly informal, e.g. *Hi there! Hi Max, How are you doing? How are things? How's it going? Speak soon. Take care. Cheers. Bye for now. Love.*
- Conduct a class discussion and give clear feedback.

EXTENSION For homework you could ask students to translate or find equivalents for the Language for writing phrases in their own language(s). This raises awareness of differences in formality as it draws on the students' own knowledge and experience.

Exercise 8a
- Tell students that they are going to write an email about changed arrangements.
- Remind them that they should use phrases from the Language for writing box but also explain that there may be useful phrases in the Language for speaking box on page 42.
- Ask them to read the three options carefully and go through any problem vocabulary.
- Tell them to choose one option and write the email for it. Remind them to write clearly as another student is going to read it. If you have access to computers, these emails could be done on screen to be a more authentic experience.

EXTRA SUPPORT For students who need extra support, help them decide whether the option they have chosen is informal or not. Help them to decide which text in exercise 6 is a good model for their email. Encourage them to use the structure and phrases from the model. (Option one is more formal, option two less formal and option three will depend on the students in the class and how well they know each other.) If you think that they will struggle alone with this writing task, you could put them into pairs to do it.

Unit 4   87

- Monitor their writing closely and assist where necessary.
- Give a time limit for the task if necessary.

EXTRA CHALLENGE Encourage fast finishers to check their grammar and spelling. If possible, put two students together who have written the same email and ask them to compare how they both did the task. They could find similarities and differences between the two emails. If they have written different emails, they can still compare them and discuss why they think the phrases they have chosen are suitable.

Exercise 8b

- Ensure the students' emails are exchanged widely around the class so that they receive emails from students they haven't been working with.
- They now each have a new email which they need to write a reply to. They can choose to 1) accept and confirm the new arrangements or 2) explain why the new arrangement is not possible for them and make an alternative suggestion.
- If you think students would benefit from discussing the task, you could put them into pairs to write the replies.
- Set a time limit and monitor and assist if necessary.

EXTRA CHALLENGE Fast finishers should be encouraged to write two alternative email responses for the same email as outlined above.

- Encourage students to check their grammar and spelling.
- Return the replies to the original writers to read.
- Conduct class feedback. Ask students how effective the email exchanges were, e.g. *Was the email you received easy to understand? Was it written in a logical order like the examples in exercise 6? Do you feel it was the right level of formality? Why/Why not?*

EXTRA ACTIVITY For extra speaking practice you could use the original emails from exercise 8a again. Put students into new pairs and ask them to 'telephone' each other to accept or change the arrangements, using phrases from the Language for speaking box. Tell them to turn their chairs so that they are sitting back to back which helps them pretend that it's a phone conversation, not face to face. Remind them to think about the level of formality. Monitor and give feedback.

4.5 Video

Esplorio

VIDEOSCRIPT

Social media has changed the world we live in.
Over a billion people are on social media sites, such as Facebook, Linkedin and Instagram and many of them use it every day. It is now the most popular activity on the internet.
People spend a quarter of their online time on a social network, and mobile technology means people can access their social media accounts from anywhere at any time.
So, people are living more of their lives – especially their social lives – online.
This means that people now have a detailed record of much of their lives, because social networks record what people say, when they say it and where they say it. But a lot of this information is rarely in one place.
This is where Esplorio can help.
Esplorio brings together all your social media content to create a travel diary. It shows everywhere you have been and lets you click on a location.
Once you create an account you can connect your social networks. Esplorio then turns all your information into a travel diary.
Tim Fernando started the company when he was at University and Essa Saulat joined later.
Tim travelled a lot, but found that his photos were all on different social media sites. So, he invented a website that collected them all in one place.
He took his idea to Isis Innovation, a company that turns the university's most exciting research into successful business ideas.
They gave Tim and Essa a place to work and helped them develop their product. They also helped create a business strategy.
In the future, Esplorio are going to expand. They're introducing a 'recommendations' tool next year. The website will use your current information to suggest where you might want to go in the future.
Esplorio is just one example of the social media explosion. Entrepreneurs like Tim and Essa are starting new social media companies all the time all over the world.
Some will only last a few months, but some will change the way we live and work. And one thing is for sure, this phenomenon isn't going to end soon.

VIDEO ANSWERS

Exercise 1
Internet: site, social media, website account, click, connect
Business: company, product, strategy, expand, entrepreneur

Exercise 3
1 social 2 travel 3 map 4 pictures 5 university
6 recommendations

Exercise 4
a T
b T
c F (In the future Esplorio will recommend places to you based on your information.)
d F (Entrepreneurs are creating social media tools all the time all over the world.)
e T

Review

ANSWERS

Exercise 1a
1 doing
2 to do
3 watching
4 doing
5 to buy
6 to visit

Exercise 2a
1 I'm meeting
2 We're probably going to look at
3 I'm getting
4 I'm seeing
5 We're meeting
6 We're going to see

Exercise 3a
1d download films
2c use social media
3b pass your driving test
4a leave home
5g shop online
6h spend time abroad
7f choose your career
8e do online banking

Exercise 4a
22 in your twenties, in your early twenties, about twenty
59 in your fifties, in your late fifties, middle-aged
70 elderly
35 in your thirties, in your mid-thirties
16 in your teens/a teenager

Exercise 5a
1 present
2 bus
3 texts
4 shoes
5 married
6 home

Exercise 6a 4.15

ANSWERS/AUDIOSCRIPT 4.15

A Are you doing anything on Friday night?
B No, I don't think so. Why?
A Do you fancy coming round for dinner?
B That sounds great. Oh, hang on, did you say Friday?
A Yes, is there a problem?
B I'm sorry, but I can't make Friday. I'm meeting a friend from university.
A No problem. How about Saturday instead?
B Saturday? That'd be great.

ANSWERS
1 a   2 e   3 f   4 c   5 g   6 d   7 h   8 b

Exercise 6b

POSSIBLE ANSWERS
a Are you free
b Sounds great.
c I'd love to.
d I'm afraid
f Would you like to come round
h Could we meet

A Are you free on Friday night?
B Yes, I think so. Why?
A Would you like to come round for dinner?
B I'd love to – oh hang on, did you say Friday?
A Yes, is there a problem?
B I'm afraid I can't make Friday. I'm meeting a friend from university.
A No problem. Could we meet Saturday instead?
B Saturday? Sounds great.

Unit 4   89

5 Stuff and things

Unit overview

Language input

Articles (CB p47)	• *They hide the container.* • *Teachers at a school in England.* • *It contained information.*
Quantifiers (CB p48)	• *Only a few people have a bank account.* • *Lots of Kenyans have a mobile phone.* • *Does it offer enough benefits?*
Grammar reference (CB pp142–3)	

Vocabulary development

Adjectives for describing objects (CB p46)	• *ordinary, valuable, brand new …*
Money (CB p48)	• *credit card, wallet, receipt …* • *save up, in debt, owe …*
Suffixes (CB p51)	• *arrangement, suitable, computer …*

Skills development

Reading: Understanding linkers for reason and result (CB p50)

Speaking: Explaining words you don't know (CB p52)

Writing: Email (3): returning an online product (CB p53)

Video

Documentary: The Dubai Mall (Coursebook DVD & CB p54)

Vox pops (Coursebook DVD & TG p261)

More materials

Workbook	• Language practice for vocabulary, pronunciation, grammar, speaking and writing
Photocopiable activities	• Grammar: Money talks (TG p212 & TSRD) • Vocabulary: Auction (TG p230 & TSRD) • Communication: What are you going to do? (TG p248 & TSRD)
Tests	• Unit 5 test (TSRD)
Unit 5 wordlist (TSRD)	

5.1 Your world in objects

Goals
- Describe objects
- Use articles

Lead-in
- Write *stuff* and *things* on the board and elicit the difference (= basically the same meaning but *stuff* is informal and uncountable, *things* is neutral and plural.
- Find out if the students remember Huang Quingjun, the Chinese photographer they read about in Unit 2.2. (He took photographs of people with all their things outside their homes.) Some students may remember *possessions* as a synonym for *things you own* – if not, teach this word.

STUDY TIP Point out that students need to set aside a time each week when they try to remember what they learned recently in their lessons. They could write a few sentences summarizing what they remember and then review the lesson to check anything they have forgotten. Research shows that language learners are more likely to remember what they have learned if they see it more than once.

- Ask: *Do you have a lot of stuff here with you in class? Are all the things in your bag or pocket important? Why/Why not?* They could discuss these questions in pairs or small groups.

Vocabulary & Listening   adjectives for describing objects

Exercise 1
- Students read the instruction.
- You could demonstrate the activity by bringing in one or more of your own possessions to show to the class.
- Students work alone on this task.
- Put them into pairs to compare their answers.
- **EXTRA CHALLENGE** Students could ask their partners questions to get more information.
- Conduct a class discussion.

Exercise 2a 5.1

> **Audio summary:** Four different speakers each describe an object which is important to them.

- Ask students to look at the photos of different possessions.
- Tell them that they are going to hear four people talking about their favourite possession. They should write speaker 1–4 next to the photo of their possession.
- Play track 5.1.
- Go through the answers together.

ANSWERS
1 d
2 b
3 a
4 c

AUDIOSCRIPT 5.1
Sandra My favourite possession is definitely my scooter. It's brand new. I only got it a few weeks ago. Riding it is great fun and the feel of the cool wind is wonderful, especially in this hot weather. And just looking at it brings a smile to my face. I love the colour and the design of it and it's so bright and shiny! The seat's made of leather so it's very comfortable to ride.

Omar My favourite possession is my smartphone. It's just an ordinary one, nothing special, but I use it all the time, for making calls, writing notes, sending emails, checking stuff on the internet – everything really. It's so useful I can't imagine life without it. It's very thin and light so it's easy to carry around and it's got a plastic cover to protect it.

Helena My favourite possession is this ring. It's antique and it's gold. It's not very valuable – not worth much money – but it's very special to me. It was my grandmother's. She gave me it before she died. It's got a dark blue stone with a black spot on it so it looks like an eye. My grandmother believed it gave her good luck. I love it because it reminds me of her. It's really, really small – tiny, in fact! She obviously had very small fingers!

Marcus My favourite possession is a round box. It's made of a kind of pale grey metal. It sounds strange, but I don't know what's inside it! The box is called a time capsule. My parents gave it to me when I was a baby, but I can't open it till I'm 25. They put special objects in it. It contains personal things, and objects which will tell me about life in the year I was born. It's amazing. It's quite large and really heavy. I can't wait to see what's inside!

Exercise 2b
- Refer students back to exercise 1a. Ask them to choose one of the reasons why each object a–d is important to each person.
- You could put them in pairs to discuss this.
- Check answers together. Encourage students to remember what each person said.

ANSWERS
1 b
2 c
3 a
4 a

Exercise 3 5.1
- Tell students to decide which object each one describes.
- Students work alone on this task but ask them to check their answers in pairs.
- Tell them that you are going to play the track again so they can check their answers.
- Play track 5.1.
- Go through the answers together if necessary.

ANSWERS
1 smartphone   4 ring
2 ring   5 scooter
3 time capsule 6 smartphone

Exercise 4a
- Focus students' attention on the words in bold in the sentences in exercise 3.
- Tell them that they need to categorize these words by adding them to the mind map. Point out that the first one has been done as an example.

Unit 5   91

- Students work alone on this task.
- Go through the answers. At this point you can point out that when we describe the kind of material we often use *be made of* e.g. *It's made of metal. They're made of plastic.*

ANSWERS
Material: metal
Age: brand new
Size/shape: tiny, thin
Opinion: ordinary, valuable, special
Colour: pale grey
Weight: light

Exercise 4b

- This exercise is the same as exercise 4a but uses new sentences from the listening.
- In pairs, students add the bold words to the mind map.
- Go through the answers together and drill the /e/ sound in 'leather' and the /k/ ending of *antique*.
- **EXTENSION** Ask the students to work with their partner and add two more words to each category on the mind map. Elicit suggestions from the class and confirm which category they belong to. Drill any mispronounced words.

ANSWERS
Material: leather, plastic, gold
Age: antique
Size/shape: large
Opinion: useful, personal, amazing, comfortable
Colour: dark blue
Weight: heavy

Pronunciation adjective word stress

Exercise 5a 5.2

- Students need to focus on the pronunciation of the vocabulary from exercises 3 and 4.
- Students can work alone, but will get more pronunciation practice if they work in pairs and say the words aloud.
- Tell them to count the syllables and decide the stress pattern for each of the words. Model the example so they understand that each circle represents a syllable and the large circle is the stressed syllable.
- Tell them to listen to the recording to check their answers.
- Play track 5.2.
- Check they have the correct answers.

ANSWERS/AUDIOSCRIPT 5.2 & 5.3
plastic [Oo, 2]   ordinary [Ooo, 3]
useful [Oo, 2]   special [Oo, 2]
amazing [oOo, 3]   comfortable [Ooo, 3]
personal [Oo, 2]   valuable [Ooo, 3]

Exercise 5b 5.3

- Tell students to repeat the words after they hear them.
- Play track 5.3 as many times as necessary. Pause and repeat individual words which are causing problems until the pronunciation sounds natural.
- **WATCH OUT!** You can highlight that sometimes it appears that a syllable is missing in certain words. *Comfortable* /ˈkʌmftəbl/ only has three syllables though when students break it down they often find four. *Valuable* /ˈvæljuəbl/ and *ordinary* /ˈɔːdnri/ are also contracted in pronunciation. Not all words with these spelling patterns (*-able* and *-ary*) are contracted in this way. Other examples of adjectives are *fashionable* /ˈfæʃnəbl/, *temporary* /ˈtemprəri/.

Exercise 6a

- Tell students to choose one of their favourite objects but keep it a secret. Other students will need to guess what it is.
- Check students understand that 1) they know that this is a written exercise and 2) they remember NOT to use the name of the object in their sentences.

ANSWERS
Students' own answers

EXTRA SUPPORT Focus students' attention on the sentences in exercises 3 and 4b and tell the students to use these as model sentences which they can adapt for their own object.

- Set a time limit for them to write the sentences.

EXTRA CHALLENGE Fast finishers should think about the order of their sentences – the obvious clues should be read out last.

Exercise 6b

- Put students into small groups. Ask them to take turns to read out their sentences to the other students in their group.
- The students who are listening should guess the object.
- Monitor for good use of adjectives to describe things. Note any pronunciation difficulties with the adjectives.
- Set a time limit to the end of the activity when most groups have almost finished.
- Conduct class feedback. Praise good use of adjectives and correct any pronunciation problems.

Reading & Grammar articles

Exercise 7a

- In pairs, students look carefully at the photos and discuss what they show.
- Conduct a class discussion – elicit ideas, but do not confirm any of them yet.

Exercise 7b

> **Text summary:** An article about time capsules (special containers that people fill with objects typical of the time they are living in, so future generations can learn about life at that time).

- Ask students to read the text in order to check the ideas they had about the photos.
- Go through any unknown vocabulary and explain anything students still do not understand about time capsules.

Exercise 8

- Tell students to read the questions.
- Allow them plenty of time to read the article again and discuss their answers with a partner.
- Conduct a class discussion of the questions. Encourage students to explain their reasons.

EXTENSION Further questions you could ask: *Can you think of any disadvantages of putting objects in a time capsule?* (One problem is that technology changes quickly and it may not be possible for people in the future to play recordings, for example. Also recordings may decay over time.) *How long should a time capsule be left before opening it? Why?* (There will be different answers for public time capsules and those given as presents.)

Exercise 9

- Ask students to read the Grammar focus box on articles.
- If necessary, go through the uses of *a/an*, *the* and no article, using the examples which are given.
- Ask students to read the text again and decide which use each of the highlighted words shows. You could do the first one together as an example. *'The objects.'* How about use 3? No, because they are not general but specific ones. Use 2b? No, because this is plural, not one thing. Use 2a? Yes – 'The objects' refers back to 'objects' in the previous sentence so we have read about this before.
- Students work alone but check their answers with a partner.
- Go through the answers together, referring back to the Grammar focus box whenever necessary.

ANSWERS
Use 1 a school, a baby
Use 2a the objects, the container, the baby
Use 2b the history,
Use 3 People, newspapers, information

- Refer students to *Grammar reference* on p142. There are three more exercises here students can do for homework. See answers in next column.

Exercise 10

- Students read a website post about making a time capsule as a present and comments from people with suggestions about what objects to put in it.
- Tell them to complete the sentences with the correct article in each case. Sometimes they will not need an article and should complete the space with a cross (X).
- Students work alone on the task.
- Allow them to check their answers together in pairs. If they have different answers, they should refer to the Grammar focus box to decide which is correct.
- Go through the answers, eliciting why if possible.

ANSWERS
1 an 2 a 3 a 4 the 5 – 6 – 7 a 8 a 9 the
10 – 11 the 12 – 13 the

Exercise 11a

- Elicit how many objects they need to choose (six).
- Put students into small groups to do this task.
- Tell them to decide the focus of their time capsule. Is it about their town, country or the whole world this year?

EXTRA SUPPORT To simplify the task, write a list on the board of ten possible objects to choose from. (Suggestions: a newspaper, a map, recordings of TV programmes, news, current music, photos of famous people and details of why they are famous, money, technology such as a smartphone with instructions, books published this year, catalogues, receipts for things people often buy, all kinds of tickets, your personal diary for the year, photos of the people who made the capsule, a letter to the people who open it.)

FEEDBACK FOCUS (FOR AFTER 11C) Monitor the discussions, focusing on their use of articles. Note down any problems.

- Give them a time limit to the end of the activity so that all the groups finish at the same time.

EXTRA CHALLENGE Give fast finishers another suggestion from the list above so that they have to discuss if it might be better to include it and leave out one of their six chosen objects. Example: *What about including a photo of your group with a little bit of writing about each of you?*

- When all groups have made their decisions, give them time to decide how to present them to the class, i.e. which group member will present each object. Remind them to explain their reasons for choosing each object too.

Exercise 11b

- Groups present their six objects to the class.
- Ask listeners to make notes about the objects and reasons.
- After each presentation, invite questions from the class.

Exercise 11c

- Conduct a vote on which group has the best time capsule and why. Give that group a class round of applause.
- Do correction of errors with articles. Refer the students back to the Grammar focus box to decide why there is a mistake and how to correct it.

GRAMMAR REFERENCE ANSWERS

Exercise 1
1 a
2 a
3 a
4 an
5 an
6 a
7 a
8 an

Exercise 2
1 The
2 –
3 The
4 –
5 the
6 –
7 the
8 the

Exercise 3
1 a
2 the
3 an
4 a
5 an
6 the
7 the
8 The
9 A
10 the
11 the
12 –
13 the
14 –

Unit 5   93

Background note: The Guinness Book of World Records states the earliest time capsule was created by Thornwell Jacobs of Oglethorpe University, Atlanta USA in May 1940. It is the size of a room and will not be opened until 8113! In 1990 the International Time Capsule Society (ITSC) was set up to record details of all time capsules in the world.

5.2 It's all about the money

Goals
- Talk about money
- Talk about quantity

Lead-in
- Write *money* on the board.
- Put the students into pairs to brainstorm verbs which we use with the noun *money* (e.g. *raise, spend, save, earn, borrow, invest, waste, lose, make, steal, owe, need, lend*).
- Elicit verbs and make a mind map around the central word *money*. Ensure that they are pronouncing this word correctly /ˈmʌni/ so it rhymes with 'funny'.

Vocabulary & Speaking   money

Exercise 1
- Put students into pairs.
- Ask them to look at the sets of words about money and discuss the difference between them with their partner.
- Conduct a class discussion and explain the differences yourself if there is any confusion.

Exercise 2a
- Match the first question and response together to demonstrate the task if necessary.
- Encourage students to work together in pairs so that they can help each other with unknown words or phrases.
- Monitor carefully to hear any vocabulary they are having difficulty with.
- Go through the answers together. Focus on the words and phrases in bold and use concept questions to check that all students understand what they mean. Example: *If you borrow money, is that money yours or somebody else's? Are they giving the money to you as a gift?* Drill pronunciation of any difficult words.

WATCH OUT! The word *change*: students typically learn this as a verb meaning 'to make or become different'. In this lesson it is used as an uncountable noun which means 'coins rather than paper money'(see answer a). You could also point out that it can be a money verb meaning 'to exchange money for the same amount in different coins or notes', e.g. *Can you change this £10 note into two fives?* Or it can mean 'to exchange money into the money of another country', e.g. *I need to change these Euros into Dollars.*

ANSWERS
1 g   2 b   3 f   4 h   5 e   6 a   7 c   8 d

Exercise 2b
- Students work in pairs.
- Tell them to take turns to ask and answer the questions in exercise 2a.
- Allow plenty of time for this speaking practice.
- Conduct a class discussion. Ask if any of the students were surprised by their partner's answers. Elicit interesting answers.
- Correct any pronunciation mistakes you have noticed with the new vocabulary.

Grammar & Reading   quantifiers

Exercise 3
- Write on the board *a cashless society* and elicit that this means a society without cash. You could make a general comment that many countries around the world are starting to use other methods of payment instead of cash.
- Put students into pairs and tell them to think about any disadvantages of a cashless society that they can think of.
- Monitor and ask them to think about what they use cash for and what problems they might have if they didn't use cash. They can also think not only about themselves but other groups in society.
- Elicit some of the disadvantages they have thought of.

Exercise 4

Text summary: An article about cashless societies, taking Sweden as an example of a country where cash is used less and less. The article also discusses the use of mobile banking.

- Tell the students to read the article and find out whether the disadvantages they discussed are mentioned in it.
- Allow enough time for them to read the article carefully.
- Check which disadvantages they found in the article, together with any that they didn't find. You could ask whether they learned anything new from reading the article.

ANSWERS
Disadvantages mentioned in the text are:
Elderly people find it hard to use the new technology.
Small businesses have to pay bank charges when their customers pay by card.

Exercise 5
- Ask students to read questions 1–4 and answer them.
- Put them into pairs discuss their answers.
- Allow plenty of time to work on the task.
- Go through the answers together.

EXTENSION You could put students into small groups to discuss their answer and reasons for question 4.

EXTRA ACTIVITY Working in pairs, students find out how 'cashless' their partner's life is. Tell them to find out how often their partner pays in cash and how many cashless transactions their partner makes via computer or smart phone. This is an extension of exercise 2a but students have now read the article and have a different perspective on the discussion. It will be less repetitive if they are with a different partner to the one in exercise 2a.

ANSWERS

1. 1661 Sweden became the first country to use banknotes.
   110 The number of bank robberies in Sweden in 2008.
   16 The number of bank robberies in Sweden in 2011.
   20% Under 20% of Kenyans have a bank account.
   95% Over 95% of Kenyans have a mobile phone.
2. Elderly people (as they may need some help with the technology) and small businesses (as they have to pay a little money to the bank each time somebody pays them using a card).
3. It saves time (as they no longer need to travel long distances to pay a bill). There is less danger of being robbed as people carry less cash.
4. Students' own answers.

Exercise 6

- Write the noun *quantity* and elicit the meaning or a translation of the word. Teach the grammar word *quantifier* (= a word which describes the quantity of something.)
- If necessary, elicit the difference between countable nouns and uncountable nouns.
- Check that they understand they must find the example nouns in the text. Point out the example.
- Students work on this task alone, then check their answers with a partner.
- Go through the answers together.

ANSWERS

2	cash	9	businesses
3	countries	10	help
4	crime	11	notes
5	Kenyans	12	cash
6	time	13	benefits
7	people	14	change
8	money		

Exercise 7

- Ask students to read the Grammar focus box about quantifiers.
- They choose the correct option to complete the rules.
- Students work alone on the task.
- Go through the answers together. Ask concept questions as you go through the answers to check that all students understand the rules in the Grammar focus box. Example: *Show them a wallet with no cards and say 'I don't have some credit cards.' Is that sentence correct?* (No, because we usually use 'any' in negative sentences.)
- The Grammar box states *a few* and *a little* = a small amount. You should elicit which one we use with countable and which with uncountable nouns – refer students to exercise 6 if necessary.
- Also check that they understand the negative context of *too much/too many*. Example: *If I say 'I have too much work to do' does this mean that I have the right amount, or more or less than the right amount?* (more) *Is it a problem for me?* (Yes)
- Refer students to *Grammar reference* on p143. There are four more exercises here students can do for homework. See answers on p96.

ANSWERS

1	some	4	small
2	any	5	negative
3	can	6	positive

Exercise 8a

- Ask students to read and complete the text which consists of three responses to the article they read.
- They need to choose the correct option in each case.
- Students work on the task alone.
- Go through the answers together.

ANSWERS

1	a lot of	7	a few
2	much	8	some
3	enough	9	any
4	a lot of	10	a lot of
5	many	11	many
6	some	12	any

Exercise 8b

CRITICAL THINKING The students have already given their opinions in relation to living in a cashless society (exercise 5) but in this exercise they are asked to respond to other people's opinions and reasons which they may not have thought of before. It is good to point out that they are practising a valuable skill in their second language.

- Put students in pairs to discuss which of the three people they most agree with and why.
- Conduct a class discussion on the topic.

Exercise 9a

- Focus students' attention on the table and give them an example sentence of your own, using items from each column.
- Students work alone to write four true sentences about themselves.
- Monitor the accuracy of their sentences, especially 1) that they are using the right quantifiers for countable and uncountable nouns and 2) that they are correctly using the quantifiers in positive and negative sentences.

EXTRA SUPPORT You could help less confident students by eliciting some of the rules for quantifiers that they studied in exercise 7 before they start making sentences. Examples: *Which quantifiers can we use with the negative 'don't'?* (many, much, any, enough). *Which quantifiers can only be used with uncountable nouns?* (much, a little)

ANSWERS
Students' own answers.

Exercise 9b

- Put students into small groups. Ask them to read out their sentences to each other and compare them.
- Conduct a class discussion. Ask *Were any of the sentences very different or totally opposite? Did any of your group have very similar sentences?*

Exercise 10a

- Ask students to read the instruction carefully.
- At this point, it's a good idea to find out whether asking direct questions about money is acceptable or not in the students' culture. Point out that it can be a sensitive area to discuss. In Britain for example, people don't usually ask direct questions such as *How much do you earn?* or *How much do you pay each month on your mortgage?*

Unit 5   95

- Highlight that the survey is about *spending habits* not just about shopping (i.e. they can ask *What method of payment do you use for paying your rent/mortgage, school fees, electricity bills?* etc.).
- Remind them that they need to make three more questions so the survey has six questions in total.
- Put the students into pairs to write the questions.

EXTRA SUPPORT Encourage students who need extra support to use the sentences in exercise 9a as a basis for their questions.

- Monitor and check the questions they have written. Make sure they are correct grammatically and that they are acceptable to ask.

Exercise 10b

- Tell students to interview other members of the class. If it is a small class, they can interview all the students. Otherwise, you will need to divide the class into two or even four parts so that the interview stage is not too long.
- It is a good idea to give time for students to decide in their pairs how they are going to carry out the survey. For example, they could each survey half of the students or they could ask all the students three questions each. Remind them that they will need to make a note of the answers.
- You could set a time limit at the beginning of the activity or monitor carefully and set a time limit to the end of the activity so that they all finish asking questions at the same time.
- Ask students to sit together again in their original pairs.
- Now they have a few minutes to talk in their pairs and analyse the results of their survey. Focus their attention on the prompts to help them present the results to the class.

WATCH OUT! Elicit that these prompts are followed by the plural form of the verb, e.g. *A lot of us like … , Some of us spend …* . Students sometimes add a third person 's' but remind them that the prompts refer to 'us' so take the verb form they use with 'we'.

- Go round and monitor the pairs. Assist any students who are struggling.

EXTRA CHALLENGE For fast finishers, tell them that they should think about what the results tell us about the class. For example, *All of us have a credit card so we are all happy to pay for things on credit. A lot of us like shopping with other people. Perhaps this shows that we prefer to ask other people about things before we buy them.*

Exercise 10c

- Students present their results to the class.
- Note they will all have asked questions 1–3 so you could elicit the results of these questions from the class, rather than having each pair repeat them.
- As they are listening to the presentations, students could make notes of any results they find surprising or interesting.
- Conduct a class discussion of the presentations. Praise good, clear presentations with accurate use of the quantifiers.
- Conduct any necessary error correction.

GRAMMAR REFERENCE ANSWERS

Exercise 1
1. any
2. any
3. any
4. some
5. some
6. any

Exercise 2
1. a lot of
2. a few
3. a little
4. a lot of
5. a few
6. a lot of

Exercise 3
1. don't have enough
2. don't keep too much
3. are too many
4. gets too much/hasn't got enough
5. aren't enough

Exercise 4
1. A lot
2. enough
3. any
4. a lot of
5. a little
6. much
7. lots of
8. too much
9. some

5.3 Vocabulary and skills development

Goals
- Understand linkers for reason and result
- Understand and use suffixes

Reading understanding linkers for reason and result

Lead-in
- Ask students: *Do you think you could live with fewer possessions than you have now? Would your life be better or worse?*
- Put them into pairs to discuss these questions.
- Conduct a whole class discussion. Encourage students to give reasons for their opinions. Remember there is no right or wrong answer.

Exercise 1
- Ask students to read the quotation and think about the answers to the questions.
- Put them in pairs to discuss their answers.
- Conduct a class discussion. You could contrast this quotation with the title of the previous lesson 'It's all about the money'.

ANSWERS
Students' own answers

Exercise 2a
- The focus of this part of the lesson is on linkers and how they help us to read a text more easily.
- Two key words the students will need are *reason* and *result* so check that they understand these first. Elicit that the reason comes before an action and the result is what happens after an action.
- Tell students to read the Unlock the code box.
- When they have read it, tell them to cover the box. Ask them or write on the board 'When you read "because" does this link to the reason or result?' Ask them questions about the other linkers.

EXTRA CHALLENGE With a strong group you could tell them to take turns to test each other in pairs by asking the question *What does X link to?* (replacing X with a different linker each time).

WATCH OUT! It seems illogical but *For this reason* does not link to the reason for the action but rather to the result. Example: *My hair was too long. For this reason I went to the hairdresser.* Ask students to try replacing this phrase with other linkers to show that it is similar in meaning to *so, therefore* and *as a result*.

Exercise 2b
- Ask students to read sentences 1–4.
- They need to choose the correct linkers in each sentence. There are always two correct and one incorrect.
- Students work on this task alone, then check their answers in pairs.
- Go through the answers together.

ANSWERS
1 So, Therefore
2 since, as
3 because, since
4 For this reason, As a result

Exercise 2c
- Ensure students understand the three parts to this task. You can highlight them in the example which has been done for them.
- Students work on this task alone.
- Go through the answers together.

EXTENSION Ask the students how you could write sentence 1, keeping the same meaning but using *because*. Tell them they may need to change some words around. If they are having difficulty, give them the first two words: *She bought a new sofa because her sofa was getting old.* Do the same with sentence 2, *I sold the jacket because I hardly ever wore it and I needed some money.* Ask *Which other linkers could we use in the place of 'because' with the same meaning?* (as, since) Ask students to do the same with sentence 3 but this time choose a linker of result: *They didn't accept cards. As a result/so/for this reason/therefore we paid in cash.* This exercise helps students to practise changing the order of sentences with reason or result in them.

ANSWERS
1 Linker: so
  Reason: Her sofa was getting old
  Result: she bought a new one.
2 Linker: Therefore,
  Reason: I hardly ever wore the jacket and I needed some money.
  Result: I sold it.
3 Linker: because
  Reason: they didn't accept cards.
  Result: We paid in cash

Exercise 3a

Text summary: An article about a couple who decided to choose a minimalist lifestyle, i.e. to live with fewer possessions. The wife describes why and how they got rid of unwanted things and how their life has changed as a result.

- Ask students to read the text and find eight linkers. They need to circle the linker and, as in exercise 2b, underline the reason and put a dotted line under the result.
- Students work alone on the task.
- Allow plenty of time but remind them that they do not need to understand the whole text, just focus on the linkers and how the writer has used them.
- Encourage them to check their answers with a partner.
- Go through the answers together.

ANSWERS
Linker: *For this reason*
Reason: Possessions can take up a lot of space … we might worry about security
Result: more and more people are choosing a 'minimalist lifestyle'
Linker: *So*
Reason: our flat was full of stuff … couldn't find anything … couldn't close the cupboards
Result: we went minimalist
Linker: *As a result*
Reason: we sold … we hardly ever used
Result: our book collection went from 300 down to six … we gave away … and I even sold …
Linker: *as*
Reason: my wardrobe is the size of a suitcase
Result: Choosing clothes in the morning is easy
Linker: *As a result*
Reason: when I buy something I ask myself, 'Do I need this?'
Result: I've saved lots of money
Linker: *because*
Reason: they think our lifestyle isn't enjoyable any more
Result: Others worry
Linker: *Therefore*
Reason: We have more time now for important things
Result: we're happier than before
Linker: *since*
Reason: there aren't too many of them
Result: I love my possessions more

Exercise 3b
- Tell students to read the questions.
- Students work alone on this task and write the answers to the questions.
- Allow them to check in pairs if you wish.
- Go through the answers together.
- Check that all students understand the meaning of *minimalist* /ˈmɪnɪməlɪst/ and can pronounce it.

Unit 5   97

- In question 2, *get rid of* is a useful three part phrasal verb so check they fully understand the meaning. Example: *How can you get rid of something you don't want?* (give it away, sell it, throw it away, etc.) Ask: *When was the last time you got rid of something? What was it and why?*

ANSWERS
1 Because their flat was too full. They couldn't find anything and they couldn't close the cupboards or drawers.
2 Because they hardly ever used them.
3 Because she asks herself 'Do I need this?'
4 Because they think their life isn't enjoyable any more.
5 Because they have more time for important things, like family and travelling.
6 Because there aren't too many of them and she uses everything she has.

Exercise 4

- Put students into small groups to discuss what they think about the four decisions Rachel made.
- When they have discussed in their groups, elicit some opinions from the class. Encourage them to try to explain their reasons.
- Praise the accurate use of *because*, *so* and any other linkers they use in this exercise.

ANSWERS
Students' own answers

Vocabulary & Listening suffixes

Exercise 5a

- Tell students to read about suffixes in the Vocabulary focus box.
- Check that they understand that the suffixes change the words grammatically into a different part of the word family. Use the example *enjoy* in the box to show this.
- Elicit the verb form of *arrangement* (arrange), and the noun form of the adjective *beautiful* (beauty).

Exercise 5b

- Ask students to complete the table by adding a suffix to each verb or noun/verb and writing the new word in the next column. Elicit the first answer from the class as a demonstration if you wish.
- Remind them that when they have completed the table they should find the words in the article to check their answers.
- Students work on this task alone. Then go through the answers together.

ANSWERS
1 possession
2 decision
3 computer
4 equipment
5 stressful
6 comfortable
7 enjoyable
8 digital

Exercise 6

- Tell students to add the new nouns and adjectives (1-8) from exercise 5b to the suffix table.
- Tell them to add more words they know which have these suffixes. They could work with a partner on this task.

- Go through the table together checking the words from exercise 5b first. Make sure students are pronouncing these words well, especially in terms of word stress.

PRONUNCIATION You can point out that the suffix is never the stressed part of the word. This is an important pattern to know.

- Now check the other words which students have thought of. Are they in the correct column? Are they spelt correctly? Can the students pronounce them? Encourage them to peer teach the meanings of any words they added.

ANSWERS
-ment: equipment; *-ion*: possession, decision; *-er*: computer; *-ful*: stressful; *-al*: digital; *-able*: comfortable, enjoyable

DICTIONARY SKILLS Encourage students to use dictionaries for unknown words. Remind them that good dictionaries will tell them what part of speech a word is (noun, verb, adjective, etc.) which is essential information. Over time they will be able to decide which part of speech a word is by noticing the suffix.

Exercise 7a 5.4

Audio summary: A conversation between a couple, discussing objects they could get rid of.

- Tell students to think about how they would describe the three objects in the photos.
- Tell them that they are going to hear a couple discussing which things to get rid of. Tell them to tick the objects they keep.
- Play track 5.4.
- Go through the answers together. Ask students to try to remember the reasons for keeping or getting rid of the items.

EXTENSION Ask if students can remember: Thinking about the two objects they agree to get rid of – how are they going to do it? (give away the bag, sell the e-book reader)

ANSWERS
Keep: the Japanese knife (It's essential … No, I'm not getting rid of that.)

AUDIOSCRIPT 5.4
F I've got some things here that I don't think we really need. Maybe we could get rid of them?
M Like what?
F Well, like this Japanese knife that you bought. It takes up so much space in the drawer, and it's not very useful.
M Not very useful? It's essential!
F Essential for what?
M For chopping vegetables!
F Erm … how often do you chop vegetables?
M Not very often.
F Exactly! Let's get rid of it.
M Ooh no … I'm not getting rid of that.
F Oh. OK then. And then there's this bag of yours.
M Keep it. It was a present from my mother.
F But you never use it.
M You never know … one day I might.
F I don't think so. It isn't suitable for work … and it isn't …
M Keep it. It's quite fashionable, you know.
F I … yes, it's fashionable, but, it isn't really … well, it isn't really 'you', is it?

M But it'll be a disappointment to her if we throw it away.
F She'll never know. Anyway, I'm not going to throw it away. We can give it to somebody. Somebody will like it.
M Fine.
F Now, what about this e-book reader? We don't use it any more.
M You're not throwing that away. It cost us a lot of money.
F We can't keep everything, you know! We've got a newer model now, remember? We don't need this old one.
M But it's in very good condition.
F Well, that's fine. We can sell it. Get some money for it. I'll put it on eBay tomorrow. I'm sure we'll get a buyer for it.
M Alright then.

Exercise 7b
- Ask students to remember which object each statement 1–7 is describing.
- Students can work alone or in pairs on this task.
- They should write a, b or c next to each statement.

Exercise 7c 5.4
- Tell students that they're going to hear the discussion again so that they can check their answers.
- Play track 5.4 again.
- Check that they all heard all the answers.

ANSWERS
1 b   2 c   3 a   4 c   5 a   6 b   7 b

Exercise 7d
- Ask students to add the words in bold to the table in exercise 6.
- They are building up a number of examples of each of the suffixes.
- You could take this opportunity to drill the pronunciation of *comfortable* and *fashionable* again.

ANSWERS
-ment: disappointment; *-ion*: condition; *-er*: buyer; *-ful*: useful; *-al*: essential; *-able*: suitable, fashionable

Exercise 8a
- Tell students to read questions 1–5 and complete them with the correct form of the words in brackets, using suffixes.
- Students work on this task individually.
- If you wish, ask them to check their answers in pairs (but make sure they don't ask and answer them yet).
- Go through the answers together.

ANSWERS
1 disappointment
2 fashionable
3 suitable
4 possessions
5 decisions

Exercise 8b
- In pairs, students take turns to ask and answer the questions.
- Monitor their conversations and note any pronunciation difficulties with the words with suffixes.
- Conduct class feedback and also pronunciation practice if necessary.

5.4 Speaking and writing

Goals
- Explain words you don't know
- Write an email to return an online product

Lead-in
- With books closed, ask the class *Have you ever been in a situation when you needed a certain word in English but you didn't know it and you didn't have a dictionary?*
- Elicit any experiences. *What was the situation? What word did they need and why? How did they feel? What did they do?*

Listening & Speaking   explaining words you don't know

Exercise 1a
- Focus students' attention on the photos.
- Put students into pairs to talk about the photos and name the objects. Tell them not to worry if they don't know the English words for all of the items.
- Don't tell them the words for the items now. You can tell them that they will find out from the listening.

ANSWERS
a light bulb   b mosquito repellent plug   c matches
d candles   e headphones   f voice recorder

Exercise 1b
- Ask students to read the instruction.
- Tell them to discuss with their partner different things they can do in this situation.
- Elicit suggestions from the class.

POSSIBLE ANSWERS
Use a dictionary or translation app on your phone.
Ask someone who knows the language well for the name of the thing.
Describe the thing carefully, including saying what it is for.
Draw a picture of it or mime it.

Exercise 2 5.5

Audio summary: Conversations in shops. Three conversations in three different shops with different customers each time. Each customer needs a specific item but cannot remember/doesn't know the word in English.

- Tell students that they are going to hear three different conversations in shops.
- The first time they listen, they need to try to understand which photo from exercise 1a matches the object the customer wants to buy.
- Play track 5.5.
- Go through the answers, eliciting first the correct photo and then the name of the object.

ANSWERS
1 (photo f) a voice recorder
2 (photo d) candles
3 (photo b) a mosquito repellent plug

Unit 5   99

AUDIOSCRIPT 5.5
Conversation 1
SA1 Hi, can I help you?
C1 Yes, I hope so … I'm looking for … erm … one of those little machines … I don't know the name … but, er, you use it to record things.
SA How big is it?
C1 Oh, er, it's quite small. It fits in your hand or your pocket. It looks like a mobile phone.
SA Oh, yes, I know what you mean. It's called a voice recorder. You use it for recording meetings and interviews and things?
C1 Exactly! That's what I'm looking for! I'm a student, you see, and I want to record my lessons with it.
SA Ah yes. Good idea, yes … but, no, I'm afraid we don't sell them here. Why don't you try the electronics store around the corner? They probably sell them.
C1 OK. I will do. Thanks!
Conversation 2
SA2 Morning.
C2 Morning.
SA Can I help you? Are you looking for anything in particular?
C2 Yes, erm, do you sell er, Ah … what's the word? Sorry … I've forgotten the word in English. Er … They make light.
SA2 Do you mean a light bulb, an electric light bulb?
C2 No, no, no. It's not electric. It's … Ah, what's it called!? It's long and thin, like a stick and you burn it and it gives light. You need them when there is no electricity.
SA Ah, you mean a candle!
C2 Yes, a candle! Of course!
SA2 Yes, we do. They're over there on the left, next to the matches.
C2 Thank you very much.
SA2 You're welcome.
Conversation 3
C3 Excuse me. Can you help me? I've got a problem with, you know, with mosquitoes in the apartment where I'm staying.
SA3 Oh yes, it's a very bad time of year for mosquitoes!
C3 Yes. I'm look for something … I don't know the word in English. It's a thing which you put into the wall, you know. You plug it into the electricity point and the mosquitoes don't like it and they go away. Do you know what I mean?
SA3 Yes, yes, I do. A mosquito repellent plug. Yes, we do have those. If you'd like to follow me, I'll show you what've got.
C3 Great. Thank you.

Exercise 3a 5.6

- Ask students to match one sentence beginning 1–9 with a suitable ending a–i. All of the sentences come from the conversations they have just heard.
- Students work on this task alone.
- Tell them to check their answers with a partner. Then listen to the track again and check their answers.
- Play track 5.6 again.
- Confirm any answers they may have missed.
- **WATCH OUT!** A common error students make is to ask: *How is it called?* or *I don't know how it is called in English*. Point out clearly that we do not use 'how' but instead we use 'what'

with 'called'. This is similar to asking: *What is the name of this in English?* (It is correct to ask: *How do you say it in English?*)

ANSWERS
1 b 2 c 3 a 4 i 5 h 6 d 7 f 8 g 9 e

AUDIOSCRIPT 5.6 & 5.7
1 You use it to record things.
2 It looks like a mobile phone.
3 Exactly! That's what I'm looking for!
4 I've forgotten the word in English.
5 What's it called?
6 It's long and thin, like a stick.
7 I don't know the word in English.
8 It's a thing which you put into the wall.
9 Do you know what I mean?

Exercise 3b 5.7
- Ask students to repeat the phrases to ensure they have good pronunciation.
- Play track 5.7 more than once if necessary, pausing whenever you need to. It is important that the students have clear, natural pronunciation of these useful phrases.

Exercise 4
- Put students in pairs.
- Give them time to practise all the conversations, taking both roles.
- If you feel that there are still some pronunciation problems, correct them with the class, then re-pair the students so they are working with someone different and ask them to do the exercise again.

Exercise 5
- Focus students' attention on the Language for speaking box.
- Also remind them of the work they did in lesson 5.1 on adjectives to describe things. In pairs they could try to remember adjectives for size, shape, material, colour and weight. Elicit the phrase we use to describe material: *It's made of …*.
- Now tell students to take turns to describe one of the other objects in exercise 1a so that their partner can identify it.
- Give them enough time to describe one or two objects.
- Monitor to ensure they are using some of the phrases and that they are correct.

EXTRA CHALLENGE You could ask students to have a conversation similar to one of the ones they have just heard where they are asking for one of the objects in a shop.

- Conduct a class discussion about how easy or difficult it was to describe the object. *Which phrases were most helpful? Which phrases helped your partner to guess the object?*

SMART COMMUNICATION In many cases, the most important thing about an object you may need is what it is used for. If you don't know or remember the word but you don't have time to describe the object in detail, start by explaining what the object is for: *You use it to …* and *It's a thing that/which you use to …* This is often enough to get your message across.

Exercise 6

- Put students into pairs of one Student A and one Student B.
- Tell Student As to turn to page 127 and Student Bs to look at page 132.
- They need to have a shop conversation like they heard in the recording.

FEEDBACK FOCUS Monitor their discussions and focus on how clearly the customer explains which item he/she wants. Make a note of any students who use the checking and confirming phrases well.

- When they have finished the task, give feedback on good use of the phrases, including the checking and confirming phrases.

EXTRA ACTIVITY You could give each student a photo of an object you think they will not know the English word for (cut up an old catalogue or print some images from the internet). They should memorize the object and then give the photo back to you.
Set up a whole class or small group mingle activity where they need to explain their object to as many people as possible within a time limit, e.g. 10 minutes. They can count a conversation as a success if the other person says *OK, I know what you mean* (as the listener probably won't know what the object is called either). If someone does not know, they can give up and move on to another student.
Before they start, remind them to use the phrases from the Language for speaking box. When they have finished, find out who was the most successful. They can translate the words for the objects for homework and share them during the next lesson if they wish.

Reading & Writing email (3): returning an online product

Exercise 7

- Put students into pairs to discuss the question with their partner.
- When they have had enough time, get all the students' attention and elicit experiences from the class.
- Write reasons for returning an object in a list on the board.

POSSIBLE ANSWERS
Reasons for returning an item:
It is faulty (damaged, doesn't work).
It is the wrong model, colour, size etc.
A part is missing. The order is not complete.
It is not acceptable quality.

Exercise 8

- Tell students that they are going to read two emails about products bought online.
- Ask them to read the questions and find the answers in the two emails below.
- Allow enough time for students to read through the emails although they do not need to read in detail to answer these questions.
- Go through the answers together.
- Elicit or teach *a refund* /ˈriːfʌnd/ (= you receive the money back that you spent on the object) and *a replacement* (= you receive another object to replace the one they sent you – this could be the same or a different colour/model etc. as you require). Drill pronunciation if you wish.

ANSWERS
1 A The colour and shape of the watch are completely different from the photo on the website, and he didn't get a presentation box.
   B The leather is very thin and there isn't room for many coins.
2 A He wants the seller to send the correct watch and a presentation box.
   B She wants to return the purse and get a refund.

Exercise 9

- Tell students to read the instruction and the functions 1–4.
- They need to match each highlighted word in the text with one of the functions. You could do the first one as a demonstration together. *Which function is 'I recently ordered'?*
- Students work alone on this task. Then go through the answers together.

ANSWERS
1 I recently ordered
   I ordered
2 It is completely different from the photo on the website.
   I didn't receive the box.
   I'm afraid I'm not happy with it because …
3 Could you please send me …
   As a result I'd like to return/get a refund.
4 Yours faithfully
   Many thanks

Exercise 10

- Tell students that they are going to learn about punctuation. Elicit what this means then tell them that the focus is on commas.
- Tell them to read the Language for writing box about commas.
- When they have read the information, they should read Fabiola's email again and find the three mistakes she has made when using commas.
- Students work alone on this task.
- Go through the answers together and elicit the corrections. (In each case the comma should be a full stop or it could be a linker – see answers below). Point out that the comma after 'Also' is correct as explained in rule 2 in the Language for writing box.

PRONUNCIATION You could demonstrate that when reading aloud, usually where there is a comma, there is a pause, e.g. *Also, the website says*. Of course, this lesson focuses on writing but pauses are important when speaking and this is a useful aspect of pronunciation to know and practise, particularly if any students need to give presentations or speeches in their work life or as part of their studies.

ANSWERS
I ordered a purse from your website. It arrived yesterday but I'm afraid I'm not happy with it because the leather is very thin. I think it's going to break very quickly. Also, there isn't room for many coins.

Exercise 11a

- Tell students to read the four questions in the bullet points.

Unit 5   101

EXTRA ACTIVITY Tell students to think about what they need to include in this email and write questions about it. Give an example: *What product did I buy online?* They could think of questions in pairs.

STUDY TIP Point out that thinking about what questions the piece of writing will answer is a valuable technique to use when planning for writing.

- Encourage them to make notes relating to the four questions first. Assist students who find it difficult to use their imagination.
- When they start writing their emails, give them plenty of time. They can use the example emails as models for their writing.

EXTRA CHALLENGE Tell stronger students to cover the example emails and just use the phrases from exercise 9 to structure their email. You could also tell them that they should include linkers for reason and result to help the reader understand the email more easily.

- Monitor all students' writing carefully and notice how far they are in the exercise.
- Encourage all students to check that any commas they have used are in the right place. They can also check their spelling now.

Exercise 11b

- Put students into pairs and tell them to swap their emails.
- Ask them to read their partner's email then answer the questions in 11b.
- Tell them to share these answers with their partner. Also, they should say whether they think the email is clear and makes a good impression. If there is time, they can tell their partner anything they particularly liked about the email.
- Collect the emails to mark and give feedback or do correction at the beginning of the next lesson.

5.5 Video

The Dubai Mall

VIDEOSCRIPT

Dubai is a wealthy city. When it first became part of the independent United Arab Emirates, most of this money came from oil.
But Dubai didn't have as much oil as its neighbours so it concentrated on trade and finance. This policy has made the city an international centre of business and commerce. This economic success has also made Dubai a very popular tourist destination.
Tourists come here to see buildings like the Burj Al Arab – the only 7-star hotel in the world – and the Burj Khalifa – the world's tallest structure.
But the majority of tourists come for the shopping. The city's shopping centres are some of its most popular tourist attractions.
Dubai Mall, at the base of the Burj Khalifa, is the largest shopping centre in the world.
It has 1,200 shops and attracts more than 750,000 visitors every week.
Consumers can buy almost anything here. There are a lot of clothes shops, gadget shops and some fantastic department stores.
But the Dubai Mall doesn't just sell consumer goods; it sells a whole shopping experience.
You can find many of these shops in other major cities, but only Dubai's malls offer so many other attractions. This is the secret to Dubai's success as a shopping destination.
Dubai is a very hot country, so people often spend a lot of their time in these air-conditioned malls. And they don't just come here to shop, they come here to socialise too.
The Dubai Mall is also a centre of leisure and entertainment. In fact, some of the city's most popular tourist attractions are based here.
This is the mall's Dubai Aquarium.
The mall uses it for its incredible collection of 140 types of sea creatures.
Dubai Mall also has the best in multimedia entertainment. It has got 22 cinema screens and in Sega Republic, there are 14 exciting attractions with more than 170 games.
There's an Olympic-sized ice rink, too. It's in the middle of the complex. People come here to skate and to cool down.
Dubai Mall is open late, so many visitors come here in the evening. They eat, meet friends and watch the mall's world-famous fountain show.
It's easy to see why the Dubai Mall is such a popular tourist destination.

VIDEO ANSWERS

Exercise 4
1 trade and finance
2 the shopping
3 in the world
4 it's very hot outside
5 the multimedia centre
6 the ice rink
7 aquarium
8 fountain show

Review

ANSWERS

Exercise 1a
1 a few 2 some 3 a 4 – 5 a 6 a 7 some
8 the 9 – 10 the 11 the 12 the 13 a 14 –
15 lots of 16 the 17 – 18 the

Exercise 2 5.8
1 amazing
2 heavy
3 valuable
4 gold
5 light

AUDIOSCRIPT 5.8

1 large	tiny	amazing	thin
2 heavy	pale grey	blue	dark brown
3 metal	valuable	leather	plastic
4 comfortable	useful	gold	ordinary
5 antique	brand new	old	light

Exercise 3a
1 rent
2 spend
3 saving
4 wallet/purse
5 amount

Exercise 4a
1 -able
2 -ful
3 -ment
4 -able
5 -al
6 -ial
7 -ment
8 -able

Exercise 5b 5.9
1 called
2 forgotten
3 name
4 use
5 to
6 made of
7 know what

AUDIOSCRIPT 5.9

A I'm making a pizza. I need a … er, what's it called? Oh, I've forgotten the name in English. You use it to cut cheese into very small pieces.
B A knife?
A No. It's made of metal, and you move the cheese up and down against it. Do you know what I mean?
B A grater!

Unit 5 103

6 People

Unit overview

Language input

Making comparisons (CB p57)	• *People think introverts are not as sociable as extroverts.* • *The newest ideas often come from introverts.* • *Are you happier in one-to-one situations than in a group?*
Present perfect simple and past simple (CB p58)	• *Saroo lost his mother when he was five.* • *He has found his mother.* • *Have you ever missed your stop?*
Present perfect simple with *just*, *already* and *yet* (CB p62)	• *I've just got here.* • *Winter has already arrived in Moscow!* • *Have you seen any good matches yet?*
Grammar reference (CB pp144–5)	

Vocabulary development

Adjectives for describing character (CB p56)	• *tidy, honest, creative …*
Family (CB p58)	• *twins, father-in-law, cousin …* • *get married, get engaged …*
Adjective prefixes (CB p61)	• *unnecessary, impolite, disorganized …*

Skills development

Listening: Recognizing linkers in fast speech (CB p60)

Writing: Responding to news on social media (CB p62)

Speaking: Giving and responding to news (CB p63)

Video

Documentary: Nettlebed (Coursebook DVD & CB p64)

Vox pops (Coursebook DVD & TG p261)

More materials

Workbook	• Language practice for vocabulary, pronunciation, grammar, writing and speaking • Reading for pleasure • Review: Units 5 & 6
Photocopiable activities	• Grammar: Comparisons (TG p213 & TSRD) • Vocabulary: Speed friendships (TG p231 & TSRD) • Communication: Dominoes (TG p249 & TSRD)
Tests	• Unit 6 test (TSRD) • Progress test: Units 4–6
Unit 6 wordlist (TSRD)	

6.1 The quiet revolution

Goals
- Describe character
- Talk about similarities and differences

Lead-in
- Put an image of a famous person you think all the students will know on the board or just write his/her name, e.g. *Barack Obama, David Beckham*.
- Give students questions to discuss in pairs: *What do you know about this person? What do you think of him?*
- Monitor carefully and note down any adjectives for describing character that they use.
- Write these words on the board and elicit that they are adjectives. Ask *What do these adjectives describe?* (character) The students may use the word *personality* and this is fine because these words are often used interchangeably.

Vocabulary & Reading adjectives for describing character

Exercise 1a
- Tell students to read the descriptions 1–10 and match each one to one of the adjectives in the box.
- **WATCH OUT!** In description 2 there is an adjective *nervous* which is a false friend in many languages. If necessary, check that they know this does not mean *angry*.
- Put students into pairs to do the task.
- **EXTRA SUPPORT** The students will be able to peer explain some of the unknown vocabulary but if good dictionaries are available, ask them to look up words neither of them knows.
- Go through the answers together. Drill the pronunciation of the words, including word stress.

Exercise 1b
- Tell students to work in pairs. One person reads out half of the questions from exercise 1 and the other, with book closed, says the adjectives. Then they swap roles.

ANSWERS
1 quiet /ˈkwaɪət/
2 shy /ʃaɪ/
3 sociable /ˈsəʊʃəbl/
4 creative /kriˈeɪtɪv/
5 tidy /ˈtaɪdi/
6 patient /ˈpeɪʃnt/
7 confident /ˈkɒnfɪdənt/
8 clever/smart /ˈklevə/ /smɑːt/
9 honest /ˈɒnɪst/
10 lazy /ˈleɪzi/

Exercise 2
- Students read words a–d then find an adjective from exercise 1 which is the opposite.
- Go through the answers. Again, drill these new words.

ANSWERS
A clever/smart B lazy C sociable D tidy

Exercise 3 6.1
> **Audio summary:** Three individual speakers talk about the character of a person they know.

- Tell students that they are going to hear three different speakers describing somebody they know.
- The students' task is to find two adjectives from exercises 1 and 2 which describe each person (Max, Lena and Nico). Note: The speakers don't use these adjectives. It isn't an exercise in hearing the words but in understanding which words apply to each person, based on the description.
- Play track 6.1.
- Put students into pairs to check their answers. Encourage them to give evidence for their answers from the recording, e.g. *I think Lena is … because her sister said …* .
- Go through the answers together.

ANSWERS
Max: tidy, honest
Lena: clever/smart, sociable
Nico: creative, hard-working

AUDIOSCRIPT 6.1
Speaker 1
I share a flat with another student called Max. The thing about Max is that he likes everything to be in the correct place. So he always washes up straight after eating, puts the dishes straight back in the cupboard, never leaves anything on the floor … you know. He even puts his books in alphabetical order in the bookcase! The other thing about Max is that he never, ever tells a lie. So for example, if he doesn't like something I'm wearing, he'll tell me he doesn't like it. But then when he says he likes something I know he really means it.
Speaker 2
My younger sister Lena's in her last year at school. She's one of those people who's good at everything. She gets top marks in most of her subjects. And the thing is, she doesn't even try very hard. I'm not saying she's lazy – she does work, but you know, she's just a natural. She's also a real people person. She's always at parties or out with her friends. Sometimes I don't see her for days!
Speaker 3
I run a business with a guy called Nico. It's a kitchen design business. Nico's the one who does the designs. He always comes up with really interesting and unusual ideas. Our kitchens are very different from most kitchens – that's why our customers are so happy with what we do. And Nico works very long hours too – we both do – we rarely leave the office before seven or eight o'clock at night. But, you know, in these difficult economic times, we feel lucky to have so much work, so of course we don't mind putting in the hours.

Exercise 4a
- Ask students to think of a person they know well.
- Tell them to write down some adjectives from the lesson which apply to his/her character. Tell them they will need to describe their person to another student, NOT using these character adjectives.
- Students work alone on the task.

ANSWERS
Students' own answers

EXTRA SUPPORT Students who need extra support will benefit from planning time. Tell them they can make notes about the person they are going to describe but not write a full description. Also, make the task more specific if necessary, e.g. *Choose two adjectives*.

Unit 6   105

EXTRA CHALLENGE Stronger students should practise supporting what they say with examples.

Exercise 4b

- Put students into pairs.
- Tell them to take turns to describe their person.
- The student who is listening needs to say which adjectives apply to that person. They may ask questions to get extra information to help them decide.
- Conduct a class discussion. Ask *Did your partner describe their person well, so you could guess the adjective?* Elicit good examples from the class.

EXTRA ACTIVITY You could provide pictures of famous people for the students to look at and discuss what kind of character they think they have and why.

Exercise 5a

- Write *introvert* and *extrovert* on the board and ask if any of the students know the meaning. If so, they could give an example of typical behaviour of these kinds of people.
- Ask the students to read the definition and the sentences.
- They should think about the sentences alone and decide whether they think they are true.
- Conduct a class discussion. Encourage students to give reasons why they think the sentences may/may not be true.

> **Background note:** Susan Cain (who herself is an introvert) was a corporate lawyer before becoming a writer. Her book *Quiet: The Power of Introverts in A World That Can't Stop Talking*, published in 2012, became a New York Times best seller and has been translated into over 35 languages.

Exercise 5b

> **Text summary:** An article about the qualities of introverts, based upon the findings of Susan Cain in her book *Quiet*.

- Tell students to read the article and find out whether the sentences in exercise 5a are true.
- Give them plenty of time to read the article and find the answers.
- Go through the answers together.

ANSWERS
1 false – 'a third to half of us are introverts'
2 false – 'they (introverts) are just as confident as extroverts'
3 false – they are happier to spend time alone, creating ideas or solving problems.

Exercise 6a

- Check that students understand the three headings a, b and c.
- Allow plenty of time for students to make notes.
- Elicit ideas from the class.

Exercise 6b

- Students have a chance to think about the ideas in the article and express opinions about them.

CRITICAL THINKING You could ask the students to do this in stages: reflect on what they have read, link it to their own experience and apply the information they have got from it.

Reflect *Have you ever thought about this before? What information in the article was new to you?*
Link to experience *Do you know anybody who is an introvert? If so, do they fit the characteristics in the article? Does this make you think the ideas in the article are true or not?*
Apply the information *The last paragraph says that leaders who have read the book 'Quiet' are changing their practices. What can they do to make life better for introverts?*

ANSWERS
a They are just as confident as extroverts.
  They are quieter than extroverts.
  They are sociable but prefer being with close friends or family.
  They enjoy spending time alone.
b They need time to think carefully before they speak or act.
  Schools, universities and workplaces are less interested in them.
  50% of a student's grade is based on speaking well in class.
  Job adverts often ask for 'good communication skills'.
c They are good at creating new and unusual ideas, and solving problems.

Grammar & Speaking making comparisons

Exercise 7a

- Check students know the meaning of *comparative* and *superlative* but don't go through the rules for making comparisons as they are going to study this in exercise 7b.
- Point out that each of these adjectives can be found in the article, but in a different form. They should write down how it appears in the article.
- Give them plenty of time to read the text again to find the words in comparative and superlative forms.
- Elicit the answers and write them on the board.

ANSWERS
quieter
the newest
the most unusual
happier
less interested
not as/just as confident as

Exercise 7b

- Ask students to read the Grammar focus box about making comparisons and allow them plenty of time for this.
- Tell them that the forms they found in exercise 7a now need to be added in the correct place in the Grammar focus box because they are the examples of the rules.
- Students work alone or in pairs on this task.
- Go through the answers together.
- At this point, ask the students if they have questions about any of the grammar rules and deal with any confusion.

ANSWERS
1 quieter
2 happier
3 less interested
4 newest
5 most unusual

- Refer students to *Grammar reference* on p144. There are three more exercises here students can do for homework. See answers in next column.

EXTRA ACTIVITY You could write the following sentences on the board to test their understanding. Each sentence has a mistake and they need to find and correct it.
a) She's more quieter than her sister. (*quieter* – already comparative because it has *-er* ending so *more* is not needed.)
b) The weather was badder than last summer. (*bad* is an irregular adjective so you need *worse*.)
c) He's the happyest person I know. (You need to change the spelling to *happiest*.)
d) Alex is more creative that Jonathan. (Students quite often use *that* or *then* instead of *than*.)

Pronunciation *as* and *than*

Exercise 8a 6.2
- Check that students understand this is a dictation exercise.
- Play track 6.2.
- Students write down the four sentences. Play the track again if necessary, pausing when you need to.
- Check the sentences and elicit that *as* and *than* are not pronounced fully in the sentences. *Than* is pronounced /ðən/ and *as* is pronounced /əz/. They have already heard the schwa sound in previous lessons. You can elicit that these are weak forms, which occur when we speak quickly.

ANSWERS/AUDIOSCRIPT 6.2 & 6.3
1 My sister's cleverer than me.
2 My brother isn't as confident as my sister.
3 I'm taller than my parents.
4 My youngest brother isn't as lazy as I am.

Exercise 8b 6.3
- Tell students to focus on getting the rhythm right as they say the sentences.
- Play track 6.3 for them to listen and repeat. You may need to play it several times to ensure natural pronunciation.

Exercise 9a
- Tell students that they are going to find out whether their partner is an introvert, an extrovert or an ambivert. Elicit what they think 'ambivert' means. (= a person who has characteristics from both kinds of character, ambi- as a prefix means both, e.g. *ambidextrous*)

WATCH OUT! Ambivert is a technical term which even most native speakers would not know or use. If a student thinks he is an ambivert, it is better to say *I'm a bit of both*.

- Ask students to read the questionnaire and complete it using the adjectives in brackets. Point out that sometimes they also need to add *as* or *more*.
- Students work alone on the task.
- Go through the answers together.

ANSWERS
1 happier
2 as interested
3 easier
4 as enjoyable
5 better
6 as confident
7 more patient
8 closest
9 as loud
10 slower

Exercise 9b
- Tell students to do the questionnaire with a partner. They should make a note of their partner's answers.
- Monitor carefully and ensure they are collecting their partners' answers, not their own.

Exercise 9c
- Students can now analyse their partners' answers.
- Students turn to page 128 and read the analysis.
- Ask them to present the results to their partner and discuss whether they are true or not and why.
- Conduct a class discussion.

CRITICAL THINKING Ask students what they think of questionnaires of this kind. *Is this one more or less accurate than others you have seen/tried? Why?* (Students may feel this questionnaire is based upon research by an author and so more reliable. Realistically, it is very limited due to the fact that is only ten questions long.)

Exercise 10a
- Tell students to choose members of their family and make notes, using the questions to help them. Point out that they should describe their character, not physical appearance.

EXTRA SUPPORT Ask them to focus on one member of their family only. (They can do this several times in order to maximize their practice.)

- Monitor their note-writing carefully and allow them plenty of time for this preparation stage.

Exercise 10b
- When students have prepared, put them into small groups to tell each other about their families. Encourage them to ask each other questions if anything is not clear or they want more information.
- Monitor their conversations, focusing on comparative and superlative forms. Note good examples and mistakes too.

Exercise 10c
- Ask the question in c to the class and elicit some answers.
- Do error correction. Read out and praise good examples.

EXTRA ACTIVITY You could teach them the prepositional phrases *similar to* and *different from*, e.g. *I am most similar to my mum because … I am very different from my brother because …*. In new small groups they could talk about family members they are similar to and different from and why.

GRAMMAR REFERENCE ANSWERS
Exercise 1
1 Type A people are more worried about status than Type B people.
2 Type B people are more satisfied with life than Type A people.
3 Type B people are calmer than Type A people.
4 Type A people are angrier than Type B people.
5 Type B people are more patient than Type A people.
6 Type A people have worse health than Type B people.

Exercise 2
1 Gary is lazier than Sue
2 I am the cleverest in my family.
3 Javier is more sociable than Maria.
4 The men in the class are shyer than the women.

Unit 6   107

5 My chair is the biggest in the office.
6 This car's the largest in the showroom.
7 My house is further/farther from the school than yours.

Exercise 3
1 My friends are not as introverted as me.
2 My grandparents are not as well educated as my parents.
3 My children are not as creative as her children.
4 Helen is not as confident as others in the family.
5 Rome is just as interesting as Rio. OR Rio is just as interesting as Rome.

6.2 A long way home

Goals
- Talk about family
- Talk about experiences

Lead-in
- Put students into pairs or small groups to brainstorm vocabulary for different members of a family. Give them a time limit of just one or two minutes.
- Monitor and correct any spelling mistakes you see.
- Praise the pair/group with the longest list.

Vocabulary & Speaking   family

Exercise 1 6.4
- Focus their attention on the Family vocabulary quiz which they are going to do in small groups.
- Ask them to look at the three different sections. Check they understand what to do for each section. In section 1, it is not dictation. They have to decide which word is being explained by the definition. In section 3, highlight that they need to focus on the underlined sounds. You could ask them *In this section is your group going to be quiet or noisy?* Noisy – as they will need to say the words aloud to work out/decide if the sounds are the same or different.
- Put them into groups of two or three to do the quiz.
- Play track 6.4 for section 1.
- Students continue with sections 2 and 3 of the quiz in their groups.
- Monitor to check what pace they are working at and give a time limit to the end of the activity when many groups are close to finishing.

AUDIOSCRIPT 6.4
Number one: your male child is your … what?
Number two: your mother's or your father's sister is your … what?
Number three: your sister's or brother's son is your … what?
Number four: your mother's father is your … what?
Number five: your grandmother's mother is your … what?
And finally, number six: your aunt or uncle's child is your … what?

Exercise 2 6.5
- Tell the students to listen to check their answers.
- Play track 6.5.
- As a class, go through any answers that they didn't hear.
- Let them check their scores out of 20 marks.

EXTENSION You could play the final section of the recording again for students to repeat the pronunciation of the words.
PRONUNCIATION Draw their attention to section three – the words 'uncle', 'mother' and 'son'. The sound /ʌ/ often corresponds to the letter 'u' as in 'uncle' but another letter which is sometimes pronounced /ʌ/ is 'o'. Elicit other examples: *money, Monday, month, brother, another, wonder, come, something, done, front*. If students are interested, point out that the 'ou' spelling in 'cousin' in section three of the quiz is also pronounced /ʌ/ and give them some other examples: *young, touch, double, enough*. Advise them to record useful groups of words like this with similar spelling and pronunciation patterns in their notebooks.

ANSWERS

Section 1	Section 2	Section 3
1 son	1 b	1 D
2 aunt	2 b	2 S
3 nephew	3 a	3 S
4 grandfather	4 a	4 D
5 great-grandmother	5 a	5 S
6 cousin	6 b	6 D
	7 b	
	8 a	

AUDIOSCRIPT 6.5
Here are the answers to the quiz:
Question one, number one: your male child is your son and that's spelt S-O-N.
Number two: your mother's or your father's sister is your aunt. And that's spelt A-U-N-T.
Number three: your sister's or brother's son is your nephew and that's N-E-P-H-E-W.
Four, your mother's father is your grandfather and that's one word, grand G-R-A-N-D father.
Number five: your grandmother's mother is your great grandmother. So that's G-R-E-A-T grandmother … and we join the words 'great' and 'grandmother' with a hyphen, a little line.
And finally, number six: your aunt or uncle's child is your cousin and that's spelt C-O-U-S-I-N.

Question two, number one: the word for two married people or two people in a relationship is a couple.
Number two: a child with no brothers or sisters is an only child.
Number three: two children born on the same day are twins. Half brother and half sister have a different meaning: your half brother is a brother who has either the same mother or the same father as you.
Number four: a mother or father who looks after their children alone is a single parent.
Number five: The word for the people in your family is relatives. Your parents are just your mother and father.
And number six: if you take a child into your family and the child legally becomes your child you adopt the child.
Number seven: before you get married you get engaged, that means you agree, formally, that you are going to get married. You get divorced only if your marriage goes wrong. Get divorced means legally end your marriage.
And, finally, number eight: a woman who is married to your father, but isn't your mother, is your stepmother. We can also say stepfather, stepson, stepdaughter, stepsister and stepbrother. Your mother-in-law is your husband or wife's mother.

And finally, question three: pronunciation. Listen carefully.
One: father-in-law /ɔː/ aunt /ɑː/. The sound is different.
Two: mother /ʌ/ uncle /ʌ/. It's the same.
Three: cousin /ʌ/ son /ʌ/. That's also the same.
Four: father /ɑː/ daughter /ɔː/. That's a different sound.
Adopted /ɪd/ related /ɪd/. That's the same.
And number six: divorced /t/ separated /ɪd/. That's different.
And that's all the answers to the quiz! Now add up your score. How did you get on?

Exercise 3

- Ask students to read the instructions. Check the meaning of *close to* if necessary.

WATCH OUT! Students may want to know the difference between *eldest* and *oldest*. Explain that *eldest* is only used with people and usually with people who are related to each other, so it is much more specific. We can use *oldest* about anything, including people.

- Students work alone to write down the names, a), b) and c). They should have five names in total.
- Put them into pairs to do the speaking task. Read the example aloud to the class.

EXTRA ACTIVITY To extend this speaking practice, you could ask them to think of stories involving these family members which they can tell each other.

Grammar & Listening present perfect simple and past simple

Exercise 4a

Audio summary: A conversation between two friends (one male, one female) about a true story one of them heard on the radio.

- Tell students to read the instruction. Ask questions to check their understanding if necessary: *So who are the main characters in this story you're going to listen to?* (a boy and his mother) *Is it a true story?* (yes)
- Tell them to look at the words in the box and, in pairs, predict why they might be important in the story.
- You could elicit ideas from the class, but do not confirm any of them yet.

Exercise 4b 6.6

- Tell them to listen to the story and check their ideas.
- Play track 6.6.
- Reassure them that although there may be some parts they didn't hear or didn't understand fully, you will play the story again.

ANSWERS

A waterfall : This is a landmark which he remembers from his childhood and when he sees it on Google Earth it helps him find his home village.
Google Earth: This programme is the technology which helps him locate his mother.
An Australian couple: He was adopted by an Australian couple and taken to live in Hobart, Tasmania.
A train: He fell asleep on a train and woke up in Kolkata.

AUDIOSCRIPT 6.6

F I've just listened to a really interesting programme on the radio.
M Yeah?
F It was an interview with a man who lost his mother when he was boy and has recently found her again after twenty-five years, using Google Earth.
M Really? How did he do that?
F Well, this man – his name's Saroo Brierley – was from a small village in India. When he was only five years old he was on a train with his older brother. He fell asleep and woke up 14 hours later, alone, in Kolkata.
M So, couldn't they take him home again?
F Well, no, because he didn't know the name of his village. He was too young. So he lived on the streets of Kolkata. After a while he was adopted by an Australian couple from Tasmania.
M So he moved to Tasmania?
F Yes, and he says in the interview that he has always been very happy in his new family. He's done well in life: he's been to university, he's found a good job. But while he was growing up he started to think more and more about his family in India. So he decided to try to find his old home on Google Earth.
M Right … yeah … so … how … ?
F Well, he knew he was on the train for about 14 hours, he knew the speed of Indian trains. So he knew his village was about 1200 km from Kolkata. He drew a big circle on a map around Kolkata and every night for four years he sat at his computer, looking at satellite images of the landscape. Then suddenly he recognized a waterfall, where he played as a child.
M Incredible!
F So he travelled to Khandwa, the village near the waterfall. He got to the village and found his old house …
M Wow …
F But his mother didn't live there anymore. But some neighbours helped him to find her. Can you imagine the meeting? Apparently she couldn't speak for some time. She believed her son was dead after all these years.
M What an incredible story!
F Yeah, he's written a book about it. It's called *A Long Way Home*.
M I'd really like to read that.
F Me too.

Exercise 5 6.6

- Tell students to read the sentences 1–6.
- Point out that they need to listen and decide if the sentences are true, false or if we don't know, in which case they should write a question mark.

EXTRA CHALLENGE Stronger students can try to remember from the first time they heard the story and decide T, F or ?. Then they can listen to check their answers.

- Play track 6.6 again.
- Go through the answers with the class. Encourage them to refer to the recording as evidence for their answers, i.e. *This sentence is true because the woman said …* .

Unit 6   109

ANSWERS
1 True
2 False – He has always been happy.
3 ? We only know that he was adopted but we don't know if he has adopted a child.
4 False – he saw a waterfall.
5 True
6 ? None are mentioned but we don't know.

Exercise 6a
- Tell students that they are going to do some grammar work.
- Students work alone to identify the tenses of the sentences in exercise 6.
- Go through the answers together.

ANSWERS
1 past simple
2 present perfect simple
3 present perfect simple
4 past simple (and past continuous)
5 present perfect simple
6 present perfect simple

Exercise 6b
- Focus students' attention on the Grammar focus box.
- Tell them to read the rules and complete them by choosing the correct option.
- Students work alone to do the task.
- Go through the answers together.

ANSWERS
1 past simple
2 present perfect simple
3 have

- Refer students to *Grammar reference* on p145. There are two more exercises here students can do for homework. See answers in next column. (Exercise 3 will be done later, in section 6.4.)

Exercise 7a
- You could complete the first dialogue together as a demonstration.
- Students work alone to complete the dialogues.
- Check answers as a class by asking pairs of students to perform the dialogues.
- For each dialogue, encourage students to refer back to the grammar rules by asking checking questions. Example: *In dialogue 1, why is the response in the past simple?* (because the speaker is talking about something that happened at a specific time in the past: a couple of years ago after a very tiring day at work.)

ANSWERS
1 Have fallen, did, got
2 Have tried, downloaded
3 Have travelled, have taken
4 Have found, contacted
5 Have lost, left, gave, called

Exercise 7b
- Students practise the dialogues together in their pairs. This is to give them pronunciation practice and to drill them in the structures needed in exercise 7c.

Exercise 7c
- Tell students to read the information about when we use the present perfect simple and when we use past simple.
- Ask if they had noticed this pattern in any of the dialogues in exercise 7a? (All of them are like this except dialogue 3.)
- Ask one pair to act out the example dialogue.
- Students take turns to ask and answer the questions in pairs.
- Monitor carefully, paying most attention to the students' use of the tense forms. Note any points for correction or discussion.
- Give a time limit to the end of the conversations if necessary.
- Conduct error correction when they have all finished their conversations.

GRAMMAR REFERENCE ANSWERS

Exercise 1
1 kept
2 known
3 made
4 been
5 left
6 taken
7 thought
8 written
9 read
10 put
11 bought
12 given

Exercise 2
1 Have you ever been, went
2 visited, Have you ever had
3 have/has never bought
4 Have you and your wife (ever) eaten, we have
5 has never been
6 Have you ever read, saw

Exercise 3
1 About 30% of students in my class have already applied for a job.
2 Have you checked your emails yet?
3 Helen has never played computer games online.
4 We've just started using Twitter.
5 I've already seen the news today.
6 Adam has just updated his blog.
7 We haven't got an email from the hotel yet.

6.3 Vocabulary and skills development

Goals
- Recognize linkers in fast speech
- Understand and use adjective prefixes

Listening & Speaking recognizing linkers in fast speech

Lead-in
- Write the word *rude* on the board.

- Elicit that it is an adjective. Ask: *If I think that you're rude, do I have a good opinion or a bad opinion of you? What is the opposite adjective?* (polite)

Exercise 1a
- Tell students to look at the pictures and read the instruction.
- Put students into pairs to do this task.
- Conduct class feedback to find out the range of feeling about rudeness. The responses may show that not everyone feels the same about different types of behaviour. You can point out that some behaviour is culturally acceptable in some places and not in others. It may also depend on how you were brought up by your parents/family.

Exercise 1b
- In their pairs, students think of two examples of bad manners and two examples of good manners.
- Elicit examples from the class and encourage discussion.

EXTENSION Extra questions you could ask: *How do people learn good manners? Is it a teacher's job to teach good manners to children? Why do some people have bad manners? Is it worse if a woman has bad manners? Do you think some things we think of as 'good manners' are in fact unnecessary? Could you be friends with someone who has bad manners? Do you know anyone who has bad manners? If someone was behaving with bad manners near you, what would you do?*

SMART COMMUNICATION Good manners may be reflected in the way we speak to people. Before travelling to another country it is helpful to talk to someone from that country about how to greet and say goodbye in the best way, differences in how you speak to older and younger people, safe and taboo topics of conversation, etc. For example, in Britain it is common to say 'please' and 'thank you' several times in any shop transaction or when buying a ticket on the bus.

Exercise 2a 6.7
- Tell students to read the Unlock the code box about recognizing linkers in fast speech as you play the recording.
- Play track 6.7.
- Check that students understand the main point, which is that in order to catch linkers in fast speech, they should not expect to hear the full forms.
- You could play the track again and encourage the students to try to say these shortened forms of the linkers.

AUDIOSCRIPT 6.7
When we speak quickly we sometimes don't pronounce parts of words. This is especially true with very common words, like the linkers *and, but, because, so* and *for example*.

but	sounds like	'bt'
because	sounds like	'cos'
for example	sounds like	'frexample'
and	sounds like	'n'
so	sounds like	's'

Exercise 2b 6.8
- Point out that in this exercise they have to count the number of words in each sentence or phrase and write the number down. Make sure they understand how to count the contractions.

- Play track 6.8. If the students need it, play it a second time.
- Go through the answers together.

ANSWERS
1 3 words
2 5 words
3 7 words
4 7 words
5 8 words
6 8 words

AUDIOSCRIPT 6.8
1 Friends and family
2 He's clever but lazy.
3 I like him cos he's honest.
4 I enjoy winter sports, for example, skiing.
5 She was ill, so she stayed at home.
6 I'm tired cos I got up early.

Exercise 2c 6.9
- Tell students you're going to play a different track.
- Their task is to complete the sentences. They need to write more than one word and sometimes several words.
- Play track 6.9. You may need to play it more times but ask them to check their answers in pairs before you do.
- Go through the answers together.

ANSWERS
1 but expensive.
2 cos he forgot my birthday.
3 but unhappy.
4 so we took a taxi.
5 Tuesday for example.
6 so we stayed in.
7 cos of my bad foot
8 A passport for example?

AUDIOSCRIPT 6.9
1 It's nice but expensive.
2 I was upset because he forgot my birthday.
3 He's rich but unhappy.
4 There were no buses, so we took a taxi.
5 Let's meet next week. Tuesday for example.
6 The weather was awful, so we stayed in.
7 I can't run cos of my bad foot.
8 Have you got any ID? A passport, for example?

Exercise 3a 6.10

> **Audio summary:** Three people individually talk about manners in both their own and a different country.

- Tell students that they are going to hear sentences from a recording of three different speakers talking about manners.
- They need to complete the sentences 1–8 with as many words as they hear. Students work alone on the task – they should read 1–8 before you play the recording.

EXTRA SUPPORT Ensure students know the vocabulary in these sentences before you play the track. Check *a mask* and *interrupt*.

- Play track 6.10, more than once if necessary.
- Go through the answers together.

Unit 6 111

ANSWERS
1 I often go
2 for example, when they
3 so they don't
4 But I've heard
5 So when I'm
6 Because I don't
7 but I've
8 Because it means

AUDIOSCRIPT 6.10
1 I'm from New Zealand but I often go to Japan on business.
2 When people are ill, for example when they have a cold…
3 They wear a mask so they don't give the cold to other people.
4 But I've heard that in other countries …
5 So when I'm with my English friends …
6 Because I don't want to be impolite …
7 I'm from Hong Kong but I've lived in the UK …
8 Because it means you're really enjoying your food …

Exercise 3b
- Students read the phrases. Check together the meaning of 'blow your nose'.

Exercise 3c 6.11
- Tell students that you're going to play the full recording of three different people talking about manners in their own culture and in another country.
- They should tick the topics that the people talk about.
- Play track 6.11.
- Go through the answers together.

ANSWERS
wearing a face mask, interrupting, eating noisily

AUDIOSCRIPT 6.11
1 Karina
I'm from New Zealand, but I often go to Japan on business. The first time I had a business meeting there I was very surprised cos two women in the meeting were wearing a mask across their mouth and nose. I thought, 'Mmm, that's a bit unnecessary. Are they worried I'll pass a terrible illness to them?' But later I learnt that in Japan, when people are ill, for example, when they have a cold, they wear a mask so they don't give the cold to other people. It's a way of showing respect to others. This seems like very good manners to me and I think everybody should wear a mask when they're ill!

2 Stefano
Well, I'm Italian and when I'm with my Italian friends and family and we're having a really interesting conversation we get excited and we all speak at the same time. But I've heard that in other countries it's bad manners to talk when another person is speaking. So when I'm with my English friends for example, I try very hard not to interrupt because I don't want to be impolite, but, the thing is, for Italians it isn't rude to interrupt – in fact it's the opposite – it's our way of showing that we're really interested.

3 Mike
I'm from Hong Kong, but I've lived and worked in the UK for many years. One of the big differences between here and Hong Kong is table manners – you know, the way people eat their food. So for example, Chinese people often make loud slurping noises when eating noodles. Noodle restaurants in Hong Kong are very noisy places – it sounds like a competition to see who can slurp the loudest! For us slurping your noodles is a polite thing to do cos it means you're really enjoying your food, but unfortunately here in the UK it's really bad manners!

Exercise 4 6.11
- Ask students to read the questions first.
- Play track 6.11 again.
- Students write their answers.
- Go through the answers together.

ANSWERS
1 She thought that the women wearing the masks were afraid of catching an illness from her. She learnt later that they had a cold and were trying to avoid passing it on to other people.
2 He tries not to interrupt when other people are speaking.
3 Because it shows that you are really enjoying your food.

Exercise 5
- Ask students: *For Mike, eating noisily is good manners. Is this good manners or bad manners in your culture?* Elicit answers and conduct a discussion.
- Tell them they are going to talk more about what is good and bad manners.
- Ask them to read the four phrases which will be useful in their discussions. Drill pronunciation.

WATCH OUT! In this lesson, the students learnt that linkers are often not fully pronounced in fast speech. All these phrases contain 'to' which is also often shortened to /t/ before a consonant sound. Practise this, e.g. *It's OK to call your boss …* or *It's rude to blow your nose …*

PRONUNCIATION Also remind students of lesson 4.3 where they learnt about linking sounds. When 'to' is followed by a word beginning with a vowel sound we use a linking /w/ sound. Practise this, e.g. *It's polite to/w/eat …* or *It's rude to/w/interrupt.*

- Put students into small groups for this task. They can discuss the ideas in exercise 3a as well as exercise 5.
- Monitor their discussions. Ask them to give reasons why something is good manners or not and to explain what may happen if a person behaves in this way. They will need to use linkers and you can focus on whether they pronounce them naturally in shortened form. Note down sentences to use as examples in feedback.
- Give a time limit to the end of the activity so all students finish their discussions at the same time.
- Conduct class feedback.

FEEDBACK FOCUS Write some of the students' sentences on the board and elicit pronunciation. Make sure the linkers are pronounced naturally.

EXTRA ACTIVITY If you have a multicultural class, you could ask the students to think of anything else which is considered bad manners in their country so that they can advise their classmates. This would be a very useful exchange of information in case any of the students travel to different countries.

- Ask a monolingual class whether they think their country is strict or relaxed about manners. They should give reasons for their opinion, together with examples.

Vocabulary adjective prefixes

Exercise 6
- Tell students to read the instruction. Then elicit the answer from the class.

ANSWERS

im- and *un-* mean 'not'. It changes the adjective to mean the opposite.

Exercise 7a
- Ask students to read the Vocabulary focus box.
- Ask them some checking questions: *As well as the prefixes im- and un-, which other prefix is mentioned?* (dis-). *Does this have the same function?* (Yes, it makes the adjective have the opposite meaning.) *Why do we sometimes use 'a bit' before an adjective with a negative prefix?* (To make it sound more polite.)
- Ask them to write the opposite for each of the adjectives 1–10, using negative prefixes.
- Encourage the students to check in pairs.

ANSWERS

1 unpleasant
2 unusual
3 impatient
4 dishonest
5 unlucky
6 impossible
7 unfair
8 unfriendly
9 unhealthy
10 unnecessary

Exercise 7b 6.12
- Tell students they can listen to check their answers.
- Play track 6.12.
- To focus on pronunciation, play the recording again and ask the students to repeat the pairs of adjectives. Elicit that the word stress remains the same in these adjectives with or without a negative prefix.

AUDIOSCRIPT 6.12

1 pleasant unpleasant
2 usual unusual
3 patient impatient
4 honest dishonest
5 lucky unlucky
6 possible impossible
7 fair unfair
8 friendly unfriendly
9 healthy unhealthy
10 necessary unnecessary

STUDY TIP Encourage students to learn the adjectives from today's lesson and keep one or more vocabulary pages for recording more adjectives with negative prefixes that they read or hear. It's always a good study habit to find out and record the opposites of words as you learn them (whether they have negative prefixes or are completely different words).

- If you ask the students how they know which negative prefix to choose for each adjective, they often reply 'this one just sounds right'. This is good, as it shows they are developing an ear for the language and by recording and learning vocabulary they build a base for making this 'sounds right' judgement. (It is especially helpful with negative prefixes because although there are patterns, there are few rules for building words in this way.)

Exercise 8a 6.13
- Ask students to read the conversation to themselves and notice the prefixes.
- Tell them you're going to play the track so that they can listen and repeat the sentences.
- Play track 6.13, pausing where necessary. Students repeat.
- You could put them in pairs to practise a few more times.

AUDIOSCRIPT 6.13

A He wasn't very polite.
B True. He *was* a bit impolite.
A That wasn't very kind.
B You're right. It *was* a bit unkind.

Exercise 8b
- Explain that they are going to have mini conversations like the one they just practised, using the sentences 1–5 as a starting point.
- If necessary, elicit how they would respond to the first sentence as a demonstration.
- Put students into pairs.
- Monitor their conversations for accuracy. Make sure they are using *a bit* to make their responses polite.
- Ask pairs of students to act out each of the conversations in order to go through the answers.

ANSWERS

1 He is a bit disorganized.
2 It was a bit unnecessary.
3 He is a bit impatient.
4 We have been a bit unlucky.
5 It was a bit dishonest.

Exercise 9a
- Tell students to read the instruction. Check they understand the two things they need to do in this exercise, 1) add a prefix and 2) complete the sentence.
- Students work alone on this task.
- Go through the prefixes for each sentence to check they have the correct answers.

ANSWERS

1 im-
2 un-
3 im-
4 im-
5 un-
6 un-

Exercise 9b
- Put students into small groups to compare their sentences.
- To maximize their speaking practice, ask them to respond to each other's sentences, saying whether they think and feel the same and giving reasons or examples if possible.
- Conduct a class discussion.

6.4 Speaking and writing

Goals
- Give and respond to news
- Present perfect simple with *just*, *already* and *yet*

Unit 6 113

Lead-in

- Write the word *news* on the board.
- As a whole class or for discussion in pairs/small groups, ask students how they get news about what is happening in the world (internet, TV, newspapers, radio, etc.).
- Ask *How do you get news about your friends and family?* (email, text, letter, phone, meeting face to face, social media)
- You could elicit verbs which go well with *news* – *get, receive, find out, give, tell, share, hear, watch, read*.

Writing & Grammar   responding to news on social media

Exercise 1
- Ask students to read the sentences.
- Tell them to pick the sentence which best describes them and think about why.
- Put students into pairs to compare their chosen sentences.
- Conduct a class discussion. Ask students if their use of social media is similar to or different from their partner's.
- You could elicit (from sentence 3) the meaning of 'Life is too short' in relation to using social media. (= that using social media is a waste of time.)

Exercise 2
- Tell students to read the expressions in the box.
- Ask them to complete the posts using the expressions.
- Go through the answers together.
- **WATCH OUT!** Elicit that 'thing' in *You lucky thing!* really means 'person'.
- At this point in the lesson, check students know which situations you can use each expression for. If appropriate, use translation to help them.

ANSWERS
1. You lucky thing
2. Best of luck
3. Bad luck
4. Congratulations
5. Love the pic

Exercise 3
- Ask students to read the posts again.
- Students work alone to find expressions to match a, b and c.
- Allow them time to check their answers in pairs if you wish and then go through them together.

ANSWERS
a. Best of luck! Fingers crossed!
b. Well done.
c. Get better soon. Get well soon. Wishing you a speedy recovery.

Exercise 4
- Tell students they are going to analyse informal style. Ask them to read the list of different features they need to underline. Check they understand these features.
- Students work alone on this task. Then go through the answers together.

ANSWERS
Exclamation marks: there are many of these throughout the posts.
Short forms of words: fab, pic
Comments in brackets: (You'll be fine!)
Informal expressions: Have a fab time! You're a star!
Missing out words: Interview this afternoon. Broken my shoulder. Got the job! Winter already? Thinking of you. Wishing you a speedy recovery.

Exercise 5
- Tell students that the key words in the next exercise are *just*, *already* and *yet*.
- Ask them to read the Grammar focus box.
- Tell them to complete the rules about using *just*, *already* and *yet* by choosing the correct option.
- When they have finished, go through the answers together.

ANSWERS
1. before
2. before
3. end

- Refer students to *Grammar reference* on p145. There is one more exercise here students can do for homework. See answers on p110.

Exercise 6
- Tell students to use the prompts to make full sentences, using the word in brackets.
- Students work alone on this task.
- Go through the answers together.

ANSWERS
1. They have not/haven't announced the winner of the competition yet.
2. The police have already arrested a man for the robbery.
3. My brother has just got engaged.
4. Have you started your new job yet?
5. She has/'s just bought a motorbike.

Exercise 7a
- Tell students that they need to write posts similar to those in exercise 2, e.g. *Interview this afternoon. Wish me luck!*
- Remind them that they need to write clearly as another student is going to read their posts. They should leave plenty of space for other students to write comments (see layout of the posts in exercise 2.)
- Allow them plenty of time to write their posts. (Note: they do not need to try to use the expressions from exercises 2 and 3 now as these are for responding.)
- Monitor and offer guidance and correction where necessary. This is a creative task but the posts are very short so it should not take a long time.

ANSWERS
Students' own answers

Exercise 7b
- Put students into small groups. Ask them to swap their posts with another student in their group.
- Now they need to respond to the posts. Encourage them to use the expressions from exercises 2 and 3.

114

EXTRA ACTIVITY Another way to do this would be to display the posts around the room in a gallery so that all the students can walk around and read as many as possible, responding in writing on the posts when they wish. You could set a minimum amount of response, e.g. *you must write a response on at least three people's posts.*

- Conduct a class discussion of the posts.

Listening & Speaking giving and responding to news

Exercise 8a
- Ask students to look at the photos.
- Students think about how to describe what has happened in each case. You could put them in pairs to talk about it.

Exercise 8b 6.14

> **Audio summary:** Five different conversations between two people. In each case, one person shares good or bad news and the other person responds to it.

- Ask them to listen to five conversations and decide which conversation matches each photo a–e.
- Play track 6.14.
- Go through the answers together.

EXTENSION You could ask them which they think is the best news and which is the worst news. Ask them to give reasons.

ANSWERS
1 d   2 c   3 a   4 b   5 e

AUDIOSCRIPT 6.14
One
F1 Hey, I've got some good news … Pati's had her twins!
F2 Oh, wow! What's she had?
F1 A boy and a girl.
F2 Oh how wonderful! What are their names?
F1 Thomas and Rose.
F2 Ahh. Have you seen them yet?
F1 No, I'm seeing them tomorrow!

Two
M Hiya. Are you OK?
F No, not really. I've just failed my driving test.
M Never mind. You can try again soon.
F Yeah, but I've already taken it three times. That was my fourth test!
M Oh dear. I'm sorry.

Three
M Hi Tanya, it's me. I'm on the train. Listen, I've got bad news … .
F What?
M A tree has fallen on the track ahead of us.
F Oh no! Are you OK?
M Yeah, yeah I'm fine. But I'm going to be very late home. I'm not going to be back in time for the concert tonight.
F Ah, what a shame!
M I know. I was really looking forward to it. Maybe somebody else can go with you?
F Maybe. It's a bit late but I'll send out a few texts.
M Yeah. I'm really sorry.
F Oh, don't worry – that's life. At least you're safe!

Four
M Hey, Neena. Guess what?

F What?
M I've just won the prize for best young ice hockey player in the region.
F That's fantastic! When did you find out?
M Just now.
F Congratulations! I'm really happy for you.

Five
M Have you heard the news? About the fires in Australia?
F No. What's happened?
M There've been some terrible forest fires in Western Australia. It's a really serious situation.
F Have people died?
M No, I don't think so, but hundreds of houses have burned down and thousands of people have left their homes.
F That's awful.
M Yes, terrible.

Exercise 9a 6.14
- Ask students to read the expressions 1–15.
- Tell them that they need to listen to the conversations again and tick which expressions are used.
- Play track 6.14 again.
- They could check their answers in pairs. Tell them to say which conversation they heard each expression in.
- Go through the answers together.

ANSWERS
Students should have ticked all expressions except 4 (What a pity!) and 13 (That's great news!).

Exercise 9b
- Tell the students to categorize the 15 expressions according to their function a, b or c.
- Put them into pairs to discuss the task.

EXTRA ACTIVITY Put students into pairs and give them just one function a, b or c which they have to find all the expressions for. (Then you could put three different pairs together to share their answers.)

- Go through the answers as a class. Point out that these are categorized in the Language for speaking box.
- You could check students' understanding by asking some questions. *Why do we say 'I've got some good news' and not 'I've got a good news' even when we have only one thing to tell somebody?* (because news is always plural). Point out that we often use *news* with no article. *What is the right response if someone says 'Guess what?'* (What?) *Which expression means don't worry, don't be upset or it's not important?* (Never mind.)

ANSWERS
a I've got some good news.
  I've got bad news.
  Guess what?!
  Have you heard the news?
b What a pity!
  Never mind.
  Oh dear. I'm sorry.
  Oh no!
  What a shame!
  That's awful!
c Oh wow!
  How wonderful!
  That's fantastic!
  I'm really happy for you.
  That's great news.

SMART COMMUNICATION You have to be careful to pick the right level of response, particularly to bad news. When the

Unit 6   115

news is bad but not terrible, *Oh dear*, *What a pity!* and *What a shame!* are appropriate. For more serious bad news, these are not strong enough and the most appropriate phrases would be *That's awful!* and *I'm so sorry (to hear that)*.

Pronunciation intonation in short expressions

Exercise 9c 6.15
- Ask students to read the information about intonation.
- Tell them to listen to two different ways to say the same response.
- Play track 6.15.
- Elicit their reactions. Make sure they understand that the model they are aiming for is example a) – rising intonation.
- Tell them that they are going to practise saying the phrases in 9a after the audioscript. Remind them to copy the intonation pattern.

AUDIOSCRIPT 6.15

a That's fantastic!
b That's fantastic.

Exercise 9d 6.16
- Play track 6.16. Pause where necessary and repeat if the students' intonation pattern is not similar to the recording.
- You could conduct a class discussion about how important intonation is in the students' own language(s).

AUDIOSCRIPT 6.16

1 I've got some good news.
2 Oh wow!
3 How wonderful!
4 What a pity!
5 Never mind.
6 Oh dear. I'm sorry.
7 I've got bad news.
8 Oh no!
9 What a shame!
10 Guess what?
11 That's fantastic!
12 I'm really happy for you.
13 That's great news!
14 Have you heard the news?
15 That's awful!

Exercise 10a
- Tell the students to read the instruction.
- Model the response plus follow-up question, then students work alone on the task.
- Allow them plenty of time to think of follow-up questions.

EXTRA SUPPORT Write possible follow-up questions for the first two examples so that they can just match them. Examples: *Where are you going? How long is it for? Who are you going with? Was it insured? Where were you when it happened? Have you told the police?* Then they can think of their own follow-up questions for 3 and 4.

- Monitor and check carefully that they are remembering to use a response expression and then a follow-up question.

POSSIBLE ANSWERS
1 That's wonderful! Where/When are you going?
2 Oh no! Where was it? Have you told the police?
3 Congratulations! When's the wedding?
4 That's awful! Have many people lost their homes? Has anybody died?

Exercise 10b
- In pairs, ask students to take it in turns to give the news and respond with their responses and follow-up questions.
- Monitor for good use of intonation.
- Give feedback on their pronunciation if necessary.

Exercise 11a
- Students work alone to write their own pieces of news.
- Monitor to check their grammar is good and help them with vocabulary they need.

ANSWERS
Students' own answers

Exercise 11b
- This is a class mingle activity to maximize the number of times they give and respond to news.
- Highlight the last part of the instruction, 'repeat news you have heard from other classmates'. In the recording they listened to, two of the people were sharing news which wasn't about them but about another person or situation. The students now practise passing on news which is not about them but just something they have heard.
- Ask three students to act out the example dialogue.
- Start the class mingle. Monitor and stop the activity if you feel the intonation is too flat. Point it out and restart the activity.
- If necessary, set a time limit to the end of the activity so it is easy to get their attention.
- Conduct a class discussion. Ask students to tell the class the most interesting pieces of news they heard. You could ask the students whose news it is, whether the news is real and, if so, respond appropriately.

6.5 Video

Nettlebed

VIDEOSCRIPT
Hi, I'm Catherine. Today I'm in the small English village of Nettlebed. I'm here to see the childhood home of Ian Fleming.
Fleming was a very successful writer with an extraordinary life. If you haven't heard of him, you've almost certainly heard of his most famous creation – James Bond.
Fleming wrote fourteen James Bond books in his lifetime. These books were made into films and James Bond became a global phenomenon.
But Ian wasn't the only writer in his family. In fact, for a lot of Ian's life his older brother Peter was much more successful.
Peter Fleming was a British adventurer and travel writer. He wrote a series of travel books about his adventures in

Brazil and Asia. The books were very popular and have sold well ever since.

When they were young, Peter and Ian spent a lot of time here in Joyce Grove.

Joyce Grove is a large manor house in Nettlebed. It belonged to Peter and Ian's grandparents. When they were young, the boys came here all the time. They loved exploring the house's large garden and woods.

As boys they were very similar. They were both adventurous and just as competitive as each other. Peter and Ian became close friends after their father's death, but there was always competition, too. Both boys went to Eton, a very expensive school near London. Peter was more academic than Ian, but Ian was sportier, excelling at athletics.

After school, Peter went to university and graduated with a first-class degree in English.

Ian left school early. He became a journalist and then he became a stockbroker. But he didn't do very well at either. As Ian failed to become a journalist or a banker, his brother became a famous travel writer.

During the war, both Ian and Peter worked in intelligence. This experience had a big influence on both of them and when the war ended, they both wrote books about the secret services.

Peter was first. He was living here on the family estate when he wrote *The Sixth Column*, an espionage novel set in post-war Britain. He dedicated the book to Ian. Then he encouraged his publisher to print Ian's first James Bond book – *Casino Royale*.

Peter influenced a lot of Ian's writing. Peter often edited Ian's work and even suggested character names, like Miss Moneypenny. They were very close friends until Ian died in 1964.

Peter himself died seven years later in 1971. He is buried here in the churchyard, less than half a mile from the house where he grew up with Ian.

VIDEO ANSWERS
1 Ian Fleming; James Bond/Daniel Craig; MI6
3 Answers may vary in wording
   a Nettlebed is an English village/the childhood home of Ian Fleming.
   b Peter Fleming was Ian Fleming's brother.
   c Joyce Grove was Ian and Peter's grandparents' home.
   d Peter and Ian went to school at Eton / a very expensive school near London.
   e During the war, Peter and Ian worked for British Intelligence (MI6).
   f Peter Fleming is buried in Nettlebed / the churchyard in Nettlebed / near his childhood home.
4 a B   b P   c B   d B   e P   f I   g P   h I   i B   j P

Review
ANSWERS

Exercise 1a
1 The tallest
2 better
3 larger
4 The oldest
5 shorter

Exercise 1b
Sentence 3 is not true. Women use 20,000 words a day. Men use 7,000.

Exercise 2a
1 d   2 a   3 f   4 e   5 c   6 b

Exercise 3a
1 dishonest   2 unusual   3 impolite   4 impatient
5 disorganized

Exercise 4a
1 confident
2 smarter
3 hard-working
4 creative
5 sociable
6 lazy
7 untidy
(Not needed: patient, honest, shy)

Exercise 5 6.17
1 D   2 S   3 S   4 D   5 D   6 S   7 S   8 S

AUDIOSCRIPT 6.17
1 She's my mother's sister. She's my grandmother.
2 I've got no brothers or sisters. I'm an only child.
3 He's married to my mother, but he's not my father. He's my stepfather.
4 They're engaged. They're married.
5 She's my half sister. She's my cousin.
6 He's my husband's father. He's my father-in-law.
7 They're twins. They were born on the same day to the same mother.
8 They're married. They're a couple.

Exercise 6a
1 Guess
2 some
3 How
4 What
5 for
6 That's

Unit 6

7 Travel

Unit overview

Language input

Prediction (*will*, *might*) (CB p66)	• In 2045, the line will extend to Osaka. • It won't open until 2027. • In the future, some of us might fly to work by train.
***Something, anyone, everybody, nowhere,* etc.** (CB p68)	• I need something to eat. • I haven't seen anything like this before. • Nobody's serving food.
Grammar reference (CB pp146–7)	

Vocabulary development

Transport (CB p66)	• *public transport, bus pass, traffic jams …*
Holidays (CB p68)	• *accommodation, souvenir, currency …* • *book your flight, hire a car, apply for a visa …*
***-ed* and *-ing* adjectives** (CB p71)	• *I feel tired.* • *It was a really exciting film.*

Skills development

Reading: Recognizing paraphrasing (CB p70)

Speaking: Checking into a hotel (CB p72)

Writing: Short notes and messages (CB p73)

Video

Documentary: Beijing subway (Coursebook DVD & CB p74)

Vox pops (Coursebook DVD & TG p262)

More materials

Workbook	• Language practice for vocabulary, grammar, pronunciation, speaking and writing
Photocopiable activities	• Grammar: Big changes (TG p214 & TSRD) • Vocabulary: Pefect pairs (TG p232 & TSRD) • Communication: The great hotel race (TG p250 & TSRD)
Tests	• Unit 7 test (TSD)
Unit 7 wordlist (TSRD)	

7.1 On the move

Goals
- Talk about transport
- Make predictions

Lead-in
- Put students into pairs.
- Tell them to find out as much as possible about their partner's journey to college today.
- Elicit some information about different students' journeys to college. You could find out who had the easiest, longest, most complicated journey, etc.
- You could also find out whether any of the students had a different journey today to their usual journey. Why? What happened?

WATCH OUT! *I came to school by foot* is a common mistake. We use the preposition *by* with many other types of transport (e.g. by car, by bus, by train, by taxi, etc.) but the correct prepositional phrase for walking is *on foot*.

Vocabulary & Speaking transport

Exercise 1
- Put students into pairs to discuss the three questions. You may need to give a time limit for the brainstorming in question 1.

EXTRA CHALLENGE Ask fast finishers to go back to question 3 and give detailed reasons for their answer. They could also ask their partner's opinion of the public transport in their town, city or area.

- Conduct class feedback, eliciting different types of transport in answer to question 1. Check pronunciation and spelling whenever necessary.

EXTENSION You could also elicit which prepositions are used with each type of transport (*by* is most common) and which verbs are commonly used with each (*get, catch, take*, etc.). Point out any combinations which don't work well, for example that we *get* or *take a taxi* but we don't *catch a taxi*.

Exercise 2 7.1

Audio summary: Three different speakers each talk about transport in their cities and give information about the type of transport they use.

- Tell students they have to match the people's preferred type of transport to their name.
- Play track 7.1.
- Go through the answers together.

EXTRA CHALLENGE You could ask students to remember any other types of transport each person mentioned in addition to their preferred type.

ANSWERS
Kazimierz – bus
Elise – train
Aldo – bike

AUDIOSCRIPT 7.1
1 Kazimierz
I do have a car, but I only really use it to go to the supermarket or to visit friends who live out of town. I use public transport whenever possible. There's so much traffic on the road already and I don't want to add to that. The bus is the most convenient form of transport for me as there's a bus stop very close to my apartment. Bus fares are expensive, but I have a bus pass which makes it cheaper. I buy a pass once a month and then I can use the bus as many times as I want. Buses are greener now than in the past. They're quieter, they use less fuel and create less pollution.

2 Elise
I work mostly from home but once or twice a week I have to travel to another city for work. It's about an hour from where I live. I have a choice between taking the bus or the train. The bus is much cheaper than the train, but the journey is much slower as there are often bad traffic jams on the motorway. So I take the train. The trains are reliable – they usually leave on time – and they're quite comfortable. It's expensive, but the train fares are much cheaper if you book in advance. I find travelling by train quite enjoyable, except when it's really crowded and you can't sit down.

3 Aldo
I live in a big city and as in many big cities, there's a lot of traffic. Travelling by car is very slow and it's really hard to find parking spaces in the city centre. Public transport is good, but it gets very crowded and you often can't get a seat. It's also very expensive. That's why I go everywhere by bike. Luckily, I live in a city which is very good for cycling. For example, the main roads have special cycle lanes. To be honest though, I usually avoid the main roads and cycle in the quieter streets because they are safer and there is less pollution.

Exercise 3
- Students focus on words and phrases which are highlighted in bold in sentences 1–8.
- Point out that some sentences have more than one word or phrase to match to a meaning, e.g. *in sentence 1 there are two phrases in bold*.
- Give them plenty of time to match the words and phrases to their meanings a–l.
- Encourage them to use dictionaries if they are available.
- Go through the answers as a class.
- Drill pronunciation of the words and phrases in bold.

STUDY TIP If students note down vocabulary in their notebooks, encourage them to mark the stress on phrases. Each word of two syllables or more has its own stress which should be marked, but also there is usually one word in a phrase which is stressed more than the other(s) so it's a good habit to mark this stress as well. They should decide on a marking system, e.g. dots over stressed syllables and underlining under the stressed word in a phrase. (From this exercise: public transport, main roads, bus fares, bus pass, traffic jams, book in advance)

Unit 7   119

ANSWERS

a convenient
b in advance
c reliable
d crowded
e public transport
f greener
g fuel
h traffic jams
i pollution
j bus pass
k main roads
l fares

Exercise 4

- Put students into small groups.
- Ask them to discuss whether sentences 1–8 are true for them and the transport systems where they live.

EXTRA SUPPORT Give students who need extra support some thinking time in order to choose which sentences are true for where they live. Tell them to tick true sentences.

- Monitor their discussions.

EXTRA CHALLENGE Fast finishers can be encouraged to change the sentences to make them true for their own situation.

- Conduct a class discussion about public transport, parking, traffic jams and cycling.
- If most students know the town/city where the college is located, you could extend the discussion to talk about the local transport system.

WATCH OUT! We don't use *cycle* as a noun to describe the form of transport. It is almost always used as a verb, e.g. *I cycle to work* or in a compound noun, e.g. *cycle lanes*. The form of transport is a *bike* or *bicycle*.

Grammar & Reading prediction (*will, might*)

Exercise 5

> **Text summary:** An article about a new kind of train called Maglev (MAGnetic LEVitation) powered by magnets, which exists in Shanghai, China.

CRITICAL THINKING Ask students to study the photo and headline to help them imagine what the article will be about. Doing this helps them make a connection to what they have already seen and already know. Then it should be easier to notice in the text what is the same and different from their current knowledge and extract the most important points.

- Students read the questions.
- Give them plenty of time to read the text and find the answers.
- Go through the answers with the class.
- Encourage students to explain where they found the answer in the text.

ANSWERS

It is unusual because it has no wheels. It uses powerful magnetic levitation to move and floats above the tracks. The writer thinks it may become popular in the future if somebody finds a cheaper and simpler way to build the tracks but at the moment it is very expensive.

Exercise 6

- Ask students to read gapped sentences 1–5.

- They may benefit from trying to predict what kind of word or words are missing from each sentence (noun, number, adjective, etc.). Point out that there may be one or two words missing.
- Allow plenty of time for students to read the text again in order to complete the sentences.
- Allow them to check their answers in pairs, then go through the answers together.

EXTENSION The sentences use different words to those used in the article but the meaning is the same. For example sentence 1 says *raise them up* and the text says *lift them*. Ask the students to find other phrases in the sentences which have equivalents in the article: cause less pollution – create less pollution, use fuel – burn fuel, at present – currently, the journey takes 90 minutes – it takes 90 minutes to travel, the big disadvantage of – there is one major problem with, the high cost of building – it is incredibly expensive to build.

ANSWERS

1 powerful magnets
2 smoother, quieter
3 pollution
4 90 minutes
5 the tracks

Exercise 7a

- Ask students to read the three sentences and choose which predictions are strong.
- Conduct a class discussion of the answers. You can elicit that we know sentence 3 is less sure because the speaker uses *might*. (The Grammar focus box in exercise 7b explains fully.)

ANSWERS

1 and 2 are strong predictions, 3 is less sure.

Exercise 7b

- Tell students to find and underline examples of *will*, *won't* and *might* in the article. Ask them to read the Grammar focus box carefully and choose the correct option to complete the rules.
- Students work alone on this task.
- When they have finished, go through the sentences and then the rules together. You can use the sentences they have underlined to check they understand the rules.

EXTRA ACTIVITY You could also help visual learners by drawing a line vertically on the board and labelling it with *will* at the top and *won't* at the bottom. Elicit that *probably will* should be in the top half near *will* and *probably won't* in the bottom half near *won't*. *Might* and *might not* should be a little above the half way point. You can talk the students through this using the words *certain* and *more certain/less certain* to explain the difference between the words and phrases.

ANSWERS

Example sentences:
Trains will go from Tokyo to Nagoya in 40 minutes.
It won't open until 2027!
Then, in 2045, the line will extend to Osaka.
Why will it take so long?
The Tokyo to Osaka line will cost 91 billion dollars.
Maglev technology probably won't replace other forms of transport.

Somebody might find a cheaper and simpler way to build the tracks.
In the future, some of us might fly to work by train.

GRAMMAR FOCUS BOX ANSWERS
1 without
2 future
3 not sure
4 less

- Refer students to *Grammar reference* on p146. There are three more exercises here students can do for homework. See answers in next column.

Exercise 8

- Students work alone to complete the conversations with *will*, *won't*, *might* or *might not* and the verb in brackets.
- Put students into pairs to check their answers together.
- Ask some pairs to read the dialogues aloud so that you can go through the answers as a class.

ANSWERS
1 might not get, won't have to
2 will (you) get, might take, might go
3 will come, will (probably) arrive
4 won't cost, might be

PRONUNCIATION If you stress *might* in a sentence it makes you sound less sure. Model for the students *I might buy a car* and *I might buy a bike* (with *might* stressed a lot more in the second sentence). Elicit from students which they think is more likely to happen (buying a car). Ask students to make two of their own sentences with *might* and try to express to a partner, using pronunciation only, which one is less sure. Finally, elicit some pairs of sentences from the whole class and ask them to identify which is less sure.

Exercise 9a

- Ask students to read the predictions 1–6 about transport in the future.
- Put them into small groups to discuss how likely they are and predict when they might happen.
- Monitor their discussions.

FEEDBACK FOCUS Encourage them to use the target grammar – *will*, *won't*, *might* or *might not*. Make a note of any problems with making predictions.

CRITICAL THINKING Encourage students to use what they know about the topic to support their predictions. It is more convincing to use evidence such as what has already happened or what is happening now, e.g. *… because in my home town some people are already using electric cars.* Tell them for each prediction to try to think of a *because* statement.

Exercise 9b

- Tell students to make some more predictions in their group about the future of transport. There are topics to guide them.
- Allow plenty of time for the groups to complete this task and encourage them to write down their predictions.
- Monitor for accuracy.

Exercise 9c

- Put two groups together so that they can read out, compare and discuss their predictions.

- Again, monitor how they are using the grammar they've studied for making predictions.
- When they have had enough time to discuss, get all the students' attention and conduct a class discussion, eliciting just a few of their predictions and encouraging other students to give their opinions.
- Conduct feedback on these exercises.
- Do error correction of any mistakes you collected from exercises 9a, 9b and 9c.

EXTRA ACTIVITY Ask the students to write two short paragraphs about 1) the journeys they have to make and how they make them now and 2) how they predict they will make these journeys in the future, or how their journeys might be different in the future. They could do this writing in the classroom and hand it to you for marking or you could give them this task as homework.

GRAMMAR REFERENCE ANSWERS
Exercise 1
1 will carry
2 will probably be
3 won't disappear
4 will transport
5 will take
6 probably won't be/will probably not be

Exercise 2
1 We might use flying cars one day.
2 John might be tired when he arrives.
3 Our ferry might not be on time.
4 Cars might not need drivers in the future.
5 There might be international airports in all towns.
6 Do you think the Arctic might become a popular holiday place?
7 They might not serve food on the plane.

Exercise 3
1 will
2 Will
3 might
4 'll
5 won't
6 will
7 might

7.2 Getting away

Goals

- Talk about holidays
- Use *something*, *anyone*, *everybody*, *nowhere*, etc.

Lead-in

- Write *holidays* on the board.
- Ask the students *What does this word make you think of?* and *How does it make you feel?*
- Put them in pairs to share ideas.

Vocabulary & Speaking   holidays

Exercise 1

- Put students into pairs to read and discuss the questions.

Unit 7   121

- Conduct a class discussion. You could ask *Does anyone have a partner who goes away a lot on business? Is there anybody in the class who does not organize their own trips? Does anyone have a partner who said that planning a trip makes them feel stressed?* Encourage them to give as much information as possible.

Exercise 2

- Students read the phrases in the list.

EXTRA SUPPORT If you think a lot of these phrases are new to your students, you could spend time now eliciting and explaining the meanings of any unknown phrases.

- Focus students' attention on the diagram. Check that they understand what the middle section of the diagram is for.
- Students work in their pairs to fill the diagram.
- Monitor and give a time limit to the end of the activity when some pairs have almost finished.
- Go through the answers together.

ANSWERS

Before you travel:
Book your flight
Buy travel insurance
Apply for a visa
Get foreign currency

During your trip:
Lie by the pool
Buy souvenirs
Try the local food
Experience the local culture
Go sightseeing
Explore the area

Both:
Hire a car
Read a guidebook
Read online reviews
Choose your accommodation

Pronunciation word stress

Exercise 3a 7.2

- Tell students that the focus at this point in the lesson is on pronunciation.
- Ask them to mark the main stress on the words as they listen.

EXTRA CHALLENGE With strong students, you could ask them to mark the stress before you play the track, so they just check their ideas.

- Play track 7.2. Students mark the word stress.
- It's a good idea to go through the answers together, counting syllables and visually marking the stress on the words on the board if possible.

ANSWERS/AUDIOSCRIPT 7.2 & 7.3

accommodation
souvenir
insurance
currency

culture
foreign
apply
review

Exercise 3b 7.3

- Ask the students to listen again and repeat the words.
- Play track 7.3, pausing where necessary. You may need to play it more than once.
- Concentrate not only on the words' stress but also on words which are typically mispronounced: *culture* /ˈkʌltʃə(r)/ and *foreign* /ˈfɒrən/.

EXTENSION You could highlight that *-ture* at the end of a word is often pronounced /ʃə/ and give them some other examples: picture, nature, furniture, lecture. It is useful to point out patterns in the language whenever possible.

Exercise 4

- Ask students to read the questions 1–5.
- Check they know the meaning of *a last-minute person*.

EXTRA SUPPORT Students who need extra support can be given thinking time in order to prepare their answers to the questions. It is not a good idea for them to write them down, though, because this is primarily a speaking exercise.

- Put students into small groups to discuss their answers to the questions.
- Monitor and check that their pronunciation of the new vocabulary is good.
- If you have time, you could elicit some of their answers and encourage the rest of the class to ask further questions to get more information.

Grammar & Listening *something, anyone, everybody, nowhere, etc.*

Exercise 5

Background note: Manga is a specific kind of comic produced in Japan with a very particular style – typical characters have very large eyes and a lot of hair. There are many types of manga and it is read by people of all ages. It is very popular in Japan, the USA and France. The most popular manga comic characters are made into animated TV series called Anime.

- Focus students' attention on the photos and read the instruction aloud.
- Elicit ideas about what a Manga café is like.
- If you have access to the internet, you could show them some images of Manga cartoons.

Exercise 6 7.4

Audio summary: A podcast where one speaker describes his experience of a Manga café in real time as it happens.

- Ask students to check they know the meaning of all the words and phrases.
- Tell students to listen to the podcast and tick the different things you can do.
- Play track 7.4.
- Put students into pairs to check their answers.
- Go through the answers together.

ANSWERS

stay overnight
read comic books
buy comic books
watch videos
eat
drink

AUDIOSCRIPT 7.4

Here I am in Tokyo. It's 11 p.m. and I'm standing outside a *Manga Kissa*. What, you might ask, is a *Manga Kissa*? Well,

122

kissa is a Japanese word for café and Manga are Japanese comic books. And this is where I'm going to stay the night. But don't worry, I've done my research and according to my guidebook, Manga cafés are a good choice if you're looking for somewhere cheap to spend the night. Manga cafés are everywhere in Japan. In the past, they were places where you could go to read Manga for a few hours and escape the busy streets. Now they have become something different. They offer internet access and computer facilities as well as manga books. They're open 24 hours and they sell food and drinks. People often use them as a cheap form of accommodation – you pay per hour for your time in the café, but it's much less expensive than a hotel. So, I'm going to stay the night in a Manga Kissa. Well, as they say, 'You have to try everything once!' Let's go inside.

So here we are inside the café. There are walls and walls of Manga books displayed from floor to ceiling. There are thousands of them! I haven't seen anything like this before! According to the guidebook, Manga is popular with men and women of all ages in Japan, not just teenagers. They are a very important part of Japanese culture and Manga artists are very respected. There are quite a lot of people here. Some look like travellers, but a lot of people are local. Some are reading, but most people are watching videos and playing games on computers. Nobody's serving food but if I need something to eat there are loads of vending machines. Wow … there's an enormous choice. All kinds of soft drinks, pot noodles, ice cream … .

So I'm now outside my room. I'm just taking off my shoes – everyone leaves their shoes outside the room – and now I'm going to have a look inside. Well, it's not exactly a room – it's tiny and the walls only reach as high as my shoulder. And the bed's not really a bed, but a kind of long, flat seat, like a bench … but there's a blanket. It's not exactly five star accommodation, but I've got my own personal, private space and that's what matters. I think I'm going to sleep very well in here.

Exercise 7 7.4

- Point out that they need to take notes to answer questions 1–3 as there is a lot of information in the podcast about them.
- Play track 7.4 again. You may need to play it more than once for students who need extra support. If necessary, pause between each section.
- Go through the answers together.

POSSIBLE ANSWERS

1 In the past you could read Manga there. Now they have the internet and computers. They are open 24 hours and you can sleep, eat and drink there.
2 Some people are travellers. A lot of people are local. Some are reading. Most are watching videos and playing games on computers.
3 It's tiny. The walls are low. The bed is a long flat seat, like a bench.

Exercise 8

- Ask students to read the questions and discuss them with a partner.

- Conduct a class discussion. You could ask whether there is any place similar to a Manga café in the students' home country/countries.

Exercise 9 7.5

- Students read the words in the box, then work alone to complete the sentences.
- Play track 7.5 to check.
- Go through the answers together if you think they may not have heard some of them.

WATCH OUT! You could highlight that *one* and *body* at the end of these words have the same meaning. Also, point out that the words beginning with *every* take third person singular verb forms NOT plural, although they refer to more than one person, place or thing. All the words studied in this grammar focus take third person singular.

- Note: These examples from the podcast are all positive (affirmative) statements. The students will learn about negative sentences and questions in the next exercise.

ANSWERS

1 somewhere
2 everywhere
3 everything
4 anything
5 Nobody, something
6 Everyone

AUDIOSCRIPT 7.5

1 Manga cafés are a good choice if you're looking for somewhere cheap to spend the night.
2 Manga cafés are everywhere in Japan.
3 You have to try everything once!
4 I haven't seen anything like this before!
5 Nobody's serving food – but if I need something to eat there are loads of vending machines.
6 Everyone leaves their shoes outside the room.

Exercise 10

- Focus students' attention on the Grammar focus box. Tell them to complete the rules with the words *affirmative* and *negative*. (Check the meaning of *affirmative* if necessary.)
- Students work on the task alone.
- Encourage them to check their answers with a partner.
- Go through the answers together.

ANSWERS

1 affirmative
2 negative
3 affirmative

- Refer students to *Grammar reference* on p147. There are three more exercises here students can do for homework. See answers on p124.

Exercise 11

- Students work alone. Then go through the answers together.
- As you check the answers, ask extra questions to check the students understand the grammar, particularly if they make mistakes. For instance, *In number one, is this an affirmative or negative statement?* (negative – couldn't). *Why can't we use 'nowhere' here?* (because 'nowhere' is already negative and therefore takes a positive verb form).

EXTENSION You could ask questions about the content of these reviews: *Do you think these reviews are positive or negative? Which words tell you this?* (positive – They say 'a

Unit 7   123

great way to experience modern Japanese culture. Everyone should try it' and 'Cool place to stay'.) *Did these travellers experience any problems?* (The first person couldn't find anywhere else to stay and says it was basic. The second couldn't read the Manga comic because it was in Japanese). *Do these travellers think Manga cafés are good for everyone?* (Review 1: Yes. Review 2: No. 'For someone who wants to try something different.')

ANSWERS

1 anywhere
2 someone
3 everything
4 Everyone
5 someone
6 something
7 anything
8 everything

Exercise 12a

EXTRA ACTIVITY Before starting this exercise, you could explain that it's a quiz about cities. Put students into pairs to discuss which cities the two photographs were taken in.

- Elicit ideas from the class.
- Tell students to complete the quiz. Point out that, to complete the sentences, sometimes they will need to write the first part of the words and sometimes the second part.
- When they have finished, go through the answers 1–8 together.

ANSWERS

1 Every
2 where
3 some
4 body/one
5 every
6 body/one
7 where
8 no

Exercise 12b

- Put students into pairs to compare their ideas about which cities are described.
- They can check their guesses by reading the answers on page 128.
- Conduct a class discussion.

CRITICAL THINKING Ask which information in the descriptions helped them to choose each city. It is an important skill to be able to pick out the information which supports your guess or opinion from a text or a piece of listening. This kind of critical thinking is required in higher and further education and often necessary in business too. It also builds confidence in exams because if students practise this skill/technique, they have evidence for their answers.

Exercise 13a

- In their pairs, students secretly choose another famous city and make four sentences about it using the prompts/sentence starters.

EXTRA SUPPORT Students who need extra support can use the texts in 12a as a model for their own sentences, just changing the facts/information.

- Make sure all the students write down their sentences.
- Monitor their work closely to ensure they are using the target words from this lesson's grammar focus. Note any mistakes for correction later.

EXTRA CHALLENGE Stronger pairs could try to make it more challenging for their classmates to guess the city by ordering the information so that the easiest or most obvious comes last.

- You may need to give a time limit to the end of the activity so that all pairs finish at the same time.

Exercise 13b

- You could do this as a whole class activity. However, if the class is large, divide it into smaller groups. If you separate the pairs and regroup them, they will all get the opportunity to read out their sentences about their secret city.
- Ask students to read out their sentences clearly to their group or the class.
- Students who are listening guess which city is being described.
- Ask students to explain which pieces of information helped them guess the city (practising critical thinking).

GRAMMAR REFERENCE ANSWERS

Exercise 1
1 anybody
2 Nobody
3 somewhere
4 everywhere
5 anywhere
6 anything
7 Everything
8 anyone
9 Everyone

Exercise 2
1 anyone
2 No one
3 everywhere
4 nothing
5 somewhere
6 Everyone
7 anywhere
8 anything

Exercise 3
1 somewhere
2 anything
3 nothing
4 nowhere
5 no one
6 everyone
7 everywhere
8 nothing

7.3 Vocabulary and skills development

Goals
- Recognize paraphrasing
- Understand and use *-ed* and *-ing* adjectives

Reading recognizing paraphrasing

Lead-in
- Ask students which places they think are the coldest places in the world where people live.
- Allow them to brainstorm in small groups.
- Elicit ideas from the class and make a list of places.

- Ask them which climate they prefer to live in and whether they think they would be able to live in a very cold place. Encourage them to give reasons.

Exercise 1a
- Ask students to look at the places in the box and use them to label the map of the world.
- Go through the answers. Display them on a map of the world if available.
- Drill pronunciation of the places if necessary.

ANSWERS
1 New York
2 the Sahara
3 the Amazon
4 Paris
5 Tokyo

Exercise 1b
- Ask students to discuss in pairs which of these five places on the map is the hottest and which is the coldest. They should order them from 1–5 (1 = the coldest).
- Students turn to page 128 to check their answers.
- You could ask them whether they are surprised by any of the answers.

ANSWERS
1 New York 2 Paris 3 Tokyo 4 the Sahara
5 the Amazon

Exercise 1c
- In pairs, students ask and answer the questions about cold places.
- Conduct a class discussion. If students come from different places, you could find out which person comes from the coldest city. Otherwise, elicit information about cold places they have visited.

EXTENSION Students could brainstorm the sorts of problems they might have living in a cold city. If they have difficulty thinking of possible problems, give them some topics to guide them: work, transport, health, clothing, relationships, etc. Elicit some ideas from the class. You could also ask them for any solutions to these problems that they can think of.

Exercise 2a
- Focus students' attention on the Unlock the code box.
- When they have read the information and examples, ask questions to check understanding: *When a writer uses paraphrasing, is he talking about the same thing or two different things?* (the same) *If he is writing about the same thing, why does he use different words?* (to avoid repetition which can be boring and is not good style) *What problem can this cause for you when you read?* (You may think he's writing about two different things.)

Exercise 2b
- Do the first sentence together as a class to demonstrate the activity. Elicit which part in the second sentence is about a place in the first sentence. Underline it clearly if displaying it on the board. Using different colour pens may help to make it easier to notice and remember.
- Students work alone on the task.

- Monitor and assist as necessary but encourage them to use dictionaries, if available, to find out the meaning of unknown words.
- Allow them to check their answers with a partner.
- Go through the answers together.

ANSWERS
1 the French capital, Paris
2 this great river, The Amazon
3 the desert, the Sahara
4 the country, Japan

Exercise 3a

> **Text summary:** An article about the city of Yakutsk in Russia which may be the coldest city on earth. It is written in the first person by a visitor to the city who describes what it is like to live in such a cold place.

- Tell students NOT to read the text yet.
- Focus their attention on the photos and the title.
- Students work in pairs to predict eight words or phrases that they think will be used in the text and write them down in a list. You could remind them that they learnt about predicting before you read in Unit 1 of this course.

EXTRA CHALLENGE Encourage stronger students to predict common collocations rather than just single words. Example: If they have the adjective 'freezing', ask *Freezing what?* to prompt them to make a phrase (freezing temperatures, freezing conditions, etc.).

- If there is time, elicit some of their words and phrases and write them on the board. Alternatively, put two pairs together to share their word lists and find out whether any of the predicted vocabulary is the same.

STUDY TIP By now, predicting before reading any text should be an automatic habit for students. If you don't think it is, remind them frequently to look at any pictures and headlines first, then spend a moment predicting silently to themselves before they read.

Exercise 3b
- Students read the article, noticing any vocabulary that they predicted in exercise 3a.
- Allow enough time for them to read the article thoroughly.
- Elicit any words which they had successfully predicted. Drill pronunciation if necessary.

WATCH OUT! The students know the noun *degree* when it means a qualification you get from university. In these pages it is a different word, used in the plural form *degrees*, and refers to temperature (degrees celsius) but the spelling and pronunciation are the same.

EXTENSION If students brainstorm possible problems of living in a cold place in exercise 1c, they could point out those which they thought of that are mentioned in the text. You could ask them what questions about other problems they'd like to ask someone from Yakutsk if they had the chance.

Exercise 4
- Focus students' attention on the words in a–d which are also highlighted in bold in paragraphs 1–3 of the article.

Unit 7 125

- They need to find what each of these phrases refers to in the text. You could find the first one together as a demonstration: *When it says 'the Russian city' which city is it referring to?* (Yakutsk)
- They work alone on the task.
- Allow them to check with a partner if you wish.
- Go through the answers together. Remind them that these are examples of paraphrasing.
- You could ask them to draw arrows from the bold phrases to what they refer to (as in the Unlock the code box – this shows that these all refer backwards in the text to something already mentioned.

ANSWERS
1 Yakutsk
2 −50°C
3 Yakutsk
4 Yakuts

Exercise 5

- Students focus on paragraphs 4 and 5 which have underlined words.
- Ask them to find a word or phrase after each underlined word which means the same thing. Point out that the instruction says 'later in the sentence or in the next few sentences'.
- Do one example together as a demonstration if necessary.
- Students work alone on the task.
- Go through the answers. Highlight how boring it would be if the writer didn't use paraphrasing: *I put on all the things that I packed. I'm wearing 14 things.* Or *I don't feel too bad. But soon, I start to feel bad.*

ANSWERS
1 things, items of clothing
2 bad, terrible
3 Moscow, the capital
4 journey, trip

Exercise 6

- Put students into small groups to discuss.
  EXTRA SUPPORT Allow students extra time to read the article again with this in mind. You could ask them to find and underline three interesting facts to discuss.
- Conduct a class discussion. Ask them to suggest interesting facts.
  EXTRA SUPPORT Write sentence starters on the board if necessary: *I think the most interesting fact is … , It is interesting that …* or *The fact that … is really interesting.*
  EXTENSION You could also ask *Would you like to visit Yakutsk? Why/why not?*

Vocabulary -ed and -ing adjectives

Exercise 7a

- Students read the information about -ed and -ing adjectives in the Vocabulary focus box.
- Tell them to answer the questions (1 and 2) about the sentences (a and b).
- Go through the answers together. To check they understand the meanings of the words, elicit other times when people feel *disappointed* and elicit other things which can be *frightening*.

- To check they understand the difference between these two kinds of adjectives ask: *In sentence 2, how is the person feeling?* (frightened) *What is causing him to feel like this?* (the pain)
- If you think it would help your students, give them two more examples: 1) *My uncle is very interesting.* 2) *My uncle is very interested.* Ask: *Which sentence is about my uncle's character?* (1, because he makes me/other people interested in him) *Which sentence is about my uncle's feeling?* (2) *Which sentence could we add the phrase '… in history' to?* (2, because history is a subject which makes my uncle feel interested: *My uncle is very interested in history.*)

ANSWERS
1 b
2 a

Exercise 7b

- Students look at the article *The coldest city on Earth?* again and underline any -ed or -ing adjectives they find. (There are two more.)
- Elicit which adjectives the students found.
  WATCH OUT! Not all the -ed and -ing words in the text are adjectives. For example, *visiting* is a gerund, *arrived* is a past participle, *packed* is past simple form, *wearing* is part of the present continuous form.

ANSWERS
embarrassing, surprised

Exercise 8

- Students work alone to choose the correct form.
- Go through the answers together.
- If students have made any mistakes, refer them back to the Vocabulary focus box, explain and ask concept checking questions. For example: In sentence 2 'It' and 'we lost the match' are about the situation so we need an -ing adjective. *Why do you think it wasn't surprising that they lost the match?* (the other team was better, they hadn't practised enough, the other team was playing in their home stadium, some of the players on the team were ill so they had fewer players than the other team, etc.) *Which adjective do we need if this sentence starts with 'I wasn't' instead of 'It wasn't'?* ('surprised' because it is my feeling.)

ANSWERS
1 excited
2 surprising
3 worrying
4 annoyed
5 fascinated

Exercise 9

- Point out to students that the box contains the beginning of some common adjectives.
- Students work alone to complete the sentences, choosing the -ed or -ing ending of the adjective.
- If necessary, remind them to think about whether the adjective is describing someone's feeling or describing a person, situation or thing.
- Allow them to check their answers in pairs if you have time.
- Go through the answers together.

126

PRONUNCIATION If any students are making pronunciation mistakes with the *-ed* endings, this is a good time to correct them. They should only be pronouncing the ending as /ɪd/ when it follows a /t/ or a /d/. Ask them to look through all the *-ed* adjectives in exercises 8 and 9 to find which ones need an ending pronounced as /ɪd/ (excited, fascinated, disappointed.) Drill all the *-ed* adjectives to ensure they are pronouncing them well.

ANSWERS
1 embarrassed
2 frightened
3 exciting
4 bored
5 relaxing
6 disappointed
7 confusing
8 amazed

Exercise 10a
- Students write their own sentences using adjectives from exercises 8 and 9.

EXTRA CHALLENGE Ask students to write true sentences about themselves, their families, friends and places they know.

- Monitor their writing carefully. Elicit any corrections of the adjective forms from the students as you monitor. Make sure some sentences contain *-ed* and some contain *-ing* adjectives.

ANSWERS
Students' own answers

EXTRA CHALLENGE Fast finishers can write extra sentences with other adjectives or using the same adjectives with the other ending.

Exercise 10b
- Put students into pairs.
- Highlight that they need to read their sentences aloud to their partner but must NOT say the adjective.
- Demonstrate how to do this by reading one of the example sentences from the Vocabulary focus box, making a 'beep' noise instead of the adjective.
- Tell them to take turns.
- Their partner will guess the missing adjective.
- Make sure they choose the correct adjective ending. Encourage the writer of the sentence to explain if his partner makes a mistake with this grammar.

EXTRA CHALLENGE If they wrote true sentences (see extra challenge in exercise 10a) they should ask and give extra information about them.

EXTRA ACTIVITY You could ask students to write sentences similar to the ones in this exercise, leaving a line or gap where the adjective should be. They could try to use the other ending for each of the adjectives this time. These sentences could be written in class or for homework. Once you have checked them for accuracy, they can be used to test the students' memories in a few lessons' time.

7.4 Speaking and writing

Goals
- Check into a hotel
- Write short notes and messages

Lead-in
- Put students into pairs.
- Ask them to discuss what they can see in the two photos.
- Conduct class feedback, eliciting similarities and differences between the photos. Elicit/teach useful vocabulary: *reception desk, receptionist*.
- Ask questions to check the meaning of *check in*: *Do you check in when you arrive or when you leave?* (arrive) *What does the receptionist ask you to do when you check in?* (register, give your car registration number, give credit card details, etc.) Elicit the phrasal verb for leaving a hotel (check out) and ask *What do you have to do when you check out?* (pay, return the keys etc.)

Listening & Speaking checking into a hotel

Exercise 1
- Tell students to look at the words and phrases in the box and in the list below. You could point out that sometimes we shorten *bed and breakfast* to *B&B* (b and b).

EXTRA SUPPORT Allow students who need extra support time to look up these words in dictionaries or go through the meanings with them if dictionaries are not available.

- Ask them to discuss both questions with their partner. Encourage them to give as much information as possible about 'why' for each question. Remind them that they are explaining their preferences and therefore there is no correct answer. In fact, they may even have different preferences according to whether they are travelling alone, for work, arranging accommodation for a family trip etc. This could be interesting to discuss.
- Conduct a class discussion about the advantages and disadvantages of the different types of accommodation.
- Elicit what students think is important and not important when choosing accommodation. Encourage them to give reasons for their choices.

WATCH OUT! Although the word *hotel* is used in a number of languages, the pronunciation in English may be different because we strongly stress the second syllable. Drill the students if necessary.

> **Background note:** In the UK, as well as hotels there are bed and breakfasts (B&Bs) or guesthouses. These are less expensive and you usually stay in a room in a private house. Breakfast is included, but evening meals often are not.

Exercise 2a
- Students read the instruction.
- Tell them to predict Lars' and Carmen's questions about the things in the box. They can do this alone or in pairs.
- Monitor their work to check that they are forming correct questions.

Unit 7   127

POSSIBLE ANSWERS
Is there a charge for Wi-Fi?
Do I need a code for it?
What time's breakfast?
Where is breakfast?
Can we check in now?
Can we leave our luggage?
What time is checkout?

Exercise 2b 7.6

> **Audio summary:** Two different conversations; one in a hotel and the other in a hostel. Both conversations are between a receptionist and a guest who is checking in.

- Tell students to listen to the recording to find answers to their questions.
- Play track 7.6.
- Conduct class feedback. Ask whether the speakers asked the questions that they had predicted. Were there any other questions?

AUDIOSCRIPT 7.6
Conversation 1
L   Hi, I'd like to check in, please.
R   Yes, of course, do you have a reservation?
L   Yes, my name's Lars Meyer.
R   OK, Mr Meyer. So that's a double room for three nights?
L   Yeah, that's right.
R   Right, so could you fill in the registration form please? And I'll just need to take a copy of your passport and a credit card. OK, thank you, and could you sign here and here. Right, here's your key. It's room two zero six on the second floor.
L   Thanks. And please could I just check a couple of things about the room?
R   Yes, of course, go ahead.
L   Is Wi-Fi available in the room?
R   Yes, it is.
L   And is there a charge for it?
R   No, it's free of charge to all our guests.
L   OK, that's great. Oh, and will I need a code?
R   Yes, you'll find the code on the desk in your room.
L   OK, thanks. Oh yeah, and what time's breakfast?
R   Breakfast's between 7 and 10 in the main restaurant on the ground floor.
L   OK thanks very much, that's great.
R   You're welcome. Enjoy your stay!

Conversation 2
C   Hi there, we've got a room booked in the name of Rodriguez. Please could we check in?
R   Sorry, what was the name again?
C   Rodriguez … Carmen Rodriguez.
R   Just a second, let me check. Yeah, yeah I've got the booking here, but I'm afraid you're a bit early.
C   Oh …
R   The room's not quite ready yet. Check-in's at two o'clock.
C   Oh, I see, so …
R   So, er, could you come back around two and your room'll be ready then.
C   OK, no problem. But is there somewhere we can leave our luggage? We've got quite a lot of stuff.
R   Yes, you can leave it behind reception. I'll get someone to help you with that.

C   OK, thanks, and it'll be safe there … ?
R   Yeah, yeah someone'll be here all the time.
C   OK, so we'll check in later then, when we come back.
R   Yeah, that's fine.
C   Oh, and er, … can I just ask you, what time is checkout?
R   You have to vacate the room by ten.
C   Check-out is 10 a.m.? Quite early then.
R   Yeah.
C   OK, so we'll maybe …

Exercise 3 7.6

- Ask students to read sentences 1–9 and ask whether there are any words they are unsure about. Encourage peer-teaching or explain meanings yourself.
- Tell them to listen again and write L, C or R for the person who says each sentence.

EXTRA CHALLENGE Stronger students could try to remember who said which sentence before listening again. They then listen to check their ideas.

- Play track 7.6 again.
- Confirm any answers they may have missed.

ANSWERS
1 L   2 R   3 R   4 L   5 L   6 R   7 C   8 R   9 C

Exercise 4 7.7

- Ask students to repeat the phrases after the recording to ensure they have good pronunciation.
- Play track 7.7 more than once if necessary, pausing whenever you need to. Encourage them to make helpful marks on the sentences to show the most strongly stressed words and any linking between words. You can highlight that when *check in* and *check out* are verbs the stress is on the preposition – check **in**, check **out**. When they are nouns the stress is on *check* – **check**-in, **check**out.

AUDIOSCRIPT 7.7
1   I'd like to check in, please.
2   Do you have a reservation?
3   Could you fill in the registration form, please?
4   Is Wi-Fi available in the room?
5   Is there a charge for it?
6   Sorry, what was the name again?
7   Is there somewhere we can leave our luggage?
8   I'll get someone to help you with that.
9   What time is checkout?

Exercise 5

- Students read the instruction and turn to page 162.
- In pairs they practise the conversations.
- Monitor carefully. Give them time to practise both conversations, taking both roles.
- If you feel that there are still some pronunciation problems, correct them with the class, then re-pair the students so they are working with someone different and ask them to do the exercise again.

Exercise 6

- Tell the students that they are going to have a similar conversation now but without the script.

- Point out that the phrases they need are in the Language for speaking box and give them time to read through the phrases again.
- Put students into different pairs if possible. One student is Student A and the other Student B.
- They turn to the relevant page (Student A page 128 and Student B page 132) and act out the conversation.

SMART COMMUNICATION Checking into a hotel is one situation when you can predict the kind of questions you will need to ask and the questions people will ask you. It is a good idea to prepare in advance by having questions ready so that you do not waste time unnecessarily. In situations like this, *Can I just ask you … ?* and *Could I just check … ?* are useful phrases to signal to the listener that you need information. Also, it is a good idea to repeat the information or paraphrase it in order to check that it's correct. Example:
C: … what time is checkout?
R: You have to vacate the room by ten.
C: Checkout is 10 a.m.?

Writing short notes and messages

Exercise 7
- Put students into pairs.
- Tell them to read the all the different notes and messages a–g.

EXTRA CHALLENGE Ask stronger students to cover sentences 1–7 and individually think about what each message tells the reader and why the person sent each one. This means that they will have to find their own way to explain the function of each message or note. Then they can check how close their explanations were to the reasons 1–7.

- Ask students to work in their pairs to match each note or message with the reason for writing 1–7.
- Go through the answers together.

EXTENSION Ask students to think about the kind of notes and messages they write in their private lives and for work. Do they write any in English? Ask them to imagine notes or messages they might need to write in English if they were travelling in another country. Elicit ideas from the class.

ANSWERS
1 f 2 d 3 e 4 a 5 b 6 g 7 c

Exercise 8
- Tell students to read the Language for writing box.
- Go through the three features which are mentioned if necessary.
- Students read the notes and messages in exercise 7 again. They find and underline examples of the features.
- Allow them to check their answers with a partner.
- Go through the answers together.

ANSWERS
1 I'm just arriving at the bus station.
  The traffic is terrible.
  Do you want me to get you anything?
  An/the engineer is on his way.
2 Shall we/Could we cut the last part?
3 v long = very long
  1 hr = 1 hour

Exercise 9
- Students work alone, deleting words in sentences 1 and 2 to make them into messages.
- You could ask them to cover the messages in exercise 7 until they have finished. Then they can read messages b and c again to check their answers.
- Conduct a class discussion on the kind of words which they crossed out. Refer to the Language for writing box as necessary.

Exercise 10
- Explain to students that they need to turn the sentences into short notes or messages.
- Students could do this task alone or in pairs.
- Monitor which words they are leaving out.
- Go through the answers together.

ANSWERS
1 Coffee machine out of order. Use machine on 2nd floor.
2 In city centre. Want me to get currency for holiday?
3 Working late tonight. Home at 8.00.
4 Thanks v much for dinner invitation Sat night. Love to come. See U then.
5 Missed bus. There in 1 hr.
6 See U at station Tues. Train leaves 7.30.

Exercise 11
- Students read the three situations.
- Tell them to write the first message or note to their partner.
- Students 'send' a message to their partner and their partner writes a reply.
- Monitor carefully and note any points for correction.

EXTENSION You could see how many times they can reply to each other with a message or note. If they are having difficulty, tell them that they have to change the arrangement for some reason so they need to send another message.

- Conduct a class discussion on how easy or difficult it is to write notes and messages like this in English. Ask some pairs to read out their chain of messages.
- Do any necessary error correction.

EXTRA ACTIVITY If you have time and think your students will benefit, put them into new pairs and ask them to repeat the message writing exercise choosing a different situation from exercise 11.

Unit 7 129

7.5 Video

Beijing subway

VIDEOSCRIPT
Everything about Beijing is big and busy. It's a bustling metropolis that covers 16 districts over almost 17,000 square kilometres.
As the country's capital, Beijing is China's political and cultural centre. You can find the country's government buildings, its biggest businesses and many of its most famous landmarks here.
And everywhere you look, there are people. Beijing has got a population of over 21 million people. Every day they cross the city to get home, get to work or get to school.
A city this busy needs an efficient transport network. But Beijing is an ancient city with very narrow streets – too narrow for today's traffic.
Many people choose to cycle around the city, but to get somewhere faster they can use the Beijing Subway.
This fast rail network is the oldest metro system in China. It started in 1969 with one line that was 24 kilometres long. Today it has 17 lines with almost 465 kilometres of track.
Each week around 10 million people use the subway. It is one of the busiest and most crowded metro systems in the world.
The population of Beijing is growing all the time. Experts predict it will continue to grow.
So the Chinese government are going to expand the railway. But this won't be easy and will take a lot of work. The plan is to have 30 lines with 450 stations and over 1,000 kilometres of track.
Beijing isn't the only city in China expanding its metro system. All over the country, cities are building or improving their subways. By 2050, the country will account for almost half of the world's metro lines, but Beijing will still be one of the busiest and the biggest in the country.

VIDEO ANSWERS

Exercise 1
Suggested answers:
Photo 1 busy traffic in the city; busy traffic on narrow streets
Photo 2 a map of subway lines; the metro system in Beijing
Photo 3 A train coming into a subway station; people crossing the city on the subway

Exercise 3
Suggested answers:
a The video shows people in cars, buses, taxis but mentions also bicycles (shows rickshaws) and the metro system.
b Because Beijing is an ancient city and its streets are too narrow for traffic.
c They want to expand it to more lines, more stations and more tracks.

Exercise 4
a 16   b 21   c 1969   d 10 million   e 30   f 1,000
g 2050

Review

ANSWERS

Exercise 1b
1 won't
2 might
3 will
4 will
5 will
6 might not
7 might

Exercise 2a
1 Everybody
2 nowhere
3 somewhere
4 everyone
5 anything
6 anything

Exercise 3a
1 When the trains are **crowded** you sometimes have to stand.
2 On long journeys I try to avoid motorways and **main roads** and use quieter routes.
3 **Fares** keep going up in my city – the metro in particular is getting very expensive.
4 I hate sitting in a **traffic jam** for hours without even moving.
5 I buy my **bus pass** every month. It's cheaper and more convenient.

Exercise 4a
1 visa
2 souvenirs
3 flight
4 sightseeing
5 accommodation

Exercise 4b
1 apply for a visa
2 buy/choose souvenirs
3 book/choose a flight
4 go sightseeing
5 choose/book accommodation

Exercise 5a
1 relaxing
2 embarrassed
3 annoying
4 frightened

Exercise 6b 7.8
1 like
2 fill
3 form
4 available
5 charge
6 checkout
7 someone

AUDIOSCRIPT 7.8
A I'd like to check in, please. The name's Samson.
B OK, Mr Samson, that's a single room for two nights. Could you fill in the registration form, please?
A Of course. Is Wi-Fi available in the room?
B Yes, but there's a small charge for it.
A I see. And what time is checkout?
B You have to leave your room by 11.00 a.m.
A OK, great.
B Room 604. I'll get someone to help you with your bags.

Unit 7 131

8 Language and learning

Unit overview

Language input

Ability (*can, be able to*) (CB p76)	• Bilingual children can speak two languages. • The brain is able to repair itself.
Obligation, necessity and permission (*must, have to, can*) (CB p78)	• All teachers must have a Masters degree. • Parents have to pay a small fee for books. • Teachers can earn a lot of money.
Grammar reference (CB pp148–9)	

Vocabulary development

Skills and abilities (CB p77)	• map reading, telling jokes, making decisions … • He's brilliant at solving problems. • She's OK at fixing things. • I'm useless at remembering people's names.
Education (CB p78)	• maths, drama, literature … • Was your school strict? • How do you feel about taking exams?
Make* and *do (CB p81)	• make a noise • do sport

Skills development

Listening: Understanding connected speech (2) (CB p80)	
Speaking: Asking for clarification (CB p82)	
Writing: Completing a form (CB p83)	

Video

Documentary: Career change (Coursebook DVD & CB p84)	
Vox pops (Coursebook DVD & TG p262)	

More materials

Workbook	• Language practice for grammar, pronunciation, vocabulary, speaking and writing • Listening for pleasure • Review: Units 7 and 8
Photocopiable activities	• Grammar: A little learning (TG p215 & TSRD) • Vocabulary: Robot sales (TG p233 & TSRD) • Communication: A bit lost (TG p251 & TSRD)
Tests	• Unit 8 test (TSRD)
Unit 8 wordlist (TSRD)	

8.1 The amazing human brain

Goals
- Talk about ability
- Talk about skills and abilities

Lead-in
- Put an image of a human brain on the board.
- Elicit the word *brain*. Ask the class to brainstorm anything they know about the human brain and write their suggestions on the board. To help them think of ideas, you could prompt them: *Size? Colour? What does it do? How does it work? Are human brains better than computers?* etc.

Grammar & Listening   ability (*can, be able to*)

Exercise 1a
- With books closed, explain to students that they are going to see some words and they need to say the colours they see, not the words. They should say the colours as fast as they can.
- Put students into pairs to do the activity.

Exercise 1b
- Students read and discuss the questions with their partner.
- When they've talked about what happened, they look at the information at the bottom of the page.
- Conduct a class discussion.

Exercise 2a
- Tell students that they are going to listen to a radio programme about the human brain.
- **EXTRA ACTIVITY** You could refer students back to the ideas they had in the lead-in and ask them to choose some things they think might be mentioned in the radio programme. This encourages them to practise the skill of prediction before listening.
- Put the students into pairs and ask them to read the statements 1–6 and decide whether they are true or false.

Exercise 2b 8.1

> **Audio summary**: A fairly long extract taken from a radio programme about the human brain. The radio presenter interviews a neuroscientist who answers questions about commonly held beliefs about the human brain.

- Play track 8.1 so that they can check their answers.
- Go through the answers together, checking that they heard the relevant information. You could ask them to try to remember what the speaker said.

ANSWERS
1 F ('The truth is that we use all of our brain. We don't use all of it at the same time, but even for a small action like moving your little finger, we use a large part of it.')
2 T ('At birth, the average brain of boys is 12 to 20% larger than that of girls.')
3 F ('According to research, however, it isn't true.')
4 F ('Oh, definitely. Many children grow up in bi-lingual homes and can speak two languages equally well. In fact some research says that speaking two languages can actually improve your brain.')
5 T/F ('In some cases, the brain can repair itself; in other cases the brain isn't able to repair itself. It depends on how serious the problem or brain damage is. So this is sometimes true and sometimes false.')
6 F ('No, of course they can't!')

AUDIOSCRIPT 8.1
On today's programme we're talking about the brain. The brain is an amazing organ. It can learn. It can remember. It can think. But there are many myths about the brain, stories a lot of people believe, but which are not true. My guest today is neuroscientist Dr Gerry Fernandez.
Dr F Good morning.
P … and I'm hoping he'll be able to tell us what's true and what's not.
Dr F I'll certainly do my best!
P OK, so first question: is it true that we only use 10% of our brains?
Dr F Ah yes, the 10% myth! This is one of the most common myths about the brain, but don't believe everything you hear! The truth is that we use all of our brain. We don't use all of it at the same time, but even for a small action like moving your little finger, we use a large part of it.
P Not true then?
Dr F I'm afraid not!
P Alright, now my next question is: are boys' brains bigger than girls' brains?
Dr F Surprising as it may sound, this is true! At birth, the average brain of boys is 12 to 20% larger than that of girls.
P Really? So, does that mean boys are more intelligent?
Dr F Er … no, it doesn't.
P OK, next question. Can you remember things better if you listen to classical music?
Dr F Ah, you're talking about the 'Mozart' effect. Many people bought classical music CDs after hearing this myth in the 1990s. According to research, however, it isn't true. But who knows, you might enjoy the music anyway!
P Absolutely! My next question is: can babies learn more than one language at the same time?
Dr F Oh, definitely. Many children grow up in bi-lingual homes and can speak two languages equally well. In fact some research says that speaking two languages can actually improve your brain.
P Ah, interesting. And what about this? Is the brain able to repair itself?
Dr F In some cases, the brain can repair itself; in other cases the brain isn't able to repair itself. It depends on how serious the problem or brain damage is. So this is sometimes true and sometimes false.
P Right, OK, thank you. And my final question for you today is: can computers read our minds?
Dr F No, of course they can't! But it's an interesting question, because scientists believe computers will soon be able to scan our brains and put our thoughts into words. They won't be able to understand the thoughts, though.
P So how will that help us?

Unit 8

Dr F People will be able to dictate letters and search the internet just by thinking.
P Oh, I see Brilliant. And that also means people with speech pro.blems might be able to communicate just by thinking.
Dr F Exactly.
P That's amazing! Well, thank you Dr Fernandez for helping us separate the facts from the myths.
Dr F My pleasure.

Exercise 3   8.2

- Ask students to read the sentences 1–3 from the audioscript.
- Tell them that you will play the last part of the programme again so they can complete the sentences.
  EXTRA CHALLENGE Students can try to remember the sentences and complete them before they listen. Then they can just check their answers.
- Play track 8.2.
- Check they heard the key words. Elicit whether these sentences are talking about now (the present) or the future. (future).

ANSWERS
1 able
2 won't
3 might

AUDIOSCRIPT 8.2

Dr F No, of course they can't! But it's an interesting question, because scientists believe computers will soon be able to scan our brains and put our thoughts into words. They won't be able to understand the thoughts, though.
P So how will that help us?
Dr F People will be able to dictate letters and search the internet just by thinking.
P Oh, I see. Brilliant. And that also means people with speech problems might be able to communicate just by thinking.
Dr F Exactly.
P That's amazing! Well, thank you Dr Fernandez for helping us separate the facts from the myths.
Dr F My pleasure.

Exercise 4

- Focus students' attention on the Grammar focus box.
- Students read the information about *can* and *be able to*, then complete the rules with the words 'present' and 'future'.
- Go through the answers together.
  WATCH OUT! A common student error is *will can* which you need to be aware of and correct to *will be able to*.

ANSWERS
1 present
2 future

- Refer students to *Grammar reference* on p148. There are three more exercises here students can do for homework. See answers on p135.

Exercise 5

- Before students complete the article, point out that they should only use *be able to* when *can* or *can't* are not possible. When they use *be able to* they should be careful to use the correct form.
- Students work alone on this task.
- Encourage them to check their answers in pairs if you wish.
- Go through the answers together. Elicit why they have chosen each form (asking them about present/future and positive/negative, referring them back to the Grammar Focus box if necessary).

ANSWERS
1 can
2 can't
3 be able to
4 be able to
5 won't be able to
6 can't
7 will be able to
8 will be able to
9 will be able to
10 be able to

Exercise 6

- Ask students to complete the sentences. Point out that they need to use *can/can't*, or *be able to* together with their own ideas.
- Put students into small groups or pairs to compare and discuss their sentences, particularly sentences 1–3.
- Monitor carefully during the writing and discussions to check they are using the target grammar forms accurately.

ANSWERS
Students' own answers

Vocabulary & Speaking skills and abilities

Exercise 7a

- Go through the meaning of *communication* and *practical* with students if necessary.
- Tell them to read the words and phrases and decide whether each one is an example of communication skills, practical skills or thinking/learning skills. Some could be part of more than one skills group.
- Allow plenty of time for the students to work with a partner, discussing and categorizing the words and phrases into the three groups.
  EXTRA SUPPORT This is a good time to encourage students who need support to use dictionaries to check unknown vocabulary in the words and phrases. With a group where you think most students will have difficulties, you could go through the vocabulary together before they start.
- Go through their answers as a class.
  EXTRA CHALLENGE Stronger students may be able to give reasons for their choices, especially when they think that a word or phrase can be in more than one group.
- Drill the pronunciation of any problem vocabulary.

ANSWERS
Communication skills (C): learning languages, telling jokes, explaining things clearly, making speeches, organizing events, map reading
Practical skills (P): taking care of people, fixing things that are broken, organizing events, map reading
Thinking/learning skills (T): understanding how things work, solving computer problems, following instructions,

making decisions, remembering people's names/historical or scientific facts, organizing events, map reading, spelling

Exercise 7b
- Students read the instruction and then add their own ideas.
- They could compare their ideas in pairs or small groups.

Exercise 8a
- In pairs, students order the phrases.
- Find number 1 (*brilliant at*) together as an example.
- Allow students time to discuss the order.

ANSWERS
1 b   2 c   3 g   4 a   5 f   6 e   7 d

Pronunciation *at*

Exercise 8b 8.3
- Tell students to listen to the track you are going to play and check the order of their answers.
- Play track 8.3 so they can check the order.
- Play track 8.3 again so that they can listen carefully to how 'at' is pronounced.
- Elicit that this is another example of a weak form in connected speech and that we don't pronounce 'at' with a full /æ/ sound. The word *at* is linked strongly to the consonant sound which comes before it in each case and is pronounced /ə/ in a relaxed way with a schwa.

ANSWERS/AUDIOSCRIPT 8.3 & 8.4
1 He's brilliant at solving computer problems.
2 I'm really good at fixing things.
3 She's good at spelling.
4 She's quite good at map reading.
5 I'm OK at following instructions.
6 He isn't very good at telling jokes.
7 I'm terrible at remembering people's names.

Exercise 8c 8.4
- Tell students to repeat the sentences and try to focus on getting the pronunciation of *at* right as they say them.
- Play track 8.4 so that the students can repeat the sentences. It is likely that you will need to play it several times to ensure good, natural pronunciation.

Exercise 8d
- Elicit the answer to the question.
  EXTENSION You could point out that it's a very common pattern – preposition followed by *-ing* form – and elicit other examples, e.g. *worried about going, interested in learning, tired of working, looking forward to seeing*, etc.

ANSWER
After *at* we use the *-ing* form of the verb

Exercise 9a
- Ask students to read the instruction carefully and point out that the end goal is to find out who they have most in common with in their group.
- Put them into small groups.
- With a weaker group, drill the question starters so that they can say them naturally.
- Allow plenty of time for this group speaking practice.

FEEDBACK FOCUS Monitor to check that the students are using the phrases from exercise 8a to explain clearly how good they are at doing the different things. Also note any good, natural pronunciation of *at* in connected speech, together with any problem pronunciation.

Exercise 9b
- Get all the students' attention and conduct a class discussion.
- Find out within the groups which students had the most in common.
- Conduct any necessary error correction and praise good examples of *at* and the *good at* phrases.

GRAMMAR REFERENCE ANSWERS
Exercise 1
1 will be able to
2 will be able to
3 might be able to
4 might not be able to
5 will be able to/can
6 might not be able to

Exercise 2
1 Can you remember any good jokes?
2 Lucy won't be able to pass the exam tomorrow.
3 I can study and care for the children.
4 Adriana can't attend the event, unfortunately.
5 Listen carefully and you will be able to understand everything.
6 Will robots be able to have conversations with us one day?

Exercise 3
1 Will scientists be able to
2 won't be able to
3 can
4 can
5 will be able to
6 Will I be able to
7 can
8 can
9 won't be able to

8.2 The secrets of a successful education

Goals
- Talk about obligation, necessity and permission
- Talk about education

Lead-in
- Put students into pairs or small groups and ask them to focus on the title of this lesson; *The secrets of a successful education*. Ask them to discuss for a minute what they think the lesson is going to be about.
- Elicit some ideas from the class.
- Check all the students can pronounce successful /sək'sesfl/ correctly.
- You could also ask students to discuss in pairs whether they think their own education as a child/young person was successful or not and give reasons.

Unit 8   135

Vocabulary & Speaking education

Exercise 1

EXTRA ACTIVITY Put students in pairs or groups to brainstorm vocabulary for school subjects. If necessary, give them a few to help them start, e.g. *chemistry, mathematics*. You could give them a time limit to add a competitive element.

- Ask students to read the subjects in the box. (If they did the extra activity, ask them whether they had thought of all of these subjects.)
- In pairs, tell them to check that they and their partner both know all the vocabulary and then discuss the questions.

EXTRA CHALLENGE Encourage strong students to give information about why they didn't do some of the subjects (they weren't available, they didn't choose them, etc.), why they enjoyed or didn't enjoy certain subjects and why they think certain subjects are particularly useful or useless.

- Monitor the discussions and note any interesting answers. Also note any pronunciation problems with this vocabulary to correct as a class. (Students may not know that in abbreviations such as IT and PE, we stress the final letter.)
- Conduct a class discussion and drill pronunciation of any problem words.

EXTENSION You could ask students to think again about the subjects they studied and talk in pairs about how good at each subject they were, remembering the phrases from 8.1 exercise 8a.

EXTRA ACTIVITY We often enjoy subjects we are good at. What other factors can help students to enjoy a subject? Elicit ideas from the class.

Exercise 2a

- Tell students to read questions 1–8 carefully.

EXTRA SUPPORT At this point you can go through unknown vocabulary with students who need extra support or tell them to use dictionaries to check any unknown words and phrases.

- Students work alone to match questions 1–8 with answers a–h. (They may need their dictionaries for vocabulary in these answers too.)
- Go through the answers together.
- Drill pronunciation of any difficult words, including word stress in long words such as *qualifications* /ˌkwɒlɪfɪˈkeɪʃnz/.

WATCH OUT! Question 7 asks about *taking exams*. It may be useful to check that students know the difference between *take* and *pass* an exam as this is a false friend in some languages. (take = do or sit an exam, pass = be successful)

ANSWERS
1 f 2 a 3 h 4 d 5 b 6 g 7 c 8 e

Exercise 2b

- Put students into pairs to ask and give real answers to the questions.
- Remind them that they should try to find out as much information as possible from their partner.

- Monitor the discussions, note any pronunciation problems and give a time limit to the end of the activity when most students have discussed almost all the questions.
- Conduct feedback, drilling any problem pronunciation. Ask the students to tell the class their partner's most interesting answer.

EXTENSION If your students enjoy debates, you could conduct a class discussion of questions 4 and or 5. Students should be encouraged to give examples to support their views.

Grammar & Reading obligation, necessity and permission (*must, have to, can*)

Exercise 3

- Ask students to read the list carefully and go through any vocabulary which is unknown.
- Check that students understand that when they score each point in the list, 1 is low importance and 5 is high.

EXTRA SUPPORT You could give them some time to think individually which score they give each thing before they start discussing.

- Put them into groups to discuss how important each thing is. If they can't agree, encourage discussion but point out that it is fine for them to have different opinions. They should support their opinions with reasons and examples.
- They may also need to specify what some of the things mean for them, e.g. *lots of homework – How much? And study for many hours a day – How many?*
- Conduct class discussion. You could find out the top three things for the class.

Exercise 4

> **Text summary:** Two factfiles on different education systems: Finland and Shanghai.

- Tell students that they are going to read about the education systems in Finland and Shanghai.
- Ask if any of them know about or have experience of these places. (There is some information in the background notes which you could share.)
- Students read both factfiles to find which things in the list are mentioned.
- Go through the answers together.

ANSWERS
regular exams, well-qualified teachers, lots of homework, studying for many hours a day, regular sport/exercise, strict rules (an enjoyment of learning is implied by 'willing to work hard')

Exercise 5

- Students need more time to read the text again for specific detail.
- Ask them to read sentences 1–6, paying close attention to the use of *can*, *must* and *can't* (in sentences 1, 3, 5 and 6).
- Point out that the information is not only true or false but may also be unknown.
- Go through the answers with the class.

STUDY TIP This exercise includes not only *true* and *false* but also *don't know*, which makes it more realistic. Texts often don't answer all our questions about the story or topic they cover. It is a good idea to think about what questions we need to find the answer to before reading a text. If it doesn't provide all the answers, then we can then do further research online or in printed material to try to get a complete picture of the topic.

PRONUNCIATION Make sure that when students read out the sentences they are pronouncing *can* and *can't* clearly. Of course there is a huge difference in meaning between these words but this can be lost in pronunciation. To ensure that the listener hears the difference you could suggest they make *can* /kən/ with a short, relaxed /ə/ sound and make *can't* /kɑːnt/ sound much longer with long /ɑː/ sound and also pronounce the final /t/.

ANSWERS
1 F (All education must be completely free.)
2 T (Schools can't charge money for anything, including meals.)
3 T (Teaching is a well-paid profession.)
4 T (There is strong competition for university places.)
5 ? (We only know that it's true in Finland.)
6 F (The text says 'at least an hour a day' so they can do more than an hour.)

Exercise 6

- Conduct a class discussion of the question or put students into small groups to discuss.
- Conduct a class discussion, eliciting the things which most surprised them. Encourage them to explain why.

Background note: PISA (Programme for International Student Assessment) started in 2000 and a new survey is conducted every three years. Assessments are carried out on 15-year-old students and they test mathematics, science and reading. The most recent survey tested 510,000 students in 65 countries.
Finland is a country in the north of Europe and a member of the European Union. Although it is the eighth largest country in Europe, the population is only around 5.5 million.
Shanghai is the largest city in China (and one of the largest in the world) with a population of around 24 million.

Exercise 7

- Focus students' attention on the Grammar focus box.
- Tell them to read the rules and examples carefully.
- Ask questions to check understanding if necessary. Example: *In rule 1 all teachers must have a Masters degree Would it be the same meaning if we replace 'must' with 'have to'?* (yes). *In rule 4 teachers can't give more than an hour and a half of homework would it be the same meaning if we replace 'can't' with 'mustn't'?* (yes) *Would it be the same meaning if we replace 'can't' with 'don't have to'?* (no – *don't have to* means it is not necessary so in this sentence it would allow teachers to give more than an hour and a half of homework if they wish).
- Students work alone to underline *must, have to, don't have to, can, can't* and *mustn't* in the text.

- They should match each underlined example with a rule in the box.
- Put students in pairs to share their answers.
- Go through the answers together as a class, referring to the rules in the Grammar focus box.

ANSWERS
Rule 1: Students only have to do a maximum of half an hour's homework a day. All education must be completely free. Parents have to pay a small fee for books and uniforms. All buxibans must close at 10pm. Students must do physical activity.
Rule 2: Students don't have to wear uniforms.
Rule 3: Students can go home.
Rule 4: Schools can't charge money for anything. Builders mustn't make noise. Teachers can't give more than an hour and a half of homework.

- Refer students to *Grammar reference* on p149. There are three more exercises here students can do for homework. See answers on p138.

Exercise 8a

- Students work alone to complete the facts about education systems, choosing from the options given.
- Check the answers together. If students make mistakes, refer them to the Grammar focus box in your eliciting and explaining.

ANSWERS
1 must
2 can't
3 don't have to
4 must be able to
5 have to

Exercise 8b

- In pairs, students discuss the facts in exercise 8a in relation to their own country.
- Monitor their discussions and note any difficulties students have explaining obligation, necessity and permission.

WATCH OUT! Students often find *don't have to* and *mustn't* confusing, so check carefully that they are using these correctly. If necessary, ask students to think of examples from their own work place or educational setting, e.g. *My company provides laptops when we need to travel so I don't have to have my own laptop* (but I can if I want to) or *I mustn't have my mobile phone switched on during meetings.*

- Conduct error correction if necessary.

Exercise 9

- Students use the grammar studied in this lesson to complete the sentences (1–6).
- Monitor to make sure they are producing correct sentences.
- Students compare their sentences in pairs.
- You could drill the word *jewellery* as this pronunciation is not easy /ˈdʒuːəlri/.

ANSWERS
Students' own answers

EXTENSION Encourage students to discuss their opinions of these sentences, e.g. *What do they think about school uniforms? Do they think parents should pay for school meals?*, etc.

Unit 8 137

Exercise 10a
- Students read the examples. Check they understand the word *perfect*.
- Put the students into small groups to write some rules for a perfect education system.

CRITICAL THINKING If students focus on different stages of education or different people involved in education, they will practise critical thinking. You could ask different groups to think about different education contexts, e.g. primary school, secondary school, university studies OR to think from the perspective of different people, e.g. a secondary school student, a university undergraduate, a primary school teacher, a parent of a child at primary school, a university professor, etc.

- Monitor to make sure they are producing correct sentences.

Exercise 10b
- Students present their group's ideas to the class.

EXTRA SUPPORT Give specific planning time so that the groups can divide their presentation between the members and practise what they are going to say.

- If students have prepared different contexts or perspectives (see critical thinking tip above), the listening groups can try to decide which context or perspective it is.
- Conduct any necessary error correction, particularly if they make mistakes using the modal verbs from this lesson.

EXTENSION Conduct a class discussion on the topic *Can education be perfect? Why/ Why not?* Students may need some time to brainstorm ideas in pairs before discussing.

EXTRA ACTIVITY In some countries *home-schooling* is popular. Parents teach their own children at home or form small groups of families in order to teach them outside the standard school system. You could put the students in small groups to discuss whether this happens in their own countries and to write some rules for parents and children who decide to do home-schooling. Conduct class discussion.

GRAMMAR REFERENCE ANSWERS

Exercise 1
1. can
2. don't have to
3. can
4. mustn't
5. don't have to
6. don't have to
7. have to
8. don't have to

Exercise 2
2. don't have to
3. have to/must
4. must/have to
5. can
6. can't

Exercise 3
1. I must remember to give Mr Simons a card.
2. You don't have to go to the library – the book's online.
3. We mustn't/can't be late for the test today.
4. Can we all have a holiday next week?
5. Students must/have to attend three lectures a week.
6. Do students have to study maths until they leave school?

8.3 Vocabulary and skills development

Goals
- Understand connected speech (2)
- Understand and use *make* and *do*

Listening & Speaking understanding connected speech (2)

Lead-in
- Ask students to look at the words and pictures on these pages.
- Tell them to think about and discuss with a partner what the words might have in common.
- After a few minutes, explain that some people were asked for their favourite word and these are the answers.
- Ask them to decide which of the words they like best, either because they like the meaning, the sound or how the word looks.

Exercise 1
- Put students into groups to discuss questions 1 and 2.
- Elicit some answers from the class, including the reasons why they like the different words.
- You could tell them your own favourite word in English and why you like it.

Exercise 2a   8.5
- Tell them that you are going to play the track so that they can complete the sentences.
- Allow them to check their answers in pairs.
- Play track 8.5 again if any students did not write down all the words.

ANSWERS
1. went out
2. smells like

AUDIOSCRIPT 8.5
1. They went out when it started to snow.
2. This smells like chocolate.

Exercise 2b   8.6
- Explain that the focus of this part of the lesson is listening and pronunciation.
- Tell them to listen to the information about connected speech and at the same time read the Unlock the code box about understanding connected speech.

PRONUNCIATION You could remind them that they studied connected speech in Unit 4 and elicit the two linking sounds they focused on: /w/ e.g. so/w/old and /j/ e.g. high/j/up.

AUDIOSCRIPT 8.6
When a word ends in a consonant and the next word starts with a vowel sound, speakers link the words together so they sound like one word. This can make it difficult to understand.

| went in | *sounds like* | wentin |
| the sound of it | *sounds like* | thesoundofit |

Sometimes words that end and start with consonants are also linked the same way:

let's leave   *sounds like*   letsleave

Exercise 2c 8.7

- Tell the students you are going to play another recording. They need to listen and complete sentences 1–6.
- Play track 8.7.
- Go through the answers together.
- Then talk about or elicit which sounds are connected. Play track 8.7 again to give them another opportunity to study the connected speech.

ANSWERS
1 smell of it
2 leave it
3 was an old
4 was worried, was late
5 it's icy
6 gives, a lot of

AUDIOSCRIPT 8.7
1 He likes the smell of it.
2 You can't leave it in the house.
3 It was an old house.
4 I was worried because it was late.
5 Be careful, it's icy.
6 She gives me a lot of presents.

Exercise 3 8.8

Audio summary: Seven people talk individually about their favourite word in English and why they like it.

- Tell students that you're going to play them a different recording now.
- They will hear seven different people talking about their favourite word.
- Students listen and number the words in order.
- Play track 8.8.
- Go through the answers together.

ANSWERS
1 d tomorrow
2 e care
3 a happiness
4 c octopus
5 g probably
6 b blossom
7 f snow

AUDIOSCRIPT 8.8
1
Tomorrow's my favourite word. Tomorrow will be a brand new day, it doesn't matter what happened in the past. I like the pronunciation of this word. It seems full of possibilities leading to a bright future.
2
Care: it's a very short and simple word but it means a lot. It sounds very open, as is everybody who cares.
3
Happiness: this is my favourite word because I like the sound of it. It makes me feel good when I hear it. You have to smile when you say it and it's one of the first words that I learnt in English.
4
Octopus: When I started learning English at the age of 10, my dad always helped me with my homework and I thought his English was very good. Then one day I was telling him all the new words we'd learnt that day in class, and when I said 'octopus', he just looked at me and said, 'Octopus? I've never heard that before. What is that?' I got very excited: this was the first time in my life I knew something and my dad didn't! It is a wonderful moment in any child's life, and octopus has been my favourite word ever since.
5
Probably: Why? Because it's the best answer to give when you don't want to answer a question or make a decision.
6
Blossom: I really like the word blossom, because I think it sounds as gentle as the thing it represents. It makes me think of young flowers and crisp, sunny spring mornings.
7
Snow – because I like the quiet snow world. It's white and clean and I love freezing weather. Also, I remember having fun when I was a child and it snowed.

Exercise 4a

- Allow plenty of time for students to read the two questions. Make sure they understand the focus of each question.
- In pairs, students discuss the questions and note down their answers.

EXTRA CHALLENGE Strong students should try to remember the answers. Then they will just need to listen and check.

Exercise 4b 8.8

- Play track 8.8 again.
- Go through the answers together.

ANSWERS
1 tomorrow, care, happiness, probably, blossom
2 octopus, snow, happiness

Exercise 5 8.9

- Tell students to listen to these sentences from the recording and complete them.
- Point out that they need to add one to three words per space.
- Play track 8.9. You may need to play it more than once.
- Go through the answers together. Highlight the words which are linked and elicit how they link together in connected speech.

EXTENSION Play track 8.9 again so students can repeat and practise linking consonant to vowel and consonant to consonant. Pause and repeat where necessary.

ANSWERS
1 one day
2 telling him
3 in class
4 because I like
5 white and
6 and I love
7 one of
8 learnt
9 full of
10 It's a very
11 means a lot
12 makes me think
13 flowers and

Unit 8 139

AUDIOSCRIPT 8.9

a Then one day I was telling him all the new words we'd learnt that day in class.
b Snow – because I like the quiet snow world. It's white and clean, and I love freezing weather.
c It's one of the first words that I learnt in English.
d It seems full of possibilities leading to a bright future.
e It's a very short and simple word but it means a lot.
f It makes me think of young flowers and crisp sunny spring mornings.

Exercise 6

- In the groups they started the lesson in, students discuss the questions.
- Conduct a class discussion, particularly eliciting tips about how to remember new words.

STUDY TIP Research has shown that students need to see new vocabulary a number of times in order to remember it effectively so you could advise your students to try some of the following:
Recording vocabulary visually in a mind map, recording vocabulary in memorable sentences – including a person or place you know well – can help you remember, making your own gap fill exercises to test yourself after a week or two, making small cards with words or phrases on one side and a translation or definition on the other which can be used as a quick memory aid, putting vocabulary on sticky notes in different places where you live or work so that you are constantly exposed to them.

Vocabulary & Speaking *make* and *do*

Exercise 7

- Students read the instruction and sentences 1 and 2.
- They work alone to choose the correct option.
- Elicit answers from the class.
- You could ask the students how they knew which was correct. As with all collocations, these combinations need to be learnt by heart. Translation sometimes helps but cannot be relied upon as the collocations are often not the same. (For *make* and *do*, the Vocabulary focus box in exercise 9 will help.)

ANSWERS
1 make
2 do

Exercise 8a 8.10

Audio summary: Six short conversations, each between two people. They include collocations with *make* and *do*.

- Students read the options a–f.
- Tell them you're going to play the six short conversations and they should decide which topic matches each conversation.
- Play track 8.10. Play it more than once if necessary.
- Encourage students to check in pairs and then check answers together.

ANSWERS
a 3   b 1   c 6   d 5   e 2   f 4

AUDIOSCRIPT 8.10

1
A Shh, don't make a noise. It's really late. You'll wake the children.
B OK, I'll be as quiet as I can.
2
A It says here in the newspaper that more than 60% of young women don't do enough exercise.
B Is that because men generally do more sport than women?
A I don't know – it doesn't say.
3
A Oh, I don't know what to do – I hate making decisions.
B I always make a list of the advantages and disadvantages, and then decide.
4
A Oh no, I've made a mistake – look.
B No you haven't, you're doing it really well.
A Well, I don't think I've done a good job.
5
A Right, that's it. I've done the washing up, the ironing, and the hoovering.
B That's great, darling. Would you like me to make you a cheese sandwich and a cup of tea?
A Yes, please, can I have a piece of cake, too?
6
A I've just read a book about Mark Zuckerberg.
B Isn't he the man who started Facebook?
A Yeah, they say he made billions of dollars before he was 30.

Exercise 8b 8.10

- Play track 8.10 again for them to hear and write down expressions which include *make* or *do*.
- Elicit expressions from the class.

ANSWERS
make a noise
do enough exercise
do more sport
making decisions
make a list
made a mistake
doing it really well
done a good job
done the washing up, the ironing, and the hoovering
make you a cheese sandwich and (make) a cup of tea
made billions of dollars

Exercise 8c

- Demonstrate the activity using *a noise* as an example if necessary. Elicit the correct column in the table.
- Students work alone to complete the table.
- Encourage students to check their answers in pairs.

ANSWERS

do	make
exercise	a noise
sport	a decision
sth well/badly	a list
your homework	a mistake
	a sandwich
	money

140

Exercise 9
- Ask students to read the information in the Vocabulary focus box.
- Students work alone to add the extra words to the table.

ANSWERS

<u>do</u>	<u>make</u>
a course	a phone call
homework	friends
nothing	a meal
a job	
an exam	

Exercise 10
- Explain that they don't need to answer the questionnaire, only complete the questions with *make* or *do*.
- Students work alone to complete the task.

WATCH OUT! Students may not have noticed they need to change the form of *make* or *do* for some questions. When most students have finished, ask them to check this carefully. Elicit that these are irregular verbs and check they remember the past simple and past participle forms.
- Go through the answers together.

ANSWERS
1 make, do
2 done, made, done, made, done
3 make, do
4 made, make, does
5 do, make

Exercise 11a
EXTRA SUPPORT If you think they need it, allow students two to three minutes quiet time to think about their own answers to the questionnaire. This will make it easier and quicker to answer when another student asks them.
- Put the students into small groups and give each student just one question to ask. Instruct them to ask all the students in their group and remind them to find out more details too, making a note of any interesting information.

EXTRA CHALLENGE Organize the activity as a whole class mingle for students who need more challenge. Explain that each group is a research team and they need to do the questionnaire to find out information from the whole class. Each group is responsible for deciding how they are going to conduct the research and record the answers. (You need to give them a time limit for the activity and this will take more time than if they do it within their small groups.)
- Monitor carefully as they ask their questions. Make sure they use *make* and *do* correctly.

Exercise 11b
- Ask students to work in their groups and decide on the five most interesting pieces of information they heard.
- Point out the sentence starters and examples and ask them to plan how they will report their information to the class.
- Students report to the class.
- If you wish, encourage further discussion of topics which seem to be of most interest to the class.

EXTENSION Students could choose several of the *make* or *do* phrases from the table and write their own questions to ask a partner. You will need to check that the questions are grammatically correct. They could ask their questions at the end of this lesson or at the beginning of the next lesson as a revision activity.

8.4 Speaking and writing

Goals
- Ask for clarification
- Complete a form

Lead-in
- Write the word *clarification* (noun) on the board. Elicit or point out that another word in this word family is *clear* (adj) so *clarification* is to make something clear.
- Ask them *When you don't understand something in English, do you usually think it's your fault?* Then ask *If this happens in your own language, do you usually think it's your fault?*
- Elicit reasons why they may not understand something in their own language (the other person doesn't explain well, they speak too quietly or too quickly, the topic is something they don't have enough knowledge about, etc.).

Listening & Speaking asking for clarification

Exercise 1a
- Ask students to look at the pictures and discuss the question in pairs.
- Go through the answers and check the students know the words *connection* and *signal* in relation to mobile phones.

ANSWERS
a The woman is travelling and has problems with her mobile phone connection/signal.
b They are at a concert and the music is very loud so they can't communicate clearly.
c They are in a lecture theatre where they need to be quiet so they are whispering and this causes a communication problem.

Exercise 1b
- Students share their own experiences with a partner.

EXTRA SUPPORT If you think they will have difficulty thinking of a personal experience, put students into small groups rather than pairs and include one strong student in each group who can start the activity.
- Monitor carefully and encourage all students to ask further questions to get more information.

EXTRA CHALLENGE You could also prompt them to remember the 'reacting to news' vocabulary from Unit 6 – *Oh no!, Oh dear!, What a shame* – which may be useful in these conversations.

Exercise 2 8.11

Audio summary: Three different conversations where the speakers have a communication problem and need to ask for clarification.

Unit 8   141

- Tell students they are going to hear the three conversations.
- Ask them to listen and match the conversations with the pictures. They should also identify the problem.
- Play track 8.11.
- Go through the answers together.

ANSWERS

1 a: Woman on train, trying to talk to her colleague Thomas in his office. They can't hear each other very well because of the bad mobile phone connection on the train.
2 c: Two university students are sitting at the back of a lecture theatre. Female student is having problems following the lecture. This may be because of her language proficiency; the speed of delivery and the complexity of the lecture.
3 b: Two friends are at a rock concert. They can't hear each other because the concert is very noisy.

AUDIOSCRIPT 8.11

Conversation 1
T Hello, Thomas Smith.
H Hi there, it's Helen. I'm just ringing to let you know what time I get in.
T Hello? Hello? Are you there? You're breaking up. Sorry, what was that?
H Oh sorry, I'm on the train. I keep losing the signal so we might get cut off. Can you hear me now?
T No, no not really, it's a really bad connection. Could you repeat that, please, and please could you speak up?
H Right OK, IS THAT BETTER? Well um my train gets in at 11 so I'll see you about half past. I'll come straight to your office. Is that OK?
T Yeah, yeah that's fine. OK, see you soon then. Bye.
H Bye.

Conversation 2
F Please could I ask you a favour? Could I borrow your lecture notes after class?
M Yeah, OK, but why?
F Well, I'm afraid I can't follow this lecture very well. I mean, what does she mean by 'the literature'? Please could you explain? Sorry, I'm a bit lost.
M Oh, I see. Yeah, of course, you can borrow them. And don't worry, I'll explain after class.
L Shh … Is everything all right there at the back?

Conversation 3
A They're really good, aren't they? I saw them a few years ago in …
B Pardon?
A I said, I saw them a few years ago in Germany before they were famous.
B Sorry, what did you say? I can't hear a word.
A Oh, never mind. It's too noisy in here. I'll tell you later.

Exercise 3 8.12

- Tell students to read the phrases and then play the conversations again so they can complete them.
- Play track 8.12.
- Students complete the sentences. Then go through the sentences together.

- Check that they understand that *breaking up* in this context means *the signal is bad so I can't hear you*. Also elicit or explain that *speak up* means *speak more loudly*.

WATCH OUT! Check that they realize you can be physically lost in a town or city but also *lost* in the sense of not understanding or not being able to follow an explanation.

ANSWERS

1 breaking   5 lost
2 repeat   6 say
3 up   7 noisy
4 mean

AUDIOSCRIPT 8.12

1 You're breaking up.
2 Could you repeat that, please?
3 Please could you speak up?
4 What does she mean by 'the literature'?
5 Sorry, I'm a bit lost.
6 Sorry, what did you say?
7 It's too noisy in here.

Exercise 4a

- Students work alone to match the expressions to one of the functions (a–e).
- Go through the answers together.

ANSWERS

a 2, 6   b 3   c 4   d 5   e 1, 7

Exercise 4b

- Tell students to turn to the audioscript on page 162 and focus on the phrases in italics.
- Students work alone to match these phrases to the functions.
- Go through the answers together.

ANSWERS

a Sorry, what was that? Pardon?
b Please could you speak up?
c Please could you explain?
d I'm afraid I can't follow.
e I keep losing the signal. It's a really bad connection.

Exercise 5a

- Focus students' attention on the Language for speaking box and point out that the phrases are organized under the same functional headings they've been using for matching.
- Now ask them to look at exercise 5a and point out that the phrases 1–5 are **responses** to one of the phrases in the box. They must decide which phrase(s) from the box cause a person to respond in this way. Point out that they are making mini-dialogues.
- Students work in pairs to find the first phrase in each one.
- Allow plenty of time for the task. Monitor and check that they are doing it correctly.

EXTRA CHALLENGE Encourage fast finishers to check the box and responses again to find any other possible phrases.

- Go through the answers together.

POSSIBLE ANSWERS
1 Could you repeat that, please? Please could you speak up?
2 It's a really bad connection. You're breaking up.
3 I'm afraid I can't follow. Sorry, I'm a bit lost/confused.
4 What do you mean by … ? Please could you explain … ?
5 Please could you explain … ?

Exercise 5b
- Ask students to focus on their pronunciation now.
- In pairs, they practise the phrases and responses from exercise 5a.
- Monitor carefully. Note any pronunciation problems.
- Conduct class feedback and if necessary drill phrases with the whole class. Encourage them to mark both sentence stress and intonation (using arrows) on the phrases in the Language for speaking box.

EXTRA ACTIVITY If you think it is necessary, put the students into new pairs to practise the phrases more.

SMART COMMUNICATION The way *sorry* is used here may be new to the students but it is common to use this word to ask for clarification. The important thing is that we use rising intonation. (*Sorry* with falling intonation is apologizing.)

Exercise 6a
- In pairs, students decide who is Student A and who is Student B, then turn to the relevant page of the book (Student A: p128 or p129, Student B: p133).
- Answer any queries they have about the role-play.
- Allow students time to decide what to say and practise.
- Monitor and correct any errors with individual pairs now.

Exercise 6b
- Put two pairs together who have prepared different dialogues.
- Students act their dialogues for the other pair.
- The pair who are listening should identify the communication problem.

CRITICAL THINKING When both pairs have performed their dialogues, they can ask each other why they chose certain phrases and discuss other ways to solve the communication problem more quickly, simply or clearly.

- Conduct a class discussion. You could ask *Which communication problem is the most annoying? Which is the most difficult (or the easiest) problem to solve?*

EXTENSION Students can think of another possible communication problem and create their own role-play to perform to the class using the Language for speaking.

Writing completing a form

Exercise 7
- Students read the questions and discuss in pairs.
- Conduct class feedback. Make a list or mind map of different types of forms on the board (application forms for jobs, courses or to join an organization/open an account, forms for visa/passport/driving licence, booking and order forms, information request forms, complaint forms).

Exercise 8
- Students look at both forms.
- Go through the answers. Ask how they identified the kind of form.

ANSWERS
A is a form to apply for a student visa to the UK.
B is a form to book a scuba-diving holiday.

Exercise 9
- Remind students to use both forms to complete the activity.
- Do the first one as a demonstration with the class. Point out that sometimes there is more than one answer.
- Students work alone on the task.
- Go through the answers together.
- There are some important points you could check they know: 1) The meaning of *put a cross in the box* and *delete as appropriate*. You could also elicit or teach *tick* and *circle*, which are sometimes used instead of *cross* and *delete*. 2) That *Ms* is pronounced /məz/ and is used for both married and unmarried women.

ANSWERS
1 family name, surname
2 first name, given name
3 date of birth, D.O.B.
4 next of kin
5 sex, gender
6 N/A
7 place of birth
8 occupation
9 signature
10 Mr/Mrs/Miss/Ms/Dr
11 medical conditions
12 required fields
13 marital status
14 CAPITAL LETTERS

Exercise 10 8.13
- Tell students there are six mistakes in form B. Ask them to find mistakes in the way the form has been filled in.
- Tell them they're going to listen to Adam talking to an adviser and they need to correct the wrong information on the form.
- Play track 8.13.
- Go through the answers together.

ANSWERS
There is no title indicated – need to delete as appropriate.
Email address: a**d**w29@yahoo.com (not atm29yahoo.com)
Date of birth: **13** not 30
Gender: **M** not F
Next of kin contact number: 07902815**3**46 (missing number)

AUDIOSCRIPT 8.13
P Hello, Action Holidays, Pippa speaking, can I help you?
A Yes, erm, I'm interested in going on the scuba-diving course in Thailand, but I'd like to check if it's suitable for complete beginners?
P Yes, that's not a problem at all. It's, er, suitable for all levels. When would you like to go?
A Well, do you have any places left on one of the January courses?
P Just let me check … Yes, the first one's on the sixth of January. It's a one week course and we've got two places left. Would you like me to reserve a place for you now?
A Yes, please, that'd be great.
P OK, can I just take down a few details then? So, could I have your full name please?

Unit 8   143

A Adam Wright.
P OK, sorry, could you repeat that, please?
A Adam Wright, W-R-I-G-H-T.
P Thanks. And what's your email address?
A It's adw29@yahoo.com.
P OK, and, er, your date of birth?
A Erm, the thirteenth of August 1996.
P Thanks. And your daytime telephone number?
A Er, do you mean my mobile number?
P Yeah, that's fine.
A It's 07905 …
P 07905.
A 232 …
P 232.
A 634.
P 634. OK. And who's your next of kin?
A Sorry?
P Next of kin … Who do we contact in an emergency? A family member, perhaps?
A Oh OK, my mother, Dorothy Wright.
P And her contact details?
A Yeah, OK. Her mobile number's 07902 815 346.
P Thanks. Oh, and do you have any medical conditions or allergies?
A No, nothing that I know of.
P OK, that's great. So, that's all booked for you. I'll send you an email with all the details. Please check they're correct and then pay the deposit online. You also need to book your own flight and send us your flight numbers as soon as possible. Oh, and don't forget, you must get travel insurance which covers you for scuba diving. So, er, thank you for booking with Action Holidays. I hope you enjoy your trip!
A OK, thanks for your help.
P You're welcome. Bye.

> **Background note:** Incorrect information is likely to be the most serious mistake, but many recruitment agencies/employers will automatically reject application forms for jobs which contain grammar or spelling mistakes.

Exercise 11
- Students read the question and discuss in their pairs.
- Elicit some answers from the class and encourage them to give reasons for their choice.

Exercise 12a
- Focus students' attention on Form A, which they now need to complete.
- Students work alone on the task.
- Monitor and assist any students who are having difficulty.
- Give a time limit to the end of the activity.

Exercise 12b
- Students read the Language for writing box. Tell students to check their forms for accuracy.

Exercise 12c
- Students exchange forms with a partner and use the checklist to make sure their partner's form is correct.
- Elicit any common problems.

  EXTENSION You could a conduct class/small group discussion: *What are the most serious mistakes to make on a form?*

8.5 Video

Career change

VIDEOSCRIPT

Kate Olivia O'Brien is an actress in New York City. For her, every day is different.
She has performed in Shakespearean plays, pantomimes and one woman shows.
Today, she is performing in *A Midsummer Night's Dream*, and later this week she's rehearsing and performing for another play.
But it wasn't always this way. She has only lived in New York for a year. Before that, she had a very different job in London.
I was a talent agent in London. It sounds very exciting, but it was very, very stressful. I worked in an office from half past nine in the morning until half past six in the evening. After work, I often went to TV studios for recordings that lasted hours. Even when I went home, I had to phone and email people all the time. It was 24 hours a day, 7 days a week.
I have dual citizenship, so it was easy for me to move from England to the States. I went to university in California, where I studied theatre and creative writing. So, I decided to move somewhere different and New York seemed like the perfect place.
I love it here. It's a fantastic city and a great place to be an actor. I can be very creative here, which was very difficult in my old job. In my old job, every day was the same, but as an actor I'm able to work and do all kinds of different things. I really enjoy the process and I work with a lot of talented people.
But was it difficult for Kate to start a new job in a new city?
The New York acting scene is very different to London and it's always hard to live in a big city when you don't know it very well. I was very nervous when I started, but I had a few friends in New York and they helped a lot. I meet a lot of new people in my work too, and of course New York is a very exciting city so it's easy to have fun here!
But acting isn't easy. I have to go to a lot of auditions, and I must always perform as well as I can. The work is very irregular too and I miss my old salary. In London, I didn't have to think about money, but as an actor I never know when and where I'm going to work. This also means I can't book many holidays because I won't always be able to go!
So, does she regret her decision?
I'm my own boss, so I have a lot more control over my life. But the most important thing is I'm doing what I want to do. I enjoy every day and although acting is difficult, I always look forward to the challenge. So I definitely made the right choice.

VIDEO ANSWERS
2 Students' answers will vary.
4 1 b 2 a 3 b 4 a 5 b

Review

ANSWERS

Exercise 1a
1 can't
2 might
3 can't
4 will be able to
5 will be able to

Exercise 2a
1 don't have to
2 have to/must
3 can
4 mustn't/can't, have to/must
5 don't have to/can

Exercise 3a
1 jokes
2 things
3 children
4 directions
5 events

Exercise 4a
1 education
2 qualifications
3 take exams
4 maths
5 do well in
6 grades
7 degree

Exercise 5a 8.14
make: decisions, lists, phone calls, your bed
do: exams, exercise, homework, housework, nothing, sport

AUDIOSCRIPT 8.14
decisions
exams
exercise
homework
housework
lists
nothing
phone calls
sport
your bed

Exercise 6a
1 Sorry, what did you say?
2 Please could you speak up a bit?
3 I'm afraid I'm a bit lost.
4 Could you repeat that, please?/Please could you repeat that?
5 Sorry, you're breaking up.

Unit 8   145

9 Body and mind

Unit overview

Language input

if + present simple + will/won't/might (CB p86)	• If your handshake is too strong, you will seem rude. • If you get it wrong, you might give a bad impression.
Present tenses in future time clauses (CB p89)	• If it rains, they won't cancel the course. • When the course finishes, we'll feel exhausted.
Grammar reference (CB pp150–1)	

Vocabulary development

Body and actions (CB p86)	• hug, nod, shake hands …
Health and fitness (CB p88)	• mental health, do exercise, be active …
Verbs and prepositions (CB p91)	• depend on, worry about, believe in …

Skills development

Listening: Using sequencing words to understand (CB p90)	
Speaking: Asking for help and giving advice (CB p92)	
Writing: A formal covering letter (CB p93)	

Video

Documentary: Sports scholarship in the USA (Coursebook DVD & CB p94)	
Vox pops (Coursebook DVD & TG p263)	

More materials

Workbook	• Language practice for vocabulary, grammar, pronunciation, speaking and writing
Photocopiable activities	• Grammar: Before we start, … (TG p216 & TSRD) • Vocabulary: What's happening at the park? (TG p234 & TSRD) • Communication: I'd like a second opinion, please! (TG p252 & TSRD)
Tests	• Unit 9 test (TSRD) • Progress test: Units 7–9
Unit 9 wordlist (TSRD)	

146

9.1 The rise and fall of the handshake

Goals
- Talk about greetings
- Talk about possible situations and the results

Lead-in
- Write *greeting* on the board.
- Elicit the meaning of this noun and elicit the verb form *to greet someone*.
- Ask students to look at the title of the lesson *The rise and fall of the handshake* and check understanding of *handshake* by asking students to demonstrate.
- Encourage them to discuss what the title means. Elicit ideas but tell them they will find the answer later in the lesson (in the reading text).

Vocabulary & Speaking body and actions

Exercise 1

Background note: In the UK, sticking your tongue out is a rude gesture, which is mainly done by children. It seems that the origin of this greeting in Tibet is connected with religion and magic. You stick out your tongue to prove it isn't black which would mean you were a demon or had been practising black magic. These days it is a sign of respect towards the person you are greeting.

- Students read the instruction.
- Put them into pairs to match the greetings 1–9 with a country.
- **EXTRA SUPPORT** Weaker students may find it easier to look at the photos first and match them with one kind of greeting from 1–9.
- Monitor and encourage the students. They will probably need to make some intelligent guesses about the greetings.
- Tell them to look at the photos (a–e) and identify the greeting in each one.
- Go through the answers together. You could ask whether any of these greetings seem unusual or strange to them.

ANSWERS
1 Argentina (photo c)
2 China
3 the UAE (photo d)
4 the USA (photo e)
5 Cambodia (photo b)
6 Tibet
7 Mozambique
8 Germany
9 Maoris (in New Zealand) (photo a)

Exercise 2
- In pairs, students test each other on the bold words in exercise 1. Ask two students to read out the example as a demonstration.
- Monitor and make sure their explanations and definitions are accurate.

EXTENSION It is possible for you to test the class or for students to test each other by performing the actions. This can be fun and memorable but it is important to be culturally sensitive as students may not want to perform some of the actions.

Exercise 3

Background note: In the UK and USA, friends and families often hug and kiss, male friends usually shake hands or pat each other on the back/shoulder, male friends may greet female friends with a kiss on the cheek, female friends often hug and/or kiss on the cheek. Handshakes are used by men and women in business or when the people don't know each other. Younger people sometimes use 'high fives' (clapping your palm against your friend's palm in the air) or bump fists.

- Put students into small groups to discuss questions 1 and 2.
- Monitor and give students a time limit to the end of the activity.
- Conduct class discussion, eliciting interesting points about greetings from the students.

EXTRA ACTIVITY You could ask students to discuss how people greet each other in the UK and USA. Elicit that there is different etiquette for different age groups and situations. Use the background note if you wish.

Grammar & Reading *if* + present simple + *will/won't/might*

Exercise 4
- Point out the numbered empty paragraph headings.
- Ask students to find a heading for each paragraph and remind them that there is one extra.
- Students work alone on this task. Then go through the answers together.

STUDY TIP In order to understand the main points of a text, it can be useful to summarize each paragraph because the purpose of breaking texts into paragraphs when we write is to move from one point to another. Students can practise the skill of summarizing paragraphs when they read news, reviews or articles.

ANSWERS
1 c
2 e
3 d
4 a
(b is not needed)

Exercise 5
- Students read the article again to answer the questions.
- **EXTRA SUPPORT** Ask students to read the questions first and go through any problems with understanding before they read the article again.
- Tell students to use dictionaries if they need them. (NB: *impression* and *germ* are explained at the end of the text.)
- Allow plenty of time for students to find the answers.
- They can check their answers in pairs if you wish.
- Go through the answers together.
- Conduct class feedback on the article.

Unit 9   147

CRITICAL THINKING It's important to reflect on what you've learned from what you read or hear. Then we can form an opinion about it. It is best to practise doing this in English rather than thinking in your own language.

- From this article students could think about these questions: *What did I learn from this article that I didn't already know? Is it surprising that handshakes have become less popular because people worry they might catch germs? Is a 'safe shake' a better idea? Why/why not?*

ANSWERS
1 The handshake was a sign of peace. It showed you were not holding or hiding a weapon.
2 'I trust and respect you and we are equal.'
3 They prefer a gentler handshake in China.
4 Because they worry that they might catch germs from shaking hands.

Exercise 6
- Students read the instruction and the example sentence, then answer the questions.
- Allow students to check their answers in pairs if you wish.
- Go through the answers together.

ANSWERS
1 present, future
2 *if* clause, main clause

Exercise 7
- Focus students' attention on the Grammar focus box and ask them to complete the rules using the words in the instruction.
- Students work alone on the task.
- Go through the answers together.

WATCH OUT! One common error is to use a future form in the *if* clause, e.g. *If you will plan to …* . This grammar structure is about possible future actions so it is a logical mistake. However, it's important to highlight that the tense in the *if* clause needs to be **present**, not future. Use the extra activity below to teach this if you wish.

EXTRA ACTIVITY Write on the board: *You will seem rude, if you will stick your tongue out in the UK.* Tell them that there is one grammar mistake and one punctuation mistake. Ask them to discuss in pairs. Elicit that *if you will stick your tongue out* should be in the present tense *if you stick your tongue out*. Elicit that there should be no comma because the comma is used when the *if* clause comes first. You could also elicit how to make the result seem less certain (change *will* to *might* in the main clause).

ANSWERS
1 present
2 result
3 first
4 might

- Refer students to *Grammar reference* on p150. There are three more exercises here students can do for homework. See answers on p149.

Exercise 8
- Ask students to read the radio programme summary which is in green in the text. If necessary, check they understand Dr Klaus's opinion.

- Point out that the rest of the text is responses made online (tweets) by people who have listened to the radio programme.

EXTRA CHALLENGE You could ask the students to read the tweets, not worrying about the gaps, and decide whether each of the four responses agrees or disagrees with Dr Klaus that we should greet each other with a fist bump. (They all disagree.)

- Students complete the tweets.
- Go through the answers together.

PRONUNCIATION Students often resist making contractions but they are important in order to sound natural and to speak quickly. Help them pronounce the contraction of *will*, modelling and drilling it with different pronouns: *I'll*, /aɪl/ *you'll*, /juːl/ *he'll*, /hiːl/ *she'll*, /ʃiːl/ *it'll*, /ˈɪtl/ *we'll*, /wiːl/ *they'll* /ðeɪl/. Then give them a short phrase to repeat, e.g. *I'll say it* and tell them to say it six times, changing the pronoun each time. They can then make three similar short phrases for a partner to use to practise in the same way.

ANSWERS
1 keep
2 won't pass
3 will think
4 refuse
5 get
6 won't be
7 don't touch
8 won't get
9 'll look
10 do

Exercise 9
- Put students into pairs or conduct whole class discussion of these questions.

EXTENSION Dictate extra questions to stimulate more discussion: 1) *In your country, what will people do if you try to bump fists?* 2) *Will people think you're rude if you don't shake their hand?* 3) *Do you think you might get ill if you touch your eyes or nose after a handshake?* Put students into pairs to ask and answer them. When they have finished, point out that the question form follows the same grammar rules as positive and negative sentences.

Exercise 10
- In pairs, students read the instruction and the examples for the activity on p129.
- They work together to write advice sentences for each pair of a and b options.
- Allow plenty of time for this task and make sure all students write the sentences down.
- Monitor carefully for accuracy in the target grammar and correct mistakes as you go round.
- When all students have finished writing sentences, put them into different pairs.
- Students take turns to use their sentences to give advice.

EXTRA CHALLENGE Stronger students can act out this part of the activity with a dialogue. They can choose one of the pieces of advice at the end of each mini role-play. You could ask some of them to perform their dialogues to the class.

GRAMMAR REFERENCE ANSWERS
Exercise 1
1 meet, won't use
2 might think, don't answer
3 'll go, we're
4 will be, arrive
5 invites, will probably expect
6 won't, don't know

Exercise 2
1 I will send a postcard if I have time.
2 What will a British person do if I don't shake his hand?
3 If you go to the party will you take a present?
4 We won't meet anyone if we don't go out.
5 My mum will be happy if you don't bring flowers.
6 Will you reply if I send you a letter?
7 Stephen will meet me at the airport if I ask him.

Exercise 3
1 —, might
2 don't, won't
3 —, will
4 might not, don't
5 will, —
6 —, will
7 might not

9.2 Going back to nature

Goals
- Talk about health and fitness
- Use present tenses in future time clauses

Lead-in
- On the board write *healthy* and *fit* and elicit the meanings. (They are near synonyms but the difference is that *fit* implies a person does exercise, whereas *healthy* is very general.)
- Elicit that these words are adjectives and ask students to give you the nouns: *health, fitness*.
- Tell them that this is the topic of the lesson.

Vocabulary & Reading health and fitness

Exercise 1
- Put students into pairs to discuss the questions.
- Conduct a class discussion. You could find out whether any students are particularly fit and ask them to explain the kind of exercise they do (what, where, how long, how often, etc.).

Exercise 2a

Text summary: An article describing a recent fitness trend called 'Paleo' which involves living like cavemen (because modern diet and lifestyle is unhealthy). Followers of 'Paleo' say it will make you fitter, healthier and happier. There is a list of things to do in order to follow this trend.

- Ask students to look carefully at the picture and say what they see. You will probably need to teach the word for the person in the picture: *caveman*. If they haven't noticed the fast food tray he is holding, ask them if there is anything strange about this caveman.
- Ask them to make predictions about the article from this picture and the title only. They could discuss this briefly in pairs.

EXTRA ACTIVITY You could ask students to predict words and phrases they might read in the text too.

Exercise 2b
- Students read the article and check whether their predictions about the content were correct.
- Elicit the gist of the text from the students: *What is this article about?*

Exercise 3
- In pairs, students discuss the questions.

EXTENSION You could ask them to focus on the different points in *How to go Paleo* and discuss what they think about each point.

- Conduct a class discussion so that all the students can share their opinions.

Exercise 4a
- When they have read the instruction, check that students understand the title of group four – mental health.
- Students focus on the words in bold in the article.
- Encourage students to ask a partner if there is vocabulary they don't know or tell them to use dictionaries if these are available. If there is a word or phrase that you think none of them will know, you could teach it before they start the activity.
- Students categorize the words in one of the four groups.
- Go through the answers together.
- Correct any pronunciation mistakes with this vocabulary – ensure they are clearly saying the plural ending /ɪz/ on *illnesses* and *diseases*. Also check that they are only saying two syllables for *natural* /ˈnætʃrəl/ and *depressed* /dɪˈprest/.

ANSWERS
1 eating: diet, natural food, junk food
2 doing/not doing exercise: fitness, active, relax, gentle exercise, cycling, weight-lifting
3 being ill: diseases, cancer, illnesses
4 mental health: stress, depressed

Exercise 4b
- Students work alone, using the words from 4a to complete the sentences.
- Go through the answers together.

ANSWERS
1 active
2 diet, natural food, junk food
3 fitness
4 depressed
5 illness
6 relax

Pronunciation *eat* and *bread*

Exercise 5a 9.1
- Tell the students that they are going to practise pronunciation and ask them to read the instruction.
- Play track 9.1 so that they can hear the different sounds.

Unit 9   149

AUDIOSCRIPT 9.1

/iː/	/e/
eat	bread

Exercise 5b 9.2

- Students write the words in the table according to the sound of the 'ea' spelling.
- Allow them to check in pairs, saying the words to each other.
- Play track 9.2 so they can check their answers.

AUDIOSCRIPT 9.2 & 9.3

/iː/	/e/
disease	health
meat	instead
easy	weather
	already

Exercise 5c 9.3

- Ask students to listen and repeat.
- Play track 9.3 and pause it when necessary so they can repeat.
- Play the track as many times as students need.

DICTIONARY SKILLS Ask students to look in dictionaries for new words with 'ea' in the spelling. They should try to add them to one of the columns in the table according to how they are pronounced. Go through these new words together.

Exercise 6

- Put students into small groups to discuss the 'Paleo' lifestyle.
- Remind them to make sure they pronounce any of the 'ea' words they use correctly.
- Monitor their discussions and give them a time limit to the end of the activity.
- Elicit from each group whose lifestyle is most or least like the 'Paleo' lifestyle and why.

Grammar & Listening   present tenses in future time clauses

Exercise 7

> **Text summary:** A short advert about 'MovNat', a fitness programme which encourages you to practise whole body movements and useful physical skills.

- Students read the advert and think about their answers to the questions.
- Go through the answers and elicit their reactions to this fitness course.

ANSWERS
MovNat is different from going to a gym because it is outside ('in the open air'). Also the focus is on natural, whole body movements and useful physical skills.

Exercise 8a 9.4

> **Audio summary:** A woman calls the MovNat enquiry line to ask for information about joining a MovNat course.

- Tell students that they are going to listen to a woman who is asking for information about MovNat. Ask them to look at the things in the list.
- Play track 9.4.
- Students listen and tick the topics the woman asks about.
- Go through the answers together.

ANSWERS
Level of fitness?
What happens in bad weather?
Dates?
Book in advance?

AUDIOSCRIPT 9.4

J Hi, I'm calling about the MovNat training course in November.
I OK, great. Are you interested in coming on the course?
J Yes, I am, but I've just got a few questions I'd like to ask.
I Right. Fire away.
J Well, the first question is, do you need to have a good level of fitness? It's just that I'm quite unfit at the moment. Does that matter? I mean, do I need to go to the gym before I begin the course?
I No, no. The course is for anybody. It doesn't matter how fit you are. When you arrive, the instructor will check your fitness level and will then divide you into two groups, beginner and intermediate.
J Right. Sounds good. I was also wondering about the weather. The course is outdoors, isn't it? It's in a park. What will happen if it rains or snows? Will you cancel it or will it be indoors?
I Erm, no. With MovNat you need to practise your skills in all weather conditions. That's part of our philosophy. The course will take place outside, whatever the weather. If it's raining or snowing, the experience will be even more exciting!
J OK. So is it necessary to book a place, or would it be alright to just turn up?
I No, you'll definitely need to reserve a place before you come. The courses are popular and places are limited. In fact, there are only two or three places left in November. Would you like me to book you onto the course now?
J I just need to check I can make those dates. Then I'll call and book.
I OK. Don't miss your place though!
J No, I won't. I'll get back to you as soon as I know.
I OK, sounds good. Speak to you soon, I hope.

Exercise 8b

- Put students in pairs to try to remember the MovNat instructor's answers.
- Go through the answers together.
- You could also ask *Does the woman book a place on the course?* (No, she has to check she can make the dates and says she'll call back.)

ANSWERS
Level of fitness: The course is for anybody. It doesn't matter how fit you are. There are two different fitness levels – beginner and intermediate.
What happens in bad weather: You need to practise your skills in all weather conditions. The course will take place outside whatever the weather. If it's raining or snowing, the experience will be even more exciting!

Dates: November
Book in advance: You have to book in advance. There are two or three places left.

Exercise 9a
- Students read the two halves of the sentence and match the beginnings of sentences 1–6 with the endings a–f.

Exercise 9b 9.4
- Play track 9.4 again.
- Students listen and check.
- Check that they were able to match all the sentence halves correctly.

ANSWERS
1 d 2 a 3 f 4 b 5 c 6 e

Exercise 10
- Students read the instruction and answer the questions 1–3.
- Allow them to check in pairs and then go through the answers together.

ANSWERS
1 future
2 present
3 future

Exercise 11
- Focus the students' attention on the Grammar focus box.
- Students work alone to choose the options to complete the rules.
- Go through the answers together.

WATCH OUT! Highlight very clearly the time references in the first rule because these are key to this grammar. They need to learn that we use present tenses after these time references.

ANSWERS
1 present
2 if
3 when
4 as soon as
- Refer students to *Grammar reference* on p151. There are three more exercises here students can do for homework. See answers in next column.

Exercise 12
- Students work alone to complete the conversations with the present simple or *will*.
- Allow them to check their answers in pairs.
- Go through answers together. If students make mistakes, refer to the Grammar focus box in your eliciting and explaining.

ANSWERS
1 change, will enjoy, get
2 will do, start, don't do, will hurt
3 will continue, finishes
4 leave

Exercise 13
- Students read the instruction and the sentence beginnings and endings.

- Allow plenty of time for them to complete the sentences as this is a creative task.
- Monitor and correct any errors with the target grammar.
- Give students a time limit to the end of the writing activity.

EXTRA CHALLENGE Fast finishers can write three more true sentences about themselves which must include one of the time expressions from rule 1 in the Grammar focus box. Check carefully.

- Put students into small groups to compare their sentences.
- Conduct a class discussion, eliciting the most amusing or interesting sentences. Praise good use of the target grammar.

EXTENSION Ask students to write or type the sentences out again, each one on a separate slip of paper, leaving gaps where the time expressions should be. These can be used by you as revision/testing in a future lesson. Alternatively, you could ask them to write the correct time expression on the back and put the slips in a box or bag for students to use to test themselves if they arrive early to the lesson or wish to do revision during a break.

GRAMMAR REFERENCE ANSWERS

Exercise 1
1 ⋀ I see a rare animal, I'll take a photo.   If
2 The weather will slowly get colder ⋀ autumn arrives.   when
3 We're really tired so we'll sleep ⋀ we arrive at the camp.   as soon as
4 I'll walk back ⋀ I get lost.   if
5 We'll go travelling in the Amazon ⋀ we have more money.   when
6 ⋀ a snake bites you, you will have to go to hospital.   if
7 It'll be dark soon. We'll have to return to camp ⋀ we reach the mountain top.   as soon as

Exercise 2
1 get off
2 will travel
3 reaches
4 will walk
5 hear
6 leave
7 will have
8 is/are
9 will return

Exercise 3
1 You'll feel better when you go to the countryside.
2 After we get to the waterfall, we'll see a bridge.
3 We might not see the island if it's cloudy.
4 When the sun comes out, will we go for a bike ride?
5 The leaves change colour before they fall./Before the leaves fall, they change colour.
6 As soon as the weather gets warmer, spring flowers will appear.

Unit 9

9.3 Vocabulary and skills development

Goals
- Use sequencing words to understand
- Use verbs and prepositions

Listening using sequencing words to understand

Lead-in
- Tell students that the topic of the lesson is social media.
- Put them into small groups to brainstorm all the social media sites they know.
- They could also discuss the similarities and differences between them.
- Conduct a brief discussion if you have time or just elicit names of social media sites and write them on the board.

Exercise 1a
- Put students into pairs to read the statements and decide whether they are true or false.

Exercise 1b
- Students look at the bottom of the page to check whether their answers were right.
- You could ask if any of this information is new to them.

Exercise 2a
- Tell them to read the text and complete the gaps with the words in the box.
- Remind them to change the form of the words if necessary.
- Students work alone on this task.

Exercise 2b 9.5

> **Audio summary:** A radio programme about a woman who describes how she stopped using social media.

- Tell students that you're going to play the introduction to the radio programme for them to check their answers.
- Play track 9.5.
- Students listen and check.

ANSWERS
1 worked
2 depends
3 worry
4 consisted

AUDIOSCRIPT 9.5
P Hello. This morning we are talking about social media. Ilaria di Genaro is a freelance professional photographer. She has worked for newspapers from all around the world and she depends on social media for her job. Last year she started to worry about spending too much time on it. She realized that her average day consisted of checking social media sites up to twelve times an hour. Ilaria, welcome.

Exercise 3a
- Students read the Unlock the code box about sequencing words.
- You could elicit the sequencing words from the box, write them on the board and drill pronunciation.

Exercise 3b 9.6
- Tell students to read the sequencing words in the box.
- Explain that they are going to listen to the second part of the radio interview and complete sentences a–d using the sequencing words.
- Play track 9.6.
- Go through the answers together.

ANSWERS
a Firstly
b Next
c Then
d Finally

AUDIOSCRIPT 9.6
P Can you explain – how exactly were you using social media?
I Well, I was using it in two different ways. There's the photography, which is my work, so I depend on Facebook and LinkedIn for business as I work for myself. But then I also use it to keep in touch with friends and family.
P When did you realize there was a problem?
I A friend asked me how often I checked social media sites. I counted and it was up to twelve times an hour.
P That's quite a lot. And how did you free yourself from it?
I So, firstly, I looked at how I used social media during the day. You know, things like which sites I visited and for how long.
P OK, well, that sounds like a good start.
I Yes, it was. I was shocked at how much time I spent each day on Facebook and LinkedIn. So next I thought 'I have to do something about this'. Actually, I really believed in my ability to just stop.
P And did that work?
I Absolutely not! It was much more difficult than I thought. I tried but I just couldn't do it.
P So what did you do next?
I So then I tried a special app you can use on your tablet, it's called 'Self-Control', and it tells you not to look at social media sites. But then I got a smartphone, and didn't put the app on the phone, so…
P … so you were checking Facebook on your smartphone a lot!
I Yeah, all the time. I was just spending so much time doing it. But finally I thought of a good idea and that was to give money to a local charity every time I looked at Facebook or LinkedIn.
P And it worked?
I Yes, it did, because I was giving the charity a lot of money, a lot. So I stopped and I now check social media a couple of times a day, and my emails maybe three times. I still give some money to charity but not quite as much.

Exercise 4
- Ask students to read the instruction.

EXTRA SUPPORT If necessary, elicit the different methods that Ilaria tried to limit her time on social media. (trying to control herself – believing in her ability to stop, using a special app, giving money to charity when she didn't look at it)

- In pairs, students talk about the different methods and which is easiest. Encourage them to explain their reasons.
- Conduct whole class feedback.

EXTENSION In their pairs or in small groups, they could brainstorm other ways to control or give up a bad habit. Elicit ideas from the class.

Exercise 5 9.6

- Students read the questions. Check they all understand them.
- Play track 9.6 again. You may need to play it more than once or pause it frequently so that they can make a note of the answers.
- Students write answers to the questions.
- Allow them to check their answers in pairs.
- Go through the answers together.

ANSWERS
1 Because she used it for business and to keep in touch with friends and family.
2 When she realized she checked social media 12 times per hour.
3 She couldn't just stop – it was more difficult than she thought.
4 The app told her not to look at social media.
5 She didn't put the app on her phone.
6 She was giving a lot of money to the charity.

Exercise 6

- Give students time to think of something and to think how they can explain the stages of giving it up.
- Remind them to plan how to use sequencing words (but it is better if they don't prepare in writing – just think about it).
- In pairs, tell them to explain what they gave up and how they did it.
- Monitor their discussions. Note any students who are using the sequencing words especially well.
- Conduct class feedback. Ask some students to explain to the class.

EXTENSION You could put them into new pairs to retell their partner's experience to a new person, using the sequencing words. Alternatively, you could tell them to write down what their partner told them, again making sure they use the sequencing words in their sentences.

Vocabulary & Speaking verbs and prepositions

Exercise 7a

- Tell the students that they are going to focus on prepositions used with verbs. Elicit a range of prepositions from them.
- Ask them to complete the sentences taken from the radio interview. Each gap is a different preposition.
- Go through the answers together.

ANSWERS
1 for
2 on
3 in
4 of

Exercise 7b

- Focus students' attention on the Vocabulary focus box about verbs and prepositions.
- Tell them to read the information and examples carefully.

Exercise 8

- Ask students to read sentences 1–8 and complete them using the verbs in the box. Remind them to change the form if necessary.
- Students work alone on the task.
- Allow students to check their answers in pairs.
- Go through the answers.

PRONUNCIATION Point out that many of the prepositions begin with vowel sounds and remind students that there is natural linking in pronunciation between a word ending in a consonant and the next word beginning with a vowel (see sentences 1, 2, 4, 5, 7). Drill these combinations so that students can hear that they almost sound like one word (as studied in lesson 8.3 'Unlock the code – connected speech'.)

ANSWERS
1 believe
2 dream
3 worked
4 consist
5 depend
6 belong
7 think
8 happens

Exercise 9a

- Students use the verbs and prepositions from exercise 8 to complete the table.
- Go through the answers together.

STUDY TIP The students need to learn these kinds of verb + preposition combinations by heart. A method which some students may like is to write sentences such as these examples: I worked *for forty for*eigners. I believe *in in*telligent *in*sects. She dreams *of of*fices *of*ten. He succeeded *in in*fecting the *in*ternet. These sentences work on the memory in two ways; repeating the letters (and sometimes sound) of the preposition within other words and also bringing to mind a strong image, which can be even more memorable if it is strange or surreal.

ANSWERS
1 to
2 in
3 dream
4 think
5 on
6 for

Exercise 9b

- Tell students to look at the sentences in exercise 8 again.
- Put them into pairs to discuss whether they agree with each statement and give reasons why/why not.

FEEDBACK FOCUS Monitor their discussions focusing on pronunciation – are they linking naturally? Make a note of any problems or missing linking which would help their speaking to flow.

Unit 9   153

- Give a time limit to the end of the activity to ensure all students finish the task together.
- Conduct error correction if necessary.

Exercise 10a
- Ask students to look at the words in the circles.
- Tell them to write four–six questions using these words. Highlight the example question to show them what to do.
- Give them plenty of time to think of and write their sentences. They should work alone.
- Monitor to check they are correct. Make sure they use an 'ing' form after the prepositions if they use a verb.
- Give a time limit to the end of the activity.

EXTRA CHALLENGE Fast finishers can write extra questions so that they use all the words.

Exercise 10b
- Put students into pairs to ask and answer their questions.
- Monitor their conversations to check that they are linking naturally in their questions.
- Conduct class feedback. Elicit anything interesting that they found out about each other.

EXTRA ACTIVITY You could give the students a homework challenge to choose a short news item or article in English and find one verb + preposition combination in it. Students bring their findings to the next lesson and share with the class.

9.4 Speaking and writing

Goals
- Ask for help and give advice
- Write a formal covering letter

Lead-in
- Ask students to look at the picture.
- In pairs, ask them to describe what they can see and discuss where the conversation is taking place, who the two women are and why they may be talking.
- Elicit ideas from the students and praise anyone who uses the word *advice* as this is the topic of the lesson.

WATCH OUT! In some languages advice is a countable noun but in English it is uncountable. You cannot use *advices* but rather *pieces of advice* or just *advice* in general. You could also highlight that *advice* /ədˈvaɪs/ is the noun and the verb is *to advise* /ədˈvaɪz/. Point out the difference in spelling and pronunciation.

Listening & Speaking asking for help and giving advice

Exercise 1
- Put students into pairs to discuss the questions.
- Allow enough time to discuss in detail and for students to think of examples for question 2.

EXTRA CHALLENGE Fast finishers could think of vocabulary for other people, apart from doctors, who you might ask for medical advice (nurse, pharmacist, optician, dentist, etc.).

- Elicit answers and experiences from students. Be aware that this can be a sensitive topic area and some may not wish to share real experiences but only talk in general.

Exercise 2
- Students read the instruction and, in pairs, match the problems (1–8) with advice (a–h).
- Remind them that one piece of advice may be suitable for more than one problem.
- Check that they know the meaning of *take it easy* (= relax, don't work too much). Advise them to help each other understand unknown vocabulary and also use dictionaries if available.
- Allow plenty of time for students to discuss and match.
- Go through the answers together.

ANSWERS
1 a, d
2 f
3 c, d, e, g, h
4 a, d
5 h
6 c, g
7 a, d, g
8 b, c, d, g, h

Exercise 3 9.7

Audio summary: Three different conversations where the speakers ask for medical advice.

- Tell students that they are going to listen to three conversations where people ask for medical advice.
- Ask them to read questions 1 and 2.
- Point out that they need to answer both questions about each of the different conversations.
- Play track 9.7.
- Allow students to check their answers in pairs if you wish.
- Go through the answers together.

EXTENSION You could play track 9.7 again, asking the students to make a note of the medical advice each person receives. Then go through the answers together.

ANSWERS
Conversation 1: c – a doctor's surgery, 3 (hurt back) (advice: take some tablets, don't lift anything heavy and take it easy)
Conversation 2: a – a chemist's, 2 (bitten) (advice: put some cream on it)
Conversation 3: b – A&E department of a hospital, 5 (broken arm) (advice: go to hospital for an X-ray and take some painkillers)

AUDIOSCRIPT 9.7
Situation 1
D Hello, please have a seat. So, what can I do for you?
P Well, I've had an accident and I've hurt my back.
D OK … and how did you do it?
P Actually, I was lifting some heavy suitcases out of the car when it happened.
D I see. Well, if you just want to lie down on the bed over there, I'll take a look. Tell me if it hurts. Right, well, I don't think it's anything serious, but you should take it easy and you mustn't lift anything heavy for the next few days. I'll

154

give you a prescription for some tablets. Please take this to the chemist's next door.
P OK, thank you very much. Oh, and how often should I take the tablets?
D It's two tablets three times a day before meals.

Situation 2
P Yes, can I help you?
C Yes, er, have you got anything for insect bites? Something has bitten me all over my arms and legs.
P Let's take a look … Well, it looks like a mosquito. They're quite red and sore, aren't they? You could try this cream which should help.
C OK thanks, I'll try it.
P And it's a good idea to keep your windows closed at night.
C Yeah, we always do. I don't know how they manage to get in!
P I think you should see a doctor if they get any worse.
C Right, OK. Well, thanks very much for your help.

Situation 3
D Hello there, Joseph Erickson?
P Yes. I'm his father. My son's had a terrible accident and I think he's broken his arm.
D How did it happen?
P Well, we were at a children's party and he ran into a wall. He put his arms out to try and stop himself but he was going so fast and …
D Let me take a look, Joseph. Oh yes, it's definitely broken. We call that a banana arm! He must try to keep still and we'll send him for an X-ray straight away.
P Er, I'm so worried, he's in a lot of pain.
D Don't worry, we'll give him some strong painkillers before he goes for the X-ray.
P He was having such a great time before it happened. I feel really upset.
D Well, I don't think you should feel bad. He was only having fun …

Exercise 4a 9.7

- Tell students to write D for doctor, P for patient or C for chemist next to each sentence 1–8.
- Students could do the task alone or in pairs.
- Monitor and give a time limit to the end of the activity.
- Play track 9.7 again so they can check their answers.

ANSWERS
1 D   2 D   3 C   4 P   5 C   6 C   7 D   8 D

Exercise 4b 9.8

- Tell students to focus on their pronunciation.
- **EXTRA CHALLENGE** Ask students to mark on the sentences one of the following (you choose which you think is most useful for your class); stressed words, intonation arrows or linking (consonant to vowel and linking sounds /w/ and /j/).
- Tell them that they're going to listen and repeat.
- Play track 9.8 again.
- Students repeat the sentences. Pause whenever necessary.
- If they did the extra challenge, ask them whether they marked the correct places or if they would change some of their markings.

AUDIOSCRIPT 9.8
1 You should take it easy.
2 You mustn't lift anything heavy.
3 Have you got anything for insect bites?
4 You could try this cream which should help.
5 It's a good idea to keep your windows closed at night.
6 How can I help you?
7 He must try to keep still.
8 I don't think you should feel bad.

Exercise 4c

- Students decide whether each sentence is giving advice and, if so, whether the advice is strong or not.
- Do number 1 together as a demonstration if necessary.
- Students work alone on the task.
- Go through the answers together. Elicit why students thought some advice was stronger. Point out that words such as 'must' and 'mustn't' are used to give very strong advice.

EXTENSION Decide which advice words are positive and which negative. Ask students to order the words from strongest advice to weakest. Start with the positive advice words. (Positive advice: *must, should, it's a good idea to, could* Negative advice: *you mustn't, I don't think you should*)

ANSWERS
1 a advice
2 b strong advice
3 –
4 –
5 a advice
6 a advice
7 b strong advice
8 a advice

Exercise 5

- Tell students to turn to the audioscript on p163 and practise the conversations in pairs.
- Monitor carefully and note any pronunciation mistakes.
- Conduct class error correction if necessary.

Exercise 6

- Focus students' attention on the Language for speaking box.
- Ask them how to make *You should go* sound softer. (= *I think you should go.*) Ask them to form the negative: *You shouldn't go* and again, make it softer. (= *I don't think you should go.*)
- Tell students to read the four medical problems in the box and check that they know what they mean. If necessary, teach words they don't know.
- Put students into pairs.
- Each pair chooses one problem and builds a role-play around it, using the Language for speaking box.
- **EXTRA SUPPORT** Students who need extra support could write prompts for the role-play, but encourage them not to write it all down as it is a speaking activity.
- Give a time limit for doing the role-play and monitor carefully. Help them to express themselves naturally and advise them on pronunciation as you go around the class.

Unit 9   155

- Get the students' attention and ask one or two pairs to act their dialogue to the class. The students who are listening should decide where the role-play takes place.
- Conduct any necessary error correction. Elicit whether the role-play included strong or softer advice and ask for examples if possible.

EXTENSION If you want the students to practise more, you could ask them to think of a different medical problem (from this page or their own choice) and prepare another role-play where someone asks for medical advice.

SMART COMMUNICATION It is important for students to realize that the British tend to make advice, suggestions, requests, etc. softer and indirect if possible. Many other cultures express themselves more directly. Of course, *You mustn't* is very strong advice. *I don't think you should* is much softer but language learners should be careful because in this case a British person may be politely trying to say *Don't do it!* If unsure, the best thing to do is ask questions to check how strongly the speaker feels.

Writing a formal covering letter

Exercise 7
- Students answer the questions in pairs.
- Elicit some of the students' experiences.

Exercise 8
- Students read the letter and answer the questions.
- Go through the answers together.

CRITICAL THINKING Everything in writing has a target audience and a purpose. It is a good habit to think about these two things when first reading any text. When reading a letter or email, this should be obvious but books, articles, messages, posters, etc all have audience and purpose too. When we understand who the writing is for and why, we can look at other things such as the tone of the piece of writing or how the author is feeling.

ANSWERS
1 to apply for the MA course in Chinese Medicine
2 application form and certificates

Exercise 9
- Students work alone to label the parts of the letter using a–g. Do the first together as a demonstration if necessary.
- Encourage them to check their answers with a partner when they have finished.
- Go through the answers together.

EXTRA ACTIVITY Point out that there are standard formats to writing dates and addresses and that these vary from country to country. Students can see from this example letter and the one in exercise 11 the standard formats used in the UK. You could ask students to compare just the home addresses in the two letters to highlight that in the UK we put the house number first, then the street name. In a multilingual class, students could compare the standard formats of dates and addresses used in their countries or a monolingual class could compare with the UK formats.

ANSWERS
a 2   b 8   c 1   d 6,7   e 4   f 5   g 3

Exercise 10
- Students read the letter in exercise 8 again and find expressions which are similar to 1–6.
- They work alone and underline the expressions they find.
- Go through the answers together.
- Now focus the students' attention on the Language for writing box. Give them time to read the information.
- If necessary, ask *Why does Julien use 'Yours sincerely' to end his letter, not 'Yours faithfully'?* (because he knows the name of the person.) This checks they understand the information about greetings and endings in the box.
- You could also point out that we do not use job titles on their own in greetings, e.g. *Dear Manager*. If we don't know the person's name, we use *Dear Sir/Madam*.
- Drill any vocabulary you think they will find difficult (faithfully, sincerely)

ANSWERS
1 additional information
2 Please find enclosed
3 Dear Dr Cheung
4 I look forward to hearing from you.
5 I am writing to apply for

Exercise 11
- Students read the letter.
- Elicit that it does not make a good impression because it needs to be more formal.
- In pairs or alone, students find more formal expressions from the box to replace the ones in italics.
- Go through the answers with the class.

ANSWERS
1 Dear
2 I am writing to request/I would like to request/I wish to request
3 Please find enclosed/I enclose
4 I am happy to provide any additional information that you need.
5 I look forward to hearing from you/I hope to hear from you soon.
6 Yours sincerely
7 Enclosures

Exercise 12a
- Students read the instruction and work in pairs on the task.

EXTRA CHALLENGE Ask stronger students to cover the letters on this page and only look at the Language for writing box in order to make the task more challenging and realistic.

- Monitor and assist any students who are having difficulty.
- Give a time limit to the end of the activity.

Exercise 12b
- Student pairs exchange letters, then check each other's letters.

EXTRA SUPPORT Give a checklist to students who need extra support: *Are the addresses and date in the correct format and correct places? Is the greeting formal and does the ending match? Does the letter have a good level of formality? Is the purpose of the letter clear? Can you find any mistakes in the letter?*

- Conduct class feedback. Find a pair who believe the letter they have checked is particularly good quality. Ask them to read it aloud to the class.

9.5 Video

Sports scholarship in the USA

VIDEOSCRIPT

This is Arizona State University, a major research university with almost 60,000 students.

The Arizona State Sun Devils represent the university in many different sports.

They have some of the best sports teams in the USA. They have teams in baseball, basketball, running, swimming, golf and many other sports. These teams attract some of the greatest athletes in the country.

Ike Davis, a professional first baseman who has played for the New York Mets and the Pittsburgh Pirates, was a huge star on the baseball team.

Terrell Suggs, who won NFL Defensive Player of the Year in 2011, played for the football team.

Phil Mickelson, one of the most famous golfers in the world, won several amateur golf championships while he was a student here.

ASU attracted top athletes like Phil Mickelson through sports scholarships.

Education in the USA is very expensive. At Arizona State, the average annual cost for a student is about $24,000. This includes tuition fees, books and the general cost of living.

Because of these costs, many students need financial assistance. If they don't receive this help, then they won't be able to finish their degrees. It's no surprise then that around 83% of students here receive some kind of grant, and each year universities and colleges spend around $1 billion on sports scholarships.

They invest in facilities and equipment, too. Arizona State, for example, has one of the country's best swimming and diving facilities. It has an 18-hole golf course and a 71,706-seater stadium – the Sun Devil stadium.

There's also a softball stadium, a soccer stadium and the Wells Fargo Arena, home to the Sun Devil's basketball team.

But why do universities like Arizona State invest so much on sports?

College sports are very popular in the United States. College football, for example, is the second biggest spectator sport in the country. Sporting success is a great advertisement for the university, so if they do well on the playing field, they will attract the best students.

It's great for young athletes, too. The scholarship programme gives them a chance to go to university. If they do well, they might become professional athletes. If they don't, they'll still have a degree.

Many of today's professional athletes began their career at college so, for universities like Arizona State, sport is big business.

VIDEO ANSWERS

1 1 spectator 2 scholarship 3 tuition fee 4 college
3 a) they all went to Arizona State University
   b) because education is very expensive
   c) because it is big business, and they will attract the best athletes
4 a) 4 b) 3 c) 2 d) 1 e) 5

Review

ANSWERS

Exercise 1a
1 If you drink coffee late at night, you won't sleep well.
2 You'll lose weight if you do regular exercise.
3 If you continue to eat junk food every day, you'll definitely have health problems.
4 If you eat small meals regularly through the day, you won't feel hungry.

Exercise 1b
1 b 2 a 3 c 4 d

Exercise 2a
forehead
cheek
lip
tongue
chin
shoulder
chest
elbow
hand
fist
thumb

Exercise 2b
1 cheek 2 hands 3 head 4 tongue 5 thumb
6 elbows 7 hand

Exercise 3a
1 exercise
2 stress
3 food
4 keep
5 natural
6 healthy

Exercise 4a
1 b
2 e
3 a
4 f
5 d
6 c

Exercise 5a 9.9

ANSWERS/AUDIOSCRIPT 9.9
D How can I help you?
P I'm having real trouble sleeping just now.
D OK, first of all, you should try to reduce caffeine or other stimulants.
P Right, I can probably drink a bit less coffee. Anything else?
D It's also a good idea to keep calm during the evening. No violent TV programmes.
P OK. I won't watch any. And what about at bedtime?
D Well just before you go to bed, have a bath or drink some warm milk.
P I see. Well I'll try those ideas.
D If things don't improve, come back and see me in a week.
P OK, thanks.

Unit 9 159

10 Food

Unit overview

Language input

Uses of the *-ing* form (CB p97)	• *Being a superstar is not all good news.* • *They don't like eating very sweet food.* • *Are you good at recognizing different flavours?*
The passive (CB p98)	• *Over 18 billion cans are produced every year.* • *The first cans were used by soldiers.*
Grammar reference (CB pp152–3)	

Vocabulary development

Describing food (CB p96)	• *bitter, savoury, sour …* • *baked, boiled, fried …* • *herbs, sauce, stew …*
Food containers (CB p98)	• *a box of … , a tin of … , a tube of …*
Words with more than one meaning (CB p101)	• *mark, figure, clear …*

Skills development

Reading: Understanding reference words in a text (CB p100)
Speaking: Problems in a restaurant (CB p102)
Writing: A restaurant review (CB p103)

Video

Documentary: Koreatown (Coursebook DVD & CB p104)
Vox pops (Coursebook DVD & TG p263)

More materials

Workbook	• Language practice for vocabulary, pronunciation, grammar, speaking and writing • Reading for pleasure • Review: Units 9 and 10
Photocopiable activities	• Grammar: Food facts follow-on (TG p217 & TSRD) • Vocabulary: Just a minute (TG p235 & TSRD) • Communication: Waiter, waiter! (TG p253 & TSRD)
Tests	• Unit 10 test (TSRD)
Unit 10 wordlist (TSRD)	

160

10.1 A question of taste

Goals
- Describe a national dish
- Use the *-ing* form

Lead-in
- Write on the board: *How often do you eat out?* and teach the phrasal verb *eat out* if necessary.
- Put students into pairs to ask and answer the question. Tell them to ask follow-up questions.
- Conduct a brief class discussion.

Vocabulary & Listening describing food

Exercise 1
- In pairs, students take turns to ask and answer the questions.
- Ask some students to report their partner's experiences.

Exercise 2 10.1
- Focus students' attention on the photos. Ask them to discuss in pairs which country they think each dish comes from.
- Elicit some ideas from the class.
- Tell students to listen to the recording to find out whether they were correct. Tell them to write the number of the speaker and the country name in the spaces provided on the photos.
- Play track 10.1.
- Go through the answers together.

ANSWERS
a speaker 3 Vietnam
b speaker 1 Austria
c speaker 4 Britain
d speaker 2 Morocco

AUDIOSCRIPT 10.1
Speaker 1
So this is a Sacher Torte. It's probably the most famous food from Austria. As you can see, it's a kind of chocolate cake. It's quite plain, really, and it's got apricot jam in the middle. On the top and sides it's covered with dark chocolate which has a nice bitter taste. It's often served with thick cream.

Speaker 2
OK, so this is a tagine. It's a kind of stew. There are several types of tagine. This one is quite a typical one – it's made with pieces of lamb cooked in a thick sauce with onions and spices. The tagine has some honey in it so it tastes quite sweet. The tagine itself is mild – it doesn't have chillies in it – but it tastes really nice with chilli sauce. Here in Morocco we usually eat tagine with bread.

Speaker 3
These are called vegetable spring rolls. They're really popular in Vietnam. There are many different sorts of spring roll. Sometimes the rolls are not cooked, but these ones are fried. They're filled with raw vegetables, fresh herbs and boiled noodles. You dip them into this sauce to give them extra flavour. The sauce has lime juice in it to make it sour, chilli to make it spicy and some sugar so

it's quite sweet. They are served as part of a meal or as a snack.

4
These are scones. It's a sort of cake but less sweet than a cake. They're baked in the oven and the traditional way to eat them here in Britain is to cut them in half and cover them with strawberry or raspberry jam and then put cream on top of the jam. You can also have savoury scones – scones without sugar. Cheese scones, for example, are quite popular, though my favourite are the sweet ones. You can eat them at room temperature or you can heat them in the oven. Personally, I like them warm.

Exercise 3 10.1
- Give students time to read the gapped sentences. Remind them that there may be more than one missing word.
- Play track 10.1 again so students can complete the gaps.
- Allow students to check their answers in pairs.
- Play the track again if necessary.
- Go through the answers together.

ANSWERS
1 dark chocolate
2 thick cream
3 pieces of lamb
4 honey, quite sweet
5 lime juice
6 as a snack
7 less sweet
8 at room

Exercise 4
- Focus students on the box and table. Go through the four headings, eliciting or teaching the meanings. You could drill pronunciation of *ingredient* /ɪnˈgriːdiənt/, *texture* /ˈtekstʃə/ and *taste* /teɪst/.
- Students work alone to categorize the words.
- Encourage students to discuss their answers with their partner. Monitor carefully and note problem vocabulary.

EXTRA CHALLENGE Encourage fast finishers to find pairs of opposites in the 'texture and taste' column. (mild – hot/spicy, bitter/sour – sweet, savoury – sweet.)

- Go through the answers together. Help with any problem words. Ask fast finishers to teach the opposite adjectives and explain the meanings yourself if necessary.

PRONUNCIATION Students commonly mispronounce the vowel sounds in *stew* /stjuː/, *herbs* /hɜːbz/, *honey* /ˈhʌni/, *mild* /maɪld/, *sour* /ˈsaʊə/, *savoury* /ˈseɪvəri/, *baked* /beɪkt/, *raw* /rɔː/. Help them by modelling clearly and drilling these words.

WATCH OUT! Write *dessert* on the board. Model and mark the word stress carefully. Draw attention to the difference in meaning and pronunciation between this noun and *desert*, e.g. *The Sahara desert*. Elicit or give example sentences. Drill pronunciation.

ANSWERS

Type of dish
sauce
dessert
snack
stew

Ingredient
herbs
honey
spices
lamb

Texture and taste
mild
hot/spicy
bitter
sweet
sour
plain
thick
savoury

How it is cooked/eaten
fried
baked
boiled
raw

Exercise 5

- Put students into small groups. Tell them to read the instruction. Remind them to uses the words and phrases from exercises 3 and 4.
- For a monolingual group who may have the same national dish, focus them on describing a dish they like.

EXTRA SUPPORT Allow students thinking and preparation time. Tell them not to write their description in full but just to make some notes to give them confidence.

- Choose a student in each group to start the activity. Monitor carefully.

EXTRA CHALLENGE Encourage fast finishers to ask each other questions about the dishes they've described.

- When they have finished, conduct class feedback. You could ask students in each group to report on one dish. Conduct error correction if necessary.

EXTENSION You could ask which was the sweetest, the plainest, the nicest dish or the dish with the most ingredients.

Pronunciation words with shortened vowels

Exercise 6a 10.2

- Tell students to read the information about pronunciation.
- Write *chocolate* on the board and cross out the unpronounced vowel (choc~~o~~late). You could also use finger gestures to show how *chocolate* seems to be a three syllable word but only has two syllables.
- Ask students to listen to more examples of this kind of word. Point out that these are in sentences in the recording (not isolated words).
- Ask them to cross out the vowel which is not pronounced.
- Play track 10.2.
- Go through the answers together.

ANSWERS
veg~~e~~table
straw~~b~~erry
rasp~~b~~erry
fav~~ou~~rite
diff~~e~~rent
temp~~e~~rature
sev~~e~~ral

AUDIOSCRIPT 10.2
These are called vegetable spring rolls.
Cover them with strawberry or raspberry jam.
My favourite are the sweet ones.
There are many different sorts of spring roll.
You can eat them at room temperature.
There are several types of tagine.

Exercise 6b 10.3

- Play track 10.3 so that students can listen and repeat the words.
- Play the track as many times as is necessary to help the students pronounce the words naturally with the correct number of syllables.

EXTRA ACTIVITY Ask students to write their own sentences which contain at least two of the words. Tell them to swap with another student and say the sentences, making sure they pronounce the words well.

AUDIOSCRIPT 10.3
vegetable
strawberry
raspberry
favourite
different
temperature
several

Grammar & Reading uses of the *-ing* form

Exercise 7a

> **Text summary:** An article about 'supertasters' – people who taste things differently because they have more taste buds than average. Positive and negative aspects of being a supertaster are mentioned.

- Focus students' attention on the title of the text and ask them to discuss the questions in pairs.
- Elicit some of their ideas (but do not confirm any at this stage).

Exercise 7b

- Give students a time limit for reading to check their ideas.
- Go through the answers with the class.

ANSWERS
A supertaster is a person who can taste things very well. This can be good and bad
Good: Many professional chefs are supertasters. Supertasters can be slimmer and probably don't smoke.
Bad: Common foods may taste too bitter, sweet, spicy. Supertasters sometimes avoid certain vegetables and fruit.

Exercise 8

- Ask students to read the questions.
- Tell them to find the answers in the article.
- Encourage them to discuss their answers with their partner.
- Go through the answers together.

ANSWERS
1 They have more taste buds.
2 About 25%.
3 Because coffee tastes too bitter.
4 Supertasters are often slimmer and smoking is less common in supertasters.

Exercise 9
- Put students into small groups.
- Ask them to read the question and discuss it together. Remember that they may never have thought about taste in depth before, so if they are having difficulty, ask them to think about the kinds of food they enjoy eating to help them reach a conclusion.
- Conduct class feedback.

Exercise 10
- Refer students to the Grammar focus box. Give them plenty of time to read it.

EXTRA SUPPORT Go through the uses of the *-ing* form using the examples in the Grammar focus box: elicit 1 the subject (being), 2 the verb which comes before *-ing* (like) and 3 the preposition which comes before *-ing* (at).
- Ask them to find another example of each use in the article.
- Go through the answers together.

ANSWERS
1 Supertasting is more common in women … OR Smoking is less common …
2 You may avoid eating …
3 Find out if you are a supertaster by looking in the mirror and counting …

- Refer students to Grammar reference on p152. There are three more exercises here students can do for homework. See answers in next column.

Exercise 11a
- Tell students that they are going to complete a questionnaire about being a *foodie*. Write *Are you a foodie?* on the board and elicit what they think this word means. (= a person who is very interested in cooking and eating different kinds of food) You could ask whether any of them think they are foodies and ask them to give reasons.
- Focus students' attention on the verbs in the box.

EXTRA SUPPORT Elicit the spelling rule for adding *-ing* if necessary (remove the 'e' before adding *-ing*, e.g. *take*, *taking*.)
- Students work alone to complete the questions using the correct verb in the *-ing* form. (If necessary, tell them NOT to answer the questions at this stage.)
- Go through the answers together.

ANSWERS
1 eating
2 cooking
3 eating
4 knowing
5 taking, sharing
6 talking, eating
7 watching
8 becoming
9 spending

Exercise 11b
- Students focus on the *-ing* forms in the questionnaire.
- Tell them to read the instruction. If necessary, check understanding by eliciting how they are going to mark the different uses of the *-ing* form.
- Students work alone to analyse the grammar, referring to the Grammar focus box when they need to.
- Allow them to check their answers with a partner.
- Go through the answers together.

ANSWERS
1 S 2 P 3 V 4 P 5 S,S 6 V,P 7 V 8 V 9 S

Exercise 11c
- Put students in pairs.
- Tell them to read the instruction. Point out that they need to ask follow-up questions.
- Give a suitable time limit if necessary.
- Encourage follow-up questions as you monitor.
- Conduct class feedback. You could ask whether there are any foodies in the class, according to the questionnaire. Encourage the students to discuss who is more of a foodie.

Exercise 12
- Students turn to page 129 and read the sentence stems.
- Go through any unknown vocabulary (pleasures, totally against, look forward to).
- Students complete the sentences with their own ideas.
- Monitor, assist and correct.
- Put students into small groups to share their ideas.

FEEDBACK FOCUS Monitor their discussions to ensure they are using *-ing* forms correctly. Make a note of any errors.
- Encourage students to report to the class in feedback which person they had most in common with and why.
- Conduct error correction if necessary.

GRAMMAR REFERENCE ANSWERS

Exercise 1
1 putting
2 eating
3 serving
4 baking
5 buying
6 keeping
7 drinking

Exercise 2
1 Cooking with my daughter was fun.
2 Covering the chicken with herbs was a good idea.
3 Drinking a bottle of water every day helps me stay fit.
4 Finding that restaurant was lucky.
5 Playing with knives is dangerous.
6 Eating too much chocolate isn't good for you.

Exercise 3
1 My friends and I enjoy going for a curry.
2 Did you consider inviting Sandra to dinner last weekend?
3 We avoid eating after 9 p.m.
4 My mother is good at baking.
5 I prefer eating fish to eating meat.
6 Are you thinking of making a cake for Karen's birthday?

Unit 10

10.2 Canned dreams

Goals
- Talk about food
- Use the passive

Lead-in
- Ask students to look at the photos of food and drink.
- Tell them to work in pairs and match each word in the box with one item in the photo.
- Go through the answers together.
- You could ask *Which of these things come from your country? Do you particularly like or dislike any of these things?* Elicit answers from the whole class or ask them to discuss in small groups.

Vocabulary & Speaking food containers

Exercise 1a
- Focus students' attention on the words for different food containers in the table.
- Allow plenty of time to complete the table with a word or phrase from the box. They can do this alone or in pairs.
- Go through the answers together. Correct any pronunciation errors with this vocabulary.

ANSWERS
1 chocolates
2 lemonade
3 frozen peas
4 chopped tomatoes
5 sparkling water
6 toothpaste
7 olives
8 apple juice

Exercise 1b
- In pairs or alone, students think of another thing which goes in each type of container 1–8.
- Elicit their answers and check that they are correct.
- Drill the food containers vocabulary if necessary.

PRONUNCIATION You could also point out that they all end with a consonant sound so link naturally with *of* and that because of this linking in connected speech, we pronounce *of* with a schwa /əv/. Help them practise this linking.

Exercise 2
- Ask students to look at the illustration and elicit that these are recycling bins. Check they also know the verb *to recycle*.
- They should understand the labels on the bins as they studied materials in Unit 5.
- Students discuss in pairs which bin to put each container in.
- Go through the answers together. Elicit from the pairs *What is in your bin for plastic?*

EXTRA ACTIVITY You could conduct a brief discussion in small groups or as a class on the topic of recycling: *Do you think your government cares about recycling? Do people in your country recycle the materials in exercise 2? Is recycling free?*

ANSWERS
Plastic: tube, packet
Metal: tin, can
Paper & cardboard: box, carton
Glass: jar, bottle

Exercise 3a
- Students read the instruction and think of six items.
- Monitor and make sure they are using container phrases.

Exercise 3b
- In small groups, students compare their lists and analyse their own and their classmates' eating and drinking habits.
- Conduct a class discussion. Ask each group *Is there anything surprising about the choices of the people in your group? Did many people choose the same items?*

EXTENSION Exercise 3b was about food or drink they like having in their kitchen. Ask them to think of six food or drink items that they think are essential (= absolutely necessary) for them. Again they should include the container phrases. They can include items from exercise 3a if they wish. Ask them to compare their lists of essentials.

Grammar & Listening the passive

Exercise 4
- Students read the questions and discuss in pairs.
- Conduct class feedback. Encourage them to support their opinions with reasons and examples.

SUGGESTED ANSWERS
1 Students' own answers
2 Advantages: You can store the food for a long time. It is often cheaper than fresh food.
Disadvantages: Canned food often tastes different to fresh food and the texture may be different. Canned food sometimes has chemicals added to preserve the food. Some of the vitamins and other good things in fresh food may be lost during the canning process.

Exercise 5 10.4

Audio summary: A talk about preserving food. After a brief general introduction, the talk focuses on the history of metal cans.

- Students read the instruction and definition of *preserve*. Ask them to read through the topics a–e to check they understand all the words.

DICTIONARY SKILLS You could take this opportunity to ask the students to use dictionaries to explore word families. *Invent is a verb. What is the noun form?* (invention), *Danger is a noun. What is the adjective form?* (dangerous) Knowing these connected words can help them with understanding and it is a good habit to check and make a record of different words in a word family.

- Play track 10.4.
- Students listen and tick the topics mentioned.
- Go through the answers together.

EXTENSION Encourage students to remember what was said about each topic if they can.

ANSWERS
a, b, e

AUDIOSCRIPT 10.4

Millions of years ago people hunted for food and ate it immediately. But they soon realized they could keep their food for longer if they protected it. So, the world's first food containers were made from animal skins and large leaves. Water was kept in coconut shells and dried vegetable skins.

Metal containers – or cans – were invented in 1810 by a French chef called Monsieur Appert. The Emperor Napoleon offered a prize to anyone who could find a way of keeping food safe for soldiers in battle, and that award was won by Appert. His invention preserved food beautifully but those first cans were made of iron, so they were incredibly heavy. But carrying them wasn't the only problem – opening them was almost impossible. Some cans even had instructions to open them with a hammer and a knife. Soldiers usually shot them open with their guns.

At the beginning of the 1800s, cans were made by hand. By the end of the 1800s, cans were produced by machine and made from a much lighter metal so they were easier to carry. But the problem of getting into the cans lasted much, much longer. Several can openers were invented, but they were all difficult to use and you could cut your fingers very badly. The safe modern tin opener – the sort with two rolling wheels and a turning key – wasn't invented until 1925.

Nowadays, over 18 billion cans are produced every year in the UK alone. If you put all those cans together, end to end, you could make a track to the Moon three times.

Exercise 6 10.4

- Tell students to read the sentences 1–4 before you play track 10.4 again.
- Students complete the sentences.
- Go through the answers together.

CRITICAL THINKING You could ask students whether they knew all this information before listening to the talk. It is useful for them to reflect on the fact that at the same time as they study English, they are also able to build upon their general knowledge through listening and reading in that second language. This can be very motivating for adult learners.

ANSWERS
1 vegetable
2 1810
3 soldiers
4 18 billion

Exercise 7

- Students read a–c and answer the questions.
- You could put them in pairs to discuss their answers.
- Go through the answers together.

EXTRA CHALLENGE Ask students if they can tell you the name for the grammatical form used in sentences a and c. (the passive)

ANSWERS
1 Yes, the meaning is the same. Sentence a focuses more on the cans. Sentence b focuses more on the soldiers.
2 No.

Exercise 8

- Focus the students' attention on the Grammar focus box.
- Give them plenty of time to read the information and complete the rules.
- Students work alone to choose the options to complete the rules.
- Go through the answers together as a class.
- To check students' understanding of the first rule ask *In example sentence 1, who is the agent?* (A French chef). *Where is the thing?* ('the can' comes at the end of the sentence.) *In example sentence 2, where is the agent? Why?* ('a French chef' is at the end of the sentence because it is not the focus of the sentence.)

ANSWERS
1 to be   2 by

- Refer students to *Grammar reference* on p153. There are three more exercises here students can do for homework. See answers on p166.

Exercise 9

- Students read the instruction and look again at the sentences in exercise 6.
- They work alone to underline the passive forms and identify whether they are present or past.
- Go through answers as a class.

ANSWERS
1 was kept (past simple passive)
2 were invented (past simple passive)
3 were used (past simple passive)
4 are produced (present simple passive)

Exercise 10

- Focus students' attention on the film review. Tell students to read the first two paragraphs to find out what the film is about.
- Elicit from the students that the film is about the ingredients of a tin of ravioli and in the film we visit the eight countries that the ingredients come from.

EXTRA CHALLENGE You could ask them to discuss in pairs why they think Katja Gaurlioff, the director, made this film. (The answer is in the final paragraph.)

- Tell students to read the whole review and complete it using the present simple in either active or passive form.

WATCH OUT! Remind them to look carefully at whether they need singular or plural to complete each gap. Subject verb agreement errors are common (e.g. the people who produces), particularly when students are focusing on new grammar structures.

- Monitor and give a time limit to the end of the activity when most students have almost finished.
- Go through the answers together. If students have made mistakes, refer to the Grammar focus box in order to help them understand better.

ANSWERS
1 learn
2 are taken
3 come
4 is grown
5 are grown
6 is made
7 are taken
8 is prepared
9 are transported
10 produce
11 talk
12 wants

Unit 10   165

Exercise 11
- Put students into pairs or small groups to discuss the questions.
- Elicit opinions from the class.

Exercise 12
- In pairs, students remember details about the products shown in the film.
- They make passive sentences about the products using the table. You could ask one pair to read out the example conversation to demonstrate the activity.
- When they have finished the activity, they can read the text again to check their answers.

Exercise 13
- Tell students in their pairs to decide who will be Student A and who will be Student B.
- Each student turns to the relevant page of the book and looks at the quiz questions under 10.2. (Student A: p129 and Student B: p133)

EXTRA SUPPORT Students could have time to write the passive questions down before they start the quiz. You could even pair two Student As and two Student Bs to help each other make the questions, then put them back in their original pairs to do the quiz.

- Students take turns to make full questions in the passive from the prompts and ask their partner. Remind them that they need to give the multiple choice answers too.
- When they have all finished, conduct class feedback. You could find out if any students knew all of the answers and if there were any answers which surprised them.

GRAMMAR REFERENCE ANSWERS

Exercise 1
1 Fresh pizza is sold in the local supermarket.
2 Tomatoes were introduced to Europe in the fifteenth century.
3 Where is asparagus grown?
4 Is spicy food eaten in Mexico?
5 Curry wasn't eaten in England until the eighteenth century.
6 When was butter first made?

Exercise 2
1 The restaurant is visited by many celebrities.
2 Was bread served with the soup?
3 Lemonade is usually sold in bottles or cans.
4 Bananas are not grown in Europe.
5 Are the glasses kept in this cupboard?
6 Dinner is not often served before 10 p.m.

Exercise 3
1 is taken
2 are filled
3 is done
4 are put
5 is dried
6 are packed
7 are wrapped
8 are delivered

10.3 Vocabulary and skills development

Goals
- Understand reference words in a text
- Understand words with more than one meaning

Reading understanding reference words in a text

Lead-in
- Ask students to look at the photo and describe to their partner what they can see.

Exercise 1a
- Students read the newspaper article headline and discuss questions 1 and 2 with a partner.
- Elicit some ideas from the class.

Exercise 1b 10.5

Audio summary: A radio news report which gives information about how much food is wasted, the reasons why this happens and the kinds of food we waste.

- Tell students that you are going to play them a news report on the topic which contains the answers to questions 1 and 2.
- Ask them to take notes.
- Play track 10.5.
- Encourage students to discuss the answers in pairs.
- Go through the answers together.

ANSWERS
1 People buy too much food and forget they have it. They cook too much food and can't eat it all. They don't like how it looks. They worry that it will make them ill.
2 Fresh vegetables and salad, drink, fresh fruit and bread and cakes.

AUDIOSCRIPT 10.5
P A recent report has found that one third of the world's food ends up in the rubbish bin. Here in the UK, half of the food which is thrown away comes from our homes. Here's Martin Waits, from the organization 'Taste it, don't waste it!'
M Much of the waste happens because people buy too much food, which they don't have time to cook. The food is just left at the back of the fridge or the cupboard and then it's forgotten. Another reason for wasting food is that we cook or prepare too much food, we can't eat it all and it goes in the bin. But the sad thing is, people often throw away food that's perfectly safe to eat, just because it doesn't look nice or because they're worried it will make them ill.
P According to the report, the foods we waste the most are fresh vegetables and salad, drink, fresh fruit and bread and cakes.

Exercise 2
- Students read the Unlock the code box about reference words.

- To understand reference words, students need to think carefully about what they are referring back to.
- Help them to compare the first two sets of sentences by highlighting *figure* in the first set of sentences. In this case the reference word must be referring back to a number.
- The second set of sentences show how reference words can refer back to a whole situation.
- Focusing on *the ones*, point out that in the example sentence you could replace *ones* with *apples*. Reference words are often used to avoid repetition.
- *So* is a useful reference word meaning 'also' or 'in the same way' and refers back to verbs.

WATCH OUT! Make sure the students aren't confusing this reference word 'so' with another meaning of 'so' – as a linker of result which they studied in Unit 5, 5.3 page 50. Tell them it is a different word, though pronounced and spelt the same.

Exercise 3

- Students read the instruction and focus on paragraph 1 of the article.
- Allow plenty of time for them to find the reference words and look back in the text in order to choose the correct option a–c. You could encourage them to mark the referencing as it has been done in the Unlock the code box.
- Students can check their answers in pairs if you wish.
- Go through the answers together.

ANSWERS
1 a apple
2 c only buy fruit and vegetables which look perfect

Exercise 4

- Students focus on the reference words in bold in the text and draw the referencing back to the word/s they refer to.
- Monitor and check that they are finding the correct words to underline/circle.
- Go through the answers together. If possible, bring up the text on the board and ask students to come to the board and draw the referencing on or elicit and draw the referencing yourself.
- Check that students are clear about the difference between *developed* countries and *developing* countries. Ask them which examples of these countries are given in the text. Elicit any more examples they can think of.

ANSWERS
Line 8 'so' refers to 'thrown away'
Line 8 'the ones' refers to 'fruit and vegetables'
Line 11 'this' refers to 'people buy more food than they can eat'
Line 15 'so' refers to 'waste'
Line 19 'this' refers to '95–115kg' (the weight of food wasted)
Line 20 'these' refers to 'developing countries'
Line 23 'this' refers to 'waste happens on farms during production or transportation'

Exercise 5

- Tell students to read the questions. Check any unknown vocabulary – students may need you to go through the meanings of *persuade* and *average* with them.

- Students work alone to read the text again and answer the questions.
- Go through the answers together.

CRITICAL THINKING Ask students to reflect on what they have read and discuss the topic in small groups using some of these questions to guide them: *Do you think supermarkets should sell fruit and vegetables with marks on them? Would you buy them? Do you think supermarkets should stop special offers? How could developed countries waste less food? Are you surprised that developing countries waste so much food? How could developing countries waste less food?*

ANSWERS
1 They throw them away.
2 With offers like 'buy one, get one free'.
3 a) 650 million tonnes
   b) 6–11kg
4 The hot and humid weather.

Exercise 6

- Students read the instruction. If necessary, find the first reference word together as a demonstration, circle it and find the word/s it refers to.
- Students work alone on the task.
- Allow them to check their answers in pairs if you wish.
- Go through the answers together.

ANSWERS
'that' refers to 'shopping on an empty stomach'
'This' refers to 'food which has travelled thousands of miles'
'These' refers to 'soft apples or oranges'
'So' refers to 'make great fruit juices'
'The first one' refers to 'a best before date'
'that date' refers to 'a best before date'
'this' refers to 'share with someone else'
'one of these' refers to 'a doggy bag'

Exercise 7

- Students read the tips in the text again and categorize them according to the place where you can do them, a, b or c.
- Encourage students to check their answers in pairs.
- Go through the answers together if necessary.

EXTENSION Put students into small groups to share their opinions and experience. Ask *Which of these things in the list of tips do they already do? Which things do they think they could start/stop doing? Are there any tips which they would not follow or disagree with? Why?*

ANSWERS
a Don't throw away soft or old fruit. Understand food labels.
b Avoid shopping on an empty stomach. Don't buy food which has travelled thousands of miles. Understand food labels.
c Share a starter and a dessert with someone else. Ask for a 'doggy bag'.

Unit 10   167

Vocabulary words with more than one meaning

Exercise 8a
- Ask students to read the Vocabulary focus box carefully.
- Go through it together. Elicit the meaning of *free* in the first example and in the second example.
- **EXTRA CHALLENGE** You could put students into pairs to try and think of any other words they know in English which have two different meanings.

Exercise 8b
- Students refer back to the article about food waste on page 100.
- Allow plenty of time for them to find the key words in the text and work out which meaning is correct in each case.
- Go through the answers together.

ANSWERS
1 pretty (blue sub-heading) b, quite/very
2 left (line 2) a, remaining/still there
3 mark (line 2) a, a spot or line that spoils the look of something
4 funny (line 8) b, strange
5 figure (line 19) b, a number
6 clear (line 19) b, obvious

Exercise 8c
- Put students into pairs to make sentences which illustrate the other meaning for each word. You could do the first one as a demonstration together. (e.g. *They have painted the bedroom walls pink and it looks very pretty*.)
- Allow plenty of time for this creative task.
- Monitor and check that their sentences clearly show the other meaning to exercise 8b. Help students to self-correct any errors you see.

STUDY TIP Help students learn to self-correct by indicating where there is an error, so that they have a chance to identify and correct it. If necessary, you can give extra help by saying which kind of error it is, e.g. word order, spelling, wrong part of speech, etc. When students can see what kinds of errors they commonly make, they can write their own checklist to use when they finish any piece of written work.

EXTRA ACTIVITY Ask students to imagine they are dictionary writers. Write on the board two or three of the students' sentences illustrating the same word from exercise 8b. Students discuss in small groups which one they would use as an example sentence in their dictionary. Encourage them to justify their choices, e.g. *It is shorter. It is easier to understand. It is easier to remember. It is interesting*, etc.

Exercise 9a
- Sentences 1–4 contain words in bold which can have more than one meaning. Students read the sentences and choose which meaning each word has in this sentence.
- They work alone on the task.
- Go through the answers.

ANSWERS
1 b 2 a 3 a 4 b

Exercise 9b
- In pairs, students discuss the statements in exercise 9a and decide whether they agree or disagree.
- Encourage them to give reasons and examples to support their opinions.
- Conduct class discussion of the statements. Encourage turn-taking and politeness between students in the class who have different opinions.

EXTENSION/EXTRA CHALLENGE Strong students can write new sentences for the words in exercise 9a which illustrate the other meaning of the word. Check carefully.

Exercise 10a
- Tell students to read the questions 1–4 and complete them with a word from exercise 9a.
- They should also decide which meaning each one is. Highlight the example to show them what to do.
- Students work alone on the task.
- Go through the answers together.

ANSWERS
2 way (b)
3 diet (a)
4 charge (b)

Exercise 10b
- In their pairs, students take turns to ask and answer the questions. They can also ask further questions to get more information from their partner.
- Conduct a class discussion if you have time.

10.4 Speaking and writing

Goals
- Explain and deal with problems
- Write a review of a restaurant

Lead-in
- Focus students' attention on the photos. Elicit that each photo shows a customer and waiter/waitress in a restaurant or café.
- Put students in pairs or small groups to discuss what they think is happening in the photos. Ask *Do you have any experience of these kinds of conversations, either as the customer or the member of staff?* Encourage discussion.

Listening & Speaking problems in a restaurant

Exercise 1
- Students read the questions.
- In small groups, they take turns to ask and answer.
- **EXTRA SUPPORT** With a weaker group, drill the questions to ensure good pronunciation, especially of favourite /ˈfeɪvərɪt/ and usually /ˈjuʒəli/ and restaurant /ˈrestrɒnt/.
- Conduct class feedback – ask one student in each group to report their answers to question 3. Elicit suggestions from the class for question 4.

168

Exercise 2 10.6

> **Audio summary:** There are five conversations which illustrate problem situations in restaurants. Three are common problems which customers have. The other two are situations where the customer is at fault.

- Tell students that they are going to hear five different conversations in restaurants.
- Check that they understand the task.

EXTRA CHALLENGE With a stronger group, you could also ask them to make notes of the kind of problem being discussed.

- Play track 10.6.
- Allow students time to check their answers in pairs. You may need to play the track again.
- Check answers together. If any of the problems were the same as students' suggestions in exercise 1, praise them.

EXTRA SUPPORT Ask further questions and play track 10.6 one more time for them to find the answers:
1 Why does the customer need a cloth? 2 What is the mistake on the bill? 3 Why does the customer want a different glass? 4 What mistake did the customer make? 5 Why doesn't the customer want to eat the fish?

ANSWERS
1 C   2 R   3 R   4 C   5 R

AUDIOSCRIPT 10.6

1
C Excuse me. I'm very sorry but I've just spilled my orange juice. I'm afraid some's gon,e on the floor too. Could you possibly bring me a cloth?
W Sure. That's no problem.
C I'm sorry about that.
W Oh no, don't worry. It's not your fault. It happens all the time. Would you like another juice?
C Oh yes, please. Thank you.

2
C Excuse me? Erm … there seems to be a mistake in the bill.
W Oh, is there?
C You've charged us for two coffees and we only ordered one.
W Oh, I'm terribly sorry. I'll get you another bill.
C OK. Thanks.

3
C Excuse me. Could I have another glass, please? This one's dirty. It's got lipstick on it.
W Oh, yes. So it has. I do apologize. I'll get you a clean one.
C OK, thanks very much.

4
C Excuse me. I've got a bit of a problem. I didn't know that you only accept cash and I don't have enough on me.
W Yes, it does say 'No credit cards' on the door.
C Yes, sorry. I didn't see that. Could I … , is there a cash machine near here?
W There's one a few minutes down the road.
C Would you mind waiting while I go and get some money out?
W Not at all.
C OK, I'll be back in a few minutes. Sorry.
W Don't worry about it. That's fine.

5
C Excuse me? I'm afraid I can't eat this fish. It smells funny.
W What do you mean, sir?
C I mean it smells funny. It doesn't smell fresh.
W But it is fresh. It was delivered to the restaurant this morning.
C Well, you smell it.
W Yes, you're right, sir. It doesn't smell fresh. I'm very sorry about that. I'll bring you another one.
C Er, no. I'd like to order something else, please.

Exercise 3a 10.6

- Tell the students that they are going to listen to complete specific phrases in the same conversations.
- Give them time to read the phrases.
- Play track 10.6 again.
- Go through answers with the class.

WATCH OUT! Point out, using question 7 as an example, that *Would you mind … ?* is followed by the *-ing* form of the verb.

ANSWERS
1 Could … possibly   6 do
2 your fault.   7 you mind
3 seems to   8 Don't worry
4 charged us   9 afraid
5 terribly   10 like to order

Exercise 3b 10.7

- Ask students to listen to the sentences and then repeat them.
- The focus is on natural English so point out the stress, rhythm and linking in each phrase. You may need to pause the recording to do this and/or play it several times so the students have plenty of practice.
- Play track 10.7.

AUDIOSCRIPT 10.7
1 Could you possibly bring me a cloth?
2 Don't worry. It's not your fault.
3 There seems to be a mistake …
4 You've charged us for two coffees …
5 I'm terribly sorry.
6 I do apologize.
7 Would you mind waiting … ?
8 Don't worry about it.
9 I'm afraid I can't eat this …
10 I'd like to order something else, please.

Exercise 4

- Focus students' attention on the Language for speaking box where the phrases are organized into functions. Tell them to use these phrases as they do this activity.
- Ask students to read the situations. Go through any unknown vocabulary.
- Ask them to work in pairs to plan what the customer could say in each situation. Give them plenty of time to discuss.
- Elicit answers from different pairs.

Unit 10   169

POSSIBLE ANSWERS
1 I'm afraid I can't read this menu. Could you possibly bring me a menu in English?
2 I'm afraid these people are very noisy. Could we possibly move to a quieter table?
3 There seems to be a problem. We ordered our food 30 minutes ago. Would you mind checking it, please?
4 I'm afraid my knife fell on the floor. I'd like a clean one, please.
5 There seems to be a mistake. I'm afraid I didn't order this. Could you bring … , please?
6 There seems to be a mistake. You've charged us for … which we did not order. I'd like a new bill please.

Exercise 5
- Ask students to work in pairs and use the phrases from the Language for speaking box to act out a conversation in a restaurant. Tell them to decide which of them is going to be the customer for the first conversation.
- Students can use the situations in exercise 4 as the basis for their conversations.
- Monitor carefully and note any correction points.
- You can conduct error correction before they try situation 2 or wait until they have finished more conversations.

EXTRA CHALLENGE Strong students can start using their own ideas for conversations about problems in restaurants now.
- Make sure that students in each pair swap roles for each conversation.
- Conduct class feedback. You could invite a confident pair to the front of the class to act out each situation.

SMART COMMUNICATION The British are less direct than many other nationalities when explaining problems or asking for something. In the UK, polite formulas are often used. Examples: *There seems to be a mistake.* rather than *There is a mistake.* and *I'm afraid I can't eat this.* rather than *I can't eat this.*
Around the world where English is used between non-native speakers, direct phrases can be used and are generally *not* considered impolite.

Reading & Writing a restaurant review

Exercise 6a
- Go through the vocabulary with the students. Help them with the meanings and drill pronunciation if necessary.
- Put students into pairs to discuss the order of importance. Remind them to *give reasons* for their choices.

EXTRA SUPPORT You could give each pair five small pieces of paper and ask them to write one of the things on each piece. It's easier for some students if they can move pieces of paper around to show their order of importance visually.
- Conduct class feedback. Elicit views from a few pairs, encouraging them to explain why.

Exercise 6b
- Tell students to read the sentences.
- Students match each sentence to one thing in the box.
- Check answers together.

EXTENSION You could also elicit whether each sentence is positive or negative. Ask how they know.

ANSWERS
food	(positive)
atmosphere	(positive)
value for money	(positive)
location	(negative)
service	(negative)

Exercise 7
EXTRA ACTIVITY Write *restaurant review* on the board. You could elicit the verb (to review a restaurant) and noun for the person who does this (a reviewer). Ask the students: *If you see a good review of a restaurant, are you more interested in going there? Why/Why not?*
- Students read the two reviews and answer the questions.
- Allow students to check their answers in pairs.
- Go through answers with the class.

ANSWERS
Lee Min mentions atmosphere, food, service and value for money.
Isabelle mentions location, atmosphere, food, service and value for money.
Both writers say that the food is tasty. They also agree that the atmosphere is good – though Lee Min says it is lively while Isabelle says it's cool and modern.
They disagree about the other aspects.

Exercise 8
- Highlight the two different tasks to do.
- Give the students plenty of time to read the reviews again. They may discuss their answers in pairs.
- Go through answers with the class.

ANSWERS
1 Adjectives which describe the restaurants: busy, lively, disappointing, cool, modern
Adjectives which describe the food: tasty, good value, cold
2 There isn't a huge choice of food on the menu.
It's always busy and the atmosphere is lively.
It isn't good value.
It's right in the middle of town.
The staff are friendly and helpful.

Exercise 9
- Focus the students' attention on the Language for writing box. Make sure the meaning of *apostrophe* is clear.
- When the students have read the information, ask if they have any questions about it.

EXTRA SUPPORT To check points 1 and 4, write on the board
1. the customer's food and
2. the customers' food.
Ask *How many customers does the food belong to?* Point out that the pronunciation is the same for both, so you cannot hear this grammatical difference, only see it.
- Ask students to find apostrophes in the two restaurant reviews and decide if they are type 1, 2, 3 or 4.
- Go through answers as a class. (Some answers occur more than once in the text.)

WATCH OUT! Point out that *it's* could be a contraction of *it is* or *it has* and they need to work this out from the sentence, so elicit for each answer (though in these reviews there are only examples of contracted *it is*).

170

ANSWERS
It's – type 1, contraction of it is
isn't – type 2, contraction of is not
food's – type 1, contraction of food is
You're – type 1, contraction of you are
don't – type 2, contraction of do not
diners' – type 4, the diners are plural
location's – type 1, contraction of location is
atmosphere's – type 1, contraction of atmosphere is
weren't – type 2, contraction of were not
couldn't – type 2, contraction of could not
didn't – type 2, contraction of did not
friend's – type 3, friend is singular
aren't – type 2, contraction of are not

Exercise 10
- Students work alone to correct the review.
- Ask them to check their answers in pairs. Then go through answers as a class.
- Ask students to explain their answers, referring to rules in the Language for writing box.

ANSWERS
friend's – unnecessary apostrophe (friends)
isnt – missing apostrophe (isn't)
Its – missing apostrophe (It's)
wont – missing apostrophe (won't)
foods – missing apostrophe (food's)
chefs – missing apostrophe (chef's)
friends – missing apostrophe (friends')

Exercise 11a
- Students think of a restaurant they have been to. Tell them to make notes about the different things in exercise 6a, plus anything else they like or dislike about the restaurant.
- If the students know the same restaurant, they could work together. This also gives them speaking practice.

Exercise 11b
- Ask students to write a review of the restaurant (either individually or in pairs, as set up in exercise 11a).
- Give them a suitable time limit for this writing.
- Monitor carefully, pointing out errors for the students to self-correct and helping them to express themselves.

EXTRA CHALLENGE Remind fast finishers to include information and opinion about all the things in exercise 6a. When they have finished, tell them to check their work for errors. They could look up spellings in their dictionaries. They should also check their use of apostrophes.

EXTENSION You could ask them to rewrite the review but make it opposite – so all positive comments become negative and all negative become positive. This could be a homework task.

Exercise 11c
- Instruct students to swap their review with a partner and give it a star rating, similar to the examples.
- If students wrote their reviews in pairs, they will need to swap with another pair.
- Conduct class feedback. Elicit answers to the question 'Would you like to go there?'

EXTENSION If you have extra time, you could put the reviews up around the walls like a gallery. All students could walk around and read them and decide which restaurant to visit or not to visit or decide on their top three restaurants.

10.5 Video

Koreatown

VIDEOSCRIPT
This is New York's Koreatown.
And Korea Way – a small part of 32nd Street between Fifth Avenue and Broadway – is the heart of the neighbourhood.
This area of New York is close to the Empire State Building, Madison Square Garden and Penn Station, so a lot of tourists walk through here.
This makes it a great place to do business, which many Koreans realized when they immigrated here in the 1980s. Soon the area was full of Korean shops, supermarkets and lots and lots of restaurants.
Today, Koreatown is a bright and bustling part of New York and if you want to try traditional Korean food, it's the best place in the city.
This is Miss Korea Barbecue.
They make authentic Korean food using traditional Korean methods.
And one of their most popular meals is *japchae*.
Japchae is an old Korean dish. The word is actually two Korean words. *Jap* means 'mixed' and *chae* means 'vegetables'. It was first made over 400 years ago and today it's one of the most popular dishes in Korea.
It's also a favourite in Korean restaurants abroad, so the chefs here at Miss Korea Barbecue are really good at making it.
First of all, the peppers, onions and courgettes are prepared. These vegetables are then added to the pan. Then they are all fried together over a large flame.
While the vegetables are being cooked, the noodles are boiled. These noodles are made from sweet potato, but the chefs here make many different types.
As the noodles are boiling, the dish is seasoned and sauce is added.
Once they are ready, they are all mixed in the wok.
Finally, the chefs leave everything for a few minutes because *japchae* isn't served hot, it's served at room temperature.
This is the traditional recipe, but it can be made in different ways. Some people add spices to make it hot and spicy, while others add herbs to make it more savoury. Whichever way you prefer it, *japchae* – like most Korean food – is healthy and delicious.

VIDEO ANSWERS
1 Individual answers will vary, must be nationality words.
2 a Korean restaurant   New York   a Korean dish
4 a Koreatown is very close to big New York attractions.
  b Many Koreans started doing business there in the 1980s.
  c *Japchae* is a special dish. It means 'mixed vegetables'.
  d The vegetables are fried.
  e *Japchae* is served at room temperature.
  f Some people add herbs to make *Japchae* more savoury.

Review
ANSWERS

Exercise 1
1 are consumed
2 was first brought
3 wanted
4 was sold
5 is made
6 is now used
7 were also told
8 needed

Exercise 2a
1 drinking
2 getting
3 Paying
4 buying
5 protecting
6 Spending

Exercise 3a
1 thick
2 canned
3 olives
4 stew
5 plastic

Exercise 4a 10.8
Speaker 1 b
Speaker 2 a

AUDIOSCRIPT 10.8
1
My favourite snack food is pão de queijo, which means 'cheese bread' in English. They're baked in the oven and they look like little balls. They're a popular snack and breakfast food in Brazil and Argentina. They're delicious when they're warm.
2
Churros are my favourite snack. We often eat them for breakfast in Spain. They taste a bit like a doughnut but they're long and thin. They're fried in oil and then they're covered in sugar. They're really nice if you dip them into a cup of thick hot chocolate.

Exercise 5a
1 left
2 way
3 funny

Exercise 6a
1 Would you mind giving us a quieter table, please.
2 I'm afraid this soup is cold.
3 Could you possibly bring us some more tap water, please.
4 I'm terribly sorry.
5 There seems to be a mistake in the bill.

Unit 10   173

11 World

Unit overview

Language input

If + past tense + would (CB p106)	• *If scientists took a smart pill, they'd be more likely to find cures for illnesses.* • *What would you do if you could break the law once today?*
Used to (CB p108)	• *It used to take weeks for news to travel to a different continent.* • *In the past people didn't use to send texts.*
Grammar reference (CB pp154–5)	

Vocabulary development

Global issues (CB p106)	• The environment • Advances in science and technology • Food and farming
The news (CB p109)	• *flood, hurricane, transport strike …*
Phrasal verbs (CB p111)	• *set up, put down, carry on …*

Skills development

Listening: Understanding connected speech (3) (CB p110)	
Speaking: Expressing and responding to opinions (CB p112)	
Writing: A presentation (CB p113)	

Video

Documentary: The European Union (Coursebook DVD & CB p114)	
Vox pops (Coursebook DVD & TG p264)	

More materials

Workbook	• Language practice for vocabulary, grammar, pronunciation, speaking and writing
Photocopiable activities	• Grammar: For the greater good (TG p218 & TRSD) • Vocabulary: Good news, bad news (TG p236 & TRSD) • Communication: Climate change (TG p254 & TRSD)
Tests	• Unit 11 test (TRSD)
Unit 11 wordlist (TRSD)	

11.1 Making the world a better place

Goals
- Talk about unlikely situations in the future
- Talk about global issues

Lead-in
- Write on the board *global, international, national*.
- In pairs, ask students to put the words in order from smallest area to largest. (*national, international, global*)
- Check they have the correct order and drill the words.
- Ask them to choose one of the following sentences to match each adjective: 1) It affects the world. 2) It affects my country. 3) It affects two or more countries.
- Check the answers (1 global, 2 national, 3 international). Drill world /wɜːld/, country /ˈkʌntri/ and region /ˈriːdʒən/.

Vocabulary & Speaking   global issues

Exercise 1
- Students read questions 1–3 and look at the issues in the picture.
- **EXTRA SUPPORT** Some students may need thinking time before the discussion so they can organize their ideas. Also, this is a good time for them to use their dictionaries to check some of the words in the picture.
- Put them into pairs to discuss.
- Elicit ideas from the class.

Exercise 2
- Students read the newspaper headlines a–g and match them with the global issues.
- Do the first one together as a demonstration if necessary. Remind them that more than one answer may be possible.
- Go through the answers together.

ANSWERS
a The increasing population
b Advances in science and technology/ Health and wellbeing
c The economic situation
d The environment
e Food and farming/Health and wellbeing
f Health and wellbeing
g Unemployment

Exercise 3a
- Put students into small groups to look at the vocabulary in exercises 1 and 2 and help each other understand the meanings. Try to group stronger students with weaker ones.
- Provide them with good dictionaries if they are available.
- Monitor carefully. Note any words or phrases they are having difficulty with.
- Conduct class feedback. Explain any problem words to the class. Drill word/phrases which students mispronounced.

Exercise 3b
- Students work alone to complete the statements using words from exercises 1 and 2.
- Go through the answers together.

ANSWERS
1 unemployment
2 global warming
3 health
4 population

Exercise 3c
- In pairs or small groups, students discuss which statements are true for their country.
- **EXTRA CHALLENGE** Stronger students could change the sentences to make them true for their country.
- Elicit some of their responses and conduct a class discussion of these statements.

Exercise 4
- In small groups, students read and discuss questions 1–3.
- Monitor and give a time limit to the end of the activity.
- Elicit interesting discussion points from the students.

Grammar & Listening   *if* + past tense + *would*

Exercise 5a   11.1

> **Audio summary**: A programme where three speakers from different countries have one minute each to present ideas which could improve the world.

- Tell students they are going to listen to a programme where people present their ideas for how to change the world.
- Tell them to look at the table. In this task they need to complete column 1 only.
- Play track 11.1.
- Go through the answers together.

ANSWERS
1 spend more money on developing drugs that can make us more intelligent.
2 everybody learns how to dance salsa and dances salsa every day.
3 introduce a special day, once a year, when everybody in the world gives a gift to a neighbour.

AUDIOSCRIPT 11.1
P Hello and welcome to *Ideas to change the world*. Every week we invite three people, from three different countries, to tell us – in one minute – about an idea which could make the world a better place. We will listen to the three ideas and then our guest judge will select the best one. Our judge today is Dr Miriam Kirkham, Professor of Global Studies at Chicago University. A very warm welcome to the programme, Miriam.
M Thank you.
P And now for the 60 second ideas. The first comes from Alessandro Bartoli in Italy. Alessandro, you have 60 seconds to tell us your idea to improve the world. Starting … from … now!

Unit 11   175

A My idea to change the world is to spend more money on developing drugs that can make us more intelligent. Why would this be a good idea? First of all, scientists would be more likely to find cures for illnesses like heart disease and Alzheimer's if they were more intelligent. Not just scientists, everybody would benefit from a bit of extra intelligence. It seems that higher intelligence can help to reduce a number of social and economic problems. So, I think the smartest thing we can do to make the world better is to make ourselves smarter.
P Thank you, Alessandro. And our next guest is Pilar Jimenez from Spain. Pilar you have 60 seconds, starting … now!
PJ The world would be a better place if everybody learned how to dance salsa and danced salsa every day. Why? Because when you dance, you forget about your problems. It also makes you think about your body and that encourages you to get fit. Another thing is that if you're someone who feels a lot of anger, salsa, or any dance, can turn these angry feelings into a kind of positive energy. It can make you happy. So more dancing means more happiness, more happiness means less crime and less war. So with lots of us happy from all that dancing every day, we can be more positive in the world and do great things. That's it!
P And finally, we have Dovydas Mirowski from Poland. Dovydas, you have 60 seconds to tell us about your idea, starting from now.
D I would like to change the world by introducing a special day, once a year, when everybody in the world gives a gift to a neighbour. The gift shouldn't cost a lot of money but we should choose it carefully: it could be a bunch of wild flowers, a tiny toy for the children, or a jar of home-made jam. This would be an international holiday and it would give neighbours around the world a chance to get to know each other. This idea of 'Gifts for Neighbours' wouldn't solve the world's serious problems like unemployment or global warming, but it would make the world around us feel like a kinder, friendlier place.
P Thank you very much.

Exercise 5b 11.1

- Tell students you are going to play the recording again so that they can complete part B of the table.
- Play track 11.1 again.
- Allow students to check answers in pairs.
- Go through answers together.

ANSWERS

1 cures	6 war
2 heart	7 wild flowers
3 economic	8 jam
4 fit	9 kinder
5 crime	

Exercise 6

- In small groups, students discuss the suggestions and score them out of 10.

EXTENSION Encourage them to brainstorm the advantages and disadvantages of each idea. This can help them support their scores better.

- Find out which idea the class thinks is best and why.

Exercise 7a 11.2

Audio summary: This is the second part of the same programme. The ideas are judged by an expert, scored out of 10 and then the judge chooses the idea she thinks is best.

- Tell them they will listen to the judge's opinions now and compare them to their own group discussions.
- Play track 11.2.
- Check that they have understood the judge's choice.

EXTENSION Encourage them to respond to the judge's comments/opinions if they are different to their own discussions in exercise 6.

ANSWERS

The judge chose 'giving a gift to a neighbour' day. She gave it 10/10.

AUDIOSCRIPT 11.2

P So what did you think about the idea for a pill that would make us 'super intelligent'.
M Great idea, I mean, we live in a complicated world and we need all the brain power we can get.
P True, but do you think it's likely that scientists will be able to come up with a super-intelligence drug? Isn't it rather a crazy idea?
M No, not at all. You can already buy drugs to help you to concentrate more and to improve your mental energy. This is just the next step.
P So would you take a smart pill?
M I would take a smart pill if I knew it was safe. Of course that's a big 'if'! My worry, though, is the cost. If only a few people could afford them, that would give them an unfair advantage. In exams, for example.
P Good point. So your score for a smart pill?
M Erm … 7 out of 10.
P OK. So let's move onto the second idea – that 'Everybody should dance salsa every day'.
M Well, I liked the idea that dancing can make you fit and happy. That can only be a good thing.
P Mmm, but some people aren't confident about dancing, are they?
M True, but if you danced a little bit every day then you would become confident.
P Uhuh …
M The only problem for me is that it would take a lot of effort to do it every single day. But, still, I like the idea. I'd give it 8 out of 10.
P OK, and what about the last idea … everybody should give a gift to a neighbour.
M I think it's a wonderful idea, because when you do something kind for somebody else, the other person feels good, but you feel good too. It gives you a really positive feeling. Also, giving a little gift once a year is something everybody can do. I mean, it's true that if everybody gave a gift to a neighbour once a year, it wouldn't solve the world's problems, but it would make a lot of people a little bit happier.
P So, your score for that?
M Mmm, 10 out of 10.
P Well, there you are, Dovydas. Congratulations!

Exercise 7b 11.2

- Tell students that you are going to play the track again so that they can listen and complete sentences 1–4.
- Give them some time to read the sentences.
- Play track 11.2 again.
- Go through the answers together.

ANSWERS
1 take, knew
2 could
3 danced, become
4 gave, solve

Exercise 8

- Students read the questions and answer them.
- They could do this task alone or in pairs.
- Go through the answers together.

ANSWERS
1 imaginary
2 present/future
3 past
4 would

Exercise 9

- Focus students' attention on the Grammar focus box and ask them to complete the rules by choosing the best option.
- Go through the answers together.
- Ask questions about the example sentence to check understanding: *Can scientists take a smart pill now?* (No.) *Why not?* (Smart pills don't exist yet.) *Is the speaker sure that smart pills will exist in the future?* (No.) *So is this a real or an imagined situation?* (Imagined.) *The result of taking a smart pill is probably finding cures for illnesses. Is this going to happen?* (We don't know because they don't exist yet – the situation and the result are imagined.)

ANSWERS
1 past
2 unlikely
3 first

WATCH OUT! It's really important that the students focus on the context of this grammar to understand that it does not relate to past events although there is past tense in the structure.

- Refer students to *Grammar reference* on p154. There are three more exercises here students can do for homework. See answers on p178.

Exercise 10a

- Students work alone to make the prompts into full sentences. Do the first one as a demonstration if necessary.
- Monitor and note any problems with the tenses/structure.

EXTRA CHALLENGE Ask fast finishers to check their punctuation, i.e. that they have commas where necessary.

- Go through the answers together.

PRONUNCIATION Contractions with *would*. From sentences 1 and 5, elicit that we contract *we would* to *we'd* /wiːd/. Model it and drill students, with *we'd* on its own but also in sentence 1. Say the first clause up to the comma and then gesture for the students to add the second clause starting with *we'd*. Also practise contracting *I would* to *I'd* /aɪd/. Change the sentence to *If I stopped eating meat, I'd be healthier.* and drill as before. Students drill in pairs using the sentences in exercise 10a.

ANSWERS
1 If we all stopped eating meat, we would feel healthier.
2 Crime rates would go down if guns were illegal.
3 Even if we produced no greenhouse gases at all, it wouldn't stop global warming.
4 The world would be a better place if there was/were no tobacco industry.
5 If we lived in an ideal world, we would still find something to complain about.

Exercise 10b

- In pairs, students discuss whether they agree or disagree with the statements in 10a.
- Encourage them to try to give reasons and examples too.
- Monitor and give a time limit to the end of the activity.
- Conduct a class discussion.

Exercise 11

- Make it clear to students that they have preparation time now for a group activity.

EXTRA SUPPORT Go through the sentences with weaker students to make sure they fully understand the situations before they begin the task.

- They work alone to imagine what they would do in situations 1–5.
- Monitor and check that their notes are easy to understand.

Exercise 12

- Put students into groups.
- They read the instruction and the example then take turns to ask and answer questions, using notes from exercise 11.

FEEDBACK FOCUS Check that they are using *would* in their answers and that they are making the contraction *I'd* as much as possible. Make a note of errors but also good models you can use in the feedback stage.

- Conduct class feedback.

Exercise 13a

- Ask them to read the instruction for giving a short presentation. Go through the steps with them to make sure they understand the task.
- Students work in pairs on steps 1 and 2 of the task.

EXTRA SUPPORT Students could look at the audioscript on page 164 to find a way to start their presentation, e.g. *Our idea to change the world is* . . . .

- Monitor carefully and help groups who are finding the writing difficult. Make sure they have at least one sentence using *if* + past tense + *would*.
- Give a time limit to the end of the written task.
- They read step 3 again and take it in turns to practise and time each other, aiming to make the talk 60 seconds long.

Exercise 13b

- Put two or three pairs together. Each pair chooses who will give their presentation.
- Point out the three questions to consider when listening. Make sure one person times each presentation.
- Students take turns to give and judge presentations.
- Monitor carefully and conduct a class discussion.

Unit 11 177

CRITICAL THINKING The content of a presentation is the most important thing but we also judge how it is done: *Did the speaker talk too quietly, too quickly, too slowly or with unclear pronunciation? Was it too brief or too long?* Ask students to discuss: *If you gave your presentation again, would you change anything? Why?* (You could point out that this question uses today's grammar structure.)

GRAMMAR REFERENCE ANSWERS

Exercise 1
1 had, would live
2 would be, disappeared
3 found, would
4 rose, would disappear
5 be, became
6 lived, 'd do
7 wouldn't start, had

Exercise 2
1 If unemployment wasn't high, my friends would have jobs.
2 I'd like this programme if the topic were/was interesting.
3 If politicians didn't receive a lot of money, people wouldn't be angry about it.
4 We would enjoy living here if there weren't lots of social problems in the area.
5 Farming wouldn't be difficult if the weather didn't change a lot. (OR Farming would be easy if … .)

Exercise 3
1 If everyone had clean water, people wouldn't drink from rivers.
2 If people didn't drink from rivers, fewer people would get diseases.
3 If fewer people got diseases, hospitals would be less crowded.
4 If hospitals were less crowded, the cost of health care would fall.
5 If the cost of health care fell, more would be spent on education.
6 If more were spent on education, people would do better jobs.
7 If people did better jobs, the economic situation would improve.

11.2 Breaking news
- Talk about past habits and situations
- Talk about the news

Lead-in
- If possible, prepare this lead-in by finding images of the top news stories from today. Show them to the students and ask if they know anything about them.
- If you don't have time to find pictures, just ask students if they know what the top news stories are today.

Grammar & Reading *used to*

Exercise 1
- Put students into groups to discuss the questions.
  WATCH OUT! The word *news* is uncountable. You can say *the news* and *some news* but not *a news*. Elicit or teach that you need to say *a piece of news* or *a news story/a news item/a news report* if referring to news in a countable way.
- When they have discussed in groups, find out as a class how often they check the news and how they do it.

Exercise 2
- Students look at the three pictures of news events. If necessary, teach the meaning and pronunciation of *eruption* /ɪˈrʌpʃn/ and the verb *to erupt*.
- They discuss the questions in their groups. This involves them discussing when each event happened. If they have no idea, the background note might stimulate discussion.
- Elicit from the class ideas about how long each news story took to travel to the other side of the world. Ask them to give reasons for their estimates.

Background note: Abraham Lincoln was the 16th President of USA from March 1861 to April 1865 when he was assassinated by John Wilkes Booth while he was at the theatre.
When the volcano on Krakatoa in Indonesia erupted in 1883, it destroyed two thirds of the island. The eruption is said to be the loudest noise in history and could be heard 3000 miles (4,800 km) away.
In January 2009, US Airways flight 1549 made an emergency landing on the Hudson River in New York. All 155 people on the plane got off safely.

Exercise 3

Text summary: An article which focuses on developments in how we receive news, from the first newspapers to modern technology such as Twitter. Details of the news stories in the pictures are given.

- Students read the article and check their answers.
- Go through the answers together. Elicit the reasons why each news story took that amount of time to travel across the world.

ANSWERS
Death of Abraham Lincoln: nearly two weeks, telegraph had not been invented.
Eruption of Krakatoa: minutes, using the new invention of undersea electrical telegraph wires.
Plane landing in Hudson River: minutes, people who were there posted comments and photos on Twitter.

Exercise 4
- Tell students to read the headings a–e and match each one with a paragraph in the article. Remind them that there is an extra heading.
- Students work alone on this task.
- Go through answers together.

ANSWERS
1 From the few to the many
2 From weeks to minutes
3 From the still to the moving image
4 From professional reporter to citizen journalist
Extra heading: From local to national

Exercise 5
- Students read the sentences – which are examples of the structures *used to* and *didn't use to*.

- They answer the questions alone or in pairs.
- Go through the answers together.

ANSWERS
1 no
2 more than once
3 yes
4 didn't use to

Exercise 6
- Focus the students' attention on the Grammar focus box about *used to*.
- Tell them to complete the rules with *did*, *not* and *once*.
- Students work alone to complete the rules.
- Go through the answers together.

WATCH OUT! We don't use *used to* for present habits. Examples of INCORRECT sentences: *My job is tiring so I use to go to bed early.* or *I don't use to drink coffee.* This is a common mistake – the student thinks *used to* has the same meaning as *usually* and they try to make it refer to habits in the present. Point out to them that *used to* is only about the past. Remind them they can use *usually* about present habits.

ANSWERS
1 not
2 once
3 did

- Refer students to *Grammar reference* on p155. There are three more exercises here students can do for homework. See answers on p180.

Exercise 7
- Students read the instruction. Point out that in some sentences it may not be possible to use *used to* or *didn't use to* – they have to decide.
- Do sentence 1 as a demonstration together if necessary. Ask them *Is this sentence about the past?* (Yes) *Is it true now?* (No) *Is it about something which happened only once?* (No) This means we can use *used to*. Remind them to use the negative.
- Students work alone on the task.

WATCH OUT! Students often make mistakes with the negative because they forget to use the infinitive. Example error: *Mobile phones didn't used to have cameras.* Remind them that it works the same way as other verbs in the negative.

- Go through the answers together, referring to the rules in the Grammar focus box and using questions as above if they have made mistakes.

ANSWERS
1 Mobile phones didn't use to have cameras.
2 In the 1940s, people used to listen to the radio to get the latest news.
3 (It is not possible to use 'used to' here because it is talking about something which happened only once.)
4 Before the 1850s, newspapers didn't use to contain photos.
5 (It is not possible to use 'used to' here because newspaper apps are still popular so it's still true today. Also, 'became popular' is something which only happens once.)
6 Before the telegraph, it used to take ten days by horse to deliver news across the USA.

Exercise 8
- Students read the instruction and look at the example.
- Give them time to think about how their lives have changed, looking at the ideas given and thinking about other big changes which are not on the list.
- Put students into pairs to do the task.
- Monitor carefully, paying attention to their use of the target grammar.

EXTRA CHALLENGE Remind stronger students that they can use the negative. Examples: *I didn't use to worry about my parents getting older but I do now. I didn't use to save my money until I had children.*

- Conduct a class discussion. Ask some pairs the question 'Whose life has changed the most and why?'
- Elicit corrections to any errors that you noticed while monitoring.

EXTENSION Ask students to remember and write down what their partner said. This will give you one more chance to check that they are using the grammar correctly. If you'd like to make this a more interesting activity, you could instruct them NOT to use their partner's name in any of the sentences. Then they could display them around the classroom, walk around and read each other's pieces of writing and guess which student the sentences are about. (If you number the pieces of writing before you display them, this will make them easier to refer to during feedback stage.)

Vocabulary & Speaking the news

Exercise 9
- Focus students' attention on the highlighted words in the article.
- They work alone to complete the sentences using the highlighted words.
- Go through the answers. If necessary, drill pronunciation of the /ə/ sound in *journalist* /ˈdʒɜːnəlɪst/ and the word *natural* which students may think has three syllables but is usually pronounced with two. /ˈnætʃrəl/

ANSWERS
1 social media, up to date
2 Natural disasters
3 articles
4 crash
5 journalist, report
6 reach
7 spread
8 weekly

Exercise 10
- Students read the sentences and complete them with their own ideas so that they are true for them.
- Allow plenty of time for this creative task.
- Monitor carefully to make sure their sentence endings are grammatically accurate.
- Give them a time limit to the end of the activity.
- Put them into pairs to share their sentences and compare their habits and opinions regarding the news.
- Conduct a class discussion to find out the students' opinions.

CRITICAL THINKING Choosing a side and defending your point of view. Conduct a fuller discussion of sentence 3 by splitting the class into two groups – those who chose *I think* and those who chose *I don't think*. Encourage each group to work together and make a list of their arguments, with reasons and examples. Then encourage debate between the two groups. Help them to take turns and try to ensure all students get an opportunity to speak. If they enjoy this activity, you could repeat it with one of the other sentences as the topic to practise this skill further.

Exercise 11

- Focus students' attention on the vocabulary in the box.
- Students read the instruction and categorize the vocabulary into a or b.

EXTRA SUPPORT You could put students into pairs to do this activity so that they can help each other with the meanings of words. Encourage them to use dictionaries if necessary.

- Go through the answers together.

EXTENSION Ask students to brainstorm in pairs or small groups other common events or topics which are reported in the news: other crimes, war and fighting, scientific discoveries/developments, economic changes, the lives of celebrities, death of a public figure, sport, etc.

ANSWERS
A natural disasters: flood, forest fire, hurricane
B man-made news events: election, robbery, transport strike

Exercise 12

- Put students into groups.
- Each student chooses one recent news story to explain. They may need some quiet thinking time before the group work.

EXTRA SUPPORT Weaker students could discuss in pairs before the group work in order to prepare one story together. (Also, if you used images as a lead-in to the lesson, these could be used again now as prompts for discussion.)

- Students take turns to explain their story to the group. Encourage the listening students to ask questions if they do not understand something. The speaker should also explain why this news story interested him/her.
- Monitor carefully. Note any points for correction.
- Conduct a class discussion. You could find out whether any students chose the same story.

EXTRA ACTIVITY You could ask students to search for a short news article on the internet or other English news sources. As a homework task, they can read their article and summarize it for their classmates. You could make a news bulletin display on the wall and encourage them to read each other's summaries.

GRAMMAR REFERENCE ANSWERS
Exercise 1
1 used to pass
2 used to get
3 used to trust
4 didn't use to travel
5 didn't use to be
6 used to take
7 didn't use to have
8 used to get
9 used to be

Exercise 2
1 I used to
2 My father used to
3 We didn't use to
4 Did you use to
5 Mobile phones used to
6 Did your family use to go

Exercise 3
1 A boy used to deliver our newspaper every day.
2 (not possible)
3 We never used to watch TV in the summer.
4 Did you use to do your homework as soon as you got home when you were at school?
5 (not possible)
6 (not possible)

11.3 Vocabulary and skills development

Goals
- Understand connected speech (3)
- Understand and use phrasal verbs

Listening understanding connected speech (3)

Lead-in
- Write on the board 1) *sculptor* /ˈskʌltə/ and 2) *sculpture* /ˈskʌltʃə/. Ask students *Which word is a job?* (sculptor) and elicit that a sculpture is what the sculptor makes.
- Model the pronunciation and drill the students to make sure they pronounce them well – you can just say *Number 1*, *Number 2*, etc. in random order as many times as necessary to elicit each word.

Exercise 1
- Students read the instruction and look at the photos.
- Put them into pairs to discuss the questions.
- Elicit some ideas from the class but don't confirm any of them yet.

Exercise 2a 11.3

Audio summary: An interview in two parts about a sculptor called Jason de Caires Taylor who creates life-sized sculptures of people and puts them underwater.

- Tell them that you are going to play two sentences from the interview. Ask them to listen and complete the phrases.
- Play track 11.3. You may need to play it more than once – it is important that they hear the words to complete the phrases.
- Check the answers together.

ANSWERS
1 did you go
2 I've

AUDIOSCRIPT 11.3
1 Why did you go there?
2 I've always loved …

Exercise 2b 11.4
- Students read and listen to the information in the Unlock the code box about connected speech.
- Play track 11.4.
- You could ask students whether they have noticed this when watching films in English or listening to English song words. Point out that it is not only in informal English but it is something which happens naturally as we speak quickly, no matter what the situation.

AUDIOSCRIPT 11.4
In natural speech we say common expressions, such as *I don't know, you know,* or *I want to* as a single unit. This means some sounds change or disappear at the end of one word and the start of the following word. Recognizing this will help you understand more easily; using them will develop your fluency.

In natural speech:

I don't know	sounds like	/aɪdəˈnəʊ/
I want to	sounds like	/aɪˈwɒnə/
Do you know what I mean?	sounds like	/dʒəˈnəʊwɒaɪˈmiːn/
I've been a	sounds like	/aɪvˈbɪnə/
for a while	sounds like	/fərəˈwaɪl/

Exercise 3a 11.5
- This is a dictation exercise. Explain that you are going to hear seven expressions. Tell students to listen and write what they hear.
- Play track 11.5.
- You will probably need to play the track two or three times, pausing where necessary.
- Ask students to compare their expressions with a partner.
- Go through the answers to make sure they have heard all the words.

EXTENSION You could ask them what they noticed about the phrases. Which sounds change and/or disappear when we connect the words in speaking?

AUDIOSCRIPT 11.5
1 For a long time
2 Can you tell us about … ?
3 He wanted to …
4 He's been a …
5 Quite a few …
6 You see …
7 You know …

Exercise 3b 11.6
- Tell students to listen and repeat the phrases, trying to make the changes which happen in connected speech.
- Play track 11.6. Pause it and repeat where necessary. Encourage all students to repeat each phrase.

AUDIOSCRIPT 11.6
1 Why did you go there?
2 I've always loved …
3 For a long time
4 Can you tell us about …?
5 He wanted to …
6 He's been a …
7 Quite a few …
8 You see …
9 You know …

Exercise 4
- Students work in pairs. They decide which of them is Student A and which is Student B then turn to the relevant page of the book. (Student A: p129, Student B: p133).
- This is a peer-dictation exercise.
- Monitor and note any continuing problems with producing the connected speech phrases.
- Give feedback to the class together. If necessary, drill phrases more. Use track 11.6 from exercise 3b if necessary.

Exercise 5 11.7
- Students listen to first part of the interview and answer the gist questions 1 and 2.
- Play track 11.7.
- Go through the answers together.

EXTENSION You could find out whether anybody in the class can scuba-dive and whether any of them have seen a coral reef.

ANSWERS
1 Jason has built an underwater sculpture park.
2 He wanted to bring his love of the sea and his love of sculpture together. He also wants to help the environment because the statues help coral reefs to grow.

AUDIOSCRIPT 11.7
P Good afternoon and welcome to another in the series *Fantastic Holidays*. This week, we're looking at a very unusual place to visit. Steve Jones is going to tell us all about it. So, Steve, welcome to the show!
S Thanks!
P Now, tell us a little bit about the special place you visited. Why did you go there?
S Well, you see, I've always loved the sea and diving, and this is a new and really unusual underwater place to visit, so I thought it would be perfect for me.
P You mean you have to dive to get there?
S Yes, that's the only way to see it because, you see, it's an underwater sculpture park. It was built by a sculptor called Jason de Caires Taylor in the Caribbean Sea.
P The Caribbean? Why did he do it there?
S He's always loved the sea, he's been a sculptor for a long time – so, he wanted to bring these two things together. Also, you know, the statues actually help coral reefs to grow and this helps the environment. That's very important in the Caribbean …

Exercise 6a 11.8
- Students listen to the second part of the interview to make notes about Grace Reef and Circle of Children.
- Play track 11.8.
- You may need to play it more than once.

Unit 11   181

Exercise 6b

- Put students into pairs to share their ideas.
- Monitor carefully and check that they all heard the important information.
- Conduct class feedback. Go over any of the listening which caused confusion and point out anything they missed.

ANSWERS

Grace Reef
Sixteen statues placed across a sandy area.
The weather conditions move the sand underwater so some days you can see ten statues and some days only three are not covered with sand.

Circle of children
Twenty-six statues of children. They are in a circle.
It took around six months to make.
He put down each individual statue then connected them underwater.

AUDIOSCRIPT 11.8

P OK, can you tell us about some of the pieces he's made? Are there a lot of them?
S There are actually quite a few! The first … the first piece he did is called *Grace Reef*. He placed sixteen statues across a sandy area, and it's really interesting to see how they change. It isn't so deep there and the sand moves according to the weather conditions, so you can go there one day and there'll be ten statues, you go there another day and there'll only be three.
P Wow, that sounds really interesting. Tell us a little bit about the big circle of children that he's made.
S Well that's actually made of 26 different children. It took him around six months to make and weighs … I don't know, about fifteen tonnes. And because it's so heavy, he couldn't put it all down in one piece, so he put each individual statue down and then connected them all underwater. It wasn't easy, but he didn't give up! I think he spent about a week underwater, you know, moving sand and rocks.
P That's amazing and I think I'd really like to see it!
S Yes, it's really worth a visit.
P Well, thanks for coming into the studio, Steve. If you are interested in going to this wonderful underwater sculpture park, you can find more information on our website …

Exercise 7

- Students read the questions and discuss in pairs or groups.
- Elicit responses from some of the students.
  EXTENSION You could ask students their opinions of the underwater sculpture park, e.g. *Is it stupid, clever, interesting, important … ?* Encourage them to explain why.
  EXTRA ACTIVITY With stronger students, you could ask them to work in pairs to write 1–3 questions they would like to ask Jason de Caires Taylor if they met him. Monitor and check the questions are correct.

Vocabulary & Speaking   phrasal verbs

Exercise 8

Text summary: An article giving biographical information about Jason de Caires Taylor and explaining his reasons for creating underwater sculptures.

- Students read questions 1–4 and then read the article to find the answers.
- Allow plenty of time for them to do this.
- Go through the answers together.

ANSWERS
1 When he was a child
2 In Grenada in the West Indies and off the coast of Cancun, Mexico.
3 Because he believes we need to protect the environment and solve some of the serious problems with our oceans.
4 He wants children to grow up to have a positive relationship with nature.
   He says human problems change but time and nature carry on and the coral growing on the statues 'puts paint' on them.

Exercise 9a

- Ask students to read the sentences and focus on the words in bold.
- You could put them into pairs to talk about the meanings of the words.
- Go through the meanings together.

ANSWERS
1 took up = started (doing an activity)
2 set up = made, created

Exercise 9b

- Focus students' attention on the Vocabulary focus box about phrasal verbs.
- Tell them to read the information and examples carefully.
  EXTRA SUPPORT Write on the board *He took up diving.* and elicit that this is a phrasal verb with an object. Write *He took up it.* on the board and ask whether it is a good sentence. (No, the correct sentence is *He took it up.*) Refer students to the point in the Vocabulary focus box about pronouns.

Exercise 10

- Focus students' attention on the highlighted phrasal verbs in the text.
  EXTRA SUPPORT If you think many of your students may not know the words in 1–8, give them time to use dictionaries or discuss the meanings in pairs.
- Students work alone to match each phrasal verb with a meaning 1–8. Ask them to write the infinitive forms.
- Allow students to check their answers in pairs.
- Go through the answers together.

ANSWERS
1 carry on
2 give up
3 find out
4 grow up
5 put on
6 put down
7 set up
8 take up

182

Exercise 11

- In pairs, students use the ideas in the box to make combinations with the phrasal verbs a–f.
- Highlight the example to show them what to do.
- Give them plenty of time to try out different combinations and remind them some words from the box can be used more than once.
- Go through the answers together.

ANSWERS
a) You can set up a business, a company or a meeting.
b) You can take up a sport, golf, smoking, a hobby.
c) You can find out information, facts, the answer, news.
d) You can give up a sport, chocolate, smoking, a hobby.
e) You can put on clothes, shoes, weight.
f) You can put down a book, a pen.

Exercise 12a

- Students write five sentences, leaving gaps for the phrasal verbs.
- Monitor and correct any errors. If it is not clear to you, check which phrasal verb they think fills the gap – they can whisper to you.

EXTRA CHALLENGE Encourage stronger students to write sentences using different tenses – past, present and future.

WATCH OUT! Make sure students do not use a pronoun and also an object, e.g. *I took them off my shoes.* or *I gave it up smoking.*

- Give a time limit to the end of the activity to ensure all students finish the task together.

Exercise 12b

- Put students into pairs with someone they haven't worked with in this lesson.
- Tell them to look at the example conversation. Demonstrate by reading it out with one student. The teacher should read Student A and make a noise or say *gap* loudly at the appropriate point. Then elicit the missing phrasal verb.
- Point out that they should ask follow-up questions because all the gapped sentences are true.
- Allow plenty of time for this activity.
- Monitor carefully, focusing on their use of the phrasal verbs in the sentences and in the follow-up conversations.
- Conduct a class discussion, asking some students to report on one of their partner's sentences and giving any extra information they found out.

EXTRA ACTIVITY You could ask pairs of students to write mini-conversations (on any topic) which have to include two of the phrasal verbs. (For strong students you could give an added challenge by giving them roles – two business men or a teacher to a student, etc.) Monitor for accuracy. For feedback, put two pairs together. They take turns to act out the dialogue and spot the phrasal verbs (and guess the roles if they have done the extra challenge).

11.4 Speaking and writing

Goals

- Express and respond to opinions
- Give a presentation

Lead-in

- Focus students' attention on the photos.
- Put students into pairs to decide how you say these things in English (selfies, security cameras (CCTV) and social network sites/social media).
- They could discuss why there are more of these things than just a few years ago.
- Conduct a brief class discussion.

Listening & Speaking expressing and responding to opinions

Exercise 1

- Write the word *private* on the board and elicit that it is an adjective. Try to elicit the noun from this word family *privacy*. Drill pronunciation of privacy /ˈprɪvəsi/.
- Students read the instruction and definition of privacy. They discuss in pairs.
- Conduct class feedback. If you find they don't have much to say, ask questions based on the suggestions below, e.g. *How do you feel if a stranger takes a photo of you on their mobile phone?*

POSSIBLE ANSWERS
More people than ever have a camera with them all the time because they have one on their mobile phone. People may take photos of you or your children and share them or upload them onto the internet without your permission.
When you go on a social networking site, your comments may be seen by everyone (though it is possible to send private messages.) People may post comments about you on their sites.
Security cameras record everything which happens so we are being videoed a lot of the time.

Exercise 2 11.9

Audio summary: A radio programme about privacy where an interviewer stops people in the street to ask them their opinions. There are four different interviews.

- Tell students you are going to play a recording of an interviewer asking a number of different people *Is privacy dead in our 21st century world?*
- Focus their attention on the table. Point out that the interviewer does four different interviews.
- Ask them to listen to find out whether each person interviewed agrees with, disagrees with or isn't sure about the question.
- Play track 11.9.
- Allow students to check their answers in pairs if you wish.
- Go through the answers together.

EXTENSION You could play the track again, asking students to listen for any reasons the people give for their answers. Then elicit some answers from the class (given below).

ANSWERS
1 Hannah – disagree (it's important to feel safe so she doesn't mind the CCTV cameras)
2 Mateo and Pilar – agree (They share everything online with their friends. Someone posted a video that Pilar had no control over and she didn't like it.)
3 Lena – not sure (We don't share everything. It can be good for business.)
4 Albert – agree (three million people saw someone's dinner party because his guests wrote about it on social network sites.)

AUDIOSCRIPT 11.9

I Excuse me, can I ask you a question?
H Erm, well OK, but I'm late for work, so if you're quick …
I OK, some media experts are saying privacy is dead in our 21st century world. Do you agree?
H No, I'm afraid I disagree, although you do see a lot more cameras around. I mean the CCTV ones.
I And what do you think about that?
H Well, it's important to feel safe these days, isn't it? So I don't mind too much. Anyway, I'm sorry but I have to go now.
I OK, thank you very much … . Er, excuse me, do you have time to answer a few questions?
M & P Yeah, OK …
I Some media experts are saying 'privacy is dead in our 21st century world'. Do you agree?
M Well, maybe, yeah. I certainly tell my friends everything online! What do you think?
P Yeah, that's a good point. All my friends keep in touch through Facebook too. But recently I went to a concert and I had to dance on stage. I was so embarrassed, and when I got home, someone, I don't know who, had posted a video of me dancing on YouTube! My worst nightmare and I had no control over it. Personally, I don't like that, so yeah, I agree, perhaps privacy is dead!
I OK, thanks very much … . Excuse me, could I ask you a question? … Do you think privacy is dead?
L Pardon?
I Do you think privacy is dead?
L Oh, I'm not sure about that. I haven't really thought about it before. I think we live our lives online these days, so I take your point, but we don't share everything and it can be very helpful in business, you know, to network, contact other people, but, I don't have strong views on this really …
I OK thanks … . Excuse me, can I talk to you for a moment? Do you think privacy is dead in our 21st century world?
A Oh, it's funny you should ask that! I've just read a story about a guy who had a dinner party in New York, invited 15 guests and had no idea that they were posting photos on Twitter and Instagram during the meal – turns out over three million people saw his dinner party! Can you believe it? So, yeah, that's right, no one has much privacy these days – not even in their own homes!

Exercise 3 11.9

- Ask students to use the words in the box to complete sentences 1–8.
- Students could do the task alone or in pairs.
- Monitor and give a time limit to the end of the activity.
- Play track 11.9 again so they can check their answers.

ANSWERS
1 disagree   5 sure
2 maybe   6 take
3 point   7 views
4 agree   8 right

Exercise 4a

- Students categorize the phrases in exercise 3 according to their function: a, b or c.
- Do the first one together as a demonstration if necessary.
- They could do this task alone or in pairs.
- Go through the answers together.

ANSWERS
a expressing opinions: 5, 7
b agreeing: 2, 3, 4, 8
c disagreeing: 1, 6

Exercise 4b

- Students read the extra phrases 1–7 and categorize them as in 4a.
- Go through the answers together.

ANSWERS
a expressing opinions: 1, 4, 5, 6
b agreeing: –
c disagreeing: 2, 3, 7

Pronunciation expressing opinions politely

Exercise 5a 11.10

- Tell students that they are going to focus on pronunciation now.
- Ask them to read the information which begins *When we give opinions …*
- Explain that this part of the lesson focuses on how your voice goes up and down. Teach the word *intonation* to any students who do not know.

PRONUNCIATION One of the best and most natural ways to show intonation patterns is with hand/arm gestures, rather like conducting music. This helps visual students to 'see' how the pitch of the voice changes. You could try using this technique during this lesson.

- Tell them to listen to the same disagreeing phrase said in two different ways and look at the arrows. Which is more polite?
- Play track 11.10.
- Check the answer together.

ANSWER
B sounds more polite.

AUDIOSCRIPT 11.10

a I'm afraid I disagree.
b I'm afraid I disagree.

Exercise 5b 11.11
- Students make correct sentences by putting the words in order. Start the first sentence together as a demonstration if necessary.
- **EXTRA SUPPORT** You could give them the first word in each sentence to help them start.
- Students work alone on the task.
- Allow them to check their sentences in pairs.
- Tell them to listen to the recording to check their answers.
- Play track 11.11.

AUDIOSCRIPT 11.11
1 I'm sorry, but I don't really agree.
2 Yeah, but I don't think that's true.
3 I take your point, but I'm not sure about that.
4 True, but there are other ways to look at it.

Exercise 5c 11.12
- Tell students to repeat the phrases after the recording.
- Play track 11.12. You may need to play this several times, pausing if necessary in order to make sure they have good pronunciation.

AUDIOSCRIPT 11.12
1 I'm sorry, but I don't really agree.
2 Yeah, but I don't think that's true.
3 I take your point, but I'm not sure about that.
4 True, but there are other ways to look at it.

Exercise 6a
- Tell students that they are going to have some thinking time now before discussing in groups.
- Ask them to read the comments and decide whether they agree or disagree. They should also try to think about why.
- Tell them to add one more comment about another topic of their choice.
- Monitor these extra comments to make sure they are correct and easy to understand.

Exercise 6b
- Focus students' attention on the Language for speaking box. Tell them to use these phrases in their discussions.
- **EXTRA SUPPORT** Weaker students can have a few minutes to decide how to start giving their opinion on each comment so they are ready (though they will take it in turns to start).
- Put students into small groups to discuss the comments, give opinions, agree and disagree.
- **FEEDBACK FOCUS** Monitor the discussions of the first comment and check that their responses sound polite. If necessary, get all students' attention and remind them to use the polite intonation patterns that they have practised.

Exercise 6c
- Ask students to tell you about any interesting discussions they had.
- If you wish, conduct a whole class discussion of one of the comments or ask a few students to read out their additional comments and encourage class discussion of these points.

Reading & Writing a presentation

Exercise 7
- Students read the questions and discuss them with a partner. Point out that it doesn't mean only presentations in English but also in their own language(s).
- **EXTRA CHALLENGE** Fast finishers should ask follow-up questions (Where, when, who to, how often, how long, etc.).
- Elicit the kinds of presentations which the students commonly give.

Exercise 8a
- In pairs, students brainstorm tips for using email securely.
- If they are having difficulty thinking of tips, ask them to brainstorm what can go wrong in terms of email security and this may help them think of tips to avoid it.
- Elicit some ideas from the class if you wish or move straight on to exercise 8b.

Exercise 8b
- Students read the text to check their answers.
- Go through any problem vocabulary.

Exercise 9a
- Ask students to compare the text they have read with Slide A below.
- In pairs, they discuss the differences. Then go through the differences together.

POSSIBLE ANSWERS
The information on the slide is basically the same but some points have been joined together, e.g. credit card details, user names and passwords are all personal data in the slide.
There is less writing on the slide. The sentences are short and simple. There are direct suggestions (not *you should*). These changes make it easy to read from a white board/screen.
There's a picture on the slide.
There's a heading.

Exercise 9b
- Focus students' attention on the Language for writing box. Ask them to read it carefully.
- Go through any points which they are confused about.
- They read Slide A again and find examples of things in the box.
- Go through the answers together.

ANSWERS
Short simple words and phrases: Emails are not 100% secure.
Miss out unnecessary words: If you trust sender
Avoid contractions: Do not send …
Do not use personal expressions: Only open attachments rather than You should only …
Use general words to express ideas: Personal data rather than credit card details, user names or passwords.

Exercise 10a
- Explain that they need to focus on a new presentation slide now, Slide B.
- Students work in pairs to find the problems with Slide B.

Unit 11   185

- Monitor carefully. If students are having difficulty finding problems, refer them to the Language for writing box.
- You could elicit some of these problems from the class.

> **POSSIBLE ANSWERS**
> Some errors: 'probelsm' should be 'problems', data protection is uncountable so it shouldn't have 's' at the end. Also 'go away form your desk' should be 'from'.
> The sentences are all too long and complicated. There are unnecessary words.
> 'I don't think', 'It's not a good idea' and 'you shouldn't' are personal and each contains a contraction.

Exercise 10b
- Students rewrite Slide B either in their pairs or alone.
- Monitor their writing carefully. Help weaker students to simplify the information and language.
- You could ask students to swap slides and check each other's writing, referring to the Language for writing box for guidance. Alternatively, they could read as many slides as possible. Then they could choose which slides are the most effective and explain why.

Exercise 11a
- Students work together to write their own presentation slide. The topic is *using social media* and they can choose the context *for work*, *for study* or *in your social life*.
- Put them into groups. They discuss questions 1 and 2 in order to get ideas for their slides.
- Monitor the brainstorming stage to make sure they have enough ideas.

Exercise 11b
- Students choose three tips from their ideas. They discuss in their pairs how the slide will look.
- Monitor and assist weaker students.

> **EXTENSION** If they have access to computers, they could create the slides using technology and find a suitable image to include to make the slide attractive.

Exercise 11c
- Students compare their slides with another group's slide. They should refer to the Language for writing box and consider the content, language and design.
- Monitor their discussion and encourage constructive criticism.
- Conduct class feedback.

> **CRITICAL THINKING** You could ask whether having others comment on their work has helped them to see where they could make improvements. You could ask them for other ideas about how to ensure that documents they produce in English are error free and good quality.

> **EXTRA ACTIVITY** You could ask students to write a slide from a presentation they have already given in their study or work life in English. Or, it could be a slide for a presentation they can imagine really giving in the future. This can be a homework task. It is to give them a more personal opportunity to practise creating presentation slides in English.

11.5 Video

The European Union

VIDEOSCRIPT

The European Union is a group of European countries that co-operate politically and economically.
It began in 1956, when six European countries – Belgium, France, Italy, Luxembourg, the Netherlands and West Germany – set up the European Economic Community. These countries were still suffering after the Second World War. They knew that if they worked together, each country could improve its own economy and make Europe a more stable place to live.
The benefits of this economic and political union were soon obvious, and other countries wanted to join. The EEC began to expand.
In 1993, the European Economic Community became the European Union and since then it has continued to grow. Today, the union is the largest economy in the world, accounting for 20% of global imports and exports.
But becoming a member isn't easy. If a country wants to join, it needs to pass several tests.
It needs to guarantee democracy and human rights and show it has a strong economy.
Membership of the EU also needs the backing of the people. If a country's population voted against membership, then that country wouldn't be allowed in. But once a country becomes a member, they can participate at all levels of the union.
This is the headquarters of the European Council in Brussels.
The leaders of each member state meet here at least twice every six months. While they are here they agree on the EU's goals.
The European Commission suggests new legislation that will achieve these goals. Each member state has a commissioner and each commissioner is in charge of a different department.
The European Parliament discusses and votes on new legislation proposed by the commission. Each country elects its own Members of European Parliament.
These are three of the EU's main institutions, but the EU is much bigger than this. It can be very complicated, too. After all, it isn't easy to please every country. Some countries, for example, believe the EU has too much power and that each country should have more control over its own laws and regulations.
But other countries want the EU to have more power. They believe a stronger union is better for each individual country.
But, in general, the EU has been a success. It has encouraged a spirit of co-operation and collaboration on a continent that used to be much more divided.
As its motto says, these nations are all 'United in Diversity'.

VIDEO ANSWERS
2 d is not mentioned in the video
3 a 1993
  b any three of Belgium, France, Italy, Luxembourg, the Netherlands or West Germany
  c to improve the economy, and make the region a more stable place to live
  d guarantee democracy, guarantee human rights and have a strong economy; the people of the country must want to join
  e at least twice every six months
  f the European Commission
  g because they believe each country should have more control over its own laws and regulations

Review
ANSWERS

Exercise 2a
1 Phone calls used to be a lot shorter.
2 People used to have more face-to-face contact.
3 In the past people used to have diaries and address books.
4 People used to put their photos in albums.
5 We didn't use to have all our information on just one or two devices.
6 Technology used to change more slowly.

Exercise 3a
1 high
2 Natural
3 fire
4 media
5 warming
6 create
7 financial
8 hunger

Exercise 3b 11.13
1 forest fire 2 natural disaster 3 high unemployment 4 create jobs 5 social media

AUDIOSCRIPT 11.13
The forest fire in the woods of the northern provinces is the second natural disaster to affect the region after last June's floods. The area also has very high unemployment with around 40% of under 30-year-olds out of work. Yesterday, we heard that a multinational company has decided not to build a new factory here. People had hoped this would create jobs in the region. When they heard the news, many young people wrote angrily on social media.

Exercise 4a
1 set up 2 found out 3 give up 4 take up
5 carry on

Exercise 5a 11.14
1 I think … true
2 afraid … agree
3 my opinion
4 I think you've got a point
5 take your point

AUDIOSCRIPT 11.14
1 You know **I think** this is probably **true**.
2 I'm **afraid** I don't really **agree**.
3 In **my opinion**, young people in particular find it very hard to be alone.
4 Yeah, I **think you've got a point**. I'm always on the phone or listening to something.
5 I **take your point**, we do spend more time in contact with people now, but we still have quiet moments.

Unit 11   187

12 Work

Unit overview

Language input

Present perfect simple with *for* and *since* (CB p116)	• *I've had this job since 2012.* • *She's been my boss for two years.*
Uses of the infinitive with *to* (CB p118)	• *Edison invented the employment test to recruit staff.* • *It was difficult to answer the questions.* • *Only a few people managed to pass the test.*
Grammar reference (CB pp156–7)	

Vocabulary development

Jobs, professions and workplaces (CB p116)	• *software developer, journalist, builder …* • *laboratory, factory, court …*
Job responsibilities (CB p118)	• *employ new staff, deal with customers, write reports …*
Phrases with *in* (CB p121)	• *in a mess, in trouble, in common …*

Skills development

Reading: Understanding linkers for surprising information (CB p120)

Writing: A curriculum vitae (CV) (CB p122)

Speaking: Answering questions in a job interview (CB p123)

Video

Documentary: Personal assistant (Coursebook DVD & CB p124)

Vox pops (Coursebook DVD & TG p264)

More materials

Workbook	• Language practice for vocabulary, grammar, pronunciation, writing and speaking • Listening for pleasure • Review: Units 11 and 12
Photocopiable activities	• Grammar: Do you know about your partner? (TG p219 & TSRD) • Vocabulary: Three in a row (TG p237 & TSRD) • Communication: Unusual job interviews (TG p255 & TSRD)
Tests	• Unit 12 test (TSRD) • Progress test: Units 10–12 • Exit test
Unit 12 wordlist (TSRD)	

12.1 The working environment

Goals
- Talk about jobs and professions
- Use the present perfect simple with *for* and *since*

Lead-in
- Put students into pairs and tell them they have five minutes to find out their partner's job and the jobs of other people in their family (parents, siblings, husband/wife, grandparents).
- Including the jobs of family members ensures they get practise using third person singular -s.
- Conduct class discussion, e.g. *Which person in your partner's family has the most interesting job?*

Vocabulary & Speaking   jobs, professions and workplaces

Exercise 1
- Focus students' attention on the mind map. Point out that there are three sections: A, B and C, each with an example.
- In pairs, students add the words in the box to the mind map. They can help each other to understand the meanings and also use dictionaries if available.
- Monitor and note any pronunciation problems and difficulties understanding the meanings of the words.
- Go through the answers together.
- Drill pronunciation of any difficult words.

EXTENSION   Put students into small groups. Give each group one section of the mind map (section B to the strongest students) and ask them to brainstorm more words which they can add to their section. Conduct class feedback. If possible, add them to a mind map on the board or write them in three lists.

ANSWERS
A Jobs: nurse, software developer, scientist, accountant, journalist, personal assistant (PA), administrator, judge, builder
B Professions: engineering, information technology (IT), construction, law, medical research, health care, sales, politics, administration
C Workplaces: office, building site, laboratory, factory, hospital, court

Exercise 2a
- This is a collocation exercise – students find words which go together well.
- Do the first one together as a demonstration if necessary, crossing out the word which doesn't go.
- Students work alone on this task. Then go through the answers together.

ANSWERS
1 sales
2 scientist
3 politics
4 builder
5 administrator
6 engineering

Exercise 2b
- Students read the instruction and rewrite two sentences, making them true about their own work situation.

- Monitor carefully to ensure that they are using the new vocabulary correctly. Correct any mistakes.
- Give a time limit to the end of the activity if necessary.
- Put students into pairs to compare their sentences.

EXTENSION   For further practice you could ask them to rewrite the sentences so they are true about family members' jobs (referring back to the lead-in activity if you had time to do it).

Exercise 3
- Put students into small groups to focus on section A of the mind map in exercise 1.
- They read the questions and discuss.
- Conduct class feedback: *Do you think we all agree about the most stressful job?*, etc. Elicit from different students.

Grammar & Listening   present perfect simple with *for* and *since*

Exercise 4
- Students work in pairs to prepare for the listening task. Ask them to look at the photos and discuss the questions.
- Monitor their discussions.
- Conduct class feedback, particularly to elicit advantages and disadvantages (question 3).

Exercise 5a
- Tell students that they are going to listen to a podcast about offices.
- Ask them to look at the topics in the box and think about which of these topics will be mentioned in the podcast.

Exercise 5b   12.1

> **Audio summary**: A podcast where a presenter talks about open-plan offices. The podcast includes brief interviews with two people: an architect and a sound expert. They explain some of the problems of open-plan offices and suggest possible solutions.

- Play track 12.1.
- Students listen to the podcast and check their ideas.

AUDIOSCRIPT 12.1
P I've been a newspaper journalist since 2001. I enjoy my job mostly, but … I really don't like the office where I work. It's huge and there are about 60 of us in here. We all sit here, we hear the same noises, we breathe the same air. I've worked here for five years. Or at least, I've tried to work here. But it's not easy, and here's why … .
P So why do millions of us work in open-plan offices? To find out more about open-plan offices, I spoke to architect, Nicky Delaney.
P So, Nicky, tell me – how long have we had open-plan offices? Is it a new way of working?
ND Well, no actually. Open-plan offices have been around since the late 19th century. The first ones appeared in the USA and were like schools, with workers sitting quietly at small desks, in straight rows, facing the same way. In the 1960s a new kind of office was introduced in Germany where desks were organized into work zones of different sizes, with desks facing each other. This was to encourage communication and sharing of ideas.

Unit 12   189

P But let's be honest, although it's good to communicate and share ideas, sometimes it's possible to have too much talk and it can be difficult to work. Listen to sound expert, Justin Simms, talking about the effects of noise on how we work.

JS When we do work like writing a document, a voice in our head helps us organize our ideas. Scientists say that nobody can understand two people talking at the same time – we can understand a maximum of 1.6 people talking. If somebody else is speaking, then we can't listen to that voice in our head. That means we can't work well and research has shown that the noise in open-plan offices can reduce productivity by 66%.

P And then there's the opposite problem. Open-plan offices can be too quiet, if everybody's doing their work in silence. So it can be hard to have private conversations. Justin Simms again.

JS Some companies have recently started to use something called 'pink noise'. Pink noise sounds like falling rain or wind in the trees. It's played through speakers and provides background noise, which covers the sound of other people's conversation and also covers up the sound of silence.

P So if open-plan offices can be a problem, are there alternative solutions? In the last few years, 'break out areas', where people can have informal meetings, have become more and more popular. In next week's programme, I'm going to look at this new flexible working environment. Till then, it's goodbye from me.

Exercise 6 12.1

- Give students time to read the notes carefully.
- **EXTRA SUPPORT** Ask students to predict the kind of word they need to complete each gap, e.g. *noun – person, thing, place, number* or *verb, adjective,* etc. Do the first together as an example if necessary. They could do this alone or in pairs.
- Tell them to listen and complete the notes.
- Play track 12.1 again.
- Go through the answers together.

ANSWERS
1 the USA   5 66
2 19th   6 quiet
3 ideas   7 wind
4 1.6

Exercise 7

- Put students into small groups to discuss the problems of open-plan offices (too noisy, no privacy) and think of some solutions.
- Monitor their discussions. Encourage talkative students to ask quieter students for their opinions to make sure everyone has a chance to speak. Note any points for correction.
- **EXTRA CHALLENGE** Set up the activity in the style of a business meeting with one chairperson in each group (explaining what the chairperson does if necessary) and one secretary to write down their ideas. Stronger students can also be encouraged to think of other problems of open-plan offices in addition to the ones in the podcast and discuss solutions.
- Give a time limit to the end of the activity.

- Students present their problems and solutions to the class. If you want them all to speak during feedback, regroup the students so that there is one person from each group in the new groups. Then they present to each other.
- Do any necessary error correction.

Exercise 8a

- Focus students' attention on sentences a and b from the listening.
- Tell them to answer the questions about the sentences.
- Go through the answers together.

ANSWERS
1 In 2001   3 five years ago
2 Yes   4 Yes

Exercise 8b

- Elicit or tell students that the sentences in exercise 8a are in the present perfect simple tense. Ask them to look at them again and circle *for* and *since* because these are key words.
- Tell them to read the Grammar focus box and complete the rules.
- Students work alone to choose the correct options for 1–3.
- Go through the answers together.
- **EXTRA ACTIVITY** Write on the board *I've studied English …* and ask the students to finish the sentence so it is true for them using *for*. Check sentences carefully. Ask them to finish the sentence again using *since*.

ANSWERS
1 continue now
2 since
3 for

- Refer students to *Grammar reference* on p156. There are three more exercises here students can do for homework. See answers on p191.

Exercise 9

- Students look at the phrases and decide if they go with *for* or *since*. They could do this in pairs or alone.
- **EXTRA SUPPORT** Some students benefit from physically moving pieces of paper around. You could give pairs of students some blank slips of paper and ask them to copy one phrase onto each slip. Then they could work together to make two groups of phrases on their desks.
- Monitor and if they are having difficulty, tell them to try using them in an example sentence, e.g. *I have lived here …* .
- **WATCH OUT!** A common error is *since a couple of days*. Point out to students that *a couple of days* is a period of time so we use *for* but if they want to use *since* they can say *a couple of days ago*.
- Go through the answers together.

ANSWERS
FOR: an hour, ages, a long time, a couple of days, many years
SINCE: three o'clock, we arrived here, I left school, last year, Monday

Exercise 10
- Tell students to read the title of the text. Point out that these are comments from people posted on a website.
- Ask them to complete the web postings. Highlight that if a gap has a verb in brackets, they need to choose the correct form to use: present simple, present perfect simple or past simple. If a gap does not have a verb in brackets then they should choose *for* or *since*.
- Do the first one together as a demonstration if necessary.
- Students work alone on this task.
- Allow them to check their answers in pairs.
- Go through the answers together.

ANSWERS
1 have worked
2 for
3 have had
4 since
5 worked
6 feel
7 haven't been
8 since
9 are
10 got
11 haven't had
12 for

Pronunciation *has* and *have*

Exercise 11a 12.2
- Focus students' attention on the example sentences.
- Tell them to listen to find out how *has* and *have* are pronounced.
- Play track 12.2.
- Elicit answers from the class. If possible, model the difference between /həv/ and /hæv/ and also /həz/ and /hæz/ because the students will be able to see the movement of your mouth.

ANSWERS
Has and *have* are contracted to weak forms with no /h/ sound and just /ə/ rather than /æ/.

AUDIOSCRIPT 12.2 & 12.3
How long have /əv/ you worked here?
How long has /əz/ he known her?

Exercise 11b 12.3
- Tell them to listen again and repeat.
- Play the track again. You may need to play it several times to ensure good natural pronunciation.

Exercise 11c 12.4
- Tell students that this is a dictation exercise and they have to write the four sentences they hear.
- Play track 12.4. (Play it more than once if necessary.)
- Make sure that they have written them correctly.
- You could play the track again and ask students to repeat so that they practise the pronunciation more.

AUDIOSCRIPT 12.4
1 How long have you had your phone?
2 How long has the weather been like this?
3 How long have you been awake today?
4 How long has your teacher been at this school?

Exercise 11d
- In pairs, students ask and answer the four questions.
- Ask some pairs to do one of their conversations again in front of the class.
- Praise good pronunciation of the weak forms for *have* and *has*.

Exercise 12a
- Put students into new pairs, one Student A and one Student B. They turn to the relevant page. (Student A: page 129 and Student B: page 133.)
- They work alone to write names or words in response to their prompts.
- Monitor and make sure they are only writing down words, not full sentences.
- Give them a time limit to the end of the activity.

Exercise 12b
- Students read the words their partner has written.
- They take turns to ask questions to get information about the words and names their partner has written.

FEEDBACK FOCUS Monitor their conversations, focusing on their use of the present perfect simple with *for* and *since*. Note points for correction.
- When they have finished their conversations, conduct error correction.

EXTENSION If you have extra time, you could put the students into new pairs and ask them to do this exercise again (using the same words and names). This time they can focus carefully on the pronunciation of *has* and *have* when they use the present perfect.

GRAMMAR REFERENCE ANSWERS

Exercise 1
1 Sean's Bar has served drinks since 1900.
2 Château de Goulaine has made wine for almost 1,000 years.
3 Hotel *Hoshi Ryokan* has provided rooms since 718.
4 Barts hospital has cared for patients for nine centuries.
5 Raeapteek pharmacy has sold medicines since 1422.
6 Gazzetta di Mantova has printed newspapers for many years.

Exercise 2
1 How long have you been a journalist? Six months.
2 Has your wife worked in medical research for many years?
3 Rebecca hasn't enjoyed her job since she started it.
4 Have you all studied here since last summer?
5 I haven't had this office for a long time.
6 How long have your children been at university – three or four years?
7 There has been a building site behind our house for two months.

Exercise 3
1 Lisa's been a PA for two years.
2 We've worked in this hotel since Tuesday.
3 I've wanted to be a nurse for many years.
4 I've studied law for three years.
5 My grandad has had a PC since he was 80.
6 There's been a factory next to our house since 1950.

Unit 12   191

12.2 The changing face of work

Goals
- Talk about what a job involves
- Use the infinitive with *to*

Lead-in
- Elicit or explain that the question *What do you do?* is asking for someone's job title or field of work in general. If you want to find out what things they do at work, you can ask *What does your job involve?*
- In pairs, students ask and answer *What does your job involve?* (If they are not working at present, they can ask/answer *What would your dream job involve?*)
- Monitor how well they are able to do this task. Point out that by the end of this lesson they will have learnt more vocabulary and grammar to help them talk about their job more easily and in more detail.

Vocabulary & Listening job responsibilities

Exercise 1
- Focus students' attention on the six photos. Point out that photos a, c and e are from some years ago and photos b, d, and f are their more modern equivalents, so they should look at the photos in pairs, e.g. a with b.
- In pairs, students discuss the work activities and how they have changed in the last 50 years.
- Monitor their discussions and help them with any vocabulary they need to express their ideas.
- Conduct class discussion.

ANSWERS
Photos a and b are about typing, producing documents etc. Photos c and d are about presenting information, teaching. Photos e and f are about communicating.

Exercise 2 12.5

Audio summary: Three different speakers talk about their jobs. They each explain what their job involves.

- Check students understand what they need to do.
- Play track 12.5.
- Students decide whether each speaker feels positive, negative or neutral about their job.
- Allow them to check their answers in pairs.
- Go through the answers together.

EXTRA CHALLENGE Ask stronger students to try to remember what each speaker said to support their answer.

ANSWERS
Speaker 1 negative: I guess I've just been in this job for too long.
Speaker 2: positive: It's tiring work, but I love it.
Speaker 3: positive/neutral: It's not the most exciting job in the world and I don't expect to stay in this job forever, but I'm very happy to do it for now.

AUDIOSCRIPT 12.5

Speaker 1
I work for an advertising agency. I'm a director and my job is to advise clients about their advertising campaigns. I spend a lot of time in meetings – I attend five or six meetings a day, sometimes more. And they're usually at the clients' offices, not at my own, unfortunately. I often have to give presentations at the meetings, so it can be quite stressful. I also entertain clients a lot – you know, take them to restaurants and sports events, that sort of thing. It sounds like fun, but it's difficult to relax when you're with clients. I'd prefer to be out with family or friends. I guess I've just been in this job for too long.

Speaker 2
I'm a restaurant manager. I work for a large restaurant in Las Vegas and I manage a team of fifteen people. One of my main roles is to recruit and train new kitchen and waiting staff. I also do a lot of paperwork. For example, I write a report on food sales at the end of every evening. I often don't get to bed until after two in the morning. It's tiring work, but I love it!

Speaker 3
I'm an administrator at the law court. I work in a team of four people, who I really like, and we run the day-to-day business of the court. So we set times and dates for court cases, answer phone enquiries and deal with emails. It's not the most exciting job in the world and I don't expect to stay in this job forever, but I'm very happy to do it for now.

Exercise 3 12.5
- Tell students to read sentences 1–9 which are from the listening.
- Point out that they should use words from the box to complete them. (There are two gaps in sentence 9.)
- Students work on this task alone.
- Play track 12.5 again so that they can check their answers.

ANSWERS
1 clients
2 meetings
3 presentations
4 team
5 staff
6 paperwork
7 team
8 business
9 enquiries, emails

Exercise 4
- Ask students to look at the first table.
- Do number 1 as a demonstration together if necessary.
- Students work alone to find words from the box to match to the pairs of verbs.

EXTRA SUPPORT You could elicit or teach the meanings of recruit, deal with, type up and entertain which they may not know. Drill pronunciation.

- Monitor carefully and check that they are doing the task correctly.
- Go through the answers together.

WATCH OUT! Elicit from students that *staff* is an irregular plural noun, e.g. *The staff in this office **are** happy*. We don't use *a staff* or *staffs*. When we talk about one person, we usually use *a member of staff*.

ANSWERS
1 new staff
2 customer enquiries
3 reports
4 meetings
5 clients
6 a team
7 presentations
8 the phone

Exercise 5a
- In pairs, students read and discuss the questions. Check that they understand the meaning of *challenging*.
- Point out in questions 2 and 3, they can answer in the present tense if they have experience of the activities but use *would* if they are just imagining but don't have experience of them.
- Monitor and encourage them to discuss all the activities.
- **EXTRA CHALLENGE** Encourage stronger students to try to give reasons for their answers in 2 and 3.
- Conduct class feedback. Ask some students for their answers.

Exercise 5b
- Students read the instruction and think about the people they can talk about.
- **EXTRA SUPPORT** Give students thinking time to focus on two people they know well and plan how to describe their job responsibilities. It is better if they don't write at this stage.
- In pairs, they take turns to tell each other about the people they chose and the job responsibilities they have.
- Monitor carefully. Note any points for correction.
- Give a time limit to the end of the activity.
- Invite one or two students to tell the class about their chosen person's job.
- Conduct error correction.
- **EXTENSION** Ask students to think about/remember how they answered *What does your job involve?* during the lead-in to the lesson. Give them thinking time to plan how they could use any of the vocabulary for this lesson to explain their job responsibilities more clearly or in more detail. Put them in new pairs to talk about their own job (or dream job) again.

Grammar & Reading uses of the infinitive with *to*

Exercise 6
- Students read the question. Write the example on the board and put them into pairs to think of other methods used by companies to recruit staff.
- When they have had time to discuss, elicit their ideas and make a list on the board.

POSSIBLE ANSWERS
Use a recruitment agency.
Advertise on the internet – use social media and register with specialist employment sites.
Take part in a jobs fair. Promote your company in universities and colleges.
Use personal recommendations, referrals from current staff.

Exercise 7

Text summary: An article about how companies are using new developments in recruitment to find new staff. The main focus is on using characteristics of computer games to attract young people and test their abilities, called *gamification*.

- Check that students understand that sentences 1–3 are summaries and they need to choose one of them.
- Give them plenty of time to read the article.
- Allow them to check their choice in pairs.
- Check the answer together. Elicit why it is the best summary.

ANSWER
The best summary is 3 because it is about recruiting staff through the use of technology and, specifically, computer games.

Exercise 8
- Focus students' attention on the things in 1–6. They need to read the article again and think about why these things are mentioned.
- When they have ideas about the things, they explain their reasons in pairs and check their answers.
- Go through the answers together.

ANSWERS
1 Thomas Edison was the first person to invent an employment test.
2 Gamification is when recruiters use characteristics of computer games.
3 L'Oreal is an example of a company which has used '*gamification*'.
4 Reveal is the name of L'Oreal's game, created to provide real-life problems to solve in a virtual environment.
5 Marriot is an international hotel group who created a game on Facebook to attract staff in markets outside the USA.
6 one million likes – My Marriot Hotel game got over this number of likes.

Exercise 9
- Students read the questions. Check that they understand *pros and cons* – you could elicit *advantages and disadvantages* as synonyms.
- You could organize this discussion in small groups or elicit ideas from the class as a whole.
- **EXTENSION** Make the discussion more personal. Ask them *Would you like to play a computer game as part of the recruitment process for your next job?* Encourage them to explain why/why not?

Exercise 10
- Focus students' attention on the Grammar focus box about the uses of the infinitive with *to*. Give them time to read through carefully.
- **EXTRA SUPPORT** If necessary, go through the uses with the students, asking checking questions, e.g. *What is the reason? Which is the adjective?*, etc.
- Tell them to look for and underline more examples of infinitive with *to* in the article.

Unit 12 193

- They should also decide whether each example is use 1, 2 or 3 from the Grammar focus box.
- Allow them to check their answers in pairs then go through them together. Elicit the use of each example.

PRONUNCIATION Remind students that in lesson 4.3 they learned about linking sounds in connected speech. They need to add a linking /w/ between *to* and words beginning with a vowel sound, e.g. *to* /w/ *answer, to* /w/ *add, to* /w/ *attract*. Otherwise *to* is generally reduced to a weak form /tə/ and hardly ever pronounced /tuː/ before a word beginning with a consonant sound, e.g. *to know, to work, to recruit*.

ANSWERS
1 using characteristics of games to add some fun, which has used gamification to recruit new staff, developed a game to attract young people
2 necessary to know, designed to recruit, is likely to become
3 want to work, try to solve

- Refer students to *Grammar reference* on p157. There are three more exercises here students can do for homework. See answers in next column.

Exercise 11

- Ask students to ask and answer in pairs *How many job interviews have you had?* and *Have you had a video interview?*
- Tell them to read the tips about video interviews. Point out the example of where *to* has been added. Tell them to find 8 more places to add *to*.
- Students work alone on this task.
- Go through the answers together.

ANSWERS
To make sure
Sensible to test
You need to get up
Important to make
Remember to look
Try not to look at
Forget to warn
Want to be interrupted

Exercise 12a

- Ask students to read the topics in the list and choose one of them. Try to ensure there are a number of students who have chosen each topic (not all students writing tips on the same topic).
- They should write five tips and include infinitive with *to* where possible.
- They could do the task alone or in pairs.
- Monitor and help them think of ideas and correct mistakes.

Exercise 12b

- Ask students to read out their tips to the class and discuss the best ones. This can also be organized in small groups, see below.

CRITICAL THINKING Pyramid discussions can be useful to help students explain, discuss and defend their ideas in more depth. Firstly, small groups who have chosen the same topic work together and present their tips to each other. Then they discuss and choose the five best tips. After that, put all students together and this time each group reads out their top five tips. They all discuss and choose the five best tips of all. The process also involves polite disagreement (lesson 11.4) and compromise.

EXTRA ACTIVITY Ask students to write five tips for a 'How to…' sheet on a topic of their own choosing, using infinitive with *to* where possible. This could be done as a homework task. Display them in the classroom.

GRAMMAR REFERENCE ANSWERS

Exercise 1
1 I'm writing to ask for a job.
2 John's working late to type up his report.
3 I'm going to arrive early to check my emails.
4 Mike's gone to meet a client.
5 They're doing research to find a cure for AIDS.

Exercise 2
1 It's useful to deal with emails quickly.
2 It's important to meet the department director.
3 It isn't/it's not good to wear trainers at the office.
4 It's bad to be fifteen minutes late every morning.
5 It's OK to eat at your desk.

Exercise 3
1 It's good ⋏ add some humour or a story into your presentation to keep the audience interested.
2 Audiences need ⋏ think about what you are saying so stop speaking after a joke or a statistic ⋏ give them time to respond.
3 Always remember ⋏ sound excited, and you must make your passion for the topic clear.
4 It's very important ⋏ prepare. If you manage ⋏ find time, prepare questions for your audience so that they can join the discussion.
5 Don't forget ⋏ practise your presentation in front of the mirror.
6 On the day itself, try ⋏ arrive early ⋏ check everything is working.

12.3 Vocabulary and skills development

Goals
- Understand linkers for surprising information.
- Use phrases with *in*

Reading & Speaking understanding linkers for surprising information

Lead-in

- Write the word *surprise* on the board. Ask *How does this word make you feel?* Point out that this word is neutral – surprises can be good or bad. Drill the pronunciation.
- Elicit the adjectives *surprising* and *surprised*. Remind them that they studied *-ing* and *-ed* adjectives in lesson 7.3. Check that they know *surprised* describes a feeling, e.g. *I was so surprised*. *Surprising* describes a situation, thing or person which causes that feeling, e.g. *The ending of the book was really surprising*.

194

Exercise 1

- Ask students to think about one specific interview situation they remember (for a job or a study course). It could be successful or unsuccessful.
- Put students into pairs.
- Tell them to use questions 1–4 to help them describe what they can remember about the interview to their partner.

EXTRA SUPPORT You could give weaker students some silent planning time to organize their thoughts before the speaking task.

- Elicit some experiences from the class. You could also share one of your own interview experiences and encourage them to ask you questions to get further information.

EXTRA ACTIVITY Put students into small groups and tell them to brainstorm 'how to be successful in an interview'. To help them start, you could ask them, for example, *Is it important to be on time for an interview?* (yes) They should write down a list of ideas about expected behaviour (but don't need to write full sentences). Monitor and prompt them when necessary. Suggestions: learn about the job/course before the interview, prepare answers to common questions, dress smartly, switch off your mobile phone, do not eat, drink or chew gum, speak clearly and at the right volume, sit still and sit up straight, make eye contact, smile, answer questions as fully as possible, be positive and interested about the job/course. Now ask: *If you don't do these things, what will happen?* (You will probably be unsuccessful. You probably won't get the job/place on the course.)

Exercise 2a

- Students read the information in the Unlock the code box about linkers for surprising information.

PRONUNCIATION There are a number of ways to pronounce *ough* in English. Model *although* /ɔːlˈðəʊ/ and *even though* /ˈiːvn ðəʊ/ and drill the pronunciation. You could point out that this sound is the same as in *know* or *go* and drill in phrases *although she knows* /ɔːlˈðəʊ ʃi nəʊz/ or *even though we didn't go* /ˈiːvn ðəʊ wi dɪdnt gəʊ/. Drill the other linkers too, particularly to get the stress right.

- Check that students understand the concept, if necessary: *Did he get the job?* (yes) *What happened at the interview?* (He was late.) *When you're late for an interview, do you usually get the job?*, etc. An unsurprising sentence would be *He was late for his interview, so he didn't get the job*. Elicit that *so* is a linker of result (lesson 5.3 *so, as a result, therefore*).

EXTRA CHALLENGE For stronger students, point out that all the linkers in the box are for surprising information, but they come in different places in the sentence or may be followed by different structures. Focus their attention on how each linker is used, e.g. *Instead* and *However* start a new sentence and have a comma, etc.

WATCH OUT! Students may think that the surprising information always comes in the second part of the sentence. Point out that the examples with *although*, *even though*, *despite* and *in spite of* could be written with the clauses reversed, e.g. *He got the job although he was late for his interview*. The surprising information is that he got the job, no

matter which order the clauses are in. You can check this point again after exercise 2b, using sentences 1–3 as examples.

Exercise 2b

- Students read the instruction and choose the correct option to complete the sentences.
- They work alone on this task.
- Go through the answers together.

EXTENSION You could ask them which of the actions in sentences 1–5 they think is the most surprising and why.

EXTRA ACTIVITY Put students in small groups. Ask *Do you think you would behave like the person in each sentence 1–5? If so, give an example to explain why*. Example: *Sentence 1, I would wear a heavy suit although it was hot if I went to a formal interview. Sentence 2, I would go to work despite the fact that I felt ill if I had a very important meeting*. Elicit ideas from each group. You can elicit or point out that they are using the *if* + past tense, *would* structure that they learned in lesson 11.1.

ANSWERS
1 he wore a heavy suit
2 She went to work
3 He answered his phone
4 she emailed me
5 I didn't take it

Exercise 2c

- Students complete the sentences.
- Monitor and make sure that their sentences show a clear contrast/surprising information.
- Put them in pairs to share their sentences.

Exercise 3

Text summary: An amusing text from a website about what not to do in job interviews. There are six stories, each told from the interviewer's point of view.

- Students read the instruction. Ask *Are you going to read stories by interviewers or the people who were interviewed?* (Interviewers – they are from a website for recruiters.)
- Tell students to read the title only. Ask *Are these stories about successful or unsuccessful interviews?* (unsuccessful)
- Tell students to look at the pictures and find four stories which match them.
- Students read the text and work on the task alone.
- Go through the answers together.

ANSWERS
Picture a: story 1
Picture b: story 4
Picture c: story 5
Picture d: story 6

Exercise 4

- Students read the stories again and circle any linkers for surprise in each story. Tell them also to underline the surprising information.
- Find the first linker together as a demonstration (*However*). Elicit which is the surprising information to underline. (However, this guy answered it …)
- Allow them to check their answers in pairs.
- Go through the answers with the class.

Unit 12 195

ANSWERS

1 **However,** this guy answered it, then asked me to leave my office because he needed to have a 'private' conversation.
2 **although** he turned up in shorts and a long shirt.
3 **even though** he was applying for a job at the corporate office of a shoe company.
4 **despite** he went up to every one of the interviewers and asked if we wanted an arm wrestle.
5 **but** replied 'My 23 insect tattoos' … and showed us his back
6 **Instead,** he took the whole bowl

Exercise 5

- Students read the stories one more time and match each story with one of the main points a–f.
- Go through the answers together.

EXTRA CHALLENGE Encourage students to give extra information/be specific by asking further questions, e.g. for answer A *What was he offered? How much did he take?* and for B *What was the request? Why did he ask this?*

ANSWERS

a story 6
b story 1
c story 5
d story 2
e story 3
f story 4

Exercise 6

- Put students into small groups to discuss the question.
- Conduct a classroom discussion. You could try to find out whether they agree which interviewee behaved the most strangely and why.

CRITICAL THINKING You could ask them to discuss in their groups whether they think each story is really true and give reasons why they think it is/isn't true.

Vocabulary phrases with *in*

Exercise 7a

- Students read the Vocabulary focus box about phrases with *in*.
- Elicit three general meanings of *in* from the box: professions, wearing things, time/place.

Exercise 7b

- Point out the three uses of *in* on the mind map.
- Focus their attention on the highlighted words and phrases in the text. Tell them to add them to the mind map.
- They work alone on this task.
- Allow them to check their answers in pairs.
- Go through the meanings together.

EXTENSION Elicit other combinations with *in* which could be added to the mind map, e.g. with other items of clothing or colours, with other professions, with other future time references.

EXTRA ACTIVITY Tell students to look around the classroom and choose three students. They should write a sentence about each student's clothes, using a phrase with *in* for each person. They should share their sentences in pairs and their partner should guess which students are described.

- An activity to practise phrases with *in* about professions is *Do you know anybody…?* In pairs, students take turns to ask *Do you know anybody in …?* or *Do you know anybody who works in …?* adding different professions each time. The aim is to get a 'yes' answer, e.g. *Do you know anybody in marketing? Yes, my brother's a marketing manager.*
- For talking about time, ask the class questions and they need to write answers including a phrase with *in*, e.g. *When will this lesson finish? When will your next holiday be? When will you take a test in English? When will you have grandchildren?*, etc. They can then compare their answers in pairs.

ANSWERS

A Wearing something: in shorts
B Talking about a profession: in sales
C Talking about position in time or place: in the middle, in five years' time, in front of

Exercise 8

- Students read the instruction. Tell them to work out the meanings of the phrases by looking at the rest of the sentence carefully.

EXTRA CHALLENGE Tell stronger students to cover the definitions a–f and try to discuss the meanings with a partner. Then, they can check their ideas with the definitions.

- Students could work alone on this task, but they might find it easier to discuss the meanings of the phrases in pairs.
- Go through the answers together.

ANSWERS

1 d 2 b 3 a 4 e 5 c 6 f

Exercise 9a

- Students read the instruction and complete the questions using words from the box and *in*.
- Monitor and check that they don't miss out *in*.
- Go through the answers together.

ANSWERS

1 in a hurry
2 in a mess
3 in front of
4 in charge of
5 in trouble
6 in common
7 in five years' time

Exercise 9b

- Put students into small groups.
- They take turns to ask and answer the questions.
- Monitor their discussions and try to encourage all members of each group to join in.

EXTRA CHALLENGE Encourage the students to ask follow-up questions to get more information after 'yes' answers. (*Why?, Why not?, What?, Where?, When?*, etc.)

- Conduct a class discussion. You could elicit any answers from the groups which they found interesting or surprising.

- Alternatively, you could use these sentences as the basis of a class survey. Put the students into pairs. Each pair chooses one or two sentences to ask to all of their classmates in a mingle activity. They record the answers, get extra information if possible and when they have asked everyone, discuss in their pairs how many 'yes' and 'no' answers they got. Then they present their results to the class. This information could also be made into a class poster: e.g. *Most of us are tidy. We hate it if our desks are in a mess. Only one of us has had to speak in front of a large audience. It was at a conference and there were 250 people.*

EXTENSION For homework ask students to write true sentences about themselves using fixed phrases with *in* from this lesson. Stronger students could also write sentences using *in* with general meanings as shown in the mind map. You will need to collect these pieces of writing to mark them.

12.4 Speaking and writing

Goals
- Write a CV
- Take part in a job interview

Lead-in
- Focus students' attention on the photo at the bottom of the page.
- Ask them to discuss in pairs where they think the photo was taken and what they can see.
- Elicit ideas from the class. You could teach them the word *pile* to help them describe the photo.

Writing   a curriculum vitae (CV)

Exercise 1
- Focus the students' attention on the heading. Point out that we rarely say Curriculum Vitae in full but usually say CV.
- Students read the questions and they ask and answer them in pairs.
- Conduct class feedback.

> **Background note:** LinkedIn is a business-related social media service which people use for professional networking. It was launched in 2003 and by 2013 had nearly 260 million members. The service is available in 20 languages. Members have a profile page which is like an online CV and they make and recommend professional connections with other members.

Exercise 2
- Ask students to read the headings in the box. Then go through any unknown words and phrases.
- Focus their attention on the CV of Stefan Nielsen. Tell them to add the missing headings from the box.
- Students work alone on this task.
- Go through the answers together.

ANSWERS
1. Date of birth
2. Email address
3. Education and Qualifications
4. Work Experience
5. Skills
6. Interests
7. Referees

Exercise 3
- Highlight that the next text is part of another CV.
- Explain that the writer has been too informal and they should replace the informal words in italics with more formal words from the box.
- Do the first one as a demonstration together: *Can you find a word in the box which means 'was the boss'?* (managed).
- Students could do this task alone or in pairs. If they work in pairs, encourage them to help each other understand unknown words. If alone, they could use dictionaries if available.
- Go through the answers together.
- Drill pronunciation of any of this new vocabulary which you think may be difficult.

ANSWERS
1. managed
2. training
3. developed
4. attended
5. provided
6. assisted
7. fluent
8. basic
9. good knowledge of
10. on request

CRITICAL THINKING Students can analyse these CVs by comparing them to CVs they have seen in their country. What are the similarities and differences a) in the kind or amount of information they include and b) in the layout or presentation? They could discuss in small groups or as a class

Exercise 4
- Students read the instruction.
- They write a CV based upon the example in exercise 2 and using words/phrases from exercise 3.
- Allow plenty of time for them to write a CV. If your time is limited, you could tell them to focus only on writing the Work Experience part of the CV as in exercise 3.
- Monitor carefully and assist students who are having difficulty. Help with specific vocabulary they may need and provide dictionaries if possible.
- Give a time limit to the end of the activity.

EXTRA CHALLENGE Ask fast finishers to check their spelling and punctuation (e.g. *use of capital letters for names, qualifications, job titles*). Tell them to check that they have used formal phrases to describe the work experience.

- Ask students to swap CVs and read their partner's CV. You could give them a checklist so that they can give feedback:
  The CV is easy to understand.
  The CV has enough and the right kind of information.
  The CV uses formal words and phrases.
  The CV shows good spelling.
- Monitor this student-to-student feedback and then conduct class discussion.

Unit 12

EXTENSION As homework they could spend time creating a real, full CV for themselves in English. Ask them to bring it to you to check.

Listening & Speaking answering questions in a job interview

Exercise 5 12.6
- Focus students' attention on the three job advertisements a, b and c. Tell them to read the adverts carefully.
- Explain that the woman in the photo, Danielle, applied for one of the jobs. Ask them to listen to the first part of her interview to decide which job she applied for.
- Play track 12.6.
- Check the answer together.

ANSWER
Sports writer

AUDIOSCRIPT 12.6
I Hi Danielle … Come in. Take a seat.
D Thanks very much.
I So, just to introduce myself. I'm Philippa Hart, Head of HR here at Canadian News Online. As you know, we're a new company and we're looking to build up our team of sports writers.
D Uh-huh.

Exercise 6a 12.7
- Students read the questions a–e.
- Check that they know the meaning of the word *achievement* if necessary. Drill pronunciation.
- Students listen to the next part of the interview and note down her answers.
- Play track 12.7.
- Go through the answers together.

EXTENSION You could ask students which interview questions they think are the most difficult and why.

ANSWERS
a a university degree in journalism
b worked as a sports journalist for six years
c wants to write about a range of sports, wants to get into online publishing
d creative, works quickly, good at interviewing sports people; finds it hard to say 'no'
e won award for best young sports journalist

AUDIOSCRIPT 12.7
I So, on with the interview …First of all, tell me, Danielle, what qualifications have you got for this job?
D Well, I've got a university degree in journalism, and that included not just newspaper and magazine journalism, but also radio, TV, and, of course, online journalism.
I OK, good, and how much experience do you have? In sports journalism, I mean.
D I've worked as a sports journalist for six years. My first job was working for a local newspaper in my town. I worked there for two years and then I wrote for a teenage sports magazine. I'm currently writing for a popular ice-hockey magazine called *Shoot*.
I Yeah, I know it well. So, why do you want to work for this company?
D Well, I enjoy my present job, but I'd like to write about a range of sports, not just ice hockey. Also I'd really like to get into online publishing.
I Sure, sure. And what are your strengths and weaknesses?
D Mmm, that's a difficult question. Strengths … well, I'm creative, I can work quickly when I need to, and I'm good at interviewing sports people – you know, getting them to say interesting things. Weaknesses … I find it hard to say 'no' sometimes when people ask me to do things. That means I sometimes have too many projects. But I'm working on that.
I Sounds good. And what's your greatest achievement? What are you most proud of in your career so far?
D Er, well two years ago I won an award for best young sports journalist. There was quite a lot of competition for that. You know, writers at other sports magazines – so I was quite pleased.
I Yeah, I'm sure. Now, do you have any questions about the job?
D Er, yes, I do have a few actually …

Exercise 7a 12.7
- Students read sentences 1–8 and choose the correct option for each.
- Go through unknown vocabulary: *get into, award*.
- Students work alone on this task.
- Tell them that you're going to play the interview again so they can check their answers.
- Play track 12.7 again. If necessary, go through the answers together.

ANSWERS
1 journalism
2 six
3 an ice-hockey
4 online
5 quickly
6 interviewing sports people
7 say 'no'
8 sports

Exercise 7b 12.8
- Tell students that they are going to practise pronunciation so that they pronounce the phrases in bold correctly and naturally. They need to listen and repeat.
- Play track 12.8. Pause where necessary and play it again if you think the students need more practice.

AUDIOSCRIPT 12.8
1 I've got a university degree in journalism.
2 I've worked as a sports journalist for six years.
3 I'm currently working for an ice-hockey magazine.
4 I'd really like to get into online publishing.
5 I can work quickly.
6 I'm good at interviewing people.
7 I find it hard to say 'no'.
8 I won an award for best young sports journalist.

Exercise 7c
- Focus students' attention on the questions in exercise 7 again.
- They match each question to one or more of the answers.
- Allow them to check their answers in pairs.
- Go through answers together.

ANSWERS
a 1   b 2, 3   c 4   d 5, 6, 7   e 8

Exercise 8
- In pairs, students use the phrases in bold in exercise 7a to talk about themselves.

EXTRA SUPPORT As the focus is on speaking in an interview, it is not a good idea for students to write down the sentences, but give them thinking time to plan mentally if necessary.

- Monitor carefully. Note any points for correction, especially any pronunciation errors.
- Ask some students to report on what their partner said.
- Conduct error correction.

SMART COMMUNICATION If an interviewer asks *What are your strengths and weaknesses?*, your answer needs to include a weakness but this is difficult to do! It needs to be something not very important or it can even be something quite positive but presented as a weakness such as *I find it hard to say 'no'* or *I spend too much time checking my work to make sure it is right*. It is a good idea to plan a response especially when having an interview in another language.

Exercise 9a
- Tell students they are going to role-play a job interview. In pairs, tell them to choose one job advertisement to base the role-play on.
- They decide who will be Student A and who Student B. Then they read their part of the instruction.
- Give a time limit for this preparation stage.
- Monitor carefully. Help 'interviewers' to write more questions. Encourage them to think specifically about what they need to ask in relation to the job advertised.
- Help 'interviewees' to plan answers to the questions in 6, using the Language for speaking box. Remind them to be specific to the job advertisement they have chosen.
- When they are ready, students role-play the interview in their pairs.
- Monitor the role-plays.
- Make a note of particularly good performance as well as errors for correction.

Exercise 9b
- The students in each pair swap roles and they choose a different advertisement for their new role-play.
- Guide them through the stages of exercise 9a, based upon the new advertisement.
- Monitor their preparation carefully and give a time limit to the end of the planning time.
- Ask students to role-play the interview in their pairs.
- After these role-plays do error correction from all the interviews.

Exercise 9c
- Students reflect on how well they answered questions in the interviews.
- You could put them into small groups to discuss which questions were easy and difficult.
- Conduct class feedback.

Unit 12

12.5 Video

Personal Assistant

VIDEOSCRIPT

I Liz Conibere works at Cranfield School of Management as a Personal Assistant to the International Development Director and also as the Administrator for International Development.

L The tasks I perform tend to fall into two areas. There are the tasks, the traditional PA-related tasks and these include things like organizing travel for my boss. This can be booking flights, making hotel reservations, setting up meetings for him, sorting out his insurance, his currency needs.
The other half of my job as the International Development Administrator, I do have more involvement there with organizing the main study tours that the students go on in June each year.

I What do you do on a typical day?

L When I first come in, obviously there's the normal tasks, mainly checking emails and things these days and responding to those. And then maybe if my boss is in – he doesn't always come into the office – if he's in, I would normally meet up with him to discuss anything that needs to be done, particularly, maybe he has travel to organize. And then I just have to get on really and do the work.

I What do you like about your job?

L I do like the atmosphere that revolves around the university. There's always something going on. It's very buzzy and the atmosphere is always quite positive. We have a lot of international students, more than 50% probably now, so it's always interesting to meet people from different cultures as well.

I What do you dislike about your job?

L There aren't many things that I dislike, I really enjoy the job generally. Sometimes it's difficult to get things done quickly. You have to get several people to sign things or to authorize things and sometimes this can take a while. So sometimes if you have something urgent it can be a problem to get things sorted out quickly.

VIDEO ANSWERS

1 book a flight   make a hotel reservation   set up a meeting   check email   sign a document

3 a She is a personal assistant, and administrator.
   b The atmosphere at the university / meeting people from different cultures
   c Things don't always happen quickly.

4 a T   b DS   c F   d T   e F   f DS   g T

Review

ANSWERS

Exercise 1a
1 've lived
2 haven't had
3 haven't eaten
4 've been
5 've known
6 've had

Exercise 2b
easy to give
important to find
on cards to help
images to get
questions to get
try not to give too
people really need to know
remember to breathe slowly

Exercise 3a
PA – administration
judge – law
builder – construction
scientist – medical research
software developer – IT
nurse – health care

Exercise 4 12.9
1 No 2 No 3 Yes 4 Yes 5 Yes 6 Yes 7 No
8 Yes 9 No

AUDIOSCRIPT 12.9
1 Does an accountant work in a court?
2 Do you pay a client to do work for you?
3 Does a medical researcher work in a laboratory?
4 If you recruit somebody, do you give them a job?
5 If you fill in a form, are you doing paperwork?
6 If you advise someone, do you tell them what they should do?
7 If your desk is in a mess, is it tidy?
8 If you manage a team, are you in charge of the team?
9 If you are in trouble with your boss, is he or she pleased with you?

Exercise 5
1 entertain
2 a report
3 train
4 attend
5 managed

Exercise 6a
1 in; e
2 as; c
3 at; a
4 to; b
5 into; d

Unit 12 201

Photocopiable worksheets: contents

Grammar: Teacher's notes

Unit 1	203
Unit 2	203
Unit 3	203
Unit 4	204
Unit 5	204
Unit 6	205
Unit 7	205
Unit 8	205
Unit 9	206
Unit 10	206
Unit 11	207
Unit 12	207

Grammar: Worksheets

Unit 1	208
Unit 2	209
Unit 3	210
Unit 4	211
Unit 5	212
Unit 6	213
Unit 7	214
Unit 8	215
Unit 9	216
Unit 10	217
Unit 11	218
Unit 12	219

Vocabulary: Teacher's notes

Unit 1	220
Unit 2	220
Unit 3	221
Unit 4	221
Unit 5	222
Unit 6	222
Unit 7	223
Unit 8	223
Unit 9	224
Unit 10	224
Unit 11	225
Unit 12	225

Vocabulary: Worksheets

Unit 1	226
Unit 2	227
Unit 3	228
Unit 4	229
Unit 5	230
Unit 6	231
Unit 7	232
Unit 8	233
Unit 9	234
Unit 10	235
Unit 11	236
Unit 12	237

Communication: Teacher's notes

Unit 1	238
Unit 2	238
Unit 3	239
Unit 4	239
Unit 5	240
Unit 6	240
Unit 7	241
Unit 8	241
Unit 9	242
Unit 10	242
Unit 11	243
Unit 12	243

Communication: Worksheets

Unit 1	244
Unit 2	245
Unit 3	246
Unit 4	247
Unit 5	248
Unit 6	249
Unit 7	250
Unit 8	251
Unit 9	252
Unit 10	253
Unit 11	254
Unit 12	255

Vox pops

Teacher's notes	256–258
Worksheets	259–264

Grammar

Unit 1 Three questions, three answers

Paired activity, completing questions with appropriate question words, and matching questions and answers to form short conversations

Language
Question words: *are, did, do, how, what, when, where, which, who*

Preparation: Make one copy of the worksheet for each pair.

1 Review question words by eliciting questions with the question word at the beginning. With the exception of *are* and *do* (which can only be used in the present), the questions can refer to the present or the past. Write the questions on the board, correcting any mistakes. When you have done this, erase everything from the board.
2 Divide the class into pairs. Give a copy of the worksheet to each pair, and go through the example questions and answers in the shaded cells. There are three questions and three answers based on the same topic, which, when put together, form a short conversation. Point out that each question and answer following on from question 1 has been given the number 1. Model the conversation by asking one student to read the shaded questions and one student to read the shaded answers.
3 Students decide on the question word that starts each question, then match questions and answers, numbering them to show the flow of each conversation.
4 The first pair to correctly complete all of the questions and match them to the answers is the winner.

ANSWERS

2 **How** often do you go out for dinner? *Usually once a week.* **What** kind of food do you like the most? *Chinese.* **Where** do you usually go to eat? *A very good restaurant called Sojo.*
3 **How** much did your last mobile phone cost? *Nothing. It was free with a contract.* **Where** did you get it? *From a shop in town.* **What** do you like about it? *It's very simple to use.*
4 **How** many close friends have you got? *Just two.* **How** often do you meet them? *Three or four times a week.* **What** do you usually do together? *We go to the cinema or a restaurant.*
5 **Do** you like travelling? *Yes, I love seeing different places.* **When** did you last go somewhere interesting? *Last summer.* **Where** did you go? *A lovely island called Santorini.*
6 **What** time do you usually leave home for work or college? *At about eight o'clock.* **How** do you get there? *I take a train and then a bus.* **Are** you usually on time? *Yes, but sometimes I'm a bit late.*
7 **Which/What** sport do you like the most? *I really enjoy tennis.* **Do** you have a favourite player? *Yes, a Spanish player called Rafael Nadal.* **What** do you like about him? *He's so good at what he does.*
8 **Did** you have a nice weekend? *Yes, it was great, thank you.* **Did** you do anything interesting or exciting? *No, nothing special.* **Who** did you spend time with? *Just my family.*

Unit 2 Relative clauses game

Group activity, describing people, places and things using relative clauses

Language
Relative clauses: *It's a person who/that …, It's a place where/that …, It's a thing which/that you use … + infinitive, It's a thing which/that you use for … + -ing*

Preparation: Make one copy of the worksheet for each group (maximum of six students per group). Cut up the sheets so that there is one wordlist for each student.

Non-cut alternative: Make one copy of the worksheet for each student and fold the sheets so that only one wordlist is showing. Tell students not to look at the other lists.

1 Write *Richard Branson* on the board and tell students to describe him using a relative clause, e.g. *He's a businessman who/that founded the Virgin Group.* Write *Sydney* on the board and repeat the process, e.g. *It's a place where you can see a famous opera house.* Write *car* on the board and repeat the process, e.g. *It's a thing which/that you use to get/for getting from your home to your office.* Write all the example sentences on the board.
2 Divide the class into groups. Give each group member a different wordlist. Allow students five minutes to read through their list and ask for clarification of any words they don't know or any vocabulary they might need to describe those words. They should also add two words of their own to the bottom of their list.
3 Tell students that they each have different wordlists. Explain that they must take turns to describe one word on their list, using a relative clause, for the other students in the group to guess. The student describing the word must write the name of the person who first guesses correctly in the 'Winner's name' column on their wordlist.
4 When students have finished, they add up how many times each person's name appears on all the players' wordlists to find the overall winner.

Unit 3 A new hobby

Paired activity, completing and numbering sentences to create a story

Language
Past simple: regular verbs (*jumped, moved, watched*, etc.) and irregular verbs (*began, fell, got*, etc.)
Pronunciation: *-ed* in regular past simple verbs

Preparation: Make one copy of the worksheet for each pair and cut the sheets in half.

Grammar 203

Non-cut alternative: Make one copy of the worksheet for each student and fold the sheets in half. Tell students to look at exercise 1 or 2, as appropriate.

1 Write the following verbs on the board: *climb, drop, shout, come, fall, send*. Ask students what the difference is between the first three and the last three verbs (the first three are regular; the last three are irregular). Elicit the past forms of these verbs and focus on the pronunciation of the endings of the regular verbs (/d/ for *climbed*, /t/ for *dropped* and /ɪd/ for *shouted*).

2 Divide the class into pairs and give them a copy of the first section of the worksheet. Give the pairs five minutes to look at the illustrations and discuss what is happening in each one. Then ask for feedback, or prompt them by asking questions (e.g. *Where is the teenage girl in the first illustration? How does she look? How old do you think she is in the second illustration? Where is she?*).

3 Focus on the illustration that shows the man climbing the building and explain that this is called *urban free climbing*. Ask students what they think this involves.

4 Give each pair the second section of the worksheet. Working together, students complete the sentences with the correct past simple form of the verbs in brackets, and number the sentences in order (1–16), using the illustrations in exercise 1 as a guide. In some cases, there may be more than one possible answer.

5 Give students fifteen minutes, then review the answers. In pairs, students read the story to each other. They should pay particular attention to the pronunciation of the *-ed* ending in the regular verbs.

> **POSSIBLE ANSWER**
> 1 g (grew) 2 j (moved) 3 d (didn't like) 4 m (was)
> 5 p (didn't sleep) 6 a (got) 7 o (made) 8 f (worked)
> 9 h (did) 10 k (climbed) 11 b (jumped) 12 e (needed)
> 13 n (decided) 14 l (began) 15 c (fell) 16 i (landed)

Unit 4 Let's get together

Group activity, completing diary entries and making arrangements for the future

> **Language**
> Future structures: *going to*, present continuous

Preparation: Make one copy of the worksheet for each student.

1 Write the following two sentences on the board:
I'm working/going to work on my project next week.
I'm meeting/going to meet Jo at six o'clock tonight.
Ask students to decide which of the underlined structures in the sentences can be used, and which is the best structure. (They both can; *going to work* is better in the first sentence because it is a plan or intention, and *meeting* is better in the second sentence because it has a fixed time.)

2 Divide the class into groups (maximum of four students per group). Give each student a copy of the worksheet. Tell them to decide who in their group is student 1, student 2, etc.

3 Give them five minutes to independently make notes (not complete sentences) in their diary about the activities they are going to do next week. Some activities should include a time, and they should leave five spaces blank. There is an example to guide them.

4 Tell students that they want to meet their friends next week. Working together in their groups, but without looking at one another's entries, give students fifteen minutes to try and find as many times as possible during the week when they can meet. They should do this by asking one another if they are free at various times (e.g. *Karel, are you free on Monday morning?*) and answering in the affirmative or negative (*Yes, I am. / No, I'm sorry, I'm not.*). For each negative answer, they should also give a reason, using the present continuous or *going to* (e.g. *I'm playing/going to play tennis with Carmelita.*). Students should fill in the other diaries on their own worksheet with the activities their partners are doing. It is possible that groups will find that there are no times during the week when they are all free. In this case, they should try to persuade their partners to reschedule some of their plans (e.g. *Karel, could you postpone your tennis game with Carmelita?*).

5 Tell the groups to stop and ask them how they got on. Did any of them find a time when they could all meet? Are any of them able to meet more than once?

Unit 5 Money talks

Paired activity, completing sentences and matching them to form short conversations

> **Language**
> Quantifiers for uncountable and plural countable nouns: *a few, many, much*, etc.

Preparation: Make one copy of the worksheet for each pair.

1 Write the following on the board: *any, enough, a few, a little, many, much, some*. Ask students to produce sentences with them, focusing on whether the nouns they describe are countable or uncountable.

2 Ask students to brainstorm words related to money and write them on the board. Make sure they include the following: *account, afford, balance, bills, borrow, cash, coins, debt, lend, owe, pay, rent, save*; if they don't, elicit them through examples and paraphrasing cues, or refer students to Unit 5.2 in the Coursebook.

3 Divide the class into pairs. Give a copy of the worksheet to each pair. Explain that the worksheet contains five different conversations between speakers A and B. The numbered sentences at the top show the beginning of each conversation. Students first decide on the quantifiers and money vocabulary from the box to complete the sentences, then complete the grid at the bottom of the worksheet with the correct letters to show the flow of each conversation. Remind students to be careful, because a sentence may appear to follow on from another, but may not fit in with the rest of the conversation.

4 The first pair to correctly complete all of the sentences and match them is the winner. Alternatively, set a time limit of fifteen to twenty minutes, then ask the class to stop and review their answers. The pair with the most correctly completed sentences and matches is the winner (1 point for each correctly completed sentence, 1 point for each correct match).

ANSWERS

A	B	A	B
1 (lend)	e (owe)	g (enough)	m (pay)
2 (much)	a (save)	i (borrow)	o (debt)
3 (afford)	d (pay)	j (many)	n (some)
4 (any)	b (cash)	f (few)	k (coins)
5 (bills)	c (rent)	h (balance/account)	l (account/balance)

Unit 6 Comparisons
Group activity, planning a party

> **Language**
> Adjectives (superlative and comparative forms): *bad, boring, easy, enjoyable, fast, good, happy, interesting, lazy, loud, quick, quiet, relaxed*

Preparation: Make one copy of the worksheet for each student.

1 Elicit the comparative and superlative forms of the adjectives in the *Language* box and write them on the board for reference during the activity.
2 Divide the class into groups (of any odd number). Give each student a copy of the worksheet. Tell students to independently complete exercise 1, then compare answers in their group to see how their responses differ, and if the statements are grammatically correct.
3 Tell the class that for exercise 2, they are going to organize a party in their groups. The prompts in the squares are the options that they must discuss and decide upon. For each square, students give their preference and a reason, using a sentence with comparatives/superlatives. Because they are in groups with an odd number, they can go for a majority vote if they cannot decide on an option.
4 Once all the decisions about the party have been made, students explain to the rest of the class about the kind of party they are going to organize.

Unit 7 Big changes
Group activity, predicting how a city will/might change in order to make it more attractive

> **Language**
> Predictions: *might, might not, probably won't, will, won't, will probably*, etc.

Preparation: Make one copy of the worksheet for each group (maximum of three students per group) and cut the sheets in half. You will also need some spare paper for each group.

Non-cut alternative: Make one copy of the worksheet for each group and fold the sheets in half. Tell students to look at exercises 1 and 2 or exercise 3, as appropriate.

1 Ask students to think about the college/university/school where they are studying English, and ask them what makes it an attractive place for the students who study there, and the teachers and other staff who work there. Also ask them if there is anything that makes it unattractive for those same people.
2 Tell students to imagine that the people who run the college/university/school have decided to spend a lot of money on improving it. What changes do they think they will/might make? Elicit and write on the board one sentence for each future prediction, using *might, might not, probably won't, will, won't, will probably*.
3 Divide the class into groups, giving them a copy of the first section of the worksheet and a spare sheet of paper. Give the groups between five and ten minutes to discuss the problems they can see in the illustration, paraphrasing where they don't know the exact words. Ask them about some of the problems they can see.
4 Tell them to imagine that the city council (the group of people who run the city or a city department) are going to make some changes that will make the city a more attractive place for visitors, residents and local businesses. Give students ten minutes to write, on the separate sheet of paper, all the changes that they think the council will/might implement. They should also try to explain why (e.g. *I think the council will probably close the main street to traffic to make it a safer place for shoppers.*). Ask for feedback.
5 Give each group the second section of the worksheet. Ask them to look at the illustration to see what changes the council has made. Elicit sentences describing these changes. (This is an opportunity to review the present perfect simple from Unit 6 in the Coursebook, e.g. *The council has closed the main street to traffic.*)

Unit 8 A little learning
Paired/Group activity, completing puzzles with words to reveal a mystery phrase

> **Language**
> Obligation, necessity and permission: *can, can't, didn't have to, don't have to, had to, have to, must, mustn't*

Preparation: Make one copy of the worksheet for each pair and cut the sheets in half.

Non-cut alternative: Make one copy of the worksheet for each student and fold the sheets in half. Tell students not to look at the other halves.

1 Write the following headings in columns on the board: *school subjects, exams, general education*. Ask students to think of words/phrases to go under each heading, then ask them to give you a sentence with each one. They should try to use the language of obligation, necessity and permission wherever possible (e.g. *We didn't have to wear a uniform at school.*). Continue for ten minutes, then erase the words on the board.
2 Divide the class into groups (four students per group) and sub-divide each group into pairs. Allocate each pair a letter (A or B) and give them the relevant half of the worksheet. They should not show this to the other pair. Pair A defines the words/phrases on their worksheet (a–j) or says gapped sentences, avoiding saying the words/phrases. Give the following example: for *career*, they could say, *This is a job or series of jobs that you do throughout your life. / If you want a good [blank], you have to work hard at school and college*. Wherever possible, they should try to use *can, can't, didn't have to, don't have to, had to, have to, must, mustn't*. Pair B listens, decides what the word/phrase is and completes the corresponding row in the puzzle.

3 The pairs then swap roles, with pair B defining the words/phrases on their worksheet (1–10) or saying gapped sentences, and pair A completing their puzzle. While they are doing this, write the following sentence on the board: *My college/university/school uses a system of _____ instead of exams to decide how well students are performing.*

4 When both pairs have completed their puzzles, explain that the letters in the shaded spaces in both pair A and B's puzzles form a mystery two-word phrase connected with education. This phrase can be used to complete the sentence you have written on the board. The winning group is the first one to work out what that phrase is. Encourage them to decide what it means from the context.

ANSWER
continuous assessment (a system in which the quality of students' work is judged by coursework and not by exams)

Unit 9 Before we start, …
Independent/Paired activity, completing sentences with correct verb forms and discussing answers

Language
Present simple in future time clauses
Time clauses: After / As soon as / Before / If / When + present simple + will
Future with will

Preparation: Make one copy of the worksheet for each student.

1 Give each student a copy of the worksheet and tell them to complete the sentences (1–8) and questions (9–14) with the correct form of the verbs in brackets, and any further information needed to personalize the sentences.

2 Check answers together as a class.

ANSWERS
1 Before I **go** home today, I [student's own answer (future with *will*)].
2 My colleagues/friends might [student's own answer (simple infinitive)] soon if [student's own answer (present simple)].
3 When my brother/sister/boyfriend/girlfriend **saves up** enough money, [student's own answer (future with *will*)].
4 My colleagues/friends **won't be** pleased if [student's own answer (present simple)].
5 If I/my brother/my sister **wake(s) up** late on Sunday, [student's own answer (future with *will*)].
6 As soon as I **get up** on Saturday, [student's own answer (future with *will*)].
7 Our teacher might [student's own answer (simple infinitive)] after we [student's own answer (present simple)].
8 When this lesson **finishes**, we [student's own answer (future with *will*)].
9 What **will you do** when you **get** home this evening?
10 After you **finish** this English course, what **will you do**?
11 What **will you do** if you **don't go out** this evening?
12 As soon as you **wake up** on Saturday morning, what **will you do**?
13 If you **eat out** this weekend, what kind of food **will you choose**?
14 If it **rains** tomorrow, how **will you get** to work/college?

3 Write the following on the board: *Before I go home today, I'll tidy my desk.* Ask if any students have written the same for sentence 1. Ask a couple of students to read out their sentences, and elicit appropriate comments, e.g. *Me too! Oh, not me. I won't do that.*

4 Write the following on the board: *What will you do when you get home this evening? Watch TV or do your English homework?* Ask a student the question. Encourage all plausible replies, writing a few on the board, e.g. *I'll definitely/I definitely won't/I might do my English homework. / Neither will I. / I won't do either because I'm staying at a friend's house. / I think I'll be late home tonight.*

5 Divide the class into pairs and encourage them to compare their statements, ask each other their questions and continue the conversation as naturally as possible.

6 Once the pairs have finished, elicit feedback from students as a whole class. Ask them to report on what their partner said to them, including any similarities or differences, etc.

Unit 10 Food facts follow-on
Paired activity, listening to facts and matching them to follow-on sentences, which students complete

Language
Passive voice: *are eaten, was grown,* etc.

Preparation: Make one copy of the worksheet for each pair and cut the sheets in half.

Non-cut alternative: Make one copy of the worksheet for each student and fold the sheets in half. Tell students not to look at the other halves.

1 Write the following verbs and gapped facts on the board:
eat, grow, invent, name
Over 7,000 varieties of apple _____ around the world.
More than 3 billion pizzas _____ by people in the USA each year.
The colour orange _____ after the fruit.
The ice lolly _____ by a boy called Frank Epperson in 1905.

2 Ask students to complete the facts with the correct form of the verbs (*are grown, are eaten, was named, was invented*). Then ask students what these sentences all have in common (they all use the passive voice – the first two are present; the last two are past). Ask students why the second and fourth sentences have the word *by* in them (because it tells us who does/did the action).

3 Divide the class into pairs, giving them a copy of the first section of the worksheet.

4 Tell students to look at the sentences in exercise 1 (a–l), and explain that each one follows on from a fact about food that you are going to read to them. Give the pairs ten minutes to discuss what information they think preceded each sentence, and see if there are any they can complete with the passive form of the verbs in the box. Once they have done this (it does not matter if they have not completed all of their sentences), tell them to cross out four sentences. They can delete any four they like, but it will be to their advantage to cross out four sentences that they have not completed.

5 Explain that they are now going to play a bingo-style game with their remaining sentences. Read out facts 1–12 in exercise 5, including the number. Students listen and

206

decide if any of their remaining sentences can follow on from these facts. If so, they write the appropriate number (1–12) in the boxes. If they haven't already done so, they also complete the sentences with the appropriate passive form of the verbs. Pause for a minute between facts to allow students time to do this and discuss their answers. When they have completed all eight of their sentences, they shout *Finished!* The first pair to shout out is the winner. Check answers as a class. If they have made any mistakes, the game continues.

ANSWERS
1 h (was/were grown)   2 c (is used)   3 j (are eaten)
4 e (was, served)   5 l (was, invented)   6 a (was, advertised)
7 i (are believed)   8 k (are transported)   9 f (are thrown)
10 b (is obtained)   11 d (is, used)   12 g (are employed)

6 Give each of the pairs a copy of the second section of the worksheet (or ask them to unfold it). Ask students to read the facts and review their answers.
7 Working in the same pairs, students think of and write new ways of following on from the facts. If possible, their new follow-on sentences should include a passive form.

Unit 11 For the greater good
Group activity, discussing how an interest could lead to a sequence of events that would make the world a better place in some way

Language
if + past tense + *would*: *If you worked harder, you would get better results*, etc.

Preparation: Make one copy of the worksheet for each group (maximum of three students per group).

1 On the board, write the following: *If more people grew their own fruit and vegetables, …* Ask students to give you a few examples of how this sentence could be finished using a second conditional clause (e.g. *they would be healthier.*).
2 Divide the class into groups. Give each group a copy of the worksheet and ask them to complete the sentences 1–10 in exercise 1 with words from the boxes (there are two examples given). In each case, the sentences follow on from each other in a cause-and-effect sequence.
3 Students continue to do this until the first group finishes. At this point, review the answers (one or more students can read out the sentences) and point out that the small action at the beginning (growing your own fruit and vegetables) leads to a big result at the end (the world being a more peaceful place).

ANSWERS
1 wouldn't become, were   2 didn't become, wouldn't have to   3 could spend, didn't have to
4 spent, would learn   5 learnt, could find
6 found, would earn   7 could give, earned
8 gave, would have   9 had, would be   10 were, would be

4 Students look at exercise 2. In their groups, they tell each other about one or two of their own interests. They then agree on one of these, and write it in the gap in the initial sentence.
5 Then give them fifteen to twenty minutes to work together to write a sequence of cause-and-effect sentences similar to those in exercise 1. The aim is to create a series of linking benefits which in some way (no matter how improbable or unlikely) will make the world a better place. Some groups will be able to come up with a lot of linked benefits, and others will not. If two groups run out of ideas, they could get together and exchange ideas about the things they wrote, helping each other to add more benefits.
6 When they have all finished, students read out their benefits to the rest of the class and try to persuade them that the interest they chose is the best way of making the world a better place. To make this more interesting, the other groups can challenge them if they think that some of the benefits are unlikely or impossible. The class can then vote on the interest that (if more people did it) would be the best one for making the world a better place.

Unit 12 Do you know your partner?
Paired activity, with students completing information about their partner, then asking questions to check how well they know each other

Language
Present perfect: *How long have you …? I've had … since/for …*
Past simple: *When did you buy …? When did you last …?*

Preparation: Make one copy of the worksheet for each student.

1 Tell students you are going to test them on how well they know each other, now that they have been studying together for some time. Demonstrate with a confident student, writing on the board: *[Student's name] has lived in his/her current house for thirteen years*. Ask the rest of the class if they think you are right. Ask the student, *How long have you lived in your current house?* and elicit from them if you were right or wrong.
2 Divide the class into pairs. Give each student a copy of the worksheet. Ask them to independently complete the information about their partner, without conferring. Tell students they are not expected to know all the answers and can guess any information they don't know. Where there are options to choose from, students should select one option only.
3 Once students have completed their sentences, ask them to spend a minute thinking about the questions they will need to ask their partners to find out the information. At this point, students can work together in groups to brainstorm questions (but not with the partner they have written about).
4 Students then get back into their pairs and take turns to ask each other questions. Encourage them to verify their ideas through questioning without looking at their worksheets. Monitor and correct while students are talking.
5 At the end of the activity, students count how many statements they guessed correctly and give themselves a score out of ten on how well they know their partner. Encourage feedback from the whole class, and see who scored the highest.

Grammar   207

1 Grammar Three questions, three answers

1. Work with a partner. Complete the questions in A–C with the correct question word (*are, did, do, how, what, when, where, which, who*).

2. Match the questions to the answers to make eight conversations.

Questions A

1 _What_ kind of films do you like?	2 _____ often do you go out for dinner?	3 _____ much did your last mobile phone cost?	4 _____ many close friends have you got?
5 _____ you like travelling?	6 _____ time do you usually leave home for work or college?	7 _____ sport do you like the most?	8 _____ you have a nice weekend?

Answers A

Nothing. It was free with a contract.	Yes, I love seeing different places.	Usually once a week.	Yes, it was great, thank you.
I really enjoy tennis.	I'm very fond of comedies. **1**	Just two.	At about eight o'clock.

Questions B

_____ did you last go somewhere interesting?	_____ you do anything interesting or exciting?	_____ often do you meet them?	_____ you have a favourite player?
_____ do you get there?	_____ did you get it?	_When_ did you last go to the cinema? **1**	_____ kind of food do you like the most?

Answers B

From a shop in town.	I take a train and then a bus.	Last night. **1**	No, nothing special.
Last summer.	Three or four times a week.	Chinese.	Yes, a Spanish player called Rafael Nadal.

Questions C

_____ do you like about it?	_____ do you like about him?	_____ you usually on time?	_____ do you usually do together?
_____ did you spend time with?	_____ do you usually go to eat?	_Do_ you go there a lot? **1**	_____ did you go?

Answers C

A lovely island called Santorini.	A very good restaurant called Sojo.	He's so good at what he does.	Yes, I try to see the latest films. **1**
We go to the cinema or a restaurant.	Just my family.	It's very simple to use.	Yes, but sometimes I'm a bit late.

Navigate B1 Teacher's Guide   208   Photocopiable © Oxford University Press 2015

2 Grammar Relative clauses game

Wordlist 1	Winner's name
website	
Japan	
Jackie Chan	
politician	
son	
camping	
smartphone	
aerobics	

Wordlist 2	Winner's name
Brazil	
library	
street performer	
thief	
niece	
sushi	
computer games	
suncream	

Wordlist 3	Winner's name
school	
the moon	
Mickey Mouse	
engineer	
mother	
Facebook	
rocket	
homework	

Wordlist 4	Winner's name
cinema	
motorway	
vet	
pavement artist	
cousin	
tablet	
karate	
rubbish	

Wordlist 5	Winner's name
Mars	
beach	
lawyer	
wife	
clown	
camera	
pen	
bicycle	

Wordlist 6	Winner's name
park	
Switzerland	
child	
police officer	
Johnny Depp	
washing machine	
rubber	
TV	

3 Grammar A new hobby

1 Work with a partner. Discuss what you think is happening in the illustrations.

---

2 Complete the sentences with the past simple form of the verbs in brackets.
Put the sentences in the right order (1–16) using the illustrations in exercise **1**.

a I _____ a job in an office near my home. (get)
b Sometimes he even _____ from building to building. (jump)
c Sometimes I _____ , but not very far. (fall)
d I _____ it there. (not/like)
e I _____ a hobby. (need)
f He _____ in the same department as me. (work)
g I ____grew____ up in a small village in the countryside. (grow) [1]
h He _____ an unusual activity called 'urban free climbing'. (do)
i Fortunately, I always _____ on my feet! (land)
j I _____ to London. (move)
k He _____ up buildings as if they were mountains. (climb)
l I _____ with small buildings. (begin)
m It _____ crowded, dirty and noisy. (be)
n So I _____ to join him. (decide)
o I _____ friends with one of my colleagues. (make)
p With all the noise, I _____ well at night. (not/sleep)

4 Grammar Let's get together

1 Work in small groups. What is each of you going to do next week? Make notes in your diary page.
   Write times for some of the activities. Leave five spaces blank.

Example

	Morning	Afternoon	Evening
Monday	tennis with Carmelita (9.30 a.m.)		cinema with Mark
Tuesday		shopping with friends	gym
Wednesday	visit travel agency to book holiday		Mozart concert at town hall (8.30 p.m.)
Thursday		coffee with Mum (3.15 p.m.)	
Friday	dentist (10 a.m.)	call Keira	dinner with David and Amy (7.30 p.m.)

Student 1

	Morning	Afternoon	Evening
Monday			
Tuesday			
Wednesday			
Thursday			
Friday			

Student 2

	Morning	Afternoon	Evening
Monday			
Tuesday			
Wednesday			
Thursday			
Friday			

Student 3

	Morning	Afternoon	Evening
Monday			
Tuesday			
Wednesday			
Thursday			
Friday			

Student 4

	Morning	Afternoon	Evening
Monday			
Tuesday			
Wednesday			
Thursday			
Friday			

2 Arrange a time to meet with your group.

5 Grammar Money talks

1 Work with a partner. Complete speaker A's and speaker B's sentences with words from the box.

account afford any balance bills borrow cash coins debt
enough few lend many much owe pay pay rent save some

2 Match the speakers' sentences in the grid below to make five conversations.

Speaker A

| 1 Could you _____ me £10 until tomorrow? | 2 I need a new car, but even a used one costs too _____ money these days. | 3 I'm afraid I can't _____ to go out tonight. | 4 Have you got _____ money on you? | 5 We got three _____ today – electricity, gas and water! |

Speaker B

| a Well, you'll just have to _____ up for one. | b I don't think so. I gave the last of my _____ to that man who was collecting for charity. Why? | c That's not good news. And the _____ on the flat is due tomorrow. | d Oh, don't worry. I'll _____ for dinner. | e Again? But you already _____ me £20! |

Speaker A

| f We need a _____ things from the supermarket, and I left my purse at home. | g I know, but I don't have _____ money for my bus fare. | h Already? Oh dear. How's our bank _____ at the moment? | i Perhaps I could _____ some money from the bank instead. | j That's really kind of you, but you've paid for too _____ meals out recently. |

Speaker B

| k OK, let me see. No, I've just got a few _____ . Nothing else. | l I'm not sure. I'll go online and check our _____ . | m OK, but only if you promise to _____ me back tomorrow. | n But we need to celebrate your promotion. And when you've got _____ money, you can take me out. | o They'll just say no. You're already heavily in _____ . |

A	B	A	B
1	e		
2			
3			
4			
5			

Navigate B1 Teacher's Guide   Photocopiable © Oxford University Press 2015

6 Grammar Comparisons

1   Complete the sentences with your own ideas.
   1   Having a party with friends is _____ than having a party with family.
   2   The most/least _____ part of a party is the preparation.
   3   The _____ part of the party is meeting new friends.
   4   Fancy-dress parties are _____ than formal dinner parties.
   5   Weekday parties are as/not as _____ as weekend parties.

2   Work in small groups. Plan a party. For each set of prompts, decide which option you would prefer and explain why, using comparative and superlative adjectives.

pub / restaurant / house	family / friends / family and friends	food / no food	DJ / tablet / live band
weekday / weekend	big budget / small budget	formal dress / casual dress / fancy dress	written invitations / electronic invitations
rock / pop / jazz	afternoon / evening	indoors / outdoors	decorations / no decorations
people can stay overnight / people can't stay overnight	bring your own drinks / provide drinks	party games / no party games	children / no children

7 Grammar Big changes

1 Work in small groups. Look at the illustration. What problems can you see in the city?

2 Read the information. Discuss the changes you think the council will/might make to the city.

> The city council has been given a lot of government money. They want to make the city a better place in order to attract visitors, new residents and businesses.

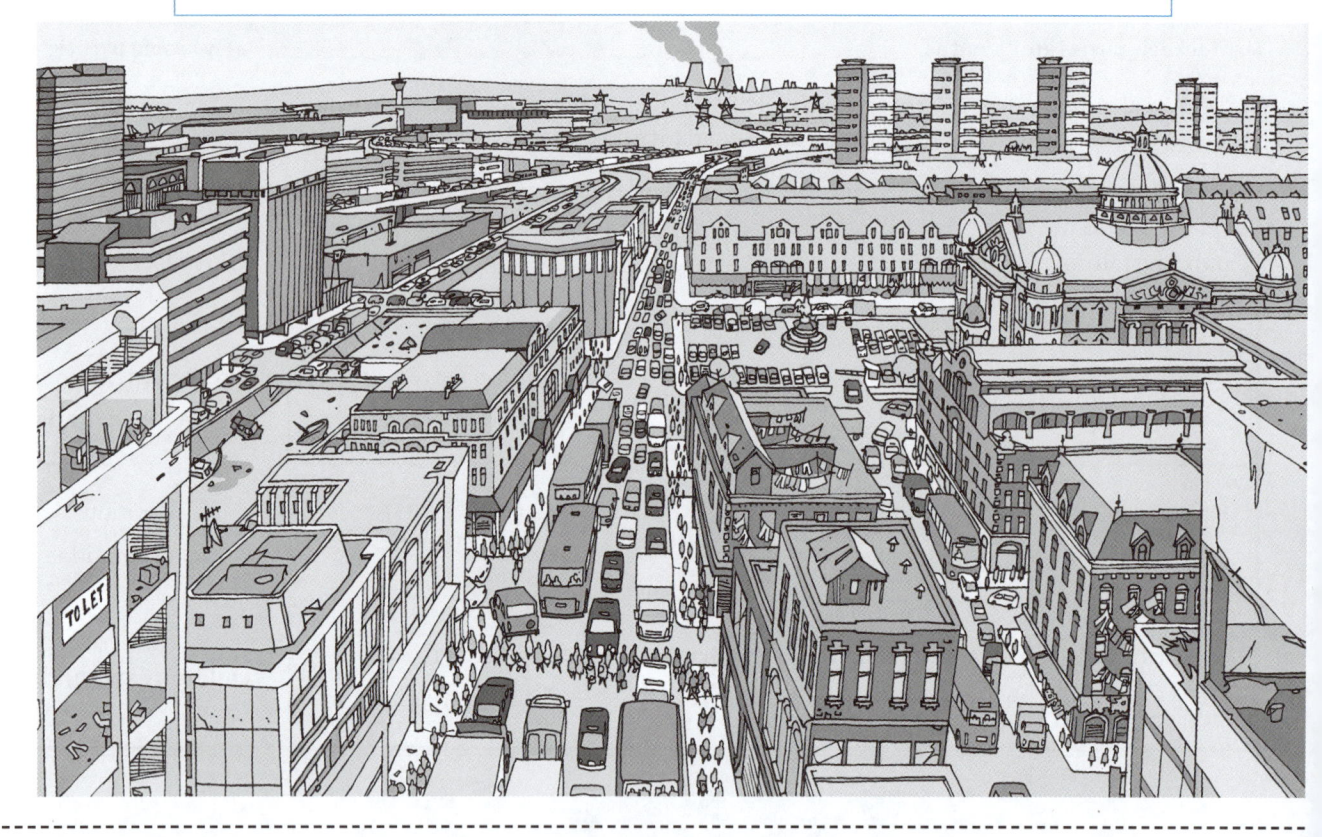

3 It is five years in the future. Look at the illustration. What changes has the council made to the city?

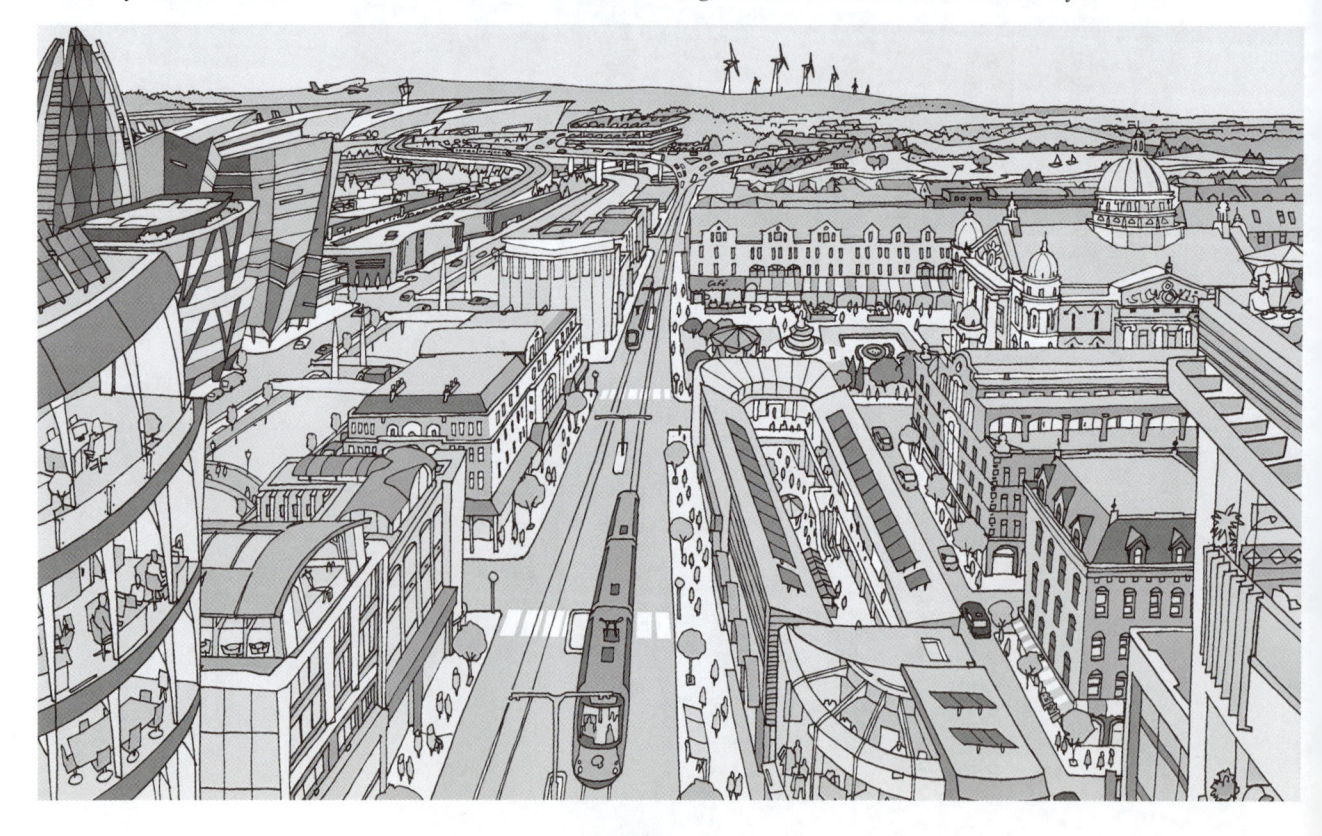

8 Grammar A little learning

Pair A

1. Define the words/phrases (a–j) for pair B, but don't say the words/phrases. Alternatively, use the words/phrases in sentences, but say 'blank' instead of the words/phrases.

   a career   b history   c grades   d success   e physical education
   f science   g drama   h relaxed   i trained   j maths

2. Listen to pair B's definitions or gapped sentences. Complete the puzzle with the words/phrases (1–10).

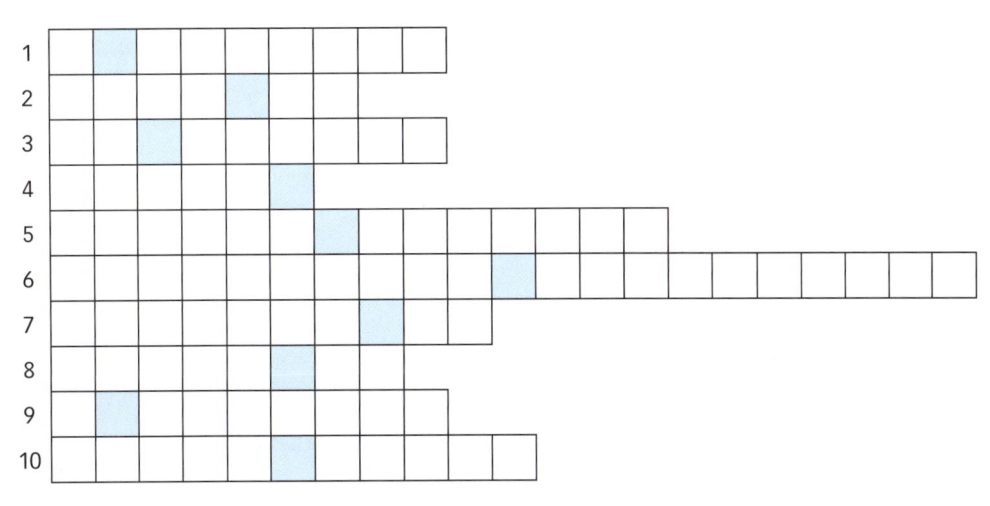

3. Find the mystery phrase.

Pair B

1. Listen to pair A's definitions or gapped sentences. Complete the puzzle with the words/phrases (a–j).

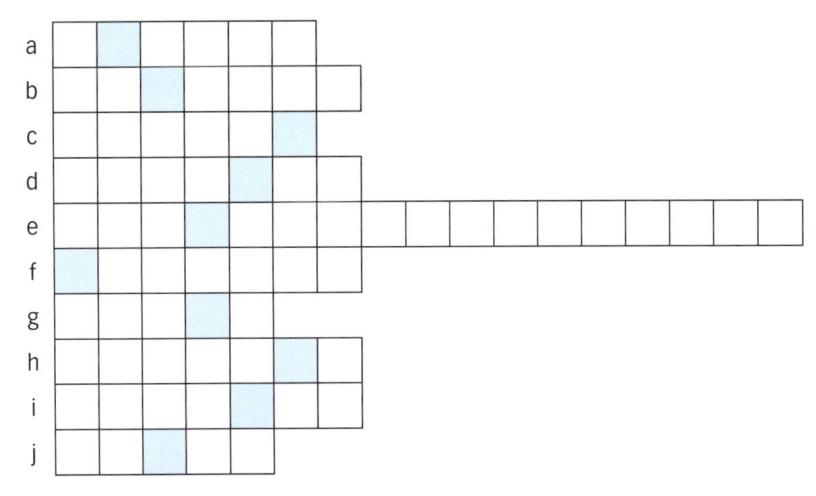

2. Define the words/phrases (1–10) for pair A, but don't say the words/phrases. Alternatively, use the words/phrases in sentences, but say 'blank' instead of the words/phrases.

   1 economics   2 uniform   3 languages   4 strict
   5 qualifications   6 information technology   7 literature
   8 homework   9 qualified   10 state school

3. Find the mystery phrase.

Navigate B1 Teacher's Guide   215   Photocopiable © Oxford University Press 2015

9 Grammar   Before we start, …

1 Complete the sentences (1–8) and questions (9–14) with the correct form of the verbs in brackets and your own ideas.

1 **Before** I _____ (go) home today, I _____ .

2 My colleagues/friends **might** _____ soon **if** _____ .

3 **When** my brother/sister/boyfriend/girlfriend _____ (save up) enough money, _____ .

4 My colleagues/friends _____ (not be) pleased **if** _____ .

5 **If** I/my brother/my sister _____ (wake up) late on Sunday, _____ .

6 **As soon as** I _____ (get up) on Saturday, _____ .

7 Our teacher **might** _____ **after** we _____ .

8 **When** this lesson _____ (finish), we _____ .

9 What _____ (you/do) **when** you _____ (get) home this evening? Watch TV or do your English homework?

10 **After** you _____ (finish) this English course, what _____ (you/do)? Start another one or do something different?

11 What _____ (you/do) **if** you _____ (not go out) this evening? Get a takeaway or cook for yourself?

12 **As soon as** you _____ (wake up) on Saturday morning, what _____ (you/do)? Go back to sleep or jump out of bed straight away?

13 **If** you _____ (eat out) this weekend, what kind of food _____ (you/choose)? Fast food or a traditional meal?

14 **If** it _____ (rain) tomorrow, how _____ (you/get) to work/college? By car or by bus?

2 Work with a partner. Compare your answers. Take turns to ask and answer the questions (9–14).

10 Grammar Food facts follow-on

1 Work with a partner. Read sentences (a–l). They come after facts about food. Discuss what you think these facts are. Complete the follow-on sentences with the correct form of the verbs from the box.

   advertise   believe   eat   employ   grow   invent   obtain   serve   throw   transport   use   use

   a It _____ originally _____ in the newspapers as a medicine. ☐
   b For example, bright red _____ from a small insect called a cochineal beetle. ☐
   c In many cases, white paint _____ instead. ☐
   d It _____ often _____ by Indian farmers to stop elephants eating their crops. ☐
   e However, it was originally very expensive and _____ only _____ in the most expensive restaurants. ☐
   f Around 15 million tonnes of it _____ away in the country each year. ☐
   g Over 1.5 million people around the world _____ there. ☐
   h In 2013, 22 million tonnes of the fruit _____ there. ☐
   i They use these colours because they _____ to make people feel hungry. ☐
   j Most of them _____ while they are still alive. ☐
   k They _____ about 4,000 miles before they reach our supermarkets. ☐
   l Unfortunately, the can opener _____ only _____ forty-eight years later. ☐

2 Cross out four sentences (a–l).

3 Listen to your teacher. Can any of your sentences follow on from the facts?
   Match the facts (1–12) to the follow-on sentences (a–l).

4 Shout *Finished!* when you have matched all eight of your sentences.

----

5 Read your teacher's facts. Write new follow-on sentences.

   1 India produces more bananas than any other country in the world.
      They are eaten in many Indian desserts, but some are also cooked and eaten as a vegetable.
   2 Milk adverts on TV rarely show real milk.
      _____
   3 Oysters are a popular, but expensive, seafood.
      _____
   4 These days, peanut butter is a cheap and popular food.
      _____
   5 A French chef invented the food can at the beginning of the nineteenth century.
      _____
   6 Tomato ketchup first appeared in our shops in the 1830s.
      _____
   7 Most fast-food restaurants have signs that are red, yellow or orange.
      _____
   8 Bananas travel a great distance from their country of origin.
      _____
   9 Many Western countries like the UK have far more food than they need.
      _____
   10 Some food colours and flavours have unusual origins.
      _____
   11 The ghost chilli is one of the world's hottest peppers.
      _____
   12 McDonald's is one of the world's biggest fast-food chains.
      _____

11 Grammar For the greater good

1 Work in small groups. Complete the sentences (1–10) with verbs/verb phrases from boxes A and B.

A

could give   could spend   didn't become   found   gave   ~~grew~~   ~~had~~   had   learnt   spent   were   wouldn't become

B

could find   didn't have to   earned   were   would be   would be   ~~would be~~   would earn   would have   ~~would have~~   would learn   wouldn't have to

One of my interests is growing my own fruit and vegetables. I think more people should do this.

Benefits

If people ____grew____ more of their own fruit and vegetables, they ____would have____ cheap, nutritious food to eat.

If they ____had____ cheap, nutritious food to eat, they ____would be____ healthier.

1 People _____ ill so often if they _____ healthier.
2 If they _____ ill so often, governments _____ spend so much on healthcare.
3 Governments _____ more on education if they _____ spend so much on healthcare.
4 If governments _____ more on education, people _____ more and get better qualifications.
5 If people _____ more and got better qualifications, they _____ better jobs.
6 If they _____ better jobs, they _____ more money.
7 They _____ more money to charity if they _____ more money.
8 If they _____ more money to charity, poorer people _____ a better quality of life.
9 If those people _____ a better quality of life, they _____ happier.
10 If more people _____ happier, the world _____ a more peaceful place.

2 Discuss your interests with your group. Choose an interest and complete the sentence. Write sentences (1–12).

One of our interests is _____ . We think more people should do this.

Benefits

1 _____
2 _____
3 _____
4 _____
5 _____
6 _____
7 _____
8 _____
9 _____
10 _____
11 _____
12 _____

12 Grammar Do you know your partner?

1 Complete the sentences about your partner. Write the correct form of the verbs in brackets.

    Ana has lived (live) in his/~~her~~ current house for _four_ ~~years~~/months.
1 _____ (live) in his/her current house for _____ years/months.
2 _____ (work/study) at/in _____ since _____ .
3 _____ (not eat) chocolate since _____ .
4 _____ (know) his/her best friend for _____ .
5 _____ (have) his/her mobile phone/watch for _____ .
6 _____ (own) his/her bicycle/car for _____ .
7 _____ (know) how to ride a bicycle/roller skate/swim since _____ .
8 _____ (not speak) to his/her mother/father/brother/sister for _____ .
9 _____ (always/want) to _____ since he/she was a child.
10 _____ (not buy) any new clothes since _____ .

2 Work with your partner. Take turns to ask and answer questions.

David has worked in the same office since 2012.

How long have you worked in the same office?

I've worked there since 2012.

Oh good! I'm right!

Karen hasn't eaten chocolate since last Sunday.

When did you last eat chocolate?

I ate some last night.

Oh no! I wrote that you haven't eaten chocolate since last Sunday.

3 Count how many you got right.

Vocabulary

Unit 1 Something in common

Group activity, speaking and writing about free-time activities and daily routine

Language
Free-time activities and daily-routine verbs: *chat with friends online, play sports,* etc.

Preparation: Make one copy of the worksheet for each group (maximum of four students per group).

1 Write the following verbs on the board: *chat, do, eat, go, have, make, play, spend, stay.* Briefly brainstorm activities that can be described with these verbs, e.g. *chat on the internet, do our homework, eat out in restaurants.* Correct any mistakes.

2 Divide the class into groups. Allocate each group a letter (e.g. group A, group B) and give a copy of the worksheet to each group. Explain that, in their groups, they should ask and answer questions to find five activities that they have in common (e.g. five activities that they all *usually* do / *occasionally* do / *do now and then*).

3 Give the groups ten minutes to take turns to write sentences in exercise 2 about these five activities (e.g. *We nearly always spend time with our families at the weekend. We occasionally go to the beach at the weekend.*). (It does not matter if they have not found/written about five things – three or four will be enough.)

4 Students in group A take turns to read their sentences to the other groups, omitting the adverbs or expressions of frequency. The other groups guess how often group A does these things. They write a sentence they think is true about one of the activities in the table in exercise 4.

5 Each group reads out its sentence, and group A tells them if they are right or wrong. Groups win 1 point for each correct sentence.

6 Repeat stages 4 and 5 with the other groups. If there are more than eight groups in the class, they should continue at the bottom of their worksheet. The winning group is the one with the most points when all the groups have had a turn.

Unit 2 Household objects

Paired activity, playing a game using vocabulary for household objects

Language
Household objects: *bed, candle, carpet, chest of drawers, cloth, cooker, dishwasher, dustpan and brush, duvet, fridge, microwave oven, mirror, pan, rug, satellite TV, sheet, sofa, tap, towel, wardrobe, wash basin, washing machine*

Preparation: Make one copy of the worksheet for each pair and cut the sheets in half. You will also need a die and some spare paper for each pair.

Non-cut alternative: Make one copy of the worksheet for each student and fold the sheets in half. Tell students not to look at the other halves.

1 Give each student a piece of spare paper and allow them two minutes to write as many household objects as they can.

2 Go through their objects as a class, giving 1 point for each unique object, e.g. if two students have *sofa,* neither student gets a point. Write objects on the board as you go through the lists to check spelling, and for reference during the activity.

3 Divide the class into pairs and allocate each partner a letter (A or B). Give them the relevant half of the worksheet and ask them to independently draw a household object in each of the nine squares in the left-hand grid. They should not show their sheet to each other.

4 Give each pair a die and explain that if they throw a 1 or a 2, they must mime the object for their partner; if they throw a 3 or a 4, they must draw the object (on the spare paper); and if they throw a 5 or a 6, they must describe the object.

5 Tell student A to throw the die and mime, draw or describe the object in square 1 in their left-hand grid, according to the number they throw. Student B writes down what they think the object is in square 1 of their right-hand grid. Students take turns – they can either swap after they have described each square, or once they have communicated all nine objects in their own grids.

6 When both students have communicated all nine objects, they check to see if their grids match.

Unit 3 Don't hide your feelings

Group activity, acting out situations for others to decide what has happened

> **Language**
> Adjectives for describing feelings: *angry, calm*, etc.

Preparation: Make one copy of the worksheet and cut it into eight cards. You will also need some spare paper for each group.

Non-cut alternative: Make one copy of the worksheet for each group and fold the sheets so that only one role card is showing (a different card for each group). Tell students not to look at the other role cards.

1 Write the following adjectives on the board: *angry, calm, confused, disappointed, embarrassed, excited, exhausted, guilty, lonely, nervous, pleased, stressed*. Briefly review them by asking students to explain what they mean and give examples of when they might experience each of these feelings. If you have time, you could also ask them to say or write a sample sentence for each one (e.g. *I was so angry when Carlos broke my new camera*.). Leave the adjectives on the board for the activity.

2 Divide the class into groups (maximum of four students per group). Give each group a card and a sheet of spare paper. They should make sure that none of the other groups sees or hears what is on the card. Allocate each group a letter (e.g. group A, group B).

3 Explain that each card outlines a different situation. Students must imagine that they are in this situation and act it out in their groups. While they are doing this, they must not say the adjective in bold on the card.

4 The groups take turns to act out their situation, while the other groups watch. After each situation, give the other groups two or three minutes to write a sentence on the spare paper about what they think is happening. They should include one of the adjectives reviewed in stage 1 to describe how the group feels (e.g. *Group A feels nervous because they are lost in a city, and someone is following them*). (Note: There are four adjectives they won't need – and more than four if you don't use all the cards.)

5 When all the groups have acted out their situations, ask each group to say what they thought was happening in each case, and how the groups felt. For each situation correctly guessed, the group who acted it out wins 1 point. Allow for some flexibility here, e.g. the students on the bus going to the airport could also be in a taxi. The winning group is the one with the most points.

Unit 4 A full life

Paired/Whole-class activity, describing life events

> **Language**
> Life stages: *In my mid-twenties …, When I was about thirty …*, etc.
> Life events: *go to university, spend time abroad, start your own business*, etc.

Preparation: Make one copy of the worksheet for each student and fold the sheet between exercises 2 and 3.

1 Ask students to brainstorm the different things that people typically do at various stages in their life (as a child/teenager, when they are in their early/mid-/late twenties, when they are in their thirties, when they are middle-aged). With international/multicultural classes, this may lead to a discussion on differences between countries (e.g. the age at which people get married).

2 Divide the class into pairs, giving each student a copy of the worksheet. Make sure that they only look at exercises 1 and 2. Tell the class to imagine that it is many years in the future, they are elderly and are looking back on their life. Give them ten minutes to tell their partner about the things they have done at various stages in their life, using the phrases in boxes A and B. Encourage them to use their own ideas, too.

3 Students then tell the class about their partner's life. They should do this from memory (although they can refer to the boxes for the life stages and events). Their partner can correct them if they make a mistake (e.g. *I didn't leave home when I was a teenager. I left home in my early twenties*.). The class should listen carefully.

4 When everyone has spoken, tell students to turn over their worksheet so that they can only see exercise 3. In their pairs, they try to remember facts about the other students in the class. They write sentences about ten of the students, including the name of the student they refer to in each one. At this stage, they should not refer back to exercises 1 and 2.

5 Each pair then reports back what they remembered by taking turns to read their sentences. They win 1 point for each correct fact, and an extra point if they added any more information. The winning pair is the one with the most points when all the pairs have had a turn.

6 As a class, students can then discuss who they think had the most interesting, exciting or fulfilling life.

Unit 5 Auction!

Paired activity, selling and buying items auctioned by other students

> **Language**
> Adjectives/Other words and phrases for talking about objects: *ordinary, useful, valuable; It makes me feel happy. Somebody special gave it to me.*, etc.

Preparation: Make one copy of the worksheet for each student. You will also need some spare paper for each student.

1 Divide the board into seven columns, and write the following headings at the top of each column: *age, material, size, weight, shape, colour* and *opinion*.

2 Ask students with mobile phones or smartphones to give you words/phrases that could be used to describe them. Write the words in the appropriate columns on the board.

3 Ask one or two students to describe their phone to you. While they are doing this, draw their attention to any mistakes they make with articles (*a*, *an*, *the* or no article). If necessary, briefly review when to use definite and indefinite articles. Do not focus on any mistakes with the adjective order if students use them in a single sentence.

4 Divide the class into pairs, giving each student a copy of the worksheet. Give students ten minutes to tell their partner about one of their favourite possessions (not a mobile phone or smartphone) and make notes on their partner's favourite possession. Ideally, the possession should have a material value, e.g. an item of jewellery, a car, an antique.

5 Students then make notes about their own possession on the spare paper, after describing it to their partner. Write the word *auction* on the board and elicit the meaning. You could 'auction' one of your own possessions at this stage, to demonstrate how an auction works.

6 Explain to students that they are now going to auction their possessions from exercise 1. Each pair takes turns to try to sell one of their two possessions, and the other pairs in the class should bid for it. This is then repeated for their second possession. They complete rows A and B of the table below exercise 4 when they sell their items. Students should try to buy as many possessions as possible (up to a total of eight items), while keeping as much money as possible. Each pair begins with £500, which reduces the more they buy. They fill in rows 1–8 of the table below exercise 4 with details of the items they buy, how much they paid, and how much money they have left.

7 When all the pairs have had a go at auctioning their items, students work out how many items they have/how much money they have left. The pair with the most items at the end of the auction are the winners. If there is a draw, the winners are the pair who have the most money left.

Unit 6 Speed friendships

Group activity, with students describing themselves using character adjectives

> **Language**
> Character adjectives: *clever/smart, confident, dishonest, hard-working, honest, impatient, lazy, loud, patient, quiet, shy, sociable, stupid, tidy, unsociable, untidy*

Preparation: Make one copy of the worksheet for each student. You will also need a strip of paper for each student and a hat or container.

1 Go around the class asking students to supply character adjectives to describe friends or family members. Write the adjectives on the board.

2 Give each student a strip of paper. Ask them to describe themselves using three of the adjectives from the board and write them on the paper.

3 Put the pieces of paper into a hat. Each student takes a piece of paper and reads out the description. The class must then guess who they think it describes.

4 Give each student a copy of the worksheet. Tell students to match the adjectives in the first column in exercise 1 (1–8) with their opposites in the second column (a–h). Check answers as a class.

ANSWERS
1 d 2 f 3 c 4 h 5 b 6 g 7 a 8 e

5 Assign each student a photo (A–H) from the bottom of the worksheet by whispering the letter to them. Ensure you assign an equal number of men and women. If you have more than eight students, you will need to assign the same photo to two or more students.

6 Tell students to imagine they are the person given and to fill in the profile in exercise 2, pretending to be that person. They can use the adjectives on the board from stage 1, but also encourage them to use their imagination.

7 When everyone has completed their profiles, brainstorm the questions needed in order to elicit the information in the profile. Also elicit questions you could ask when meeting someone for the first time. Write the questions on the board for reference if necessary.

8 Tell students to sit in two circles, with the women (i.e. people who have photos of women) in the inner circle facing out, and the men (i.e. people who have photos of men) in the outer circle facing in, so that everyone has a partner to talk to. (With odd numbers, the person who starts off without a partner can think of some more questions to ask.)

9 Students take on the personality of the photo and profile they have, and talk to the person opposite them for three minutes, asking and answering questions in the form of a conversation. After three minutes, the outer circle rotates so that everyone has a new partner. Repeat this for however many pairs you have. At the end, the 'speed friends' decide who, if anyone, they would like to meet again.

Unit 7   Perfect pairs

Paired activity, completing and matching sentences and appropriate responses

> **Language**
> Holiday vocabulary: *book your flight, choose your accommodation*, etc.

Preparation: Make one copy of the worksheet for each pair and cut the sheets in half.

Non-cut alternative: Make one copy of the worksheet for each student and fold the sheets in half. Tell students not to look at the other halves.

1 Ask students to think of different things they do when they go on holiday (including the preparation, starting from choosing where to go). Brainstorm as many ideas as possible and write their suggestions on the board.

2 Write the following pronouns on the board: *anybody, anything, anywhere, everybody, everything, everywhere, nobody, nothing, nowhere, somebody, something, somewhere*. Tell students to give you an example of each pronoun in a sentence, using a 'holiday' word or phrase from stage 1 (e.g. *We wanted to hire a car, but nobody had their driving licence with them.*). Correct any mistakes.

3 Divide the class into pairs. Allocate each partner a letter (A or B) and give them the relevant half of the worksheet. They should not show their sheet to each other. Student A begins by reading out one of their sentences. Together with student B, they decide which verb in box A can be used to complete it, making sure they use the correct form of the verb.

4 Student B then looks for a response to student A's sentence and reads it out. Together, they decide if it is the correct response. If they both agree, they then decide which pronoun in box B can be used to complete it. The first one has been done as an example.

5 They repeat stages 3 and 4 for the other sentences on their worksheet.

6 The first pair in the class to correctly complete and match all of their sentences is the winner. Alternatively, set a time limit of twenty minutes; the winning pair is the one with the most correctly completed and matched sentences within that time.

ANSWERS
2 (hire) = f (anybody)   3 (go) = g (anywhere)
4 (bought) = k (something)   5 (get) = j (somewhere)
6 (booked/chosen) = a (nothing)   7 (chosen/booked)
= i (everything)   8 (experience) = h (somebody)
9 (done) = b (anything)   10 (trying) = d (everywhere)
11 (explore) = e (nowhere)   12 (lie) = l (nobody)

Unit 8   Robot sales

Group activity, with students trying to sell a robot they have designed by explaining why it is useful

> **Language**
> Skills and abilities: *learning languages, fixing things*, etc.

Preparation: Make one copy of the worksheet for each student and cut the sheets in half.

Non-cut alternative: Make one copy of the worksheet for each student and fold the sheets in half. Tell students not to look at the other halves.

1 Divide the class into groups (maximum of five students per group) and give them a copy of the first section of the worksheet.

2 In their groups, give students ten minutes to rearrange the letters in bold to complete sentences 1–14. They then write two more useful skills or abilities. Review their answers, and ask the groups what other two skills they have written.

ANSWERS
1 reading   2 making   3 learning   4 spelling
5 solving   6 following   7 fixing   8 taking
9 explaining   10 organizing   11 remembering
12 telling   13 understanding   14 making

3 Ask the groups to tick the three skills or abilities (from sentences 1–14) that they think are the most useful.

4 Give students the second section of the worksheet. Explain that they have designed a robot that can do the skills or abilities they ticked in exercise 3 and the two skills they have written (boxes 15 and 16). In their groups, they are going to try and sell their robot to the other groups. At this point, you could give them a specific context (e.g. the groups all run a college/hospital/department store). This will help give their sales talk more of a focus, but may also make it more difficult for them to explain why the skills they have chosen are so important in the next stage of the activity. In their groups, students think of a reason why their robot's skills/abilities are so useful or important (especially in the context you have given them, if you have done so). They write the reason in the relevant spaces in the boxes, e.g. 5 *This is a useful skill because many people have computers and they are always going wrong.*

5 The groups take turns to try and sell their robot to the other groups, explaining its skills and abilities and why they think these are useful. When they have finished, the other groups award them points (1–3), based on the usefulness of the robot's skills. The winning group is the one with the most points at the end of the activity.

Vocabulary   223

Unit 9 What's happening at the park?

Paired activity, spotting the differences between two illustrations and practising the language of actions and parts of the body

Language
Actions: *clap, hug, kiss, nod,* etc.
Parts of the body: *chin, fist, forehead, shoulder,* etc.
Present continuous: *The child is … -ing. The two men are … -ing.*
There is/are …, Is/Are there …?

Preparation: Make one copy of the worksheet for each pair and cut the sheets in half.

Non-cut alternative: Make one copy of the worksheet for each student and fold the sheets in half. Tell students not to look at the other halves.

1 Divide the class into pairs. Allocate each partner a letter (A or B) and give them the relevant half of the worksheet. Tell students that they have different illustrations and that they must find the differences by describing their illustrations to each other, but without looking at each other's illustrations.

2 Give students two minutes to think about how to describe their illustration and to check any vocabulary.

3 As a whole class, elicit questions they might ask, e.g. *Have you got a …? Is anyone running/riding a bike? What is the child doing? How many … are there?* Encourage use of *In my illustration, there is/are …*

4 Encourage the pairs to sit face to face (or back to back for an extra challenge) while doing the activity, and ensure they are unable to see each other's illustrations. They should circle the differences they find.

5 When they have found the fourteen differences, they can look at both illustrations and compare their answers.

6 As a whole class, confirm answers by eliciting feedback from a few pairs.

ANSWERS

Student A	Student B
Man texting (with one hand).	Man reading a book (with both hands).
Woman on bench putting on lipstick.	Woman on bench eating a burger.
Handbag next to woman.	Drink carton next to woman.
Boy jumping off wall.	Boy balancing on wall.
Two men with bikes standing still (without helmets).	Two men cycling (with helmets).
Cyclist 1 wiping sweat from his forehead.	Cyclist 1 drinking.
Cyclist 2 resting hand on cyclist 1's shoulder.	Cyclist 2 waving.
Father and child 1 playing with a ball.	Father and child 1 clapping.
Mother lifting child 2 up.	Mother giving child 2 a drink.
Child 3 sitting on blanket, playing with balloon.	Child 3 playing with a ball.
Woman 1 at café has fair hair; wearing trousers, has bag.	Woman 1 at café has dark hair; wearing skirt, no bag.
Women at café are touching.	Women at café aren't touching.
Men greeting each other by bumping fists.	Men greeting each other by hugging.

Unit 10 Just a minute

Paired/Group activity, with students talking for up to one minute using a word prompt

Language
Food vocabulary: types of dish, ingredients, texture and taste, etc.

Preparation: Make one copy of the worksheet for each group (maximum of six students per group) and cut the sheets in half.

Non-cut alternative: Make one copy of the worksheet for each team and fold the sheets in half. Tell students not to look at the other halves.

1 Write the following headings on the board: *Type of dish, Ingredient, Texture and taste, How something is cooked/eaten*. Ask students to think of as many food words/phrases as possible for each category, and write these under the appropriate headings. Leave these words/phrases on the board for the activity.

2 Divide the class into groups and ask each group to sub-divide into two teams. Allocate each team a letter (team A, team B), giving them the relevant half of the worksheet. They should not show their sheet to each other.

3 Give teams two minutes to add three more food-related words/phrases to their grid. (Note that it does not matter if teams write down one or more of the same words as each other.)

4 Explain that team A should now give team B a grid reference (e.g. *B4*). Team B reads out the correlating word in their grid and crosses it out. Team A must then talk for up to one minute, using the given word as a prompt. Team B awards them 1 point if they are able to talk for a minute without stalling or pausing excessively (e.g. for more than ten seconds).

5 After one minute, teams swap roles, with team B giving team A a grid reference.

6 Teams repeat stages 4 and 5, taking turns to talk using the word prompts they are given. Ask them to stop after twenty minutes. The winning team is the one with the most points.

Unit 11 Good news, bad news

Whole-class activity, with students describing news events while others match them to global issues

> **Language**
> Global issues: science and technology, the environment, health and wellbeing, the economic situation, the increasing population, food and farming, employment

Preparation: Make one copy of the worksheet and cut it into the fourteen cards. You will also need some spare paper for each student.

1. Give each student a sheet of spare paper and tell them to draw a grid with three columns and seven rows. Dictate the following words/phrases related to global issues and ask students to write them in the left-hand column (one word/phrase per row): *Science and technology, The environment, Health and wellbeing, The economic situation, The increasing population, Food and farming, Employment.* (Alternatively, you could write these on the board for students to copy.)

2. Above the second and third columns of the grid, they should write *Good news* and *Bad news* (see *Answers* for how the grid should look). Explain that they will need this grid later in the activity, but that they should turn over the spare paper and use this side for the next part of the activity.

3. Give each student a card (if you have more than fourteen students, some will have to share a card). Explain that each card has the beginning of a 'good news' or 'bad news' story. Tell students that they need to invent sentences of their own to build the beginning sentence into a complete news story. Give students ten minutes to write their stories (using as many full sentences as possible) on their spare paper.

4. Students should now take turns to read their story to the class. They should begin by telling the class the number on their card and by reading the beginning sentence. When each student has finished, the others refer to their grid and identify which issue it relates to, and whether the news was good or bad. They should then write the number in the appropriate space in their grid. (If you have fewer than fourteen students, some of the spaces will remain empty.)

5. When everyone has read their stories, review answers as a class. Students award themselves 1 point for each number in its correct place.

ANSWERS

	Good news	Bad news
Science and technology	3	5
The environment	1	7
Health and wellbeing	2	9
The economic situation	12	6
The increasing population	14	4
Food and farming	11	8
Employment	13	10

Unit 12 Three in a row

Group activity, answering questions about the jobs/professions vocabulary and what a job involves to 'win' a word and race across the board

> **Language**
> Collocations: *a degree in economics, deal with, make a good impression, run a business,* etc.
> Jobs: *judge, nurse, software developer,* etc.
> Professional areas: *engineering, health care, IT,* etc.
> Workplace: *court, hospital, open-plan,* etc.

Preparation: Make one copy of the worksheet for each group (maximum of six students per group) and cut the sheets in half. You will also need a piece of spare paper for each group.

Non-cut alternative: Make one copy of the worksheet for each team and fold the sheets in half. Tell students not to look at the other halves.

1. Divide the class into groups. Sub-divide the groups into two teams, and allocate each team a letter (team A and team B).

2. Give one student in each group a piece of spare paper and ask them to draw a large 6 x 6 grid with letters (A–F) across the top, and numbers (1–6) down the side.

3. Explain that the objective of the game is to win squares to make lines of three squares in a row (lines can be horizontal, vertical or diagonal). The team that makes the most lines of three wins.

4. Team A chooses any grid reference to start (e.g. *C3*) and team B reads out the first question on their list, saying *BLANK* where the solution should be. Team A has up to one minute to guess. If they answer correctly, they can colour in the square or mark it with the letter *A*. Team B crosses the question off their list. If team A is unable to answer the question within one minute, the turn passes to team B; the square stays blank and that square can be used by team B (i.e. to block team A) or again by team A to answer a different question.

5. Teams swap roles, with team B choosing a grid reference and team A reading out the first question on their list. The game continues with teams taking turns. Each time they guess correctly, they must choose another square that is adjacent in some way to their previous square(s) (diagonally, horizontally or vertically) in order to gain three in a row. Teams can choose a non-adjacent square on the board when they start a new line, but once they have started a line, they must choose squares adjacent to this until they can make a line of three.

6. When all the questions have been asked, the team with the most lines of three wins. Any questions that remain unanswered can be discussed in teams.

Vocabulary 225

1 Vocabulary Something in common

1. Work in small groups. Take turns to ask and answer questions about the activities you do on a daily/weekly basis. Use the verbs from box B. Find five activities that you have in common.

2. Write sentences about the five activities you have in common. Use the adverbs and expressions of frequency from box A and the verbs from box B. Use each adverb/expression and each verb once only.

A

always   nearly always   usually   often   sometimes   occasionally
every now and then   rarely   don't usually   hardly ever   never

B

chat   do   eat   go   have   make   play   spend   stay

1 _____
2 _____
3 _____
4 _____
5 _____

3. Take turns to say your sentences to the other group WITHOUT saying the adverbs or expressions of frequency.

4. Listen to the other groups. Guess how often they do the activities. Write one sentence for each group in the table. Check your answers.

Group	Sentences	Right or wrong?	Points scored
A			
B			
C			
D			
E			
F			
G			
H			

2 Vocabulary Household objects

Student A

1 Write one household object in each of the squares of the left-hand grid (1–9).
2 Throw the die. Mime, draw or describe the objects in the left-hand grid for student B.

1	2	3
4	5	6
7	8	9

a	b	c
d	e	f
g	h	i

⚀ or ⚁ mime   ⚂ or ⚃ draw   ⚄ or ⚅ describe

3 Watch or listen to student B. Guess the household objects. Write your guesses in the right-hand grid (a–i).

Student B

1 Write one household object in each of the squares of the left-hand grid (a–i).
2 Watch or listen to student A. Guess the household objects. Write your guesses in the right-hand grid (1–9).

a	b	c
d	e	f
g	h	i

1	2	3
4	5	6
7	8	9

3 Throw the die. Mime, draw or describe the objects in the left-hand grid for student A.

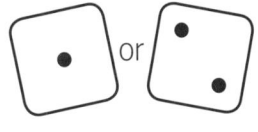

⚀ or ⚁ mime   ⚂ or ⚃ draw   ⚄ or ⚅ describe

Navigate B1 Teacher's Guide   Photocopiable © Oxford University Press 2015

3 Vocabulary Don't hide your feelings

---

*Work in small groups. Act out the situation. Do not say the adjective in **bold**.*

Your group is lost in a city. A strange person has started following you. You feel **nervous**.

---

*Work in small groups. Act out the situation. Do not say the adjective in **bold**.*

Your group is waiting at the station for a train. It was due half an hour ago, but it hasn't arrived and nobody has explained why. You feel **angry**.

---

*Work in small groups. Act out the situation. Do not say the adjective in **bold**.*

Your group is going to a rock concert to see your favourite band. You are waiting in the queue to get into the stadium. You feel **excited**.

---

*Work in small groups. Act out the situation. Do not say the adjective in **bold**.*

The film your group has just seen at the cinema wasn't very good. It was supposed to be funny, but it wasn't. You feel **disappointed**.

---

*Work in small groups. Act out the situation. Do not say the adjective in **bold**.*

Your group has taken an important exam, and you've just received the results. You all passed with good grades. You feel extremely **pleased**.

---

*Work in small groups. Act out the situation. Do not say the adjective in **bold**.*

Your group used a friend's car without asking his permission. You had a small accident and damaged it. You feel **guilty**.

---

*Work in small groups. Act out the situation. Do not say the adjective in **bold**.*

In spite of following the instructions carefully, your group can't get your new computer to work. Every time you try to turn it on, nothing happens. You feel **confused**.

---

*Work in small groups. Act out the situation. Do not say the adjective in **bold**.*

Your group is going to the airport on the bus. Your flight leaves in an hour, but you are stuck in a traffic jam. You feel **stressed**.

4 Vocabulary A full life

1 Work with a partner. Imagine it is many years in the future. You are an old man/woman looking back on your life. Take turns to tell your partner about the things you did during your life, using phrases from boxes A and B and your own ideas.

A

> When I was a (young) child, I …
> When I was a teenager, I …
> In my twenties/thirties (etc.), I …
> In my early twenties/thirties (etc.), I …
> In my mid-twenties/thirties (etc.), I …
> In my late twenties/thirties (etc.), I …
> When I was about thirty-five/forty/fifty-five (etc.), I …
> As a middle-aged man/woman, I …

B

> start my own business   have children   go to university   get a job   choose my career
> get married   leave home   retire   learn to swim   leave school   move house/flat   spend time abroad
> change career   take up a sport/hobby   pass my exams/driving test   live with my partner

2 Tell the class about your partner's life.

---

3 Work with your partner. Write sentences about ten students. Write what the students did and when they did it. Include any information you can remember.

In his late thirties, Raul started his own business. He opened a photo library. It was very successful.

1 _____

2 _____

3 _____

4 _____

5 _____

6 _____

7 _____

8 _____

9 _____

10 _____

5 Vocabulary Auction!

1. Work with a partner. Take turns to describe your favourite possession.
   Make notes in the table about your partner's possession.

What the possession is	
How old it is	
What it does (if relevant)	
What it's made of	
What it looks like (size, weight, shape, colour)	
Special or unusual features	
Why my partner likes it / Why it's important to him/her	

2. Make notes to remind you how you described your possession.

3. Auction your possessions to the class. Complete rows A and B of the table below.
   Rules
   - The minimum price you can charge is £10.
   - You can increase the price by £10 each time.

4. Buy other students' possessions. Complete rows 1-8 of the table below.
   Rules
   - You have a budget of £500.
   - You can increase the budget if you sell your possessions.
   - The aim is to buy as many possessions as possible, and have as much money left as possible.

	Possessions bought and brief description	Price paid	Money left
Example	A pen (gold and black metal); antique (about 75 years old); good condition; very nice to use	£80	£420
1			
2			
3			
4			
5			
6			
7			
8			
	Possessions sold	**Amount received**	
A			
B			
		Total	

6 Vocabulary Speed friendships

1 Match 1–8 to opposites a–h.

1 stupid
2 dishonest
3 hard-working
4 tidy
5 patient
6 shy
7 sociable
8 quiet

a unsociable
b impatient
c lazy
d clever/smart
e loud
f honest
g confident
h untidy

2 Look at the photo your teacher has given you. Complete the profile for the person.

Speed-friendship profile	
Name	
Age	
Occupation	
What kind of person are you?	
Likes	1 2 3
Dislikes	1 2 3
Describe your ideal partner	

Navigate B1 Teacher's Guide   Photocopiable © Oxford University Press 2015

7 Vocabulary Perfect pairs

Student A

1 Read out one of the sentences (1–12) below to student B. Together, decide which verb from box A is missing from the sentence, and what form it should be in.

2 Listen to student B read out a sentence. Decide if it is the correct response; if it is, write the relevant letter (a, b, c, etc.) after your sentence. Then work together to complete it with one of the pronouns from box B.

A ~~apply~~ book buy choose do experience explore get go hire lie try

B anybody anything anywhere ~~everybody~~ everything everywhere
nobody nothing nowhere somebody something somewhere

1 Do we have to ___apply___ for a visa before we go? [c]
2 Shall we _____ a car and head out into the countryside?
3 Let's _____ sightseeing today.
4 I've _____ some interesting souvenirs to take home with me.
5 I need to _____ some foreign currency before we go.
6 Have you _____ our flight yet?
7 Have you _____ our accommodation yet?
8 Let's go out tomorrow and _____ the local culture.
9 I've _____ a bit of online research in to our destination.
10 I feel like _____ some local food tonight.
11 Shall we get out and _____ the old town?
12 Let's go and _____ by the pool for a couple of hours.

Student B

1 Listen to student A read out a sentence. Together, decide which verb from box A is missing from the sentence, and what form it should be in.

2 Find a suitable response from the sentences (a–l) below and read it out to student A. If you both agree the response is correct, write the sentence number (1, 2, 3, etc.) after your sentence. Then work together to complete it with one of the pronouns from box B.

A ~~apply~~ book buy choose do experience explore get go hire lie try

B anybody anything anywhere ~~everybody~~ everything everywhere
nobody nothing nowhere somebody something somewhere

a No. There's _____ available for the day we want to travel.
b Have you? Is there _____ interesting to see or do?
c Yes. ___Everybody___ from outside Europe needs one to get in to the country. [1]
d Same here, but we've looked _____, and all you can get are sandwiches or fast food.
e Not yet. It's only 8 a.m. and _____ will be open.
f Good idea. Has _____ brought their driving licence with them?
g OK. Is there _____ in particular you'd like to go?
h Great idea. I've met _____ who has offered to take us to a traditional wedding.
i Well, I've found some nice hotels, but _____ is fully booked.
j Me too. There's _____ in South Street that gives a good exchange rate.
k Me too. I've got _____ for all of my friends.
l That sounds nice. And it's early, so _____ else will be there yet.

Navigate B1 Teacher's Guide   Photocopiable © Oxford University Press 2015

8 Vocabulary Robot sales

1. Work in small groups. Rearrange the letters in **bold** to complete the sentences (1–14).

2. Think of two more useful skills or abilities and write them in boxes 15 and 16.

3. Tick (✓) the three skills or abilities (1–14) that you think are most useful.

1 ☐ I'm good at **engdria** _____ maps.	2 ☐ I'm quite good at **agmnki** _____ decisions.
3 ☐ I'm good at **arngnlei** _____ languages.	4 ☐ I'm good at **lisgnpel** _____ words correctly.
5 ☐ I'm quite good at **visngol** _____ computer problems.	6 ☐ I'm good at **olinlowfg** _____ instructions.
7 ☐ I'm brilliant at **gnxiif** _____ things that are broken.	8 ☐ I'm really good at **ikntag** _____ care of people.
9 ☐ I'm good at **pngiexnila** _____ things clearly.	10 ☐ I'm good at **gonizirnag** _____ events.
11 ☐ I'm very good at **merirembneg** _____ names, faces and facts.	12 ☐ I'm OK at **nltlige** _____ jokes.
13 ☐ I'm very good at **eanngrstddiun** _____ how things work.	14 ☐ I'm really good at **ngkiam** _____ speeches.
15 _____	16 _____

---

4. Your group has designed a robot that can do the three skills or abilities you ticked in exercise 3 and the two skills in 15 and 16. Discuss and write reasons under the five skills/abilities why they are useful or important.

5. Describe your robot's skills and abilities to the class.

6. Listen to the other groups describe their robots. Award points.

   3 points = We think the robot's skills or abilities are all extremely useful.
   2 points = We think the robot has some useful skills or abilities, but it could be better.
   1 point = We don't think any of the robot's skills or abilities are useful.

9 Vocabulary What's happening at the park?

Student A

Student B

10 Vocabulary Just a minute

Team A

1. Complete the grid with three more words connected to food.

	1	2	3	4	5	6
A	sauce	favourite	restaurant		bitter	cookery programmes
B	cook		baked	vegetables	lamb	
C	herbs	plain	snack	savoury	boiled	hot/spicy

2. When team B gives you a letter + number reference (e.g. *B4*), tell them the relevant word from your grid (then cross it out).

3. Time team B talking about that word for one minute. Award them 1 point if they can do it without stopping.

4. Give team B a letter + number reference and talk about food and cooking for one minute, using the word they give you as a prompt.

Team B

1. Complete the grid with three more words connected to food.

	1	2	3	4	5	6
A	fried	mild		dessert	vegetarian	
B	stew	spices	flavours	sour	raw	thick
C	sweet	taste	home-cooked		dish	healthy

2. Give team A a letter + number reference (e.g. *B4*).

3. Talk about food and cooking for one minute, using the word they give you as a prompt.

4. When team A gives you a letter + number reference, give them the relevant word from your grid (then cross it out). Time them talking for one minute. Award them 1 point if they can do it without stopping.

11 Vocabulary Good news, bad news

1 Attempts to reduce pollution in our town are working.	**2** The town has been given £50 million to build a new hospital and health centre.
3 A new car that drives itself is being tested at the Road Research Centre.	**4** The government has ordered people not to have more than two children.
5 Many customers are complaining that Contel's expensive new smartphone doesn't work properly.	**6** The country's financial problems mean that people are poorer now than they were ten years ago.
7 Scientists tell us that climate change is getting worse.	**8** Thousands of cattle have been destroyed to stop a dangerous disease.
9 More people are experiencing heart problems as a result of work-related stress.	**10** For every new job in the city, there are twenty-three people applying for it.
11 A cool, dry summer means that this year's potato crop has been the best ever.	**12** Electrical goods cost 6% less than they did this time last year.
13 More than 800 new positions have been created at a new factory in the town.	**14** Recent research suggests that large families are happier than small families.

12 Vocabulary Three in a row

Group A

Take turns to say a grid reference. Listen and say a sentence or guess the word in one minute.

1. A **BLANK** writes programs for computers. (Answer: *software developer*)
2. 'To **BLANK** a business' means 'to manage or organize a business'. (Answer: *run*)
3. Someone who works in science or works in a laboratory is a **BLANK**. (Answer: *scientist*)
4. I work **BLANK** a construction company. (Answer: *for/in*)
5. Companies often **BLANK** for new staff in the newspapers. (Answer: *advertise*)
6. It's important to make a good **BLANK** at an interview. (Answer: *impression*)
7. When you teach employees a new skill, you **BLANK** them. (Answer: *train*)
8. A large office space where employees all sit and work together is called an **BLANK** office. (Answer: *open-plan*)
9. You should wear **BLANK** clothes to an interview. (Answer: *smart/formal*)
10. In ten years' time, I'd like to **BLANK** a manager. (Answer: *become/be*)
11. A **BLANK** makes the decisions in a court. (Answer: *judge*)
12. Do you need a university **BLANK** in economics if you want to work in a bank? (Answer: *degree/qualification*)
13. If you write a copy of handwritten notes on a computer, you **BLANK** the notes. (Answer: *type up*)
14. When you meet new customers, you should make **BLANK** contact with them. (Answer: *eye*)
15. **BLANK** is a kind of study that scientists carry out. (Answer: *Research*)
16. A **BLANK** is another word for a secretary, or someone who does office and administrative work for someone – perhaps for their boss or a manager. (Answer: *PA/personal assistant*)
17. When you find new staff and give them jobs, you **BLANK** them. (Answer: *recruit/employ*)
18. If you go to a meeting, you **BLANK** the meeting. (Answer: *attend*)

Group B

Take turns to say a grid reference. Listen and say a sentence or guess the word in one minute.

1. Cars or other equipment are made in a **BLANK**. (Answer: *factory*)
2. A nurse works in a **BLANK**. (Answer: *hospital*)
3. A **BLANK** works for a newspaper. (Answer: *journalist*)
4. I work in a large office, I'm **BLANK** administrator. (Answer: *an/the*)
5. He's worked **BLANK** sales all his life. (Answer: *in*)
6. Doctors and nurses work in the **BLANK** profession. (Answer: *healthcare*)
7. Sorry, I can't help you now. I'm talking **BLANK** the phone. (Answer: *on*)
8. Yesterday was very busy – I had to **BLANK** with a lot of new enquiries. (Answer: *deal*)
9. I'm in charge of a large team of people. I have **BLANK** them for two years now. (Answer: *managed*)
10. A place where scientists often work is called a **BLANK**. (Answer: *laboratory*)
11. I'll be home late this evening, as I have to **BLANK** some new clients from Japan. (Answer: *entertain/meet*)
12. I'm really nervous about the presentation I have to **BLANK** tomorrow. (Answer: *give*)
13. You have to have a degree in computer science if you want to work in the **BLANK** industry. (Answer: *IT*)
14. He was a waiter, but now he's working **BLANK** a chef. (Answer: *as*)
15. If you are an administrator, you have to **BLANK** a lot of paperwork. (Answer: *do*)
16. If you want to become a top engineer, you need a degree in **BLANK** from a good university. (Answer: *engineering*)
17. I wouldn't want to be a builder and work outside on building **BLANK** all year round. (Answer: *sites*)
18. You have to be good at maths to be an **BLANK**. (Answer: *accountant*)

Communication

Unit 1 My favourite things

Paired activity, with students guessing their partner's likes and dislikes

> **Language**
> Likes and dislikes: *can't stand, don't mind, favourite, hate, not keen on, prefer, quite like, really interested in, really into, really love*

Preparation: Make one copy of the worksheet for each student.

1 Give a copy of the worksheet to each student. Students work independently to write the phrases in the correct columns of the table.
2 Divide the class into pairs. Ask students to compare their answers with their partner. Then go through the answers with the class.

ANSWERS

✓ ✓	✓	✗	✗ ✗
prefer really love favourite really interested in really into	don't mind quite like	not keen on	hate can't stand

3 In their pairs, ask students to put their chairs back to back if possible, so that they cannot see each other or each other's worksheets while writing. Explain that they have to imagine they are their partner and complete the sentences in the box as if they were their partner. Remind them to use the *-ing* form after the phrases. They can use the illustrations to jog their memories regarding vocabulary from the unit, but they may use any vocabulary that they know, e.g. *reading, going to the cinema, listening to music*.
4 When they have finished, they can turn their chairs back, but they should not show their partner the completed worksheet. They should ask and answer to check their answers. Demonstrate with one student:
   Teacher: *Yoshiko, I wrote, 'I really love reading books.' Is that true? Do you?*
   Yoshiko: *Yes! It's true!*
   Teacher: *And I wrote, 'I'm not keen on clubbing.' Is that right?*
   Yoshiko: *Um, not really. I quite like clubbing.*
5 Complete the activity by asking students who got the most correct guesses.

Unit 2 Giving directions

Paired activity, locating places on a map and practising giving directions

> **Language**
> Directions: *Could you tell me where the (bank) is, please? Go straight along this road. You'll see the (bank) on the right. Go past the (bank) and keep going until you reach (a crossroads). Take the second left. So it's left at the crossroads? Is that right? It takes about ten minutes. You can't miss it.*

Preparation: Make one copy of the worksheet for each pair and cut the sheets in half.

Non-cut alternative: Make one copy of the worksheet for each student and fold the sheets in half. Tell students not to look at the other halves.

1 Check that students know the vocabulary for the twelve place symbols on the worksheet and write the words on the board if necessary.

ANSWERS
Student A: a post office   b coffee shop/café
c cash machine/ATM   d supermarket
e library/bookshop   f park
Student B: a cinema   b restaurant
c train/underground station   d chemist's
e petrol station   f car park

2 Elicit directions (see *Language*) by asking students how to get from college to their home. Write the language on the board for reference during the activity.
3 Divide the class into pairs. Allocate each partner a letter (A or B) and give them the relevant half of the worksheet. They should not show these to each other. Give students two minutes to independently draw or write the places on their map and to check for any vocabulary. Explain that they may end up putting their places in the same location as one of their partner's places, but that it doesn't matter if this happens.
4 Students should each have put six different places on the same map. They must now mark where their partner's places are without looking at their partner's map. Students take turns to ask, respond, locate and check the location of each place using the target language.
5 When they have finished, they check to see if their maps match.

Unit 3 What a story!

Paired activity, telling a story using prompts

> **Language**
> Telling a story: *A funny thing happened …, I had a bad experience …, I was really scared!, I was so embarrassed!, It was all OK in the end.*
> Responding to a story: *Oh no! So then what happened? You're joking!*

Preparation: Make one copy of the worksheet for each pair. You will also need some spare paper for each pair.

1 Ask the class to think of different phrases used for telling a story (*How do you start? How do you return to the subject when you've been interrupted? How do you end?*). Then ask for different phrases for responding to a story, to show you are listening and interested. (Refer students to the *Language for speaking* box on page 32 of the Coursebook if necessary.) Write their suggestions on the board and leave them there for the activity.

2 Divide the class into pairs. You need an even number of pairs, so with a small class, you may need one or two groups with more than two students. Give a copy of the worksheet and a piece of spare paper to each pair. Give students five minutes to look at the wordlists and choose the specified number of places, people, objects, etc. by ticking the relevant boxes. They should also make a list of the words they have chosen on the spare paper. At this stage, don't tell them why they are choosing these things.

3 Tell each pair to join another pair to form a group. They should exchange worksheets (but keep their list on the spare paper). Students should now look at their new worksheet and the words that are ticked. In their original pairs, give students ten minutes to think of a story that involves some or all of these words. They can add other places, people, objects, animals, etc., but they should try to use as many of the selected words as possible. They should discuss their story and what might happen in it, but not write anything.

4 Each pair takes turns to tell their story. They have a time limit of five minutes. One student tells the story (using the words on their worksheet and the phrases for telling a story on the board), while their partner responds to show they are listening and interested. While they are doing this, the other pair should listen and use their list on the spare paper to check that the pair speaking is using the words they chose, ticking the words as they are used. Each word is worth 1 point. They should also award a point each time they hear one of the phrases on the board. The winning pair is the one with the most points.

Unit 4 Where, when, what?

Paired activity, making arrangements for a day/time and a place to meet, eat and see a show or event

> **Language**
> Inviting and making arrangements: *Are you doing anything …? Are you free …? Do you fancy …? Shall we meet at …? Yes, I'd love to. I'm afraid I can't make it.*

Preparation: Make one copy of the worksheet for each pair and cut the sheets into three sections (the table, student A, student B).

Non-cut alternative: Make three copies of the worksheet for each pair and fold the sheets into three sections (the table, student A, student B).

1 Tell students that they are going to make arrangements for tomorrow night with another student in the class. Ask them what they would say to check the student is free, and how they would invite them out for dinner. Write their answers on the board.

2 Ask students what they would say to accept or refuse an invitation. Elicit that, when refusing, we usually thank the person who made the invitation, politely refuse and explain why we are refusing (and possibly suggest an alternative). (Refer them to the *Language for speaking* box on page 42 of the Coursebook if necessary.)

3 Divide the class into pairs. Give each pair a copy of the table, which they should place face up between them. Allocate each partner a letter (A or B) and give them the relevant section of the worksheet. They should not show these to each other.

4 Explain that each pair is going to arrange to meet next week. They are going to go for a meal and see a show or event afterwards. They should arrange when and where to meet, where to eat and what to do afterwards. The table shows the choices available to them. They also have notes explaining when they cannot meet, and why they cannot or do not want to go to certain places. Explain that there is only one day/time, one meeting place, one place to eat and one event that they can both manage.

5 The pairs work together to make their arrangements, using appropriate language for inviting and making arrangements (i.e. the phrases on the board or those in the Coursebook). As they make their arrangements, they should cross out the days/times, places, etc. on their table as appropriate. The first pair in the class to make an arrangement is the winner. Check answers as a class.

ANSWER
They are going to meet on Thursday evening, outside the Museum of Modern Art. They are going to eat at The Terrace, and afterwards they are going to see *Make Me Laugh* at the Comedy Club.

Communication

Unit 5 What are they going to do?

Paired activity, asking for various objects and identifying what the speaker is going to do with those objects

Language
Explaining words you don't know (including paraphrasing): *I don't remember the word. It looks like …, It's + adjective, I've forgotten the word. You use it to …*

Preparation: Make one copy of the worksheet for each pair and cut the sheets in half.

Non-cut alternative: Make one copy of the worksheet for each student and fold the sheets in half. Tell students not to look at the other halves.

1 Tell students to think of an object for which they don't know the English translation. Then tell them to imagine they have to ask for one in a shop. How would they explain what they wanted without knowing the name of the object? Elicit the fact that they would have to say they did not know the English word, then describe what it is used for and, if necessary, its size, shape and perhaps what it is similar to. Students work with a partner to try and explain the object they want using these strategies. Their partner should try to guess what they want.

2 Divide the class into pairs. Allocate each partner a letter (A or B) and give them the relevant half of the worksheet. They should not show these to each other.

3 Explain that they are each going to do three different things (situations A–C). They need four objects for each of these situations, which they will ask their partner for. Their partner will try and guess what they are going to do from the four objects they need. Whether they know the names of these objects or not, they should describe them using the method outlined in stage 1.

4 Student A describes the objects they need for situation A. Student B then decides what student A is going to do, and completes the first sentence on their worksheet.

5 Stage 4 is repeated, with student B describing the objects needed for their situation A, and student A guessing what student B is going to do.

6 Stages 4 and 5 are repeated until they have asked for the objects in all six of their situations. They can check their answers with each other when they finish. The winning pair is the first one in which both students correctly identify the three activities their partner is going to do.

ANSWERS
(Situations are listed on the worksheet.)
Student A
Situation A a pair of oven gloves, a (food) whisk, a (baking) tray and a (mixing) bowl
Situation B a sponge, a hose(pipe), a brush and a bucket
Situation C straws, (paper) cups, banner(s) and balloons
Student B
Situation A a dustpan and brush, a vacuum cleaner/hoover, a duster and a can of (furniture) polish
Situation B a (garden) spade, a trowel, a (lawn)mower and a pair of shears
Situation C a torch, a waterproof coat/an anorak, a camping stove and a sleeping bag

Unit 6 Dominoes

Group activity, choosing appropriate responses to news

Language
Introducing news: *Guess what! Have you heard the news? I've got some good/bad/interesting news.*

Responding to good news: *Congratulations! How + (adjective)!* (e.g. *How amazing/wonderful!*) *I'm really happy for you. Oh wow! That's + (adjective)!* (e.g. *That's amazing/fantastic!*) *You lucky thing!*

Responding to bad news: *How + (adjective)!* (e.g. *How terrible/awful!*) *I'm sorry. Never mind. Oh dear. Oh no! That's + (adjective)!* (e.g. *That's terrible/awful!*) *What a + (noun).* (e.g. *What a shame/pity/nightmare.*)

Wishing someone luck: *Fingers crossed.*

Preparation: Make one copy of the worksheet for each group (maximum of five students per group). Cut the sheets into the twenty dominoes. Keep an uncut copy of the worksheet for reference.

Non-cut alternative: Call out a piece of news from the worksheet; students respond appropriately. Give 2 points for a phrase that has not been used before.

1 Brainstorm good news and bad news, e.g. *Guess what! I'm getting married.* Write the ideas on the board and elicit how you might respond to them, e.g. *Congratulations!*

2 Divide the class into groups and give each group a set of dominoes. Ask students to share the dominoes equally among group members. (Some may have one more domino than others.)

3 The first student starts by selecting and putting down one of their dominoes on the table. The next student has to match the statement on the right of the domino with an appropriate response on the left of one of their dominoes (there is only one appropriate response per statement). They set down this response on the right of the original domino. If a student cannot put down an appropriate response, play passes to the next student until someone can put down the correct response. The winner is the first person in the group to use all their dominoes. Check answers as a class.

ANSWERS
The statements and responses appear in order on the uncut worksheet.

Unit 7 The great hotel race

Whole-class activity, with students mingling to practise language for checking in and out of hotels

> **Language**
> Checking in and out of hotels: *I'd like to check in/out, please. Could I check in, please? Do you have a reservation? What was the name (again)? Could you fill in the registration form, please? Is there a charge for …? Is … available in the room? Is there a … in the hotel? What time is (breakfast/checkout)? Is there somewhere I can leave my luggage? I'll get someone to help you with …*

Preparation: Make one copy of the worksheet for every six students in the class (minimum five copies) and cut each sheet into six cards. You will also need to prepare hotel signs (or ask students to prepare them) by folding five sheets of paper in half and writing the name of one of the hotels on each one: *Hotel Pluto (Paris), Minerva Hotel (Ho Chi Minh City), Jupiter Hotel (Auckland), Hotel Mars (Santiago)* and *Juno Hotel (New York)*. Also ask each student to take a sheet of blank paper and cut/tear it into six cards. They should write *room key* on three cards and *receipt* on the other three. Collect in the room keys and receipts for the moment.

Non-cut alternative: Make one copy of the worksheet for each student. The receptionists fold the sheet so they can only see their card; the travellers fold it so they can only see the relevant traveller card.

1 Divide the class into two groups: receptionists and travellers (there should be at least five receptionists). Give a receptionist card to each of the receptionists. Sub-divide the travellers into five groups and give each traveller in group 1 traveller card 1, each traveller in group 2 traveller card 2, etc. (If you have a small class, you can have one person per group or use only three or four of the traveller cards.)

2 Elicit questions a traveller might ask the receptionist while checking in/out of a hotel, and how the receptionist might reply.

3 Ask the receptionists (in pairs, if possible) to sit at five different desks around the room and give each desk a hotel sign. Give each desk an equal number of room keys and receipts.

4 Travellers travel individually, visiting each hotel, beginning with the first on their itinerary. They go to the hotel desk and check in first, asking the questions on their itinerary. The receptionists reply according to the information on their card. When the travellers have checked in, they can collect a room key. If there is a queue at the desk, they must go to the back of the queue before checking out.

5 Before the travellers can go to the next hotel, they must check out and the receptionist must give them a receipt. If you have enough receptionists for each hotel desk to have two receptionists, travellers must check out with a different receptionist. When they have a room key and a receipt, they can move on to the next hotel. The first traveller to collect five room keys and five receipts is the winner.

6 When they have finished, collect feedback from individuals about the language they used. If there is time, play the game again, reversing the roles.

Unit 8 A bit lost

Whole-class activity, with students mingling to practise asking for clarification

> **Language**
> Asking for clarification: *Could you repeat that, please? I'm a bit lost. I'm afraid I can't follow that. Pardon? Please could you explain that? Please could you speak up? Sorry, what did you say/what was that? What do you mean by …?*
> **Revision:** Asking for and giving directions

Preparation: Make one copy of the worksheet for every six students in the class and cut the sheet into six cards.

Non-cut alternative: Give each student an uncut worksheet. The tourists fold the worksheet so they can only see the tourist cards; the inhabitants fold so they can only see the inhabitant cards. Ask the tourists/inhabitants in group 1 to use tourist card 1/inhabitant card 1, group 2 to use tourist card 2/inhabitant card 2, etc.

1 Briefly revise giving directions with the class. (This is not the focus of this worksheet, but students will need to be able to do this for the activity to work.) Draw a quick sketch of a town map on the board and mark a couple of places on the map (e.g. *hotel, bank*). Ask, *How do I get to …?* and elicit the answers.

2 Reverse roles and encourage students to ask, *How do I get to …?* Try giving the answers very quickly, very quietly (so that students can hardly hear you) and using long words (e.g. *Go as far as the corner on the road that runs parallel to this one.*). Encourage students to ask for clarification using the target language. Respond to the clarification by speaking more slowly/loudly or by using simpler language.

3 Divide the class into two groups: tourists and inhabitants. Sub-divide the groups into three groups and give each tourist/inhabitant in group 1 tourist card 1/inhabitant card 1, each tourist/inhabitant in group 2 tourist card 2/inhabitant card 2, etc. (Inhabitant card 3 is the most challenging, so give this to more able students.)

4 Give students time to look at the cards and work out/rehearse what they are going to say. The inhabitants should rehearse speaking quietly, quickly or using long words; the tourists should rehearse the different phrases they learnt for asking for directions/clarification.

5 Before they start, explain that the tourists can only ask each inhabitant for one piece of information. When they have it, they should move on and ask someone else for the next piece of information they require. Ask the inhabitants to remain seated. The tourists should go around asking the inhabitants for directions. If they don't understand at first, they should ask for clarification. When they have understood, they label the places on their map.

6 After about ten minutes, ask the tourists and inhabitants to change places and exchange maps, so that they practise both roles.

7 When the tourists have all the information they need, they should sit down. This will indicate that the activity is coming to an end.

8 Give feedback by drawing a sketch of the Newton town centre map on the board. Ask students to come up and label the squares.

Communication

Unit 9 I'd like a second opinion, please!

Whole-class activity, acting out a visit to the doctor's/pharmacy

Language
Visiting the doctor's/pharmacy: *Have you got anything for …? I feel …, I've hurt/sprained/broken …, I've got a …, What can I do for you? You must/mustn't/should/shouldn't …, You could try … -ing*

Preparation: Make enough copies of the worksheet for students to have three or four cards each and cut each sheet into twenty cards. You will also need a bag or an envelope.

Non-cut alternative: Make one copy of the worksheet for each pair. Student A is the patient and student B is the doctor. Student A chooses three problems from the worksheet and visits student B to discuss symptoms, how they got the problem, etc. They then swap roles and student B chooses three different problems to discuss.

1. Divide the class into two groups: doctors and patients. Give the doctors two minutes to think of as many questions/phrases for giving advice and any health remedies as they can (e.g. *How long have you had the problem? I think you should stay in bed.*). At the same time, give the patients two minutes to think of as many health problems and questions/phrases for asking for advice as they can (e.g. *I've been feeling sick for three days. My leg hurts.*).
2. Elicit example questions/phrases and write these on the board in two columns. Check ideas and remind students when the indefinite article or no article is used. Also remind them that the present perfect simple/continuous is used to talk about health problems and that possessive adjectives are used to talk about body parts, not the definite article.
3. Place the cards in a bag or envelope and ask the patients to take a card each. Tell them they are going to visit a doctor to get some advice about the illness on their card. Elicit that if the card says *break/arm*, for instance, they should say, *I've broken my arm*. Tell the doctors that they should ask the patients questions about their illness in order to give them the best advice.
4. Encourage the doctors to suggest (or make up) remedies or treatments, and the patients to make up enough symptoms to deserve a day off work. Patients should consult one or two doctors before taking another problem card from the bag/envelope. Encourage the patients to keep trying a different doctor or exchange their cards.
5. Stop the activity and ask the doctors to get into small groups and discuss the treatments they recommended, and who was the easiest/most difficult/sickest patient. Patients should compare their experiences and decide who is the best/worst doctor and the most expensive/ridiculous treatment!
6. Ask the doctors and patients to swap roles and do the activity again.

Unit 10 Waiter, waiter!

Group activity, playing a board game to practise explaining and dealing with problems

Language
Introducing/Explaining a problem: *I'm afraid …, There seems to be a mistake. You've charged us for …, but …*
Making a request: *Could you possibly …? I'd like to …, please. Would you mind …?*
Apologizing: *I do apologize. I'm terribly sorry.*
Responding to an apology: *Don't worry about it. It's not your fault.*

Preparation: Make one copy of the worksheet for each group (maximum of four students per group). You will also need a counter for each student and a coin for each group.

1. Elicit some of the language from the *Language for speaking* box on page 102 of the Coursebook. First, act out the part of a customer by saying, e.g. *Waiter! I'm terribly sorry, but I've spilt my water.* Encourage students to give suitable replies. Continue with a few more situations, then allocate students the role of the customer, asking them what they would say in certain situations, e.g. *You've dropped your knife on the floor. What do you say?*
2. Divide the class into groups, giving them copies of the worksheet, the coins and counters. Ask students to place their counters on START. Explain that students take turns to spin the coin. Heads = move forward one square; tails = move forward two squares.
3. Point to the illustrations and explain that the student moving the counter must imagine they are the customer (for squares 1, 2, 3, 5, 7, 8, 10, 11, 12, 13 and 14) or the waiter (for squares 9 and 15).
4. The first player spins the coin and moves forward the appropriate number of squares. They then make the appropriate request, complaint or response. The player on their right must reply as a waiter or customer. If the other students in the group agree that the complaint and response are correct, the student whose turn it is may stay on the square and move forward on their next turn. If the group decides it is wrong, the student must miss a go. If another student subsequently lands on the same square, they must make a request or complaint using different phrases. The player on their right must also use a different phrase to that used by the previous player. If a player lands on a mystery square (i.e. one with a question mark), they must invent a problem and make a request or complaint about it. The student who reaches FINISH first is the winner.
5. When they have finished, round up the activity by asking students what they said for selected squares. Give feedback on any problems or errors.

Unit 11 Climate change

Group activity, with students holding discussions to practise expressing and responding to opinions

> **Language**
> Expressing opinions: *I don't have strong opinions about/views on …, I (don't) think …, In my opinion/view, …, Personally, I don't like …*
> Agreeing: *Maybe. That's a good point. That's right. Yeah, I agree.*
> Disagreeing: *I take your point, but …, I'm afraid I disagree. I'm sorry, but I really don't agree. True, but what about …? Yeah, but …*

Preparation: Make five copies of the worksheet and cut the sheets into the six cards.

Non-cut alternative: Make one copy of the worksheet for each student. Ask students in group 1 to use card 1, group 2 to use card 2, etc. All groups refer to the priorities list.

1 Say some statements from the cards, e.g. *There's going to be another Ice Age, not global warming.* Ask students to say whether they agree or disagree.
2 Divide the class into five groups. Give each member of group 1 card 1, group 2 card 2, etc. Also give each group a copy of the priorities list. (If you have fewer than fifteen students, use fewer cards to ensure that each group has at least three students.)
3 Give students some preparation time to discuss the opinions on their card. (The roles on the five cards represent a gradation of opinion, from those who deny climate change is happening, through to those who think urgent action must be taken.) Students should then look at the priorities list and decide what their priorities would be, according to the opinions they have been given.
4 Reorder students to form new groups with one person from each of the first groups.
5 Students present their arguments for or against climate change (as on their original card), agreeing and disagreeing with each other and trying to convince the others in their group. They use their opinions to argue for or against the action points on the priorities list. In their new groups, their task is to select the five action points that they consider most important. Set a time limit for them to do this.
6 After the allocated time, ask for feedback from each group – which five priorities did each group choose?

Unit 12 Unusual job interviews

Group activity, practising asking questions and giving information in job interviews, and choosing the most suitable job or candidate

> **Language**
> Job interviews: *How long have you worked …? I'd really like to get into …, I've got a university degree in …, I've worked as a … for …, What qualifications have you got for this job? Why do you want to work for this company?*

Preparation: Make enough copies of the worksheet for half the class to have one job card each (cards can be repeated).

1 Tell students that they are going to attend a job interview. Divide the class into two groups: interviewers and candidates. Give the interviewers two minutes to think of questions they might ask a candidate at a job interview, and the information an interviewer might give a candidate about a job, e.g. pay, hours. At the same time, give the candidates two minutes to think of phrases they might use to talk about their experience, and questions a candidate might want to ask about a job.
2 Elicit example questions/phrases and write these on the board in two columns. Check ideas.
3 The interviewers choose one job card each and prepare in pairs or small groups, making up details about the job, e.g. pay, holidays, working hours, and thinking of any questions relevant to the job that they can ask the candidates, using the prompts on the job card and the questions prepared in stages 1 and 2 if necessary. At the same time, candidates can prepare together for the interviews. At this stage, they will not know what job they are interviewing for, so encourage them to describe their strengths/weaknesses/achievements, and qualifications or experience they have in general, and to think of any questions about the conditions of the job they may want to ask. Encourage candidates to use their imaginations and invent details where necessary – they need a job urgently!
4 Ask interviewers to sit in a line facing candidates. Tell interviewers they have two minutes to conduct the interview. The interviewers should tell the candidates which job they are interviewing for. After two or three minutes, stop the activity. Interviewers sit still, while candidates move along to the next interviewer in the line. You may wish to repeat this up to three times.
5 Stop the activity and ask the interviewers to get together and discuss who they are going to employ for each job. They must give every candidate a job. Candidates should discuss which interview was most successful, and which job they would most like to get.
6 Encourage feedback as a whole class. Candidates give their feedback first, followed by the interviewers – do their ideas match?

Communication 243

1 Communication My favourite things

1 Complete the table below using the phrases from the box.

> prefer   really love   favourite   hate   really interested in
> really into   not keen on   can't stand   don't mind   quite like

✓✓	✓	✗	✗✗

2 Work with a partner. Imagine you are your partner. What do you think he/she likes doing? Complete the sentences.

My favourite hobby is _____.

I really love _____.

I'm not keen on _____.

I prefer _____ to _____.

I don't mind _____.

I'm really interested in _____.

I quite like _____.

I can't stand _____.

Navigate B1 Teacher's Guide — 244 — Photocopiable © Oxford University Press 2015

2 Communication Giving directions

Student A

1 Draw the places (1–6) on the map.

1. (cinema) 2. (restaurant) 3. (train station) 4. (hospital/pharmacy) 5. (petrol station) 6. (car park)

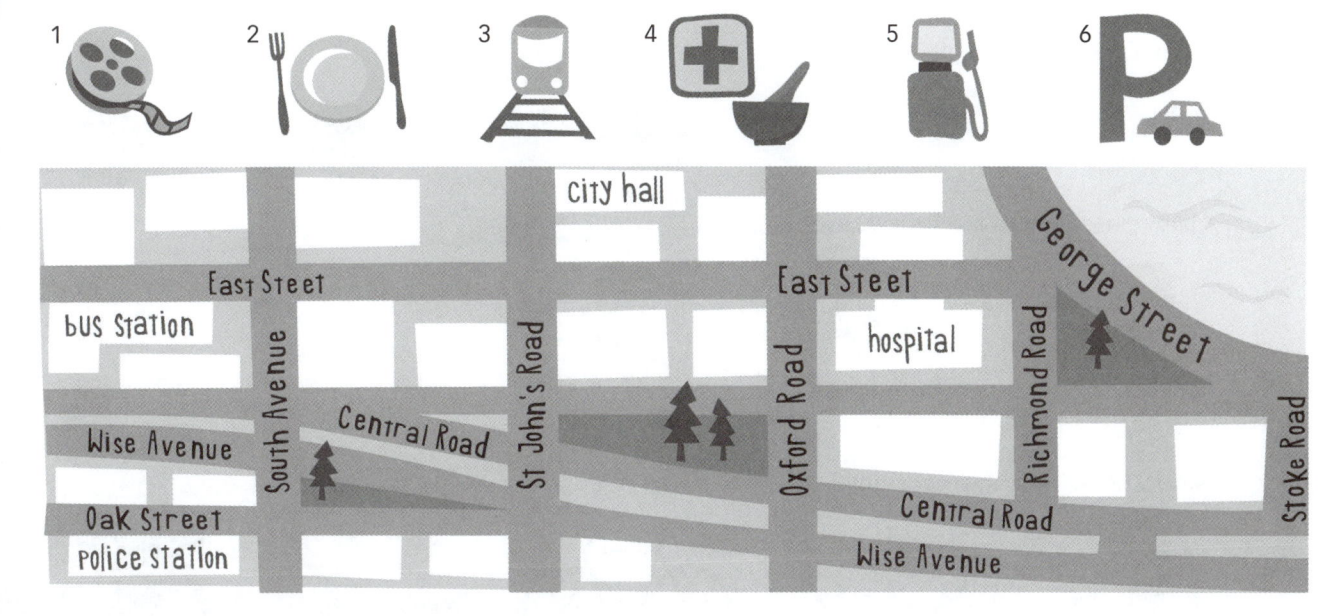

2 Ask student B where the places (a–f) are on the map.

a. (post office) b. (café) c. (ATM) d. (supermarket) e. (library/bookshop) f. (park)

Student B

1 Draw the places (1–6) on the map.

1. (post office) 2. (café) 3. (ATM) 4. (supermarket) 5. (library/bookshop) 6. (park)

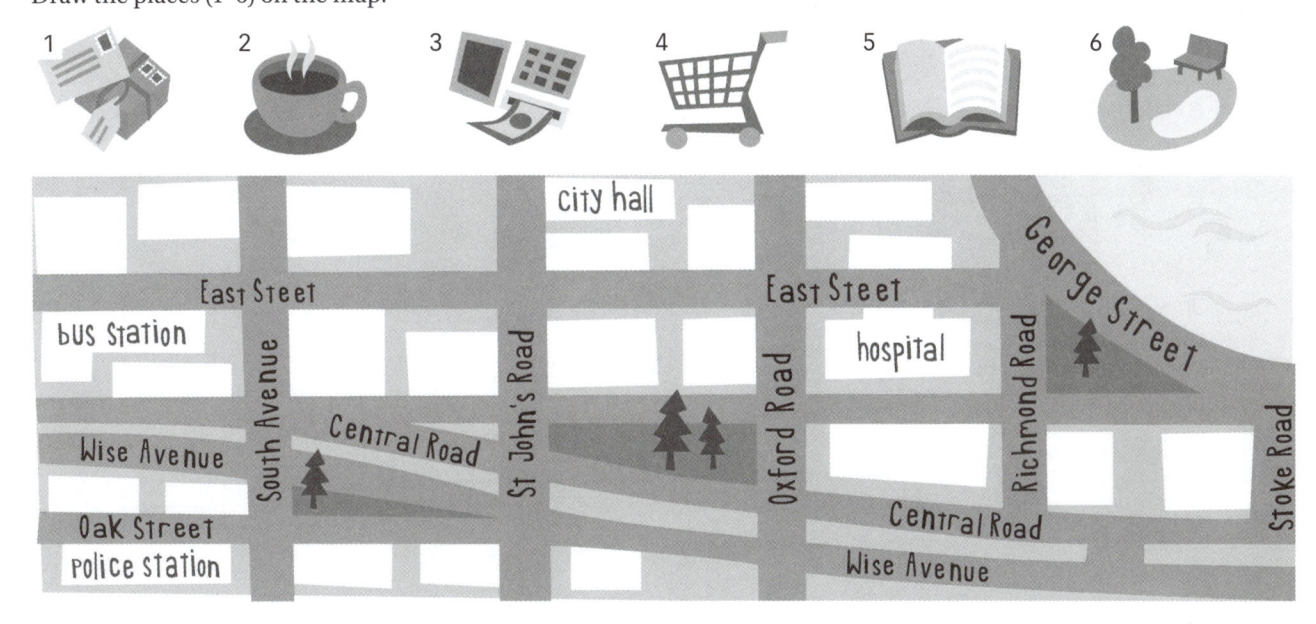

2 Ask student A where the places (a–f) are on the map.

a. (cinema) b. (restaurant) c. (train station) d. (hospital/pharmacy) e. (petrol station) f. (car park)

Navigate B1 Teacher's Guide — Photocopiable © Oxford University Press 2015

3 Communication What a story!

1 Choose and tick (✓) one place.

- [ ] an airport
- [ ] a concert
- [ ] a party
- [ ] a station
- [ ] a supermarket
- [ ] a beach
- [ ] a park
- [ ] a restaurant
- [ ] a street
- [ ] a swimming pool

2 Choose and tick (✓) two people.

- [ ] a baby girl
- [ ] a baby boy
- [ ] a small girl
- [ ] a small boy
- [ ] a young woman
- [ ] a young man
- [ ] a middle-aged woman
- [ ] a middle-aged man
- [ ] an old woman
- [ ] an old man

3 Choose and tick (✓) one object or animal.

- [ ] a ball
- [ ] a banana
- [ ] a bicycle
- [ ] a bird
- [ ] a camera
- [ ] a car
- [ ] a cat
- [ ] a credit card
- [ ] a dog
- [ ] some flowers
- [ ] a handbag
- [ ] a hat
- [ ] some keys
- [ ] a knife
- [ ] a mobile phone
- [ ] an MP3 player
- [ ] a suitcase
- [ ] a pair of shoes
- [ ] a mouse
- [ ] a wallet or purse

4 Choose and tick (✓) three emotions.

- [ ] angry
- [ ] disappointed
- [ ] frightened
- [ ] nervous
- [ ] anxious
- [ ] embarrassed
- [ ] guilty
- [ ] pleased
- [ ] calm
- [ ] excited
- [ ] in a good mood
- [ ] scared
- [ ] confused
- [ ] exhausted
- [ ] lonely
- [ ] stressed

5 Choose and tick (✓) five verbs.

- [ ] be
- [ ] drop
- [ ] lift
- [ ] rise
- [ ] take
- [ ] begin
- [ ] fall
- [ ] look
- [ ] see
- [ ] think
- [ ] climb
- [ ] get
- [ ] make
- [ ] send
- [ ] turn
- [ ] come
- [ ] go
- [ ] move
- [ ] shout
- [ ] walk
- [ ] decide
- [ ] jump
- [ ] need
- [ ] sit
- [ ] watch
- [ ] dive
- [ ] land
- [ ] push
- [ ] start
- [ ] work

4 Communication Where, when, what?

Day and time	Monday lunchtime Tuesday lunchtime Wednesday lunchtime Thursday lunchtime Friday lunchtime Saturday lunchtime Sunday lunchtime	Monday evening Tuesday evening Wednesday evening Thursday evening Friday evening Saturday evening Sunday evening
Place to meet	at the entrance to Milton Street underground station in Westmore Square in Betty's Café in Shakespeare Park outside the Museum of Modern Art	
Place to eat	Big Bang Burgers The Fat Chicken Norma's Place Pizza Palace Riverside Café The Terrace Tony's Italian Restaurant	
Show/Event	*The Glums* (musical at the New Theatre) *A Good Time* (play at the Apollo Theatre) *Hope* (action film starring Jack White at the Roxy Cinema) *Imagine This* (exhibition at the art gallery) *Make Me Laugh* (stand-up comedy at the Comedy Club) *Monsters from Mars* (horror film at the ABC Cinema) *This Time Next Year* (romantic comedy at the Alhambra Cinema)	

Student A

Arrange to meet student B for a meal and a show/event afterwards.
- You are busy on Tuesday, Wednesday and Saturday lunchtime. (What are you doing?)
- You are busy on Monday, Friday and Saturday evening. (What are you doing?)
- Milton Street underground station has lots of entrances, so you might miss each other.
- Shakespeare Park is very big and you might not find each other.
- You don't like the food at the Riverside Café.
- The Fat Chicken closed down last month.
- The pizzas in Pizza Palace are terrible.
- You don't like musicals.
- Tickets for *A Good Time* are sold out.
- You've already seen *This Time Next Year*.

Student B

Arrange to meet student A for a meal and a show/event afterwards.
- You are busy on Monday, Thursday, Friday and Sunday lunchtime. (What are you doing?)
- You are busy on Tuesday, Wednesday and Sunday evening. (What are you doing?)
- Westmore Square is very busy, so you might miss each other.
- Betty's Café is closed because it is being redecorated.
- Tony's Italian Restaurant is too expensive.
- The last time you ate at Big Bang Burgers, you became ill.
- Norma, who runs Norma's Place, is rude and unfriendly.
- You find horror films too frightening.
- The art gallery closes at 4.30 p.m.
- You hate the actor Jack White.

5 Communication What are they going to do?

Student A

1. Ask student B for the objects you need in situations A–C. Don't say what you're going to do.
   Situation A: You're going to make some cakes. You need:

   Situation B: You're going to clean your car. You need:

   Situation C: You're going to have a party. You need:

2. Listen to student B. Guess what your partner is going to do. Complete the sentences.
   Situation A: Student B is going to _____ .
   Situation B: Student B is going to _____ .
   Situation C: Student B is going to _____ .

Student B

1. Listen to student A. Guess what your partner is going to do. Complete the sentences.
   Situation A: Student A is going to _____ .
   Situation B: Student A is going to _____ .
   Situation C: Student A is going to _____ .

2. Ask student A for the objects you need in situations A–C. Don't say what you're going to do.
   Situation A: You're going to clean your house. You need:

   Situation B: You're going to do some work in your garden. You need:

   Situation C: You're going to go camping. You need:

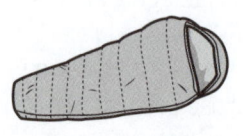

Navigate B1 Teacher's Guide   248   Photocopiable © Oxford University Press 2015

6 Communication Dominoes

How amazing! You can buy me lunch!	Helen and I are getting married in the Caribbean!	I'm really happy for you both. Can I come to the wedding?	I just failed my exam.
Oh no! Don't worry, you can take it again, can't you?	Guess what! I got that job!	How wonderful! When do you start?	My hamster died!
What a shame! Are you going to get another one?	My mum is coming to stay with us for a month.	Oh wow! That's … um … great … I think.	It's going to rain all weekend.
How awful! We won't be able to have that picnic, then.	I've got some bad news: my mobile has broken.	What a nightmare! It was new, wasn't it?	Have you heard the news? Lucy's going to teach us next week.
That's fantastic, but she gives a lot of homework.	My boyfriend just finished with me.	Never mind. He wasn't very nice to you anyway.	I've got a promotion.
Congratulations! Does that mean you're my boss now?	I had a terrible argument with my sister.	What a pity. What was it about?	I've got some interesting news: John is going out with Sally.
That's terrible! She must like boring men!	Guess what! I went back and bought those shoes!	Oh wow! Can I borrow them for the party next week?	I got a tablet for my birthday.
You lucky thing! Who gave it to you?	I've got my driving test today.	Fingers crossed. Third time lucky!	I got you a coffee.
That's great. How much do I owe you?	Guess what! Dave and I got engaged last night!	Congratulations! How did he ask you?	I lost all the photos on my camera.
Oh dear. I'm sorry. Did you download them to your laptop?	I've got some bad news: the trains aren't running today.	Oh no! I guess we won't be able to get to work, then!	I've got some good news: I won £1,000 on the lottery.

Navigate B1 Teacher's Guide — Photocopiable © Oxford University Press 2015

7 Communication   The great hotel race

Traveller card 1

Monday 28 June	Tuesday 29 June	Wednesday 30 June	Thursday 1 July	Friday 2 July
Hotel Pluto (Paris) Ask about charges for: • the mini-bar • internet access	Minerva Hotel (Ho Chi Minh City) Ask about room facilities: • TV • Wi-Fi	Jupiter Hotel (Auckland) Ask about hotel facilities: • swimming pool • gym	Hotel Mars (Santiago) Ask about times: • breakfast • checkout	Juno Hotel (New York) Ask where the restaurant is and where you can leave luggage.

Traveller card 2

Monday 28 June	Tuesday 29 June	Wednesday 30 June	Thursday 1 July	Friday 2 July
Juno Hotel (New York) Ask about times: • breakfast • checkout	Hotel Mars (Santiago) Ask about hotel facilities: • swimming pool • gym	Minerva Hotel (Ho Chi Minh City) Ask about charges for: • the mini-bar • internet access	Jupiter Hotel (Auckland) Ask where the restaurant is and where you can leave luggage.	Hotel Pluto (Paris) Ask about room facilities: • TV • Wi-Fi

Traveller card 3

Monday 28 June	Tuesday 29 June	Wednesday 30 June	Thursday 1 July	Friday 2 July
Jupiter Hotel (Auckland) Ask about charges for: • the mini-bar • internet access	Juno Hotel (New York) Ask about room facilities: • TV • Wi-Fi	Hotel Mars (Santiago) Ask where the restaurant is and where you can leave luggage.	Hotel Pluto (Paris) Ask about hotel facilities: • swimming pool • gym	Minerva Hotel (Ho Chi Minh City) Ask about times: • breakfast • checkout

Traveller card 4

Monday 28 June	Tuesday 29 June	Wednesday 30 June	Thursday 1 July	Friday 2 July
Hotel Mars (Santiago) Ask about charges for: • the mini-bar • internet access	Hotel Pluto (Paris) Ask about times: • breakfast • checkout	Juno Hotel (New York) Ask about hotel facilities: • swimming pool • gym	Minerva Hotel (Ho Chi Minh City) Ask where the restaurant is and where you can leave luggage.	Jupiter Hotel (Auckland) Ask about room facilities: • TV • Wi-Fi

Traveller card 5

Monday 28 June	Tuesday 29 June	Wednesday 30 June	Thursday 1 July	Friday 2 July
Minerva Hotel (Ho Chi Minh City) Ask about hotel facilities: • swimming pool • gym	Jupiter Hotel (Auckland) Ask about times: • breakfast • checkout	Hotel Pluto (Paris) Ask where the restaurant is and where you can leave luggage.	Juno Hotel (New York) Ask about charges for: • the mini-bar • internet access	Hotel Mars (Santiago) Ask about room facilities: • TV • Wi-Fi

Receptionist card

- *Is there a charge for …?*
  Internet access is free, but there is a charge for the mini-bar.

- *Is … available in the room?*
  All rooms have TV, Wi-Fi, mini-bar and air conditioning.

- *Is there a … in the hotel?*
  Hotel facilities: gym, restaurant

- *What time is …?*
  Breakfast: 6.30 a.m.–10 a.m.
  Checkout: 11 a.m.

- *Where …?*
  Restaurant: first floor
  Luggage: can be left at reception

8 Communication A bit lost

Tourist card 1
You want to find:
1 a bank
2 the La Vista Restaurant
3 the tourist information office
4 the museum
5 the Star Hotel
6 the post office

Ask for directions. Write the numbers of the places on the map.

Inhabitant card 1
You live in Newton. If someone asks you for information, give directions. Be friendly and helpful, but **speak very quietly**.

Tourist card 2
You want to find:
1 a bank
2 the La Vista Restaurant
3 the tourist information office
4 the museum
5 the Star Hotel
6 the post office

Ask for directions. Write the numbers of the places on the map.

Inhabitant card 2
You live in Newton. If someone asks you for information, give directions. Be friendly and helpful, but **speak very quickly**.

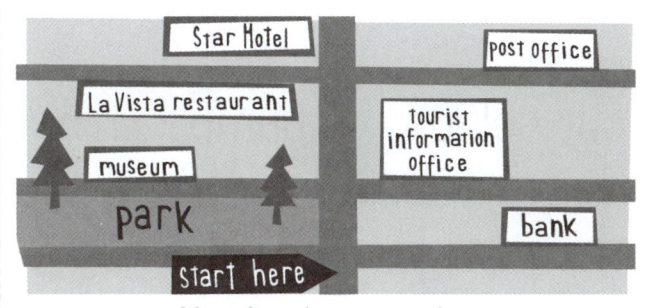

Tourist card 3
You want to find:
1 a bank
2 the La Vista Restaurant
3 the tourist information office
4 the museum
5 the Star Hotel
6 the post office

Ask for directions. Write the numbers of the places on the map.

Inhabitant card 3
You live in Newton. If someone asks you for information, give directions. Be friendly and helpful, but **use long words**, e.g.
- *parallel to* = side by side with (e.g. *It's on the street parallel to this one.*)
- *adjacent to* = next to (e.g. *It's adjacent to the post office.*)
- *in the vicinity of* = near (e.g. *It's in the vicinity of the park.*)

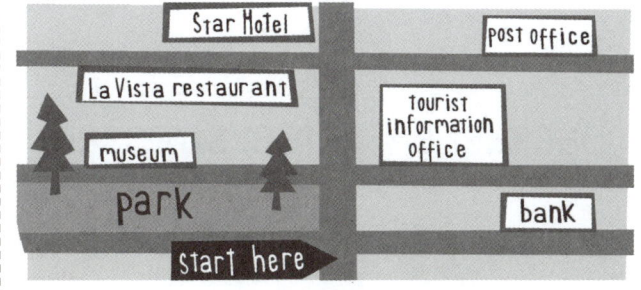

9 Communication   I'd like a second opinion, please!

a stomach ache	break / arm	a cough	sprain / ankle
a sore throat	a headache	a high temperature	a sore thumb
cut / elbow	bump / chin	feel sick	hurt / back
a sore shoulder	an insect bite	a heavy cold	feel depressed
backache	feel stressed	put on weight	feel unfit

10 Communication Waiter, waiter!

START

11 Communication Climate change

1
- You don't believe that global warming is happening.
- The world has warmed 0.7°C in 100 years, but it was that warm in the 1930s. It has been getting cooler since then.
- These changes are natural, not man-made.
- The sea level has not risen, and ice is not melting.
- There's going to be another Ice Age, not global warming.

2
- You think that global warming, if it is happening, is natural, not man-made.
- The climate has changed before. It's natural. We can't do anything to stop it.
- Only 4% of CO_2 is man-made. It's harmless, and plants and trees need it for life.
- We can't possibly get enough electricity from wind power or from the sun.

3
- You think global warming is happening, but that we can't do anything about it. We must learn to live with it.
- Taxing CO_2 and moving to wind and solar energy will take too long.
- We can't stop global warming, but we can do things to help.

4
- Science has proved that global warming is happening.
- Over 95% of scientists agree that climate change is happening.
- Global warming is caused by an increase in CO_2, produced by humans.
- Temperatures are rising faster than ever before.
- 2010 was the hottest year ever.

5
- Science has proved that global warming is happening – we need to do something fast.
- Ice is melting and the sea is rising.
- Farmland is turning into desert.
- Global warming causes hurricanes, storms and floods. These are happening more often.

Priorities list

What should we do?

- Build walls to stop floods.
- Use wind energy.
- Build houses with better heating.
- Plant more trees.
- Develop crops that can grow in cold weather.
- Save water.
- Get water to farmland to stop it becoming a desert.
- Stop people building houses near the sea.
- Use wave energy.
- Use electric cars.
- Change farms so they have more animals that can live in cold climates.
- Get better public transport (buses and trains).
- Plan to move buildings that are near the sea.
- Put a tax on CO_2.
- Use solar energy.
- Produce less CO_2.

12 Communication — Unusual job interviews

Job card 1
Window cleaner for a London skyscraper
Strengths/weaknesses/achievements
Qualifications and experience
Conditions of the job

Job card 2
Full-time babysitter for a family with six children, living on a farm
Strengths/weaknesses/achievements
Qualifications and experience
Conditions of the job

Job card 3
Head chef on the International Space Station
Strengths/weaknesses/achievements
Qualifications and experience
Conditions of the job

Job card 4
Animal dentist at your local zoo
Strengths/weaknesses/achievements
Qualifications and experience
Conditions of the job

Job card 5
Translator for horror-film subtitles
Strengths/weaknesses/achievements
Qualifications and experience
Conditions of the job

Job card 6
Tour guide for extreme safari holidays
Strengths/weaknesses/achievements
Qualifications and experience
Conditions of the job

Job card 7
Private tutor for your royal family's/president's children
Strengths/weaknesses/achievements
Qualifications and experience
Conditions of the job

Job card 8
Disneyland Paris ride mechanic
Strengths/weaknesses/achievements
Qualifications and experience
Conditions of the job

Vox pops

Aim: Each of these video worksheets aims to provide students with extra listening and speaking practice on topics connected to the unit in the Coursebook.

Preparation: Make one copy of the worksheet for each student and cut or fold in half as shown.

Unit 1 Do you live in the past, present or future?

1 Give a copy of the worksheet to each student. Students read the questions and think of their answers individually. Then divide the class into pairs and get them to ask and answer the questions.

2 Ask students to read through the questions. Then play the video, pausing after each question. At the end, play the whole video through one more time for students to check.

ANSWERS

1 a Steven   b William   c Nitin
2 a Constance   b Matthew   c William
3 a Constance   b William   c Matthew

3 Ask students to work with a new partner. Explain the task. They now discuss the questions again, and say who in the video is similar to them in their photo habits.

Unit 2 Home life

1 Give a copy of the worksheet to each student. Ask them to do the task individually. Check answers, and make sure students know how the words are pronounced.

ANSWERS

1 many   2 interesting   3 outside a city   4 live
5 work in another town

2 Play the video. Pause after each question to give students time to answer. Check answers as a group.

ANSWERS

1 1 c 2 b 3 d 4 e 5 a
2 Nitin: cosmopolitan, history
   Steven: travel, lots to do
   Matthew: villages, football
   William: diversity, culture
   Constance: seasons, hills
3 1 buildings   2 shops   3 larger   4 more   5 housing

3 Divide the class into pairs. Write the words from exercise 2, section 2 on the board. Ask students to think about which ones describe their home town. Explain the situation in section 3. Ask each pair to draw up a rough outline of a presentation, with notes on the words and images they would include. Feed back as a class.

Unit 3 Going up … One man's lift nightmare

1 Give a copy of the worksheet to each student. Go through the phrases with the class to ensure they understand them. Ask students to classify the phrases in the table by writing the number of each phrase in the relevant column. Then divide the class into pairs and ask them to compare their answers.

2 Ask students to read through the questions. Then play the video, pausing after each question. At the end, play the whole video through one more time for students to check.

ANSWERS

1 2, 3, 4, 8, 9
2 1 F 2 T 3 T 4 F 5 F 6 T 7 T 8 F

3 Ask students to work with a new partner. Explain the task and give them a moment to think about it. You could choose an example yourself and use it as a model. Students now tell their partner about a time they were nervous.

Unit 5 Your world in objects

1 Give a copy of the worksheet to each student. Divide the class into pairs. You could give a couple of examples to help, e.g. *Maybe it's because it was a gift. Maybe they love music*, etc.

2 Play the video. Pause after each question to give students time to answer the questions. Check answers as a class.

ANSWERS

1 1 d 2 b 3 c 4 a 5 e
2 1 watches television   2 isn't that good   3 camera
   4 fish   5 several violins

3 Divide the class into pairs. Demonstrate the activity with one student. Ask them to take an item from their bag and give it to you. Pretend this is your new favourite possession and make up reasons (e.g. *This was a special gift, I used it the day I got married*, etc.). Students then do the task themselves in pairs. Ask a few pairs to share their 'favourite things' and reasons.

256

Unit 6 The quiet revolution

1 Give a copy of the worksheet to each student. Ask them to do the activity individually, then discuss with a partner. Check answers as a class.

ANSWERS
1 feeling quiet, not noisy
2 going out and being with other people
3 someone who likes being with others
4 time spent alone, not with other people
5 friendly and energetic
6 stay quiet, not giving much away

2 Play the video. Pause after each question to give students time to answers. Check answers as a class.

ANSWERS
1 1 P 2 A 3 B 4 P 5 P
2 The phrases mentioned are: a, c, d, f, h.
3 Theodora, Jez, Ryan

3 Divide the class into small groups of three or four. Demonstrate by talking about times when you like to be alone (use at least some of the phrases in exercise 2, section 2). Tell students to now discuss this in small groups. Feed back as a class. Did students have similar or very different answers to each other?

Unit 7 Getting away

1 Give a copy of the worksheet to each student. Give students a few minutes to think of questions (there are two from the video written on the worksheet to get them started). Brainstorm as a class if necessary and write the questions on the board. Divide the class into pairs to ask and answer the questions.

2 Play the video. Pause after each question to give students time to do the tasks. Check answers as a class.

ANSWERS
1 1 visit some old friends   2 see the sights
  3 four days (or so)   4 in New York
  5 Madrid; Cambridge (in England)
2 1 b 2 d 3 a 4 c

3 Divide the class into groups of four or five. Ask students individually to think of a city and write it on a piece of paper. They then fold the papers and put them on the table. Demonstrate the activity. Take a piece of paper and begin: *Next summer, I'm going to [name of city]. I'm going with … We're going to … and …* Students then take turns doing the activity in their groups.

Unit 8.1 The amazing human brain

1 Give a copy of the worksheet to each student. Go over the items in the box, clarifying any unknown vocabulary. Divide the class into pairs and ask them to discuss the two questions. Feed back as a class.

2 Play the video. Pause after each question to give students time to do the tasks. Check answers as a class.

ANSWERS
1 Kimberly
2 1 T 2 F 3 T 4 F 5 F

3 Divide the class into pairs. Ask them to read the situation, then choose an item from exercise 1. Go over the useful phrases, then ask students to prepare a short role-play. Ask a few pairs to present their mini role-plays for the class.

Unit 8.2 The secrets of a successful education

1 Give a copy of the worksheet to each student. Write the words on the board in two columns (A and B). Ask students to do the task, then correct as a class. The answers below are the most likely combinations. Once you've corrected, ask students which two they think are the most important.

ANSWERS
supportive parents; inspiring teachers; broad range of subjects; self-motivation; foreign language

2 Play the video. Pause after each question to give students time to do the tasks. Check answers as a class.

ANSWERS
1 2 Emma, Dan and Sophie   2 Emma and Kimberly
  3 Sophie and Jacob   4 Jacob
2 English, Mathematics
3 1 16 2 16 3 17/18 4 18 5 17/18

3 Divide the class into pairs. Read the quote from Emma in exercise 3 or write it on the board. Ask students to discuss the questions about this. Feed back as a class.

Vox pops

Unit 9 The rise and fall of the handshake

1 Give a copy of the worksheet to each student. Students can do the task individually or with a partner. You may want to brainstorm different ways of greeting (e.g. spoken greetings, handshakes, hugs, kisses) before they start. Three of the people are from the USA. Ask students if they think their greetings will be the same or different, and ask why.

2 Ask students to read through the tasks. Then play the video, pausing after each question. At the end, play the whole video through one more time for students to check.

ANSWERS
1 1 handshake; kiss 2 different 3 *morning*; *afternoon*
   4 men; know 5 hugs; kisses
2 1 e 2 b 3 d 4 a 5 c
3 Joakim, Cindy, Elizabeth

3 Divide the class into pairs and explain the task. Students now explain how they say goodbye in different situations. You could also ask students if the rules for saying goodbye are the same as the rules for greeting in their country/countries.

Unit 10 A question of taste

1 Give a copy of the worksheet to each student. Divide them into pairs and get them to ask and answer the questions.

2 Play the video. Pause after each question to give students time to do the tasks. Check answers as a class.

ANSWERS
1 Steven O; Joakim H; Cindy H; Andrew O; Elizabeth H
2 1 a 2 a 3 c 4 b 5 c
3 1 J 2 S 3 A 4 E 5 C

3 Divide the class into pairs. Explain the situation and give students a little time to think. If they have no favourite family recipes, they can think of favourite dishes at a restaurant. Students then discuss in pairs. Feed back as a class.

Unit 11 Breaking news

1 Give a copy of the worksheet to each student. Tell them to do the first part of exercise 1 individually (write down names of people or places in the news). Then divide the class into pairs, ask them to show each other their lists and do the second part of the task. Feed back as a group.

2 Ask students to read through the tasks. Then play the video, pausing after each question. At the end, play the whole video through one more time for students to check.

ANSWERS
1 1 every day 2 once a day 3 every day
   4 every other day 5 twice or more times a day
2 1 online 2 radio 3 television 4 online 5 online

3 Ask students to work in small groups. Using the people and places they wrote down in exercise 1 (or new ones if they prefer), tell them to make a short quiz (between four and six questions) about the news. Circulate and help with the questions. Then ask groups to work with other groups and give each other their quizzes. Feed back as a class at the end. Who follows the news the closest?

Unit 12 The changing face of work

1 Give a copy of the worksheet to each student. Ask students to do exercise 1 by themselves, then to check their answers in pairs. Go over the answers as a class at the end.

ANSWERS
1 did 2 part 3 place 4 had 5 fit 6 well

2 Play the video. Pause after each question to give students time to do the task. Check answers as a class.

ANSWERS
1 b 2 c 3 b 4 a 5 b

3 Divide the class into small groups. Write the names of the jobs on the board and make sure everyone understands them. Ask students to do the first question (which job would they prefer) and compare within the group. Feed back. Repeat the process with the other question.

1 Video   Do you live in the past, present or future?

Vox pops

1   Work with a partner. Ask and answer the questions.
    1   Do you have a large collection of photos and videos?
    2   Who takes the most photos in your family?
    3   What do you take photos of?
    4   Where do you keep your photos?
    5   How do you organize your photos and videos?

2   Watch the video. Write the names.

    How often do you look at old photos and videos?
    1   Who looks at photos …
        a   once every two or three weeks? _____
        b   as often as possible? _____
        c   once every two months? _____

    What kind of photos and videos do you have?
    2   Who has …
        a   mostly photos of their grandchildren? _____
        b   lots of photos of their baby daughter? _____
        c   photos of old architecture? _____

    Where do you keep your photos?
    3   Who keeps photos …
        a   in just their phone? _____
        b   on the computer and in files? _____
        c   on their laptop or phone? _____

3   Work with a new partner. Think about what the speakers said. Whose photo habits are most similar to yours?

Steven   Nitin   Matthew   William   Constance

---

2 Video   Home life

Vox pops

1   (Circle) the correct options to complete the definitions of the word/phrase in **bold**.
    1   A **cosmopolitan** city has *many / few* people from different countries.
    2   A **fascinating** place is very *boring / interesting*.
    3   The **outskirts** are the parts *outside a city / in the city centre*.
    4   A **condominium** is a place where people *live / do sports*.
    5   A **commuter town** is full of people who *work in another town / do not travel much*.

2   Watch the video. Do the tasks.

    Where do you come from?
    1   Match the speaker to the place.
        1   Nitin   a   Pittsburgh, Pennsylvania
        2   Steven   b   Southampton
        3   Matthew   c   New Delhi
        4   William   d   Reading
        5   Constance   e   Brooklyn, New York

    What do you like about your home town?
    2   Tick (✓) the two things each speaker mentions.
        Nitin: ☐ cosmopolitan ☐ nature   ☐ history
        Steven: ☐ history   ☐ travel   ☐ lots to do
        Matthew: ☐ villages   ☐ football ☐ culture
        William: ☐ diversity   ☐ history ☐ culture
        Constance: ☐ seasons   ☐ monuments ☐ hills

    How's your town changing at the moment?
    3   (Circle) the correct options to complete the sentences.
        1   Nitin says his city has more *parks / buildings* now.
        2   Steven says there are lots of new *shops / tourist attractions*.
        3   Matthew says everything is getting *smaller / larger*.
        4   William says his city is *more / less* attractive now.
        5   Constance says her city is providing more *housing / retail stores*.

3   Work with a partner. Look at the words in exercise **2**, section 2 above. Do any of them describe your home town? Imagine you have to prepare a presentation about your town. What words and phrases would you choose? What images would you choose?

Steven   Nitin   Matthew   William   Constance

3 Video Going up ... One man's lift nightmare

Vox pops

1 Look at the phrases 1–9. Which things make you nervous? Write them in the correct column of the table below, according to how they make you feel. Then compare with a partner.

> 1 walking alone at night ☐   6 going to the dentist ☐
> 2 taking a final exam ☐   7 visiting someone in hospital ☐
> 3 speaking in public ☐   8 going to a job interview ☐
> 4 being stuck in a lift ☐   9 travelling somewhere alone ☐
> 5 being lost in a foreign city ☐

very nervous	a bit nervous	not nervous

2 Watch the video. Do the tasks.

When did you last feel nervous?

1 Tick (✓) the things from exercise 1 that the people mention.
2 Decide if the sentences are true (T) or false (F).

1 Emma did not find her youth hostel.   T F
2 Emma took the subway.   T F
3 Dan has recently moved.   T F
4 Dan didn't get the job he wanted.   T F
5 Sophie took the bus.   T F
6 Sophie went to the university by herself.   T F
7 Ezra studies computer programming.   T F
8 Jacob didn't want to make a good   T F
   impression.

3 Work with a new partner. Choose one of the situations from exercise 1. Tell your partner about it. Where were you? What were you doing? What happened?

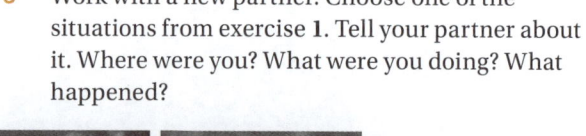

Emma   Dan   Sophie   Ezra   Jacob

---

5 Video Your world in objects

Vox pops

1 Work with a partner. Look at the photos. They show people talking about their favourite possession. For each person (1–5), guess which item from the box (a–e) they are talking about.

> a boat   b guitar   c smartphone   d tablet   e violin

1 Jez   2 Theodora   3 Elizabeth   4 Ryan   5 Craig

2 Watch the video. Do the tasks.

What is your favourite possession?
1 Were your guesses correct?
Why is it special to you?
2 (Circle) the correct options.
   1 Jez *watches television / listens to music* on his tablet.
   2 Theodora says she *is quite good / isn't that good* on the guitar.
   3 Elizabeth uses the *GPS / camera* on her phone.
   4 Ryan uses his boat to *fish / visit his friends and family*.
   5 Craig has owned *several violins / only one violin* in his life.
   Watch the video again and check.

3 Work with a new partner.

Student A: Choose one item from your bag (e.g. a pen, a notepad, a phone, a memory stick) and give it to Student B.

Student B: Imagine this is your new favourite possession. Think of reasons why and tell Student A.

Swap roles and repeat.

Navigate B1 Teacher's Guide   260   Photocopiable © Oxford University Press 2015

6 Video The quiet revolution

Vox pops

1 Look at the sentences. Do you think the people who said them are introverts or extroverts? What do the words/phrases in **bold** mean?
   1 I'm often in **a quiet mood**.
   2 I like **socialising** a lot.
   3 I'm more of **a people person**, really.
   4 I really need my **alone time**.
   5 I think I'm an **outgoing** person.
   6 I almost always **stay to myself**.

2 Watch the video. Do the tasks.

   Do you prefer spending time alone or with other people?
   1 Do the speakers prefer spending time alone (A) or with other people (P) or both (B)? Tick (✓) the correct answer.
      1 Theodora   A☐ P☐ B☐
      2 Elizabeth   A☐ P☐ B☐
      3 Jez   A☐ P☐ B☐
      4 Ryan   A☐ P☐ B☐
      5 Craig   A☐ P☐ B☐

   When do you like being alone?
   2 When do the speakers like being alone? Tick (✓) the phrases you hear.
      a after I come home from work ☐
      b during my holiday ☐
      c after I spend a lot of time away from home ☐
      d when I'm reading or when I'm studying ☐
      e at the weekend ☐
      f after I've had a hard day at work ☐
      g when I'm in a sad mood ☐
      h if I have a busy week ☐

   Do you think you are more introverted or extroverted?
   3 Which speakers say they are both introverted and extroverted?
      Theodora ☐ Elizabeth ☐ Jez ☐
      Ryan ☐ Craig ☐

3 Work with a partner. Talk about times that you like to be alone. Use the phrases in exercise **2**, section 2 to help you.

---

7 Video Getting away

Vox pops

1 Think of three or four questions you could ask someone about their plans for next summer. Then work with a partner to ask and answer each other's questions.

2 Watch the video. Do the tasks.

   What are you going to do for your holiday this summer?
   1 Complete the sentences. Use up to four words in each gap.
      1 Emma is going to _____ in Germany.
      2 Dan is going on a city break to Paris to _____ .
      3 Sophie is planning to go to Budapest on a city break for maybe _____ .
      4 Ezra is staying _____ and doing two different jobs.
      5 Jacob is going to _____ , then home to Cleveland and later to _____ .

   Who are you going with?
   2 Who are the speakers going with? Match 1-4 to a-d.
      1 Emma   a parents
      2 Dan   b by themselves
      3 Sophie c friends
      4 Jacob   d mother

3 Work in small groups. Each person writes the name of a city on a piece of paper (not their home town). Put the papers face down on the table.

   Take turns. Pick up a paper and read the name of the city. Imagine this is the destination for your next summer holiday. Tell the group who you are going with and what you are going to do.

8.1 Video The amazing human brain

Vox pops

1   Look at the items in the box. Which things would you be comfortable fixing yourself? Tell a partner.

> a computer   a shelf   a shower   a car tyre
> a bicycle   a wardrobe/closet door   a desk
> a washing machine   a mobile phone

If you can't fix one of these things, who do you ask for help?

2   Watch the video. Do the tasks.

How good are you at fixing things that are broken?

1   Which of the speakers is good at fixing things? Circle the correct name.

Emma   Sophie   Kimberly   Jacob

Do you enjoy doing it? Who do you ask for help? What was the last thing you/they fixed?

2   Decide if the sentences are true (T) or false (F).

1   Kimberly is in a new house and needs to fix lots of things.   T   F
2   Emma fixed the tyre on her dad's car.   T   F
3   Dan's father can fix things.   T   F
4   Sophie fixed the wardrobe in her dad's house.   T   F
5   Jacob helps other people to fix things.   T   F

3   Work with a partner. One of the items in exercise **1** is broken and you want your partner to help you fix it. Role-play a conversation. Use these phrases to help you.

Can you help me?   Do you have a …?
What's the problem?   Let me see.
The … is broken. I can't fix it.
Here, you hold the … and I'll …
Yes, of course. / I'm afraid I don't know.

8.2 Video The secrets of a successful education

Vox pops

1   Match the words in A to words in B to make phrases. Which two things do you think are most important for a child's education?

> A
> supportive   inspiring
> broad range of   self-
> foreign

> B
> subjects   motivation
> languages   parents
> teachers

2   Watch the video. Do the tasks.

What three things do you think are important for a good education?

1   Answer the questions. Write *Emma, Dan, Sophie, Kimberly* or *Jacob*.

1   Who says teachers are important?
    _____ , _____ and _____
2   Who says family is important?
    _____ and _____
3   Who says discipline and motivation are important?
    _____ and _____
4   Who talks about thinking critically and creatively?
    _____

Dan   Kimberly   Emma   Sophie   Jacob

What subjects do students have to study in your country?

2   Which two subjects do all the speakers mention?

> English ☐   History ☐   Mathematics ☐
> Geography ☐   Spanish ☐   Chemistry ☐
> French ☐

How long do pupils have to stay in school in your country?

3   How long do pupils have to stay in school in each speaker's country? Write the ages.

1   Emma says you have to stay in school until you are _____ .
2   Dan says you have to stay in school until you are _____ .
3   Sophie says you have to stay in school until you are _____ .
4   Kimberly says you have to stay in school until you are _____ .
5   Jacob says you have to stay in school until you are _____ .

3   One of the speakers says, 'You must stay in school until you are 16, but most people stay until they are about 18.' Work with a partner and discuss the questions.

1   Is this the same in your country?
2   Why do people stay longer in school? Why not?
3   Are young people staying in school longer now than in the past? Is this a good thing?
4   How long do you think students should stay in school?

9 Video The rise and fall of the handshake

Vox pops

Cindy: USA Andrew: USA Elizabeth: USA Steven: UK Joakim: Sweden

1 Look at the pictures of the people from different countries. How do you think they greet people in their country? Guess.

2 Watch the video. Do the tasks.

How do you greet people in your country?

1 How do the speakers greet people in their country? Complete the sentences with one word in each gap.
   1 Steven greets with a _____ or a _____ on the cheek, or a hug.
   2 Joakim says it's _____ in Sweden to the UK.
   3 Cindy usually shakes hands and says good _____ , hello or good _____ .
   4 Andrew shakes hands with _____ and with women he doesn't _____ .
   5 Elizabeth gives _____ and _____ to a good friend.

How do you greet your friends, family and colleagues?

2 How do the speakers greet friends/family/colleagues? Match the sentences 1–5 to the speakers a–e.
   a Cindy   b Andrew   c Elizabeth   d Joakim   e Steven
   1 Male friends, we hug.
   2 My dad actually kisses me on both cheeks when he sees me.
   3 Colleagues, it's the same, we shake hands.
   4 It's like they're close friends, so we might hug.
   5 The grandchildren jump up on me.

Are the rules the same for men and women?

3 Which speaker(s) think that the rules are the same for men and women?

3 Work with a partner. Discuss the questions. How do you say goodbye in the following situations?
   1 to a man you just met
   2 to a close friend at the end of a meal
   3 to a family member at the airport

10 Video A question of taste

Vox pops

1 Work with a partner. Ask and answer the questions.

Has anyone taught you how to cook?

YES — Who taught you, and what did they teach you? How old were you?

NO — Why not? Can you cook? If you can cook, did you learn by yourself?

2 Watch the video. Do the tasks.

Do you prefer eating home-cooked food or eating in a café/restaurant?

1 Which speakers prefer home-cooked food? Which speakers prefer eating out? Write H (home) or O (out) next to the names.

Steven  _____   Joakim  _____   Cindy _____
Andrew  _____   Elizabeth _____ 

Are you good at cooking?

2 Circle the correct answers.
   1 Steven's best dish is …
      a a roast dinner.   b a spicy dish.   c hamburgers.
   2 Joakim thinks he is …
      a a bad cook.   b a good cook.   c a patient cook.
   3 Cindy is good at cooking if she …
      a has time.   b feels like following directions.
      c a and b
   4 Andrew can cook …
      a general dishes.   b with a recipe.   c very quickly.
   5 Elizabeth prefers …
      a to follow recipes.   b cooking for her family.
      c eating with her family.

What's your favourite meal?

3 What is their favourite dish? Write S (Steven), J (Joakim), C (Cindy), A (Andrew) or E (Elizabeth) beside each dish.
   1 fish with vegetables _____
   2 roast chicken with potatoes and vegetables _____
   3 risotto (an Italian dish) _____
   4 simple food and Thai food _____
   5 schnitzel (an Austrian dish) _____

3 Work with a different partner. Imagine you are going to put together a book of your favourite family recipes. What dishes would you have in the book? Why? Tell your partner.

11 Video Breaking news

Vox pops

1 Think of three people or places that have been in the news recently. Write them down and show a partner. Does your partner know why they were in the news?

2 Watch the video. Do the tasks.

How often do you read, listen to or watch the news?

1 How often do the speakers read, listen to or watch the news? Circle the correct options.

1 Dan	every day	every week
2 Andrew	once a week	once a day
3 Phyllis	never	every day
4 Sophie	every day	every other day
5 Bruce	twice or more times a day	
	every two or three days	

Do you prefer to get the news from the television, newspapers or online?

2 Tick (✓) one column for each speaker.

	television	radio	online
1 Dan			
2 Andrew			
3 Phyllis			
4 Sophie			
5 Bruce			

3 Work in small groups. You are going to write a short news quiz. Think of current news stories. Use the same news stories you thought of in exercise 1 if you want. Then make five questions.

What happened in …?   What is the name of …?
Why was … in the news this week?

Work with another group. Read your questions to each other. Did you choose the same stories?

---

12 Video The changing face of work

Vox pops

1 Complete the phrases below with words from the box.

did   fit   had   part   place   well

1 I _____ a lot of research and prepared myself for the interview.
2 The director interviewed a hundred actors, but only gave one person the _____ .
3 She was so happy when she finally got a _____ at the university she wanted.
4 I _____ an interview yesterday for a job, but I didn't feel well, so I cancelled it.
5 I visited the doctor and she told me I was _____ for work.
6 My interview was two hours long, but I think it went _____ .

2 Watch the video. Circle the correct options.

What was the last interview you had?

1 Sophie had an interview this morning for …
   a a hospital.   b a university.   c a place to live.
2 Bruce had an interview for a telecoms company …
   a today.   b that he didn't get.   c as a manager.
3 Phyllis was interviewed by a famous director and …
   a got the part.   b thought it went well.
   c didn't ever act again.
4 Dan thinks his interview was …
   a successful.   b too short.   c funny.
5 Andrew had an interview …
   a for a doctor's job.   b to see if he could work.
   c to help others.

3 Work in small groups. Look at the jobs in the box and discuss the questions below.

taxi driver   television actor   video-game creator   dentist   high-school teacher

1 Which job would you prefer? Put them in order from most to least favourite and compare.
2 Which jobs would you choose for your husband/wife/father/mother? Choose one person, then put the jobs in order for that person, from most to least preferred again, and compare.